WOMEN'S FRIENDSHIP IN MEDIEVAL LITERATURE

INTERVENTIONS: NEW STUDIES
IN MEDIEVAL CULTURE
Ethan Knapp, Series Editor

WOMEN'S FRIENDSHIP IN MEDIEVAL LITERATURE

∼

Edited by Karma Lochrie and
Usha Vishnuvajjala

THE OHIO STATE UNIVERSITY PRESS
COLUMBUS

Copyright © 2022 by The Ohio State University.
All rights reserved.

Library of Congress Cataloging-in-Publication Data
Names: Lochrie, Karma, editor. | Vishnuvajjala, Usha, editor.
Title: Women's friendship in medieval literature / edited by Karma Lochrie and Usha Vishnuvajjala.
Other titles: Interventions: new studies in medieval culture.
Description: Columbus : The Ohio State University Press, [2022] | Series: Interventions: new studies in medieval culture | Includes bibliographical references and index. | Summary: "Explores literary representations of medieval women's friendships and contextualizes them in medieval history as well as the philosophy of friendship through works by Chaucer, Gower, Malory, Marie de France, female saints, late Middle Scots poets, as well as late medieval lyrics and Middle English romances"—Provided by publisher.
Identifiers: LCCN 2022006772 | ISBN 9780814215159 (cloth) | ISBN 0814215157 (cloth) | ISBN 9780814282199 (ebook) | ISBN 0814282199 (ebook)
Subjects: LCSH: Female friendship in literature. | Literature, Medieval—History and criticism.
Classification: LCC PN682.F74 W66 2022 | DDC 809/.9335220902—dc23/eng/20220412
LC record available at https://lccn.loc.gov/2022006772
Other identifiers: ISBN 9780814258361 (paper) | ISBN 0814258360 (paper)

Cover design by Susan Zucker
Text composition by Stuart Rodriguez
Type set in Minion Pro

CONTENTS

Acknowledgments vii

INTRODUCTION
KARMA LOCHRIE AND USHA VISHNUVAJJALA 1

PART 1 · VARIETIES OF SPIRITUAL FRIENDSHIP

CHAPTER 1   Female Friendships and Visionary Women
             JENNIFER N. BROWN   15

CHAPTER 2   The Foundations of Friendship: *Amicitia,* Literary
             Production, and Spiritual Community in Marie de France
             STELLA WANG   36

CHAPTER 3   Friendship and Resistance in the *Vitae* of Italian Holy Women
             ANDREA BOFFA   58

CHAPTER 4   Sisters and Friends: The Medieval Nuns of Syon Abbey
             ALEXANDRA VERINI   76

PART 2 · FEMININE SPACE, FEMININE VOICES

CHAPTER 5   "Amonge maydenes moo": Gender-Based Community,
             Racial Thinking, and Aristocratic Women's Work in *Emaré*
             LYDIA YAITSKY KERTZ   97

CHAPTER 6   Women's Communities and the Possibility of Friendship
             in the Stanzaic *Morte Arthur*
             USHA VISHNUVAJJALA   114

CHAPTER 7   Female Friendship in Late Medieval English Literature:
             Cultural Translation in Chaucer, Gower, and Malory
             MELISSA RIDLEY ELMES   135

PART 3 · NEW MODES OF FEMALE FRIENDSHIP

CHAPTER 8	Cultivating Cummarship: Female Friendship, Alcohol, and Pedagogical Community in the Alewife Poem CARISSA M. HARRIS	157
CHAPTER 9	"All These Relationships between Women": Chaucer and the Bechdel Test for Female Friendship KARMA LOCHRIE	177
CHAPTER 10	The Politics of Virtual Friendship in Christine de Pizan's *Book of the City of Ladies* CHRISTINE CHISM	197
CHAPTER 11	Prosthetic Friendship and the Theater of Fraternity LAURIE A. FINKE	219
CHAPTER 12	Conversations among Friends: Ælfflæd, Iurminburg, and the Arts of Storytelling CLARE A. LEES AND GILLIAN R. OVERING	241
AFTERWORD	Friendship at a Distance PENELOPE ANDERSON	262

Works Cited	271
List of Contributors	293
Index	297

ACKNOWLEDGMENTS

CO-EDITING A VOLUME of essays is not necessarily a recipe for friendship between and among scholars, but in the case of this volume on medieval women's friendships, it can't help but draw on our own community of friendships, past and present. Contributors in this volume represent both women scholars with whom one or the other of us has had important bonds of friendship and intellectual kinship in the past and scholars we feel lucky to have had as interlocutors in the work of "befriending past female friendships." The editors' collaboration on this volume of essays, too, bespeaks a friendship that began in the formal academic context of mentor/mentee and developed into the kind of friendship that we suspect mirrors those of many female (and male) faculty who go on to work as colleagues with graduate students with whom they have shared interests, passions, and, ultimately, friendships. We have shared the hard work, but also the exhilaration, of seeing this volume from its inception as a series of papers, through its conception, the compiling of contributors, and all the deadlines and revisions that constitute the particular challenge of edited collections, and, finally, to the joy and relief at its completion. Female friendship in the academy is crucially important, as Karma knows from her time at Princeton many years ago before female mentors were widely available in her field. Nevertheless, she, like Usha, has benefited from the support, generosity, conversations, and shared triumphs of other academic women, and we dedicate this volume to them. They know who they are.

We also thank Holly Crocker, who gave the most generous review we have ever received, and who seemed to model some of the female friendship discussed in this volume, and our editor, Ana Maria Jimenez-Moreno.

INTRODUCTION

KARMA LOCHRIE AND USHA VISHNUVAJJALA

—A woman friend is as rare as true love.

ELENA FERRANTE[1]

FRIENDSHIP HAS BEEN DEFINED, when it is defined at all, by proximity, likeness, political affiliation, public or moral good, and emotional or affective attachment.[2] With the exception of the final category, it has often been characterized in ways that are primarily or even solely available to men, and often only to those meeting other criteria such as class, religion, or race. Within these constraints, the concept of friendship sometimes comes to resemble a condition, something dictated by circumstance, rather than a bond of affection, love, or even competition, as many of us may think of it today. At the same time, in recent years, studies and news articles on health have begun to tout the benefits of friendship for our physical and mental health, although they rarely define friendship and tend to focus instead on measurable or quantifiable criteria like the number of people one communicates with each day by phone call or text message.[3]

---

1. Elena Ferrante, "A Woman Friend Is as Rare as True Love," trans. Ann Goldstein, *Guardian*, April 28, 2018, https://www.theguardian.com/lifeandstyle/2018/apr/28/elena-ferrante-woman-friend-rare-as-true-love.

2. For a recent overview, see Alexander Nehamas, *On Friendship* (New York: Basic Books, 2016).

3. Jamie Ducharme, "Why Spending Time with Friends Is One of the Best Things You Can Do for Your Health," *Time*, June 25, 2019, https://time.com/5609508/social-support-health-benefits/ (accessed June 2, 2021). The study Ducharme references that measures friendship by the number of phone calls and text messages is Suwen Lin et al., "Social Network Structure

The anthropologist Robin Dunbar, who famously posited that the number of close friendships a species was capable of maintaining depended on the size of its neocortex, concluded in the 1990s that humans were capable of about 150 close friendships, a number still referred to as "Dunbar's Number." When asked recently about research that seemed to undermine his theory, Dunbar reiterated his original claim and, according to Jenny Gross of the *New York Times*, defined a "meaningful relationship" as "those people you know well enough to greet without feeling awkward if you ran into them in an airport lounge."[4] Another recent *Times* article drew outrage from readers when it suggested that they use the pandemic to jettison friends whose struggles made them a bad influence, defining friendship as "an evolutionary advantage" and noting that "psychologists, sociologists and evolutionary anthropologists say it behooves us to take a more curatorial approach when it comes to our friends because who you hang out with determines who you are."[5] Each of the essays in this volume defines friendship in a different way—through shared values, protection, advice, physical affection, or safe spaces for difficult feelings, among other things—but each one defines friendship as something more nuanced and complex than these social science approaches construe it to be. And recent popular representations of women's friendship demonstrate that for many of us in the twenty-first century, friendship is about more than evolutionary advantages, virtuous behavior, or comfort making small talk.

If friendship after the pandemic is a matter of debate, female friendship remains even more mysterious as a category, despite its increasing popularity as a topic of novels, films, and television shows. Female friendships, if recent film criticism is to be believed, have been experiencing something of a cinematic surge since 2019 with Greta Gerwig's *Little Women*, the first major dramatic film to expand comedy's growing focus on female friendship in films like *Bridesmaids* (2011), *Spy* (2015), and *Ghostbusters* (2016), all directed by Paul Feig. The *Guardian* announced Gerwig's film and its timing as a veritable invention of sisterhood and female friendship under the title "Sister Act: From

---

Is Predictive of Health and Wellness," *PLOS One*, June 6, 2019, https://doi.org/10.1371/journal.pone.0217264.

4. Jenny Gross, "Can You Have More Than 150 Friends?," *New York Times*, May 11, 2021, https://www.nytimes.com/2021/05/11/science/dunbars-number-debunked.html (accessed June 14, 2021).

5. Kate Murphy, "How to Rearrange Your Post-Pandemic 'Friendscape,'" *New York Times*, June 7, 2021, https://www.nytimes.com/2021/06/01/well/family/curate-friends.html (accessed June 14, 2021). An earlier version of this article, published June 1, 2021, suggested that readers avoid friendships with those who are obese or who struggle with addiction because those conditions are more common among those whose friends have them.

Killing Eve to Little Women, Female Friendships Finally Get Top Billing."[6] The pairing of *Killing Eve* and *Little Women* in this title is a jarring juxtaposition: the familial nineteenth-century friendships depicted in Alcott's novel would strike most viewers as light-years distant from the BBC series' obsessive, erotic, and frightening relationship between British intelligence investigator Eve (Sandra Oh) and psychopathic assassin Villanelle (Jodie Comer). The story of female friendship framed by these two recent ventures in film and television-streaming is itself a strange and compelling riddle.

The film and television series both follow closely on the best-selling literary inquiry into female friendship by Elena Ferrante in her Neapolitan quartet of novels that explores the relationship of Lila and Lenu from childhood through adulthood. April de Angelis, who adapted the first volume of Ferrante's series, *My Brilliant Friend,* for the National Theatre in London in 2019, averred (in a curious ventriloquism of Geoffrey Chaucer's Wife of Bath, no less!), "Men have always told women's stories, and they've always put themselves right at the centre of the picture. If women had to tell the story of our lives, we'd talk about friends, really, talk about our daughters, talk about mothers, talk about grandmothers, and talk about the friendships that are important to us."[7] Indeed, as Tiziana de Rogatis notes, what is most remarkable about Ferrante's novels is their captivating representation of what she calls the "liberating messiness" of female friendship—friendship, that is, in all its intimacy, eroticism, fear, cruelty, and indispensability.[8] Ferrante herself insists on jettisoning "every literary idealization" in order to capture the sheer "disorderliness of female friendship" in her novels.[9] For Ferrante, as the epigram to our introduction suggests, female friendship is also both rare and tantamount to "true love." She further explains that "the relationship between friends has the richness, the complexity, the contradictions, the inconsistencies of love." There is also, she adds, linguistic support for her simile of female friendship

---

6. Gwendolyn Smith, "Sister Act: From Killing Eve to Little Women, Female Friendships Finally Get Top Billing," *Guardian,* December 22, 2019.

7. Quoted in Smith, "Sister Act." We allude, of course, to the Wife of Bath's rant against her husband's reading of the "Book of Wicked Wives" to her in which she exclaims that "by God, if women had written stories / As men have in their oratories / They would have written about men / More than the mark of Adam can redress" ["By God, if wommen hadde writen stories / As clerkes han withinne hire oratories / They wolde han writen of men moore wikkednesse / Than al the mark of Adam may redresse"; *Canterbury Tales,* ed. Benson, III: lines 693–96). De Angelis revises the Wife's insistence that women would call out men in their writings, suggesting that, instead, women would write about their friendships.

8. Tiziana de Rogatis, "For Elena Ferrante, What Distinguishes Conventional Male and Female Friendships? The Liberating Messiness of the Neapolitan Quartet Friendship," *LitHub,* December 17, 2019.

9. Quoted in de Rogatis, "For Elena Ferrante."

and true love. In Italian *amicizia* already collapses love into friendship by means of the root verb, *amare*, "to love."[10] The rarity of the woman friend to Ferrante's way of thinking—like that of true love—consists in its exceptionality, its marvelousness, and its scarcity.

THERE IS another kind of rarity where female friendship is concerned, however: the rarity of its consideration in scholarship, including literary scholarship, on premodern women. Virginia Woolf famously invented a female friendship in the history of letters in which the simple phrase "Chloe liked Olivia" seemed to open up worlds of pleasure and recognition that had hitherto not existed for women readers. Karma Lochrie addresses Woolf's ruminations more fully in her essay in this volume, but for the purposes of this introduction, we can sympathize with Woolf's exasperation that something is missing from accounts of literary history, even though our purview is the Middle Ages rather than the long durée of literary history.

The rarity of the female friend is not limited to accounts of literary history: it extends to the relative absence of the kind of cultural and philosophical ballast that scaffolds the history of masculine friendship as an idealized construct.

Most writers on friendship either assumed or outright insisted that masculinity was itself a condition of friendship, from the classical period to the Middle Ages and into early modernity. Female friendship was thus marginalized if not rendered inconceivable within the Western philosophy of friendship; friendship was spiritually, politically, and constitutionally unavailable to women. *Amicitia* was often deemed *by definition* a masculine virtue that excluded women. Early classical definitions conceived of friendship as primarily a public affiliation that provided the "public and political basis for civic community."[11] *Philia*, the Greek word for friendship, was originally "characterized as ethical, public, exclusively masculine, and elite,"[12] categorically excluding women, as well as nonelite citizens. In addition, Aristotle defines a more private ideal of friendship between male persons in a famous formulation: "a friend is another self."[13] The likeness between friends about which Aristotle writes is based on equality and a similitude with respect to virtue, a quality presumed to be possessed by men but not by women, as its etymology sug-

---

10. Ferrante, "A Woman Friend."
11. Ivy Schweitzer, "Making Equals: Classical *Philia* and Women's Friendship," *Feminist Studies* 42, no. 2 (2016): 339–40.
12. Schweitzer, "Making Equals," 337–38.
13. See Aristotle, *Nicomachean Ethics*, 8.8.12; Schweitzer, "Making Equals," 342.

gests.[14] Cicero likewise defined friendship in terms of "a second self . . . that become virtually one person instead of two."[15] Much later, Michel de Montaigne made explicit the exclusion of women from classical definitions of ideal friendship: "The ordinary capacity of women is inadequate for that communion and fellowship which is the nurse of this sacred bond; nor does their soul seem firm enough to endure the strain of so tight and durable a knot."[16]

Although classical models of friendship as a form of affiliation for the public good certainly survived into the early modern period, to consider them the dominant way of understanding friendship in the Middle Ages is to privilege the influence of one strand of classical philosophy—however dominant—over the written evidence that survives from the Middle Ages. The forms of friendship depicted in these texts are at times very similar to and at times dramatically different from the type valued in classical philosophy or Christian theology. The writings of Aelred of Rievaulx, a twelfth-century Yorkshire abbot who adapted Cicero's ideas for a Christian audience, are often treated as the final word on medieval friendship. Although several of the essays in this volume draw on Aelred's writings, we also note emphatically that his definition of spiritual friendship was not the only type of friendship experienced, documented, or imagined by medieval women.

The female friendships this volume considers are those evidenced in written texts. Whether they document friendships between historical women or imagine those between fictional women, this volume's essays on female friendship demonstrate that the topic of women's friendships, intimacy, communities, and affinities was, in fact, a central concern to medieval writers across genders, literary genres, and linguistic and national differences. We suggest that these friendships have long been neglected not only because of discourses privileging friendships between men but because definitions of masculine friendships have focused on those friendships grounded in likeness, virtue, and public identity; many of these friendships are between women who may not be alike, whose friendships play out largely in private arenas, or who would not be considered virtuous by either classical or Christian frameworks.[17]

---

14. See, however, Holly A. Crocker's groundbreaking intervention in masculine definitions of virtue in *The Matter of Virtue: Women's Ethical Action from Chaucer to Shakespeare* (Philadephia: University of Pennsylvania Press, 2019).

15. Cicero, *De amicitia*, quoted in Schweitzer, "Making Equals," 342.

16. "Of Friendship," in Michel de Montaigne, *The Complete Works: Essays, Travel Journal, Letters*, trans. Donald M. Frame (New York: Knopf, 2003), 167.

17. As examples, see Amanda Herbert, *Female Alliances: Gender, Identity, and Friendship in Early Modern Britain* (New Haven, CT: Yale University Press, 2014); Penelope Anderson, *Friendship's Shadows: Women's Friendship and the Politics of Betrayal in England, 1640–1705* (Edinburgh: Edinburgh University Press, 2013); and Schweitzer, "Making Equals."

No scholar has captured the sheer inconceivability of historical constructions of friendship including women more than Alan Bray. In the introduction to his important study of friendship in England from the year 1000 to the eighteenth century, Bray pauses to consider the implicit gendering of his own historical evidence:

> Am I writing about friendship or about *masculine* friendship? Curiously, this question is more difficult to answer, because friendship has been no less asymmetrical than gender itself. There is no more revealing question about the friendship of traditional society than to ask how it encompassed women.[18]

Bray acknowledges that he is indeed writing about masculine friendship, even though he finds evidence for female friendship in the seventeenth century. This volume seeks to build on Bray's question by asking the following: If medieval understandings of friendship do not encompass women, where might women's friendship reside, and under what cultural rubrics other than masculine virtue, political affinity, and civic polity might it be found? What are the conditions of its emergence and the temper of its expressions? How does it fare under the discourse of medieval misogyny? What different species of female friendship can we discern in medieval texts? Early modern writing on friendship amasses a wealth of terminology for different kinds of friendship affiliated with women and men, including "chaste friendship," "erotic" friendship, political friendship, "sworn brotherhood," and more.[19] One of the most important studies of nonsexual love and friendship in the Middle Ages is Stephen Jaeger's *Ennobling Love*, in which he argues for that secular passionate friendship that provides a diptych with spiritual friendship in medieval courtly society.[20] Jaeger's book has little to say, however, about female friendship because the friendship he examines is the masculine forerunner of courtly love. "Ennobling love" is courtly love, a cultural phenomenon which expanded on the idea of the masculine friendship as a source of self-betterment to a heterosexual ideal that included women. While women were now participants in that "ennobling love" that we call courtly love, the Middle Ages

---

18. Alan Bray, *The Friend* (Chicago: University of Chicago Press, 2003), 10.

19. For the terms for female friendship, including *chaste femme love*, see Valerie Traub, *The Renaissance of Lesbianism in Early Modern England* (Cambridge: Cambridge University Press, 2002), esp. 188–228. For sworn brotherhood, see Bray, *The Friend*, 16–17, 125–26, and 315–17.

20. C. Stephen Jaeger, *Ennobling Love: In Search of a Lost Sensibility* (Philadelphia: University of Pennsylvania Press, 1999). See his chapter "Women," 82–108.

seems to be no closer to developing a culturally legible ideal of female friendship than it was before the twelfth century.

The only major study of medieval female friendship across history consists of a volume of essays edited by Albrecht Classen and Marilyn Sandidge that includes "that still uncharted territory" of women and friendship in the Middle Ages along with essays devoted to masculine friendship.[21] One of the reasons for the relative neglect of medieval studies of female friendship, we think, is that the topic was subsumed in the movement of queer studies in the 1990s and early 2000s. For example, Lochrie's essay in the *Cambridge Companion to Medieval Women's Writing*, "Between Women," included a discussion of female friendship within the larger discussion of female homoeroticism in medieval texts. Queer medieval studies co-opted female friendship studies before there was such a thing, and, as a result, we really do not have much groundwork, theoretical or historical, for talking about female friendship as friendship in the Middle Ages. At the same time, it might seem to us as though this topic has been fully vetted because of the scattered address of the topic under queer studies. A quick search of the topic, however, reveals a surprising dearth of studies other than those we have already cited.

Meanwhile, the interest in women's friendship in other historical periods and in current popular writing continues apace without the Middle Ages. The 2017 nonfiction book *Secret Sisterhood: The Literary Friendships of Jane Austen, Charlotte Brontë, George Eliot, and Virginia Woolf*, by Emily Midorikawa and Emma Claire Sweeney, documents the largely unknown epistolary friendships these four major British women writers had with other female writers; feminist linguistics scholar Deborah Tannen's 2017 book *You're the Only One I Can Tell: Inside the Language of Women's Friendships* considers, among many other things, the detrimental effect that negative social interactions—including those with friends—have on women's health, despite the fact that they do not have a similar effect on men's health. Reese Witherspoon, posting an Instagram picture of herself with her co-stars of the 2017 HBO series *Big Little Lies* (based on the 2014 novel of the same name by Liane Moriarty), remarks of the series and her relationship to her fellow actresses: "The power of sisterhood and friendship is limitless!" *Guardian* writer Ellen E. Jones, who quotes Witherspoon, offers a somewhat different assessment of the series, if

---

21. Albrecht Classen and Marilyn Sandidge, eds., *Friendship in the Middle Ages and Early Modern Age: Explorations of a Fundamental Ethical Discourse* (Berlin: de Gruyter, 2010), 47. Even in this massive collection dedicated to friendship, only two essays address medieval female friendships explicitly: Lisa M. C. Weston, "Where Textual Bodies Meet: Anglo-Saxon Women's Epistolary Friendships," 231–41; and Sara Deutch Schotland, "Talking Bird and Gentle Heart: Female Homosocial Bonding in Chaucer's 'Squire's Tale,'" 525–42.

not the actresses' bonds with one another, as "TV's most compelling commercial opportunity yet: female friendship as a commodity."[22]

We argue that this supposedly new interest in women's friendship as a topic of art, scholarship, cinema, and even consumerism actually continues a long tradition of writing that has been neglected in scholarship until now. We can see how thoroughly a periodized understanding of women's friendship has pervaded popular thinking in examples like an NPR review of the book *Text Me When You Get Home: The Evolution and Triumph of Modern Female Friendship* that begins with the sentences "Women in the Middle Ages were excluded from many realms: the law, universities, and surprisingly, from friendship, writes author Kayleen Schaefer. The term 'friend' was reserved for the half of humanity that purportedly possessed superior morals—men— and only used to describe other men."[23] While the recent interest in women's friendship is a positive development in fiction and scholarship and nonfiction, it often relies on a false sense of periodization. With this volume, we aim to put to rest the idea that women's friendships are a particularly modern development, and with it the oversimplified narrative of historical progress between the Middle Ages and today, especially with respect to gender.

This volume is designed not only to remedy the absence of scholarly work on female friendship in the Middle Ages, therefore, but also to begin to articulate the multiform ways in which women's friendships appear in medieval literary texts, culture, and even in modern Wiccan derivatives of medieval craft societies. Like the knight in the *Wife of Bath's Tale*, who searches for an answer to the question of what it is that women most desire only to receive multiple and varied answers, we were delighted to discover in the course of assembling this collection that women's friendships in medieval literature and culture are not homogenous; nor do they necessarily track with the philosophical parameters of masculine friendships. Like Ferrante, we are interested here in the "disorderliness of female friendship," as well as its deepest sympathies, ethics, cross-species affiliations, and even its "virtual" and "prosthetic" capacities.[24] Our volume aims to generate a rich and provocative investigation into female friendships in the medieval period, but it also reserves an eye toward the present, including the recent surge in novels, movies, and stream-

---

22. Ellen E. Jones, "Is *Big Little Lies* Selling Us a Version of Consumer Feminism That Is Just Too Good to Be True?" *Guardian*, June 19, 2019.

23. Kayleen Schaefer, *Text Me When You Get Home: The Evolution and Triumph of Modern Female Friendship* (New York: Dutton, 2018); Rhaina Cohen, "'Text Me When You Get Home' Celebrates the Complexities of Female Friendship," *NPR*, February 11, 2018.

24. Laurie Finke borrows this idea of "prosthetic friendship" from David Wills, who defines it as "friendship artificially conceived or produced," in "Full Dorsal: Derrida's *Politics of Friendship*," *Postmodern Culture* 15, no. 3 (May 2005). See Finke's essay in this volume.

ing series on female friendship. In that sense, it pursues a practice of befriending past female friendships by way of considering how they might help speak to our present moment. One of the ways in which our volume straddles past and present lies in its recourse to contemporary theories of friendship, from Jacques Derrida's *The Politics of Friendship* to the work of Toni Morrison, Nancy K. Miller, and other important writers and scholars of the late twentieth and early twenty-first centuries. In addition, we recognize the wealth of feminist scholarship from the past forty years that addresses women's friendships in complex and important ways, even if we do not cite their work in our own. We are deeply aware of and indebted to their work, as we endeavor to push the inquiry into women's friendship into a past era that has remained somewhat puzzlingly immune to this vector of feminist inquiry.[25]

Rather than organizing the essays according to better-studied forms of affiliation in the Middle Ages, such as familial bonds or patronage networks, we chose to organize them according to the provocations and interventions the essays in each section are making: spiritual friendship, feminine spaces, and new modes of affinity. While each of these categories is porous and many of the essays in this volume are concerned with spiritual identity, feminine spaces, and new or emerging modes of affinity, this way of organizing the essays highlights the fact that many medieval representations of female friendship do not map easily onto existing categories of relation.

Part 1, "Varieties of Spiritual Friendship," takes up what might be the most familiar category of female friendship even though, aside from the case of Hildegard of Bingen and Richardis, scholarship has been slow to consider it. The varieties of spiritual friendships discussed in this part range widely across the temporal and the geographic, from Jennifer Brown's exploration of the famous visionaries Hildegard of Bingen and Catherine of Siena; to Stella

---

25. While any attempt to cite all the—mostly female—authors who have written on this topic over the past forty years is destined inadvertently to omit some individuals, we nevertheless wish to acknowledge as many as we can: Adrienne Rich, "Compulsory Heterosexuality and Lesbian Existence," *Signs* 5, no. 4 (Summer 1980): 631–60; Lillian Faderman, *Surpassing the Love of Men: Romantic Friendship and Love Between Women from the Renaissance to the Present* (New York: William Morrow, 1981); Audre Lorde, *Sister Outsider: Essays and Speeches* (Freedom, CA: Crossing Press, 1984); Janice Raymond, *A Passion for Friends: Toward a Philosophy of Female Affection* (Boston: Beacon Press, 1986); Mary Hunt, *Fierce Tenderness: A Feminist Theology of Friendship* (New York: Crossroad, 1992); María Lugones and Pat Alake Rosezelle, "Sisterhood and Friendship as Feminist Models," in *Feminism and Community*, ed. Penny A. Weiss and Marilyn Friedman (Philadelphia: Temple University Press, 1995), 135–46; Jody Greene, "The Work of Friendship," *GLQ: A Journal of Lesbian and Gay Studies* 10, no. 3 (2004): 319–37; and Judith Taylor, "Enduring Friendship: Women's Intimacies and the Erotics of Survival," *Frontiers: A Journal of Women's Studies* 34, no. 1 (2013): 93–113. Schweitzer provides most of these references, as well as an excellent review of feminist and queer scholarship on women's friendship; see Schweitzer, "Making Equals."

Wang's consideration of Marie de France's twelfth-century hagiography *La vie seint Audree* alongside *Eliduc* and *La Fresne*; to Andrea Boffa's discussion of Italian holy women like Clare of Rimini (d. 1346), Umiliani de Cerchi (d. 1246), and Margaret of Cortona (d. 1297); to Alexandra Verini's essay on the "absent presence" of women's friendships at Syon Abbey, a Bridgettine house established in the fifteenth century in England. Wang argues for an understanding of women's spiritual friendship not only in terms of private bonds but in terms of an *amicitia* that was public and discursive.

This volume's second part, "Feminine Space, Feminine Voices," takes especial notice of the spaces in which women's friendships become legible and the crucial role played by female audiences in the expression of female fellowship. Lydia Kertz and Usha Vishnuvajjala frame this section with their essays considering the spaces and audiences of female friendship. Kertz addresses specifically those spaces of female learning in textile production in the Middle English *Emaré*, which creates transnational connections between Muslim and Christian women in the text even as it valorizes the aristocratic Christian female body over the elite Muslim woman. Vishnuvajjala interrogates the private spaces of the fourteenth-century Stanzaic *Morte Arthur* to discover how spaces explicitly populated by women enable Gaynor's expressions of emotion and sympathy, and to suggest that fellowship among women in romance, although it might seem like so much background, is actually vital to Gaynor's rare expressions of emotion. Female fellowship, in this case, is more evident in its affective effects and gendered spaces than it is in any more conventional depiction of friendship dyads. Melissa Elmes likewise details the possible extratextual pressures and awarenesses of Middle English works by Chaucer, Gower, and Malory, arguing for a heightened late-medieval authorial orientation toward female audiences and patrons that accounts for key diversions from their source material.

The collection's final part turns to a vibrant array of secular friendships ranging from the personal and private to public and transgressive, to interspecies, to modern and prosthetic. This section, "New Modes of Female Friendship," straddles the medieval and modern by reaching out from *cummarship* in medieval alewife poems, in Carissa Harris's essay, to twentieth-century lesbian bar culture. Karma Lochrie's essay begins from the twentieth-century Bechdel test for the depiction of female friendship in contemporary cinema, to consider how three different types of female fellowship in Chaucer's *Canterbury Tales* might offer alternatives to the notion of masculine fellowship framing the tales as a whole. Christine Chism likewise maps out a kind of virtual friendship and "alternative sociality" produced by Christine de Pizan in her fifteenth-century opus, *Le livre de la cité des dames* (*Book of the City of*

Ladies). Chism's argument also affords an exciting theorizing of female readership in terms of virtual friendship that potentially expands the category of women's friendship for readers of women's text, medieval, early modern, and modern, aligning women readers across history in a sororal friendship. This section continues with Laurie Finke's provocative study of the modern Wiccan movement as it evolved from the Freemasons in terms of "prosthetic friendship." Finally, Clare Lees and Gillian Overing address the challenge of finding a "narrative in the face of absence" by considering three contemporary texts that reimagine the seventh century. They focus in particular on the possibility of friendship between abbess Ælfflæd and queen Iurminburg by way of imagining a *gemæcce,* or formal female friendship, as that concept was defined by Nicola Griffith. All the essays of this part challenge contemporary and medieval scholars to think across historical eras as well as to imagine categories of female friendship that might not easily sync with masculine models of friendship and fellowship, and that might chart new directions for theorizing female friendship tout court.

We hope that this volume is not the last word on women's friendships in medieval literature and culture, but that it charts some initial interlocutory directions for medieval scholars to begin addressing other histories and theories of women's friendships. As we write this introduction, the world is emerging from an unparalleled period of isolation because of the coronavirus pandemic, and Penelope Anderson's beautiful afterword, "Friendship at a Distance," explores how our new awareness of vulnerability, interdependence, inequality, and the necessity of caring for each other despite our differences might reshape how we think about friendship both today and in the past, arguing that studying historical representations of women's friendship "helps us imagine an equality that incorporates rather than puts aside difference." While we could not have anticipated the singular historical circumstances in which this volume would emerge when we began it, we hope that it will seize the day, so to speak, in furthering our understanding of friendships among women, both medieval and modern, both synchronic and cross-temporal.

PART 1

~

Varieties of Spiritual Friendship

CHAPTER 1

Female Friendships and Visionary Women

JENNIFER N. BROWN

THE MEDIEVAL WOMEN whose lives have come to us in most detail are the exceptional ones, those championed by powerful men, and those who were or remain controversial. In some cases—such as with visionary or mystical women—they are all three at once. And all too often the stories that survive—often hagiographies—are told by men and primarily concerned with the men with whom these women had often deep, intimate friendships. Many scholars have written about the close relationships between male writers and their female subjects, or other cross-sex friendships born from intellectual and spiritual connection.[1] But surely for many of these women, particularly those who lived or ended their lives in cloisters surrounded by other women, their friendships with their sisters and female friends were the deepest. This

---

Thank you to Karma Lochrie and Usha Vishnuvajjala for their comments on this essay. Thank you as well for the comments and suggestions by my reading group: Valerie Allen, Glenn Burger, Matthew Goldie, Steven Kruger, David Lavinsky, and Michael Sargent.

1. See, for example, the collection edited by Catherine Mooney, *Gendered Voices: Medieval Saints and Their Interpreters* (Philadelphia: University of Pennsylvania, 1999); John Coakley, *Women, Men, and Spiritual Power: Female Saints & Their Male Collaborators* (New York: Columbia University Press, 2006), and H. M. Canatella, "Long-Distance Love: The Ideology of Male-Female Spiritual Friendship in Goscelin of Saint Bertin's *Liber confortartorius*," *Journal of the History of Sexuality* 19 (2010): 35–53. My own work on the subject can be found in Jennifer N. Brown, "The Chaste Erotics of Marie d'Oignies and Jacques de Vitry," *Journal of the History of Sexuality* 19 (2010): 74–93, and *Fruit of the Orchard: Catherine of Siena in Late Medieval and Early Modern England* (Toronto: University of Toronto Press, 2018).

essay seeks to answer the question Karma Lochrie raises in her essay "Between Women": "Where [in medieval texts] were the women who formed communities with each other, engaged in deep, abiding friendship together, and experienced sexual bonds with other women?"[2] I have chosen to look at visionary women, whose specific burden of care and support is perhaps more urgent than that of other medieval religious women because of the physical and emotional toll of their raptures. In choosing a few examples from the twelfth century to the sixteenth, in various European contexts (modern-day Low Countries, Germany, Switzerland, Italy, and England), I hope to demonstrate how necessary the female friend was to the medieval visionary woman and how, by looking closely at their surviving textual evidence, we can see those friendships in stark relief.

There are many women I could consider for this essay, but I have chosen those that I feel exemplify some of the categories of women's spiritual friendship that we can glean from medieval sources and that demonstrate the nuanced relationships that surrounded and supported them: the mentor and/or mentee, the scribe and/or intellectual confidant, and a member of the visionary's close circle or community of support. The women I examine here cross these categories, and sometimes blur them, but they clearly represent close woman–woman friendships that support and make the work of the visionary possible: Hildegard of Bingen and two nuns she lived with and knew, as well as some women with whom she had an epistolary friendship; Elsbeth of Stagel and her *sisterbook* writings about Elizabeth of Töss; Catherine of Siena and the women of her *famiglia*, especially her female scribes; and, finally, the early modern Syon nun Mary Champney, a woman who inspired an anonymously authored *vita* after her death. In each of these cases, the friendship among women is not central (and is often, indeed, hidden), but between the lines of their surviving records one can piece together how these celebrated women had a network of others around them making their success possible.

Friendship has previously been examined in a spiritual context, and many of the women looked at here are known for their male friends (Hildegard and Volmar; Elsbeth of Stagel and Henry Suso; Catherine of Siena and Raymond of Capua). In Hildegard's and Catherine's cases, these friends also became the women's hagiographers. Their friendships thrived despite a tradition of *auctoritas* that agreed, as Jane Tibbets Schulenburg notes, that "it was virtually impossible for women to enter into and maintain 'pure' friendships

---

2. Karma Lochrie, "Between Women," in *The Cambridge Companion to Medieval Women's Writing*, ed. Carolyn Dinshaw and David Wallace (Cambridge: Cambridge University Press, 2003), 70–88, at 70.

with members of the opposite sex."³ The potential erotics of these relationships—imbalanced because of the notoriety of the woman visionary/saint and the hagiographer imbued with Church power and masculine authority—can sometimes be read into the *vitae* or other surviving texts. Alongside this tradition is another of "spiritual friendship," largely defined by the work of Aelred of Rievaulx in his book of that title, *De spiritali amicitia*, written in the mid-twelfth century, a text that was widely translated and disseminated.⁴ Aelred drew on classical works but reframed them in a Christian context and described how human friendship can lead to the divine. Writing at first a dialogue between two men and later a discussion among three, Aelred explains the true nature of friendship and how it opens the mind and heart to Christ: "Was that not like the first fruits of bliss, so to love and so to be loved, to help and to be helped, and from the sweetness of brotherly love to fly aloft toward that higher place in the splendor of divine love, or from the ladder of charity now to soar to the embrace of Christ himself, or, now descending to the love of one's neighbor, there sweetly to rest?"⁵ However, Aelred is clearly discussing male friendship here—the "brotherly" love he gestures toward places these friendships firmly in the monastery, although he himself documents his close relationship to his sister in the guidelines he writes for her life as an anchoress, *De instiutione inclusarum*. As Lochrie has noted, however, female-female friendship is a dangerous proposition in Aelred's eyes. For in the text he writes to his sister, he "imagines the slippery slope leading from solitary spiritual perfection to sexual and spiritual decadence through female gossip."⁶ For Aelred, spiritual friendship must involve men.

There are surely some similarities between the male, monastic friendship that Aelred envisions and those among medieval religious women. For

---

3. Jane Tibbets Schulenburg, *Forgetful of Their Sex: Female Sanctity and Society ca. 500-1100* (Chicago: University of Chicago Press, 1998), 309. See especially the entire chapter on "Gender Relationships and Circles of Friendship" for the history of Church attitudes toward friendship among men and women and how these change.

4. Marsha L. Dutton dates it between 1164 and 1167, in *Aelred of Rievaulx: Spiritual Friendship* ed. Marsha L. Dutton and trans. Lawrence C. Braceland, SJ (Collegeville, MN: Cistercian Publications, 2010), 22; for more on Spiritual Friendship, see Dutton, "The Sacramentality of Community in Aelred," in *A Companion to Aelred of Rievaulx*, ed. Marsha L. Dutton (Leiden: Brill, 2017), 246–67; as well as Domenico Pezzini, "Aelred's Doctrine of Charity and Friendship," in *A Companion to Aelred of Rievaulx*, 221–45. Nathan Lefler, *Theologizing Friendship: How Amicitia in the Thought of Aelred and Aquinas Inscribes the Scholastic Turn* (Cambridge: James Clarke, 2014), describes the classical sources and basis for Aelred and his relation to the later Thomas Aquinas's theorizing of spiritual friendship.

5. *Aelred of Rievaulx: Spiritual Friendship*, 124; The Latin can be found in Aelredi Rievallensis, *De spiritali amicitia*, in *Aelredi Rievallensis Opera Omnia*, ed. A. Hoste and C. H. Talbot (Turnhout: Brepols 1971), 348.

6. Lochrie, "Between Women," 72.

example, Marsha Dutton points out that for Aelred, the seeds of that spiritual friendship are in the work of the community and in the monastic life. In this sense, many of the women do have this kind of "spiritual friendship" that he envisioned, buoyed and supported by the women of their communities, either formal—like the Dominican nuns in sisterbooks—or informal—like the *famiglia* that surrounded Catherine of Siena.[7] In this light, Aelred envisions the spiritual friendship between Mary and Martha of Bethany as a metaphor for the perfect friendship. As Dutton notes, "These sisters appear throughout Aelred's works . . . as representatives of the contemplative and active lives and of the dynamic tension between those lives. Additionally, however, they represent the way their friendship contained Jesus concretely at its center."[8] Aelred sees in Mary and Martha the embodiment of community, of service, of prayer, and—despite their sex—of brotherly love.

I propose here that friendship among religious women, particularly visionary women, functions differently. Aelred's vision of male monastic friendship has also governed how both contemporaries and present-day readers of medieval women's lives have read these friendships among spiritual women. But by moving away from this model, we can see that there are important distinctions. Jane Tibbets Schulenburg's extensive study of female sanctity traces the ways in which friendship evolved and was seen among men and women throughout medieval Christianity. She notes that in women's same-sex friendships, there persists a "frustrating silence," but that by looking more closely at the extant evidence of holy women's lives, such as their *vitae*, "bonds of friendship seem in fact to have played a remarkably important role in the lives of these early medieval women."[9] Although since Schulenburg's book (1998) there has been more work, it has primarily focused on the erotic and queer potential and tensions of same-sex friendships in monastic settings.[10] The texts

---

7. Dutton, "The Sacramentality of Community in Aelred," 246.
8. Dutton, "The Sacramentality of Community in Aelred," 251.
9. Schulenburg, *Forgetful of Their Sex*, 349.
10. Notably, Judith M. Bennett's idea of the "lesbian-like" has been useful for many scholars to read same-sex desire in the medieval past. This has been responded to and problematized by scholars but remains an important category of understanding medieval same-sex female relationships. See "'Lesbian-Like' and the Social History of Lesbianisms," *Journal of the History of Sexuality* 9 (2000): 1–24. Other scholars have looked at the convent through the lens of queer desire. See, for example, Lisa M. C. Weston, "Virgin Desires: Reading a Homoerotics of Female Monastic Community," in *The Lesbian Premodern: A Historical and Literary Dialogue*, ed. Noreen Giffney, Michelle Sauer, and Diane Watt (New York: Palgrave MacMillan, 2011), 93–104. Most recently, Laura Saetveit Miles reads Margery Kempe and Julian of Norwich's meeting through a queer lens in "Queer Touch between Holy Women: Julian of Norwich, Margery Kempe, Birgitta of Sweden, and the Visitation," in *Touching, Devotional Practices, and Visionary Experience in the Late Middle Ages*, ed. David Carrillo-Rangel, Delfi I. Nieto-Isabel, and Pablo Acosta-García (New York: Palgrave, 2019), 203–35.

I am looking at here certainly contain these possibilities—Hildegard's letters to Richardis, for example, almost demand to be read through this lens, as her passion for and distress about Richardis are so palpable. They read like a woman's loss of a lover, not just of a friend and confidante. I do not mean to discount the erotic interpretations inherent in these examples; I believe both are true: the women in these texts are friends and they can also be lovers or potential lovers. Their friendship may not be sexual, or it may be infused with erotics, or it may be both.

Visionary women complicate some of the elements of Aelred's schematic. Women's relationships can be generational, familial, and erotic, but women's friendship intersects all of these while also carving out its own distinct space. They are also not necessarily a relationship between equals, as Aristotle argued, and they are not uncomplicated. While many of these women live in communities, they also are fundamentally apart from communal life either because of the physical and emotional toll of the visions or because of the kind of work their visions lead them to (theological, political, literary). In this way, Christ is not at the center of women's friendships. He may be at the center of the visionary woman's life and consciousness, but her friends work to make that possible for her. These friendships take the form of a community supporting the visionary, as powerful mentoring relationships, and as familial ones—modeled as sisters or mothers/daughters.

Visionary women's friends are always part of their hagiographies. Many of their visions, in fact, concern the lives or futures of friends for whom they have concern. As H. M. Canatella has noted, "Visionary experience was often a key component of medieval spiritual friendship. For example, Christina of Markyate's *vita* often described visions that she had of Abbot Geoffrey of Saint Albans, and these visions served to provide Christina with special knowledge that she could then share with Geoffrey so as to strengthen their bond of friendship."[11] But often these friendships as described in hagiographic texts are male-female, with the female visionary friend to, and championed by, the male priest who authorizes her mystical activity for a suspicious church hierarchy. The female-female friendships are less pronounced in these texts, but they are definitively there, and upon further scrutiny they show that the visionary is really dependent on the friendships of women around her in order to succeed.

THE TWELFTH-CENTURY VISIONARY Hildegard of Bingen (c. 1098–1179) is in many ways the prototypical medieval woman mystic. She entered a Bene-

---

11. Canatella, "Long-Distance Love," 48.

dictine convent in Germany at a young age, at first hid her visions, and eventually described them and wrote them down, gaining both political and religious fame as a result. Her fame comes to us through her writings but also because of her correspondence with, and sanction by, important Church leaders at the time, Bernard of Clairvaux and Pope Eugenius III among them. But Hildegard's story has the intertwining stories of other women at the margins. She is mentored by a woman, Jutta; she is encouraged by and loves deeply a nun at her convent, Richardis; and, as her fame and reputation spread, she mentors other women through epistolary correspondence, including the visionary Elizabeth of Schönau. Probing more deeply here, we can see that Hildegard's network of women is what makes her position possible and that she very well understands this to be the case.

Hildegard's hagiographer was Theodoric of Echternach (d. 1192), although he compiled much of Hildegard's life from other sources and witnesses.[12] From the first sentences of the *vita*, we are introduced to the importance of women and their friendship in Hildegard's life, as her enclosure with the anchoress Jutta is her first defining moment: "When she was about eight years of age, she was enclosed at Disibodenberg with Jutta, a devout woman consecrated to God, so that, by being buried with Christ, she might rise with him to the glory of eternal life."[13] Jutta becomes a mentor, a teacher, and a friend to Hildegard, but their relationship was already partly forged through their families. Barbara Newman notes that "Jutta's family was closely connected with Hildegard's, and her conversion provided an ideal opportunity for Hildegard's parents, Hildebert and Mechthild, to perform a pious deed. They offered their eight-year-old daughter, the last of ten children, to God as a tithe by placing her in Jutta's hermitage. As a handmaid and companion to the recluse, Hildegard was also her pupil: she learned to read the Latin Bible, particularly the psalms, and to chant the monastic Office."[14] Hildegard left her large family for a new family of two, and until other nuns joined them when they established a new convent together, Jutta must have been the most important person in Hildegard's life. Jutta's friendship and mentorship would have been foundational, but she is rarely mentioned in Hildegard's writings or *vita*, which point to a connection that is not as close a relationship as Hildegard will later forge. Franz Felten writes, "Hildegard speaks of her detachedly as a noble woman to whom she

---

12. For more on the compilation of Hildegard's hagiographic corpus, see the introduction to *Jutta and Hildegard: The Biographical Sources*, ed. Anna Silvas (Turnhout: Brepols, 1998).

13. *Jutta and Hildegard*, 140; the Latin can be found in Godefrido et Theodorico Monachis, *Vita Sanctae Hidlegardis*, in AASS, 17 Sept, V, 91–130, at 91>.

14. *Hildegard of Bingen: Scivias*, trans. Mother Columba Hart and Jane Bishop, introd. Barbara J. Newman, pref. Caroline Walker Bynum (New York: Paulist Press, 1990), 11.

was consigned in disciplina. She does not call her magistra or even mention her name."[15] However, Hildegard is quoted in her *vita*, noting that it was Jutta to whom she first entrusts her visions: "A certain noblewoman to whom I had been entrusted for instruction, observed these things and laid them before a monk known to her."[16] It is the monk, of course, whose authority will carry validation of Hildegard's visions, but it is her friend, Jutta, who is the first to know of them and who seeks out that authority.

While Hildegard's life gives us some important insight into her relationship with Jutta, Jutta's *vita*, by an unnamed author, shows us more depth in the friendship between the two women.[17] Here, we learn that after Jutta's death, Hildegard and two other nuns, "more privy to her secrets than the others," take on the intimate task of washing and preparing her body.[18] Later, Hildegard asks for and receives a vision explaining her friend's death: "When all these things had been reverently and fittingly completed, a certain faithful disciple [i.e., Hildegard] of the lady Jutta herself, one who had been the most intimate terms with her while she still lived in the flesh, devoutly desired to know what kind of passage from this life her holy soul had made."[19] The hagiographer, after describing the vision, confirms, "now the virgin to whom these things were shown was the lady Jutta's first and most intimate disciple, who, growing strong in her holy way of life even to the pinnacle of all the virtues, had certainly obtained this vision before God through her most pure and devout prayer."[20] At the end of her life, Jutta is surrounded by nuns in a convent where she herself is prioress (Hildegard succeeds her in this position), but the *vita* is careful to point out that there are special relationships here.[21]

---

15. Franz J. Felten, "What Do We Know about the Life of Jutta and Hildegard at Disibodenberg and Rupertsberg?," trans. John Zaleski, in *A Companion to Hildegard of Bingen*, ed. Debra Stoudt, George Ferzoco, and Beverly Kienzle (Leiden: Brill, 2014), 15–38, at 26.

16. *Jutta and Hildegard*, 159; "Sed quaedam nobilis femina, cui in disciplina eram subdita, haec notavit, et cuidam sibi notae monachae," *Vita Sanctae Hildegardis*, 103.

17. For speculation on the authorship of *Vita domnae Juttae inclusae*, see *Jutta and Hildegard*, 47–50.

18. *Jutta and Hildegard*, 80. The Latin can be found in Franz Staab, "Reform und Reformgruppen im Erzbistum Mainz. Vom 'Libellus de Willigisi consuetudinibus' zur 'Vita domnae Juttae inclusae,'" in Stefan Weinfurter and Hubertus Seibert, *Reformidee und Reformpolitik in Spätsalisch-Frühstaufischen Reich: Vorträge de Tagung der Gessellschaft für Mittelrheinische Kirschengeschichte Vom 11. Bis 13. September 1991 in Trier* (Mainz: Selbstverlag der Gesekkschaft, 1992), 119–88, at 184.

19. *Jutta and Hildegard*, 81–82; Staab, "Reform und Reformgruppen," 185.

20. *Jutta and Hildegard*, 83; Staab, "Reform und Reformgruppen," 186.

21. The titles of abbess and prioress and leader are all used to describe Jutta and then Hildegard, although at the beginning there was no formal convent—just women enclosed together. Some of this is laid out in Felten, "What Do We Know?," 15–38.

The three nuns who prepare her body are the keepers of her secrets, and Hildegard is given a vision of Jutta's death because of their intimacy.

Jutta's is the first friendship of Hildegard's recorded life, but it reverberates in relationships that follow, first with a nun at her convent and then later through her letters to other women and visionaries. Hildegard's first book of visions, the *Scivias,* took her ten years to write, and only then, she explains, with the help and assistance of two people: the nun Richardis von Stade, whom she mentored (Jutta's niece), and the monk Volmar of Dibodenberg. Hildegard writes in her introduction: "But I, though I saw and heard these things, refused to write for a long time through doubt and bad opinion and the diversity of human words, not with stubbornness but in the exercise of humility, until, laid low by the scourge of God, I fell upon a bed of sickness; then, compelled at last by many illnesses, and by the witness of a certain noble maiden of good conduct [Richardis] and of that man whom I had secretly sought and found, as mentioned above [Volmar], I set my hand to the writing."[22] Hildegard's friendship with Richardis consumed her, and although Richardis is credited here with giving Hildegard the courage to write her book, her letters show the depth of that friendship and the pain it caused Hildegard when Richardis left the convent to form another.

Ulrike Wiethaus notes of these letters that they "equal in tragic passion and depth the letters between Héloïse and Abelard.... The intensity of images and dramatic involvement we sense in the visions is the same we detect in Hildegard's feelings for Richardis."[23] This passion has sparked much academic discussion, casting the relationship between Hildegard and Richardis as mutually erotic or with Hildegard as a dominant figure, from whom Richardis feels she must escape.[24] Hildegard's efforts to keep Richardis with her and not moved to Bassum, where she had been elected abbess, are also the subject of many of her letters to Church figures, including Pope Eugenius. But these facts and speculations aside, we can still see the friendship at the core of what existed between these two nuns. Hildegard's book is written only with the encouragement and love of Richardis, and, as with Jutta, her work is first dependent on a woman's response before she disseminates it outward. It is hard to know what

---

22. *Hildegard of Bingen: Scivias,* 60; the Latin can be found in *Hildegardis Scivias,* ed. Adelgundis Führkötter OSB (Turnholt: Brepols, 1978), 5–6.

23. Ulrike Wiethaus, "In Search of Medieval Women's Friendships: Hildegard of Bingen's Letters to Her Female Contemporaries," in *Maps of Flesh and Light: The Religious Experience of Medieval Women Mystics,* ed. Wiethaus (Syracuse, NY: Syracuse University Press, 1993), 93–111, at 105.

24. See, for example, Kimberly Benedict's discussion of Richardis in *Empowering Collaborations: Writing Partnerships between Religious Women and Scribes in the Middle Ages* (New York: Routledge, 2004), 55–56.

Hildegard's relationship with Richardis was while they were together, because the evidence we have is in letters Hildegard wrote after Richardis has left and Hildegard's great distress therein. Her retrospective response likely colors the account of their friendship.

One of these letters shows how this departure has almost led to a crisis of faith for Hildegard: "Daughter, listen to me, your mother, speaking to you in the spirit: my grief flies up to heaven. My sorrow is destroying the great confidence and consolation that I once had in mankind.... Now, again I say: Woe is me, mother, woe is me daughter, 'Why have you forsaken me' like an orphan? I so loved the nobility of your character, your wisdom, your chastity, your spirit, and indeed every aspect of your life that many people have said to me: What are you doing?"[25] Hildegard's intense attachment to Richardis is positioned as that of both a mother and a daughter, but she also describes herself as Christlike and as an orphan in her grief. These mixed metaphors attempt to express the depth both of what Richardis meant to her and of what her loss now feels like. Peter Dronke analyzes the language of this letter, noting that it is "both intimate and heavy with biblical echoes. These can heighten, but also modify, what she is saying; they make the letter suprapersonal as well as personal. Both aspects are vital to what is essentially a harsh confrontation between transcendent love and the love of the heart."[26] That Richardis's support is so essential to Hildegard's own intellectual and visionary output further underscores what the women meant to each other. She, along with the monk Volmar, are really seen as collaborators in the *Scivias*; the visions may be Hildegard's, but the writing and formulation of them are with the help of her friends.[27]

We can see that this closeness extends to Hildegard's letters regarding Richardis and how she is addressed concerning her. At Richardis's death, her brother Hartwig, the archbishop of Bremen, writes to Hildegard with the news, acknowledging the close relationship forged between the two women: "I write to inform you that our sister—my sister in body, but yours in spirit—has gone the way of all flesh, little esteeming that honor I bestowed upon her.... Thus I ask as earnestly as I can, if I have any right to ask, that you love her as much as she loved you, and if she appeared to have any fault—which

---

25. "Letter 64: Hildegard to Abbess Richardis," in *The Letters of Hildegard of Bingen*, vol. 1, trans. Joseph L. Baird and Radd K. Ehrmann (Oxford: Oxford University Press, 1994), 143–34, at 144; the Latin can be found in "Epist. LXIV: Hildegardis ad Richardem Abbatissam," in *Hildegardis Bingensis Epistolarium*, Pars Prima I-XC, ed. L. Van Acker (Turnholt: Brepols, 1991), 147–48, at 147>.

26. Peter Dronke, *Women Writers of the Middle Ages* (Cambridge: Cambridge University Press, 1984), 157.

27. This view of Hildegard's writing is seen early in Hildegard studies and persists.

indeed was mine, not hers—at least have regard for the tears that she shed for your cloister, which many witnessed."[28] Although the relationship between Hartwig and Hildegard was obviously fraught—she blames him for Richardis's departure, and he refuses her entreaties to have her return—he recognizes the importance of his duty in letting Hildegard know and acknowledges the intimacy the women shared. Hildegard responds to him that God "works in them like a mighty warrior who takes care not to be defeated by anyone, so that his victory may be sure. Just so, dear man, was it with my daughter Richardis, whom I call both daughter and mother, because I cherished her with divine love, as indeed the Living Light had instructed me to do in a very vivid vision."[29]

Hildegard's letters reveal that she was sought out as a mentor by both lay and religious women. Although these friendships were primarily epistolary, they show tenderness and intimacy despite the formal, biblical, and metaphoric language that Hildegard favors. Beverlee Sian Rapp concludes that the language she uses in her letters is different for the female correspondents than for the men: "Such comforting and supportive language is almost unheard in Hildegard's letters to her male correspondents, but here, in a community of women, she does not hesitate to offer kind and supportive words, which may help a sister in God to deal with her troubles."[30] One unknown abbess—who appears to have previously known Hildegard in person—writes to her with affection but expresses sadness that she had not received a letter in return: "It seems clear that I must accept with equanimity the fact that you have failed to visit me through your letters for a long time, although I am greatly devoted to you. . . . For if it is not granted to me to see your beloved face again in this life—and I cannot even mention this without tears—I will always rejoice because of you, since I have determined to love you as my own soul. Therefore, I will see you in the eye of prayer, until we arrive at that place where we will be allowed to look upon each other eternally, and to contemplate our beloved, face to face in all his glory."[31] Hildegard's response is curt and a bit

---

28. "Letter 13: Hartwig, Archbiship of Bremen to Hildegard," in *Letters*, vol. 1, 49–50, at 50; "Epist. XIII: Hartvvigvs Archiepiscopvs Bremensis ad Hildegardem," *Hildegardis Bingensis Epistolarium*, 29.

29. "Letter 13r: Hildegard to Hartwig, Archbishop of Bremen," in *Letters*, vol. 1, 51; "Epist. XIIIR, Hildegardis ad Hartvvigvm Archiepiscopvm Bremensem," *Hildegardis Bingensis Epistolarium*, 30–31, at 30.

30. Beverlee Sian Rapp, "A Woman Speaks: Language and Self-Representation in Hildegard's Letters," in *Hildegard of Bingen: A Book of Essays*, ed. Maud Burnett McInerney (New York: Garland, 1998), 3–24, at 22.

31. "Letter 49: An Abbess to Hildegard," in *Letters*, vol. 1, 49–50, at 50; "Epist. XLIX: Abbatissa ad Hildegardem," *Hildegardis Bingensis Epistolarium*, 119–20.

scolding, not reflecting at all the depth of feeling revealed in the abbess's letter. As with Hildegard's relationship with Richardis, this reminds us that not all friendships go both ways, and, as with all kinds of love, it can be unrequited or unequal.

Among Hildegard's many letters to women, those to Elisabeth of Schönau have received the most attention. In Hildegard's relationship with Elisabeth, whose visions began after Hildegard was known for hers, we can see how she passes along the kind of friendship that she has received, becoming the kind of mentor that she did not have from a fellow visionary. Newman notes the similarities between the two women: "Temperamentally, Elisabeth resembled Hildegard in many ways; she shared the older women's physical frailty, her sensitivity to spiritual impressions of all kinds, and her need for public authentication to overcome initial self-doubt. Just as Hildegard had written in her uncertainty to Bernard, the outstanding saint of the age, so Elisabeth wrote to Hildegard."[32] Elisabeth reaches out to Hildegard in a lengthy and personal letter, immediately claiming a kinship and asking for advice—counsel she understands can only come from a woman in a similar position: "I have been disturbed, I confess, by a cloud of trouble lately because of the unseemly talk of the people, who are saying many things about me that are simply not true. Still, I could easily endure the talk of the common people, if it were not for the fact that those who are clothed in the garment of religion cause my spirit even greater sorrow."[33] She explains the circumstances and contents of her visions, and why they are doubted, and begs for Hildegard's advice and her stamp of approval in her closing words: "My lady, I have explained the whole sequence of events to you so that you may know my innocence—and my abbot's—and thus may make it clear to others. I beseech you to make me a participant in your prayers, and to write back me some words of consolation as the Spirit of the Lord guides you."[34]

Hildegard takes up her role as mentor and friend, encouraging Elisabeth in the face of her detractors, but also showing what she has learned as a visionary. Ulrike Wiethaus calls their relationship a "professional friendship," noting that "both women exchanged thoughts about their public 'work,' their

---

32. Barbara Newman, "Hidlegard of Bingen: Visions and Validation," *Church History* 54 (1985): 163–175, at 173.

33. "Letter 201: The Nun Elisabeth to Hildegard," *Letters of Hildegard of Bingen*, vol. 2, trans. Joseph L. Baird and Radd K. Ehrmann (Oxford: Oxford University Press, 1998), 176–79, at 176. The Latin can be found at https://epistolae.ctl.columbia.edu/letter/123.html (accessed September 23, 2019).

34. "Letter 201: The Nun Elisabeth to Hildegard," *Letters*, vol. 2, 176–79, at 179; https://epistolae.ctl.columbia.edu/letter/123.html (accessed September 23, 2019).

calling, their literal profession as visionaries."[35] Hildegard writes, warning her of temptation because she is a holy vessel, "So, O my daughter Elisabeth, the world is in flux. Now the world is wearied in all the verdancy of the virtues, that is, in the dawn, in the first, the third, and the sixth—the mightiest—hour of the day. But in these times it is necessary for God to 'irrigate' certain individuals, lest His instruments become slothful."[36] She closes by speaking to her own role as a visionary describing herself as a trumpet for God's word in order that Elisabeth can better understand her own role: "O my daughter, may God make you a mirror of life. I too cower in the puniness of my mind, and am greatly wearied by anxiety and fear. Yet from time to time I resound a little, like the dim sound of a trumpet from the Living Light. May God help me, therefore to remain in His service."[37] Hildegard uses her life as an example to Elisabeth, warning her of pride and demonstrating through her own example a language which Elisabeth can use to describe her role as visionary.

Elisabeth clearly takes her words to heart. She responds to Hildegard describing a vision and noting, "you are the instrument of the Holy Spirit, for your words have enkindled me as if a flame had touched my heart, and I have broken forth into these words."[38] Elisabeth ultimately wrote three books of her visions, the third written after this correspondence. Like Hildegard, Elisabeth would go on to lead her religious community, demonstrating how these women's friendships successively influence others.[39] Through the interconnections of Jutta, Richardis, Hildegard, and Elisabeth, we can see how these visionary women are in fact dependent on their friendships and relationships with each other and the support of women around them. The texts of Hildegard may not have existed without encouragement of Jutta and Richardis, or those of Elisabeth without Hildegard.

WE CAN SEE the outlines of visionary women's friendships a century later, again in Germany, in the phenomenon of the fourteenth-century *Schwesternbücher*, or sisterbooks. These books are records of many members of the same

---

35. Wiethaus, "In Search of Medieval Women's Friendships," 103.

36. "Letter 201r: The Nun Elisabeth to Hildegard," *Letters*, vol. 2, 180–81, at 180; "Epist. CCr: Hildegardis ad Elisabeth Monialem," *Hildegardis Bingensis Epistolarium*, 456–57, at 457.

37. "Letter 201r: Hildegard to the Nun Elisabeth," *Letters*, vol. 2, 180–81, at 181; "Epist. CCr: Hildegardis ad Elisabeth Monialem," *Hildegardis Bingensis Epistolarium*, 456–57, at 457.

38. "Letter 202/203: Elisabeth to Hildegard," *Letters*, vol. 2, 181–85, at 181; https://epistolae.ctl.columbia.edu/letter/124.html (accessed September 23, 2019).

39. María Eugenia Góngora, "Elizabeth von Schönau and the Story of St Ursula," in *Mulieres Religiosae: Shaping Female Spiritual Authority in the Medieval and Early Modern Periods*, ed. Veerle Fraeters and Imke de Gier (Turnhout: Brepols, 2014), 17–36, at 19.

convent who experienced visions and revelations, and who wrote them down collectively. Albrecht Classen explains, "We know primarily of nine major convents where this phenomenon took place, all of them located within the Dominican province of Teutonia in the Southwest of modern Germany, in the Northeast of France, and in Switzerland."[40] These books recorded the lives of exemplary sisters and served as models of holy and pious behavior for the convent, but they also allow glimpses into convent life. The simple fact of their witness—that women were moved enough to write and preserve the memory of their sisters—demonstrates an act of female friendship. Generally, the books' existences are in themselves testaments to friendship, but also their contents, as Gertrud Jaron Lewis points out, "represent a rich source of information about monastic women's friendships."[41] The books describe the extraordinary (the visions, the charisms) and the everyday interactions among the sisters. We see their daily routines and a sense that these are women of all ages making a life together. For example, Mathilde van Dijk looks closely at the sisterbook from the community Saint Agnes and Mary at Diepenveen, suggesting that the books reflect an interest in the good works and charity of the nuns, practices that reflect their pious interior lives, rather than the vision or other outsized evidence of their holiness. The examples she gives of how the leaders of the convent are described demonstrate the kindness and care among the women: "When the sub-prioress Liesbeth of Delft (d. 1423) insisted on helping to spread manure, the other sisters refused to allow it and took the spade from her. Eventually, she grabbed the mulch with both hands. . . . [Former prioress] Salome Sticken insisted on sitting with the youngest sisters in the choir, although her experience and age entitled her to a superior place."[42] However, many of the sisterbooks also support the lives and words of visionary women. The Engelthal sisterbook, for example, was formed at a Dominican monastery that was home to the German visionary Christine Ebner.

Why the sisterbooks were written and what their purposes were are somewhat unclear. They are part chronicle, part exempla, but the fact that they are written by the women of the convent in order to document the lives of their sisters is at the heart of what I am interested in here. I would like to look more

---

40. Albrecht Classen, *The Power of a Woman's Voice in Medieval and Early Modern Literatures* (Berlin: de Gruyter, 2007), 245. He notes that these convents are "Adelhausen, Diessenhofen, Engeltal, Gotteszell, Kirchberg, Oetenback, Töss, Unterliden, and Weiler" (245). For individual descriptions of these convents and the contents of their books, see Gertrud Jaron Lewis, *By Women, for Women, about Women: The Sister-Books of Fourteenth-Century Germany* (Toronto: Pontifical Institute of Mediaeval Studies, 1996).

41. Lewis, *By Women, for Women, about Women*, 222.

42. Mathilde van Dijk, "Female Leadership and Authority in the Sisterbook of Diepenveen," in *Mulieres Religiosae*, 243–264, at 259.

closely at the sisterbook of the Monastery of St. Maria in Töss, in what is today Switzerland. The community there, according to Lewis, "had its origin in a beguinage in Winterthur. . . . The Töss monastery was officially incorporated into the Order of Preachers by Innocent IV in 1245; but even prior to this date, the nuns had for several years been spiritually cared for by the friars of Zürich."[43] While a few of the sisterbooks were written in Latin (Unterlinden and Adelhausen), the book at Töss is one of the seven written originally in the vernacular German,[44] and, among its four extant complete manuscripts, one is the only illuminated copy of any of the sisterbooks.[45] One of the writers is Elsbeth of Stagel (1300–c. 1360), who, Lewis notes, "became known as a writer, scribe, and translator, but was perhaps made most famous for her spiritual friendship and literary cooperation with Heinrich Suso."[46] Many of their extant letters survive, and she may deserve credit for a large portion of Suso's work because she initially wrote down his visions and he used her text as a basis for his own.[47]

Elsbeth almost certainly wrote the life of Elizabeth of Töss, which is appended to the sisterbook and describes the visionary woman and her life at the convent. Sarah McNamer has argued convincingly that it is this Elizabeth who is the subject of the Middle English hagiographies attributed to St Elizabeth of Hungary, but not the popular St Elizabeth of Hungary who was the daughter of the king (and with whom she appears to have been confused because she was also a member of the royal family).[48] Elsbeth may have written the visions down as well, although the authorship is unclear, but she is clearly credited with Elizabeth's *vita*.[49] Elsbeth speaks with a certain pride about this royal nun, noting that she entered their order at thirteen and that she was the

---

43. Lewis, *By Women, for Women, about Women*, 21.

44. Claire Taylor Jones, *Ruling the Spirit: Women, Liturgy, and Dominican Reform in Late Medieval Germany* (Philadelphia: University of Pennsylvania Press, 2017), 57.

45. Lewis, *By Women, for Women, about Women*, 23.

46. Lewis, *By Women, for Women, about Women*, 24.

47. See, for example, Albrecht Classen, "From *Nonnenbuch* to Epistolarity: Elsbeth Stagel as a Late Medieval Woman Writer," in *Medieval German Literature: Proceedings from the 23rd International Congress on Medieval Studies: Kalamazoo, Michigan, May 5–8, 1988*, ed. Classen (Göppingen: Kümmerle Verlag, 1989), 147–70.

48. See the introduction in Sarah McNamer, *The Two Middle English Translations of St Elizabeth of Hungary* (Heidelberg: Universitätsverlag C. Winter, 1996).

49. There are no English translations of the sisterbooks. I have excerpted here from the German editions, as well as used the French translation: Jeanne Ancelet-Hustache, *La Vie Mystique d'un Monastère de Dominicanes au Moyen Age D'après la Chronique de Töss* (Paris: Perrin, 1928); *Kleinere mittelhochdeutsche Erzählungen, Fabeln und Lehrgedichte. I. Die Melker Handschrift*, ed. Albert Leitzmann (Berlin: Weidmannsche Buchhandlung, 1904), 98.

first virgin received in the order at their new foundation.⁵⁰ We know from both her *vita* and Elizabeth's *Revelations* that she develops a visionary bond with the Virgin Mary, with whom she dialogues. The sisterbook *vita* lays bare the kind of community support that allows that visionary activity to happen. In one scene of the *vita*, for example, one of the nuns has a dream vision where she sees the sisters arranged for matins, and, as they pray, their words appear to be pearls that fall from their mouths into a cup—but two pearls fall from Elizabeth's mouth for each word she utters. Although this underscores Elizabeth's holiness (the point of the *vita*, after all), it demonstrates how she is part of a communal life with women who are supporting and sharing her in her works.

The *vita* closes with an exhortation to the sisters to remember not only how Elizabeth was a model of devotional piety and excellence but how she supported and participated in the Order. Elsbeth points out how even though she was from a royal family, she lived the life of the Order in humility and poverty, an example to all the sisters.⁵¹ This emphasis on the community of nuns demonstrates how important that community is to the making and supporting of the visionary (Elizabeth) but also to the construction of the story of the community in the sisterbook. Here, the friendships among the women create a network of support that manifests itself in the text, giving the women *exempla* but also recording their lives.

CATHERINE OF SIENA is not in the formal community of a convent and her friends are mentioned in supporting roles throughout her *vita*, although we also have more direct evidence of women as her friends because they served as scribes for her, pointing beyond intimacy and a support system to an active role in shaping the life of the visionary women and her legacy afterward. This is not unique to Catherine. As we have seen, the nun Richardis acted as a scribe and collaborator for Hildegard. Another famous German mystic, Mechthild of Hackeborn, was assisted by Gertrude of Helfta (who herself was assisted by fellow nuns in the writing of her own visions). These collaborations are more than just scribal activity; the women often serve as the sounding boards for their visionary friends, the first to hear the visions as they help shape them and write them down.

In Catherine's case, women who are part of her *famiglia* of followers act as scribes for some of her many letters. Kimberly Benedict reads in the scribes'

---

50. *Kleinere mittelhochdeutsche Erzählungen*, 101.
51. *Kleinere mittelhochdeutsche Erzählungen*, 121.

notations at the ends of Catherine's letters a "provocative kind of dialogism," which uses humor to make the women's presences known: "After transcribing the holy woman's messages, the assistants would conclude with brief remarks of their own. Whereas Catherine's comments generally consist of pious instructions and exhortations, however, the scribes' messages tend to be humorous, shifting the letters' focus from the sacred to the absurd. For example, the scribes identify themselves using unflattering nicknames such as 'fat Alessa,' 'crazy Giovanna,' and 'Cecca the time-waster.' While the names are inherently silly, they are also satirical insofar as they give an impertinent twist to the humility tropes typically used by medieval religious writers."[52]

These marks of humor throughout the letters also demonstrate a sign of affection between Catherine and the women of her *famiglia*, in addition to the intimacy inherent in the scribal relationship where Catherine dictates personal thoughts. For example, in one of her letters to a woman named Monna Agnesa Malavolti, a member of the third order of lay Dominicans (as was Catherine) and a woman from an important Siennese family, Catherine encourages her to take heart and devote herself to Mary Magdalen among other female saintly role models. She and her scribe, Cecca, close the letter, written during a pilgrimage to the Dominican monastery in Montepulciano, in a way that demonstrates their close bond as well as the slippage between the writer and the scribe:

> In the name of Christ and in my name encourage and bless Monna Raniera and all my other daughters. Bless and encourage Caterina di Ghetto a thousand times for me and for Alessa and all the others who are here with me. Really, we felt like saying, "Let's make three tents here"! because truly it seems like paradise to us to be with these very holy virgins. They are so taken up with us that they won't let us leave, and we are always bewailing the fact that we are leaving. . . . I Cecca am almost a nun, because I'm beginning to chant the Office with all my might along with these servants of Jesus Christ![53]

Suzanne Noffke, who has translated and edited all of Catherine's letters, suggests that the "my name" in the first sentence is Catherine but that the "me" in the remaining parts are Cecca, her scribe and companion (Francesca di Clemente Gori). She notes that she thinks the Alessa here is Alessa dei

---

52. Kimberly Benedict, *Empowering Collaborations: Writing Partnerships Between Religious Women and Scribes in the Middle Ages* (New York: Routledge, 2004), 32.

53. Suzanne Noffke, ed., "Letter T61/G183/Dt2 To Monna Agnessa Malavolti and the *Mantellate* of Siena," in *The Letters of Catherine of Siena Volume I* (Tempe: Arizona Center for Medieval and Renaissance Studies, 2000), 4–5.

Saracini, "a close and constant member of Catherine's circle."⁵⁴ This movement from Catherine's voice ("bless . . . all my other daughters") to Cecca's ("Bless . . . Caterina . . . for me and for Alessa and for all the others who are here with me") demonstrates this close circle of women friends with Catherine at its center. Catherine is the main voice, the purpose, but she is surrounded by a group that knows her and each other well. Even Cecca's nearly humorous signoff—"I . . . am almost a nun"—shows a camaraderie and closeness among the women and their correspondence.

It is significant that the scribes for Catherine sign their names—often these women collaborators are lost to anonymity—showing that they felt themselves to be integral to Catherine's mission and messages. However, it is equally significant that the women's names appear only on her early letters and that eventually her letter writing is taken over by male scribes. The humorous epithets give way to more pro-forma signatures from Catherine, and the scribes are no longer clearly identified. The women move to the background of Catherine's life, even though they continue to travel with and support her as part of her family.

In this light, it is telling that the many women we see and know of in her letters are all but absent from her *vita*. Her mother, Lapa, and some sisters and sisters-in-law get mentioned, but the names of Alessa and Cecca are often missing although they are sometimes named as a source of a story or as an additional witness to a miracle. The women who have roles of note are those who benefited from Catherine's intercessional prayers or the miracles attributed to her. For example, in describing how Catherine cured a woman, Monna, of a possession by an evil spirit, Raymond of Capua writes: "Present at this miracle, besides Monna Bianchina, who is still alive, were Friar Santi, the holy virgin's companions Alessia and Francesca, her sister-in-law Lisa, and about a score and a half of other people of both sexes, whose names I cannot give as I have no record of them."⁵⁵

Catherine's female friends and their roles as witnesses and important sources for Catherine's life are acknowledged by Raymond at the end of his *vita*. He vouches for them as sources of reliable information in reporting on Catherine's life: "But in case I may seem to be simply misleading my readers by mentioning these people in a merely general way, I shall list their names,

---

54. Noffke, "Letter T61/G183/Dt2 To Monna Agnessa Malavolti and the *Mantellate* of Siena," 5n17.
55. Raymond of Capua, *The Life of St. Catherine of Siena by Blessed Raymond of Capua*, trans. George Lamb (Rockford, IL: Tan Books and Publishers, 1960, repr., 2003), 249; the Latin can be found in Raimondo da Capua, *Legenda maior*, ed. Silvia Nocentini (Firenze: Edizioni del Galluzzo, 2013), 318.

both the men and the women, separately. These are the people to be believed, not me! . . . Here are their names. I will begin with the women, as these were with Catherine practically all the time."[56] Here, Raymond also inadvertently demonstrates how close Catherine was to her female friends—they were with her "practically all the time." Catherine does not exist without them.

Raymond goes on to describe and praise the women closest to Catherine. He notes that Alessa (here Alessia) was the recipient of Catherine's intimacies: "Alessia of Siena, one of the Sisters of Penance of St. Dominic, though she was one of the last to put herself under Catherine's guidance, was nevertheless in my opinion the most perfect of all of them in virtues. . . . She was so assiduous and perfect that if I am not mistaken the holy virgin revealed her most intimate secrets to her towards the end and desired that after death the others should accept in her stead and take her as their model."[57] He continues to describe Francesca: "a most religious woman, united to God and Catherine in truest affection. . . . Francesca, like many others, gave me much information."[58] He closes by noting of her sister-in-law, Lisa, "Of Lisa I shall say no more, as she is still alive, and also because she was the wife of one of Catherine's brothers. I should not like the unbelievers to be able to cast doubts on her evidence, though as a matter of fact I have always found her to be the kind of woman who does not tell lies."[59]

Although studies of Catherine typically identify her in relation to the men in her life (Stephen Maconi, Raymond of Capua, Thomas Caffarini, etc.), this closer look at her letters and her *vita* demonstrates the absolutely essential role that the women in her life played—especially Alessa, Cecca, and Lisa. These women not only supported her physically as they traveled but also worked as her scribes—essential for Catherine's establishment of her reputation through her extensive letter-writing network. Finally, they serve as the sources for Raymond's *vita*, giving him the stories and the personality behind the woman he knew and championed. Even Raymond realizes how much he is in their debt.

I WOULD LIKE to conclude by looking at "The Life and Good End of Sister Marie," which describes the death of an English visionary nun after the Reformation. Compared with her more famous predecessors, named and described in this essay, Marie Champney's name has largely been lost to history. Perhaps she would have had a rich hagiographic tradition in the vein of her prede-

---

56. *The Life of St. Catherine of Siena*, 309; *Legenda maior*, 366–67.
57. *The Life of St. Catherine of Siena*, 309–10; *Legenda maior*, 367.
58. *The Life of St. Catherine of Siena*, 310; *Legenda maior*, 367.
59. *The Life of St. Catherine of Siena*, 311; *Legenda maior*, 367.

cessors if her story had taken place before the Dissolution; instead, her Life serves as a testament to the women who tried to keep that tradition somewhat alive by documenting and honoring their friend in her death; they may not have actually written her Life, but they certainly provided its details. In her Life, there are many of the themes of friendship, community support, and mutual affection that we have observed in other *vitae* and texts, but here they are more apparent as Marie and her sisters are exiled and are, in many senses, alone without some of the resources (human or monetary) available to them.

Marie was an English Bridgettine nun and had religious visions throughout her childhood. While abroad in Flanders, she had a vision encouraging her to become a nun and to remain there, so she joined the then exiled house of Syon Abbey, where the habits matched her visions and where, Ann Hutchison notes, "Mary felt she had been destined."[60] Syon in exile was not the powerful and supported community that it was in England. The nuns were having trouble finding a permanent home abroad and the exile took its toll on them emotionally, spiritually, and physically. As Hutchison describes, "Sometime in the autumn of 1578, at least ten, and perhaps more, of the younger members of the monastery were sent to England. The decision to send them had been made by the Abbess and Confessor-General at a time when Calvinists were ravaging the religious establishments in the Low Countries, attacks from which women's houses in particular suffered terrible horrors."[61] The vignettes about Marie's life focus on her return to England. The authorship is unknown, although Hutchison suggests that a likely candidate is the householder (male or female) who housed Marie in England. Marie and her sisters suffer a difficult channel crossing and then are hidden in houses throughout London with recusant Catholics, but she, like other sisters, probably because of the terrible conditions in Flanders, immediately fall very ill. They cannot maintain their community together in Protestant England, and their separation is both emotional and physical.

The description of these sisters in exile reveals how friendships were forged in that crossing and how their physical separation in various houses was overcome when their sister Marie was so deathly ill—perhaps precipitated by the loss of that community of sisters around her. As part of the Bridgettine Rule, two sisters must sit with the ailing nun night and day once it is clear that she will die. These sisters are called from other parts of the city to be with Marie: "A Thursdaye, one sister was come vp and founde her prettie and hartye, with no smale comforte to both sides. Inso much that Sister Marye

---

60. Anne M. Hutchison, "Mary Champney: A Bridgettine Nun under the Rule of Queen Elizabeth I," *Birgittiana* 13 (2002): 3–32, at 4.
61. Hutchison, "Mary Champney," 4.

called the goodman, which had fetched so quicklie vp one of her best frendes; therefore gevinge him—by comon consente—a very fayre corpus case of crimson inbrodered with golde, of her one makinge, to remember her at the holye Aulter, in fine and hansome makinge."[62] Despite the danger inherent in the sisters coming together in London, where they are essentially in hiding by living separately, they do so to usher Marie into her death.

The love they show her at her death, that they show all their sisters, truly underscores the intimacy of the nunnery and especially one in exile and peril:

> So sinkinge downe hir eye liddes, while [the priest] blessed hir and absolved her at hir passinge; never breathinge, nor gaspinge more, but holdinge the holie candle still fast in her hande, when hir holie soule was yeelded vp for hir sisters to close hir eyes and kisse their sweete Maries coarse, which was as white, as the white virgins waxe, her eyes as plumbe and as comelie as any childes in a slumber, her cheekes no leaner then in tyme of healthe, and hir cowntenaunce as asweete as the smyling babes.[63]

Although Marie is never a candidate for sainthood, the *vita*-like narrative describing her visionary past and her holy death allows us to place her among the other women discussed here. For Marie, the isolation and hardships of the recusant nuns encourages a special kind of friendship among her sisters. Unlike a nun in a convent, surrounded always by the women who support her, Marie's friends must come—at some peril—to see her to her death. These bonds are apparent in this deathbed scene where they are closing her eyes and kissing her corpse, keenly aware of the loss of their own. Like Marie, the vibrant hagiographic tradition and its associated texts about and by visionary women has become a shadow of itself. It is the end of an era.

Each of the women written about here stands somewhat outside the normal structures of a convent in addition to her outsider status as visionary and mystic. Hildegard is for a long time enclosed as an anchoress; the sister-books were written seemingly without any male or Church oversight within their Dominican convents; Catherine of Siena was a member of the Dominican third order, and Sister Marie was at first away from her homeland and then hiding within it. For all these women, the isolation of their situations led to intense female friendships with the women around them. And yet these friendships each manifest in markedly different forms: sometimes as replacement family, as mentoring or mentored, or as physical and emotional support

---

62. Ann M. Hutchison, "The Life and Good End of Sister Marie," *Birgittianna* 13 (2002): 33–89, at 73.

63. Hutchison, "The Life and Good End of Sister Marie," 85.

network. The contours of visionary women's friendships are complex, resisting the taxonomy laid out by Aelred and instead forging different bonds. Scrutiny of these texts, among others, shows that despite the idea that these women somehow were alone, lost until the men who would eventually champion them crossed their paths and recognized their gifts, we see instead women who depend on a network of other women to live the life of the visionary and what it entailed.

CHAPTER 2

The Foundations of Friendship
Amicitia, *Literary Production, and Spiritual Community in Marie de France*

STELLA WANG

RECENT SCHOLARSHIP has sought to redress the relative absence of women in the early spiritual literature of friendship.[1] Although female relationships were excluded from foundational theories on the subject, women nonetheless took part in the monastic culture of *amicitia* described by historians like Adele Fiske, R. W. Southern, and Brian McGuire, which broadly characterized the life and letters of men in orders.[2] Intimate bonds undoubtedly existed between the female religious who lived and worked in close quarters—as well as with other friends and patrons beyond their cloistered walls. This essay examines the tangible traces they left in the literary archive through the works of Marie de France. While the court poet is most known for her *Lais* about the various fates of men and women drawn together by desire and longing,

---

1. Important examples include Jane Schulenburg, *Forgetful of Their Sex: Female Sanctity and Society ca. 500–1100* (Chicago: University of Chicago Press, 1998); Mary Erler, *Women, Reading, and Piety in Late Medieval England* (Cambridge: Cambridge University Press, 2002); Karma Lochrie, "Between Women," in *The Cambridge Companion to Medieval Women's Writing*, ed. Carolyn Dinshaw and David Wallace (Cambridge: Cambridge University Press, 2003), 70–88; Laura Gowing, Michael Hunter, and Miri Rubin, eds., *Love, Friendship and Faith in Europe, 1300–1800* (Basingstoke: Palgrave Macmillan, 2005).

2. Adele Fiske, *Friends and Friendship in the Monastic Tradition* (Cuernavaca, Mexico: Centro Intercultural de Documentacion, 1970); R. W. Southern, *St. Anselm: A Portrait in a Landscape* (Cambridge: Cambridge University Press, 1990), 143–47, 161–65; Brian Patrick McGuire, *Friendship and Community: The Monastic Experience, 350–1250* (Ithaca, NY: Cornell University Press, 2010).

she was also profoundly interested in the spiritual nature of the love between women, renaming the lay once called *Eliduc* after its male protagonist to *Guildelüec and Guilliadun* because she felt the adventure concerned the women: "Eliduc fu primes nomes, / Mes ore est li nuns remuëz, / Kar des dames est avenue / l'aventure dunt li lais fu" (lines 23–26).[3] At the end of the story, Guildelüec establishes a religious order, where the two women reside together and exchange letters of friendship with Eliduc from afar. The lay can be described as a foundation narrative written at the very height of female eremitical enthusiasm in the twelfth century when spiritual communities for women, many built with female initiative and labor, reached their highest number in England and France.[4] I consider the *Lais* and the more recently attributed hagiography, *La vie seint Audree*, about the founding of Ely in light of this development.[5] I argue that these works translate the ethical ideals of *amicitia*, advanced by male monastic writers like Aelred of Rievaulx, as the mutual pursuit of spiritual growth for female lives. In these narratives, conventual institutions are represented not only as sites of retreat but as vibrant networks of talent and leadership that viewed women through their participation within community.

Following the medieval model, I focus on *amicitia* as a discursive and institutional phenomenon as much as a private one. These flourishing centers provided a rare forum where women were afforded opportunities to govern and instruct each other, sharing their skills in administration, diplomacy, and literature, among other areas. By performing public acts of service and patronage, they could create enduring arrangements to make their way of life available to other women in the future, long after their own circles of sociability had disappeared.[6] Viewing women's friendship through their relational

---

3. Text from *Lais de Marie de France*, ed. Karl Warnke, trans. Laurence Harf-Lancner (Paris: Librairie Générale Francaise, 1990). All modern translations from *The Lais of Marie de France*, trans. Glyn S. Burgess and Keith Busby (Harmondsworth, Middlesex: Penguin Books, 1986).

4. Bruce Venarde, *Women's Monasticism and Medieval Society: Nunneries in France and England, 890–1215* (Ithaca, NY: Cornell University Press, 1997), 89–132; Sharon K. Elkins, *Holy Women of Twelfth-Century England* (Chapel Hill: University of North Carolina Press, 1988); Penelope Johnson, *Equal in Monastic Profession: Religious Women in Medieval France* (Chicago: University of Chicago Press, 1993).

5. For the most comprehensive discussion, see June Hall McCash, "*La vie seinte Audree*: A Fourth Text by Marie de France?" *Speculum* 77, no. 3 (2002): 744–77. For a recent reconsideration, see Jocelyn Wogan-Browne, "Recovery and Loss: Women's Writing around Marie de France," in *Women Intellectuals and Leaders in the Middle Ages*, ed. Kathryn Kirby-Fulton, Katie Buygyis, and John Van Engen (Cambridge: D. S. Brewer, 2020), 169–191.

6. For women's patronage, see Susan Bell, "Medieval Women Book Owners: Arbiters of Lay Piety and Ambassadors of Culture," in *Sisters and Workers in the Middle Ages*, ed. Judith M Bennett (Chicago: University of Chicago Press, 1989), 135–61; Ian Short, "Patrons and Polyglots: French Literature in Twelfth-Century England," *Anglo-Norman Studies* 14 (1991): 229–49; June

and constructive roles offers an alternative interpretation of female spirituality from the traditional medieval hierarchies focused on virginity and enclosure frequently found in saints' lives and miracle collections.[7] Marie adapts the conventions of these Latinate genres, as well as those of courtly literature, to describe a fundamentally ethical model of religious participation that was available to a wider range of female experiences. Her works portray how women, lay and religious alike, could engage in spiritual friendship and the literary exchange that was its highest expression.

CONTEXT

La vie seint Audree was written during a time when female spiritual life was flourishing in England and across the Channel.[8] In the decades after the Conquest, religious institutions for women were relatively neglected, aside from a few established by bishops.[9] However, this would change with the rapid foundation of daughter houses for monastic orders in the mid-twelfth century. It was the apex of expansion and would be unmatched in later history after its decline in the beginning of the thirteenth century.[10] Female religious communities grew from twenty to more than a hundred between 1130 and 1165 in England alone, far outmatching the establishment of houses for men. In addition to the traditional Benedictine institutions, women had new choices

---

Hall McCash, *The Cultural Patronage of Medieval Women* (Athens: University of Georgia Press, 1996); Susan M. Johns, *Noblewomen, Aristocracy and Power in the Twelfth-Century Anglo-Norman Realm* (Manchester: Manchester University Press, 2018). For other late medieval studies, see Mary Erler, *Women, Reading, Piety*; and Felicity Riddy, "'Women Talking about the Things of God': A Late-Medieval Sub-culture," in *Women and Literature in Britain 1150–1500*, ed. Carol Meale (Cambridge: Cambridge University Press, 1996), 104–27. For an archaeological study of careers and social roles within female monasticism, see Roberta Gilchrist, *Contemplation and Action: The Other Monasticism* (New York: Leicester University Press, 1995).

7. The classic study is Jocelyn Wogan-Browne, *Saints' Lives and Women's Literary Culture, 1150–1300: Virginity and Its Authorizations* (Oxford: Oxford University Press, 2001). See Erler's introduction for understandings outside this model through networks.

8. R. W. Southern, *Western Society and the Church in the Middle Ages* (London: Hodder and Stoughton, 1970), 31; Janet Nelson, "Society, Theodicy and the Origins of Heresy," *Studies in Church History* 9 (1972): 65–77, at 74; Brenda Bolton, "Mulieres Sanctae," *Studies in Church History* 10 (1973): 77–85; David Herlihy, "Did Women Have a Renaissance? A Reconsideration," *Medievalia et Humanistica: An American Journal for the Middle Ages and Renaissance* 13 (1985): 1–22, at 8.

9. Elkins, *Holy Women*, 13–18; Venarde, *Women's Monasticism and Medieval Society*, 76–77; Sally Thompson, *Women Religious: The Founding of English Nunneries after the Norman Conquest* (Oxford: Oxford University Press, 1991), 191–92.

10. Elkins, *Holy Women*, xiii–iv.

between the Cistercian, Augustinian, Fontevrist, and Gilbertine orders, among others; the last was the only conventual order to be established by the English, specifically in response to female grassroots organization.[11]

The many men and women who endeavored to provide resources for the female religious life faced the pressing challenge of adapting existing infrastructure for their needs, whether that was converting the physical sites of abandoned priories, adapting rules of conduct, or producing literature providing spiritual guidance for their reading hours. This last was a question of not only translating the Latin archive into the vernacular for a wider audience but also selecting the sources and reframing its monastic material to suit their needs and circumstances. As Marie states elsewhere in the *Espurgatoire seint Patriz*, translations were undertaken so that these Latin texts could be both intelligible and fitting for lay readers: "qu'il seit entendables / a laie gent e covenables" (lines 2299–2300).[12] Saints' lives like those in the Campsey manuscript translated monastic ideals into recognizable forms for female readers within these institutions, as well as for their outside friends and patrons.

One of the most important literary discourses for communal religious life was spiritual friendship. Monastic thought on friendship was deeply influenced by the classical ideas circulating through Cicero's *De amicitia*, which celebrated a form of civic love between men. Friendship between virtuous men was important for their own benefit as well as the welfare of the *res publica*, from which women were implicitly excluded.[13] Aelred of Rievaulx adapted the Ciceronian model for the religious life, uniting its ideas of mutual will and esteem with the Pauline language of one heart and one soul (*cor unum et anima una*) to describe the vision of harmony in Christian congregations.[14] His treatise offered an important articulation of spiritual ideals of friendship and community that had always been present in varying degrees but flourished with the revival of classical learning promoted by the new cathedral schools in the eleventh and twelfth centuries. The literary legacy

---

11. Elkins, *Holy Women*, 45–51; Vernarde, *Women's Monasticism and Medieval Society*, 54–55.

12. Marie de France, *Saint Patrick's Purgatory*, ed. Michael J. Curley (Binghamton, NY: Medieval & Renaissance Texts & Series, 1993).

13. McGuire, *Friendship and Community*, xi–l. On access to Cicero's texts, see Jan Ziolkowski, "Twelfth-Century Understandings and Adaptations of Ancient Friendship," in *Mediaeval Antiquity*, ed. Andries Welkenhuysen, Herman Braet, and Werner Verbeke (Leuven, Belgium: Leuven University Press, 1995), 59–81, at 63–64.

14. Aelred of Rievaulx, *Spiritual Friendship (De Spirituali Amicitia)*, trans. Marsha L. Dutton, trans. Lawrence C. Braceland, SJ (Trappist, KY: Cistercian Publications, 2010), 60, 61, 75, 85, 114; Marsha Dutton, "The Sacramentality of Community in Aelred," in *A Companion to Aelred of Rievaulx*, ed. Dutton (Leiden: Brill, 2016), 246–67. See also Ziolkowski, "Twelfth-Century Understandings and Adaptations of Ancient Friendship," 78–79.

of this renewed interest has been well documented by the fervent epistolary exchanges that often affirmed the dedication of the writers to each other and to their shared spiritual life.[15]

Literate women inscribed themselves within these conventions, even if they foreclosed or limited the possibility of female friendship. Female religious such as Muriel of Wilton exchanged letters of friendship and verse with the Loire Valley poets like Baudri of Bourgueil and Serlo of Bayeux, describing how "friendship performed in the Lord elevates lovers."[16] Yet Baudri's praise of Muriel reminds us that female authors of her kind were still writing within a masculine discourse, writing to her in one letter: "Your words sound manly, while your voice is feminine."[17] Aelred even advised against such epistolary relationships in the *De institutione inclusarum* (c. 1162), a rule for female anchoritic life addressed to his sister. While he acknowledged that such spiritual intimacies were possible, even the original source of Edenic friendship as he described elsewhere, Aelred warned that this form of writing could engender affections of the mind that verged on the illicit and erotic.[18] On visits from other female religious, Aelred was also discouraging, urging against unnecessary intrusion.[19] Although the vocation of the anchorite was reclusive by nature, these restrictions are striking from the most important advocate of spiritual friendship. Such hesitations must have responded to avid interest from female religious who wanted to engage in the friendships that he had enthusiastically praised elsewhere, as well as imagine their possibilities through writing.

La vie seint Audree offers a vivid entry into the exclusive discourse of spiritual friendship, translating the life of Æthelthryth, a seventh-century

---

15. Julian Haseldine, "Monastic Friendship in Theory and Action in the Twelfth Century," in *Friendship in the Middle Ages and Early Modern Age*, ed. Albrecht Classen and Marilyn Sandidge (Berlin: de Gruyter, 2011).

16. Poem 138, lines 6–7: "Qui tamen in Christo conficiatur amor. / In Domino confectus amor sublimat amantes" From Baudri de Bourgueil, *Poèmes*, trans. Jean-Yves Tilliette, Baldricus Burgulianus (Paris: Les Belles Lettres, 1998).

17. Poem 137, line 10: "Dicta sonant hominem, uox muliebris erat." Holle Canatella, "Loving Friendship in Baudri of Bourgueil's Poetic Correspondence with the Women of Le Ronceray," *Medieval Feminist Forum* 48, no. 2 (2013): 5–42; Gerald Bond, *The Loving Subject: Desire, Eloquence, and Power in Romanesque France* (Philadelphia: University of Pennsylvania Press, 1995); Jane Stevenson, "Anglo-Latin Women Poets," in *Latin Learning and English Lore (Volumes I & II): Studies in Anglo-Saxon Literature for Michael Lapidge* (Toronto: University of Toronto Press, 2005), 86–107; Gabriela Signori, "Muriel and the Others . . . or Poems as Pledges of Friendship," in *Friendship in Medieval Europe*, ed. Julian Haseldine (Stroud: Sutton, 1999), 199–212.

18. Lochrie, "Between Women," 72; Elkins, *Holy Women*, 152–53.

19. Ruth Mazo Karras, "Friendship and Love in the Lives of Two Twelfth-Century English Saints," *Journal of Medieval History* 14, no. 4 (1988): 305–20, at 310.

Anglo-Saxon saint who founded the religious community at Ely. Marie's hagiography frequently figures the saint as "Dieu ami," or friend of God; variants of the term *ami* recur throughout the poem. As Brian McGuire has suggested, describing saints as *amici dei* "emphasized the worth of human bonds as part of the scheme of salvation."[20] The saint's life commemorates the importance of female friendships within that communal vision and, moreover, places Marie's work within the thriving scene of vernacular reading and literary production emerging from female religious centers. The two inscriptions on the codex of its sole extant manuscript, MS Additional 70513 at the British Library, tell us that it was likely collation literature intended for reading aloud during mealtimes for the women living at Campsey Ash priory, an Augustinian convent in Suffolk founded by two lay women in 1195.[21] The collection was also commissioned by a female lay patron, most likely Isabel of Warenne, the Countess of Arundel and, moreover, contains the only other Anglo-Norman hagiographies with known female authors from the period. Both texts were affiliated with Barking Abbey, an institution with a long tradition of female patronage and learning from the Anglo-Saxon period.[22]

Although it was not necessarily the case that Marie was writing from within this religious milieu, many of the leading historical figures that scholars have suggested for the poet's identity are women who lived in convents affiliated with Henry II.[23] One recently proposed candidate is Marie, the sister of Thomas Becket who was appointed abbess of Barking in 1173 as part of

---

20. McGuire, *Friendship and Community*, 228.

21. The two inscriptions are "Cest livere est a convent de campisse" (1r) and "Ce livre deviseie a la priorie de kanpeseie de lire a mengier" (265v). The quire of the manuscript holding the three Anglo-Norman lives composed by nuns is dated to the last quarter of the thirteenth century, and the other three *vitae* from the first quire are dated to the early fourteenth century. For Campsey Ash, William Page and H. Arthur Doubleday, eds., *The Victoria History of the Counties of England*, vol. 2 (London: A. Constable, 1903), 112. For more details on the manuscript, see Delbert Russell, "The Campsey Collection of Old French Saints' Lives: A Reexamination of Its Structure and Provenance," *Scriptorium* 57 (2003): 51–83.

22. Wogan-Browne, *Saints' Lives*, 7. For more on Barking's history, see Jennifer Brown and Donna Alfano Bussell, eds., *Barking Abbey and Medieval Literary Culture: Authorship and Authority in a Female Community* (Woodbridge, Suffolk; Rochester, NY: York Medieval Press, 2012).

23. For Marie of Reading, a monastery closely affiliated with William Marshall and William de Mandeville, the two other likely figures for "le cunte Willalme." MS. Harley 978, a manuscript of the *Lais* and *Fables*, now at the British Library, was likely copied at Reading. See Sidney Painter, "To Whom Were Dedicated the Fables of Marie de France?" *Modern Language Notes* 48, no. 6 (1933): 367–69. Of the hitherto proposed possibilities, only one historical figure, a Marie de Meulan, married to Hugh Talbot of Cleuville in Hereford and Gloucester, has no known affiliations with a religious community. U. T. Holmes, "New Thoughts on Marie de France," *Studies in Philology* no. 29 (1932): 1–10.

Henry's penance for Becket's martyrdom. She then commissioned Guernes de Pont-Sainte-Maxence's life of Thomas Becket, also found in the Campsey manuscript alongside *La vie seint Audree*.[24] Henry also had an illegitimate half-sister named Marie through their father, Geoffrey of Anjou; she was born in France and lived in England as abbess of Shaftesbury.[25] Regardless of whether a single historical Marie can be definitively identified, these biographies demonstrate the close, if sometimes complicated, relations that existed between these female spiritual communities and the powerful Anglo-Norman families that were their patrons.

A woman could enter a spiritual community later in life for a myriad of reasons, or, in the case of Marie de Boulogne, the daughter of King Stephen and abbess of Romsey, come and go at various times in her life. She was extracted from Romsey by Henry to marry Matthew of Alsace, for strategic reasons and, after having two daughters, was eventually allowed to return to the spiritual life.[26] Even the more unusual circumstances between the women in *Guildelüec and Guilliadun* might recall various stories about the early residents of Fontevrault, one of the most influential orders of female monasticism established at the beginning of the century. Philippa of Toulouse, the wife of the troubadour William IX, was a patron of Fontevrault, where she resided after her husband's affair with a young viscountess alongside, by some accounts, his first wife, Ermengarde of Anjou.[27] The social conditions that

---

24. Carla Rossi Bellotto, *Marie de France et Les Érudits de Cantorbéry* (Paris: Classiques Garnier 2009), 177–92, 81–116.

25. John Charles Fox, "Mary, Abbess of Shaftesbury," *The English Historical Review* 26 (1911): 317–26. See also Fox, "Marie de France," *The English Historical Review* 25, no. 98 (1910): 303–6; and Constance Bullock-Davies, "Marie, Abbess of Shaftesbury, and Her Brothers," *The English Historical Review* 80, no. 315 (1965): 314–22.

26. Antoinette Knapton, "A La Recherche de Marie de France," *Romance Notes* 19, no. 2 (1978): 248–53; Sara McDougall, *Royal Bastards: The Birth of Illegitimacy, 800–1230* (Oxford: Oxford University Press, 2017), 202–3.

27. For this initial suggestion, see Howard Bloch's account, though not all his details are correct. Ermengarde was neither the abbess of Fontevrault nor a nun, though she wished to be and stayed there. However, both women may have been at the abbey during Ermengarde's second stay. Bloch, *The Anonymous Marie de France* (Chicago: University of Chicago Press, 2006), 88; and *Medieval Misogyny and the Invention of Western Romantic Love* (Chicago: University of Chicago Press, 1991), 181; Georges Duby, *The Knight, the Lady, and the Priest: The Making of Modern Marriage in Medieval France* (Chicago: University of Chicago Press, 1993), 158–59. For skeptical qualifications of William's first marriage to Ermengarde as recorded in a chronicle by William of Tyre, see Ruth Harvey's painstaking study, "The Wives of the 'First Troubadour' Duke William IX of Aquitaine," *Journal of Medieval History* 19, no. 4 (January 1, 1993): 307–25. For William's repudiation of Philippa, see Linda Patersen, "Women, Property, and the Rise of Courtly Love," in *The Court Reconvenes: Courtly Literature across the Disciplines*, ed. Barbara Altmann and Carroll Carleton (Woodbridge, Suffolk: Boydell & Brewer, 2003), 41–56. For Ermengarde and Philippa's connections to Fontevrault, see Jacques Dala-

framed the entry of such women did not mean that their vows were not in earnest; nor did the influence of these religious houses end when they departed. Such women who were the audience, and even the inspiration for the *Lais*, would have found guidance in a saint's life about a former queen and charismatic practitioner of *amicitia*.

LA VIE SEINT AUDREE

As a hagiography about the foundress of Ely, *La vie seint Audree* would have offered a timely local subject for the female eremitical movement in England. Marie's source was the *Liber Eliensis*, also known as the *Historia Eliensis*, a twelfth-century Latin cartulary-chronicle about the monastery.[28] While the vita had a longer history as part of Bede's *Ecclesiastical History* in the early eighth century, the chronicle and legal inventory was undertaken over the abbey's conversion to a bishopric. The ideology of this later version was shaped by the ensuing conflict between the bishop and its residents over its rights and properties.[29] The account of the miracles, in particular, became a series of warnings against potential malefactors against Ely, especially those who would disperse its holdings. In his vita, the author uses the religious authority of its foundress to establish the superiority of the contemplative life and solder his argument about the independent status of his monastery against both royal and episcopal encroachments.[30]

Marie transforms his polemical proem to create a consciously accessible saint's life that united the active and contemplative lives for the female experience.[31] Female identities were often defined by the three estates of the

---

run, "Robert d'Arbrissel et Les Femmes," *Annales. Histoire, Sciences Sociales* 39, no. 6 (1984): 1140–60; *L'impossible Sainteté: La Vie Retrouvée de Robert d'Arbrissel (v. 1045–1116) Fondateur de Fontevraud* (Paris: Cerf, 1985), 183; and *Robert of Arbrissel: Sex, Sin, and Salvation in the Middle Ages*, trans. Bruce Venarde (Washington, DC: Catholic University of America Press, 2006), 68, 93–101.

28. E. O. Blake, *Liber Eliensis* (London: Offices of the Royal Historical Society, 1962). For a recent translation and study, see Janet Fairweather, *Liber Eliensis: A History of the Isle of Ely from the Seventh Century to the Twelfth* (Woodbridge, UK: Boydell & Brewer, 2005).

29. Virginia Blanton, "King Anna's Daughters: Genealogical Narrative and Cult Formation in the 'Liber Eliensis,'" *Historical Reflections / Réflexions Historiques* 30, no. 1 (2004): 127–49. For invented lineages and successive abbesses, see Christine Fell, "Saint Æðelþryð: A Historical-Hagiographical Dichotomy Revisited," *Nottingham Medieval Studies* no. 38 (1994): 18–34.

30. Jennifer Paxton, "Monks and Bishops: The Purpose of the 'Liber Eliensis,'" *The Haskins Society Journal* 11 (1998): 17–30; Everett Uberto Crosby, *Bishop and Chapter in Twelfth-Century England: A Study of the Mensa Episcopalis* (Cambridge: Cambridge University Press, 1994), 157–74.

31. Wogan-Browne, *Saints' Lives*, 10.

flesh, which included virginity, marriage, and widowhood. As Jocelyn Wogan-Browne has demonstrated, the hagiographies of this period often cast female saints as elective participants in a spiritual marriage to Christ, where the metaphors of betrothal and mutual desire are used to praise cloistered virginity over the other two estates. The labor of marriage and childbearing, on the other hand, were often corollaries of the active life for women. In a peroration absent from the *Liber Eliensis,* Marie's Prologue highlights the sensational fact that her saint was married not once, but twice, before her entry into the religious life. As Virginia Blanton has suggested, *La vie seint Audree* is unique in its stress on the natural state of female sexuality in the landscape of twelfth- and thirteenth-century hagiography.[32] The saint becomes a model for the private lives of lay female readers, among whom, as her narrator states more than once, would be difficult to find a young woman who had not been compelled and overwhelmed by carnal desire: "Envis seroit onkes trovee / Pucele que fust mariee, / Ke ne fust vencue et surprise / Par icel charnel coveitise" (lines 381–84). The poem ultimately suggests that she was not exemplary in spite of her married estate but rather for it: she is able to maintain her chastity within the world and its temptations and, moreover, to gain spiritual and administrative skills that would not be available to her otherwise.[33]

Although Audrey remains a virgin throughout, she models daily ascetic practices like fasting and other penitential disciplines associated with lay married status.[34] These devotional practices within daily life offer a contrast to figures like Mary the Egyptian, whose popular vita that circulated in twelfth-century collections of miracles and saints' lives like Adgar's *Le Gracial.*[35] Mary's irrepressible sexuality is its central theme, which culminates in paying her way to Jerusalem by seducing pilgrims. *La vie seint Audree* forgoes this sensational model of the repentant harlot, instead recounting a lesser known tale told in

---

32. Virginia Blanton, "Chaste Marriage, Sexual Desire, and Christian Martyrdom in *La Vie Seinte Audrée,*" *Journal of the History of Sexuality* 19, no. 1 (2010): 94–114.

33. For honorary virgin martyrs, see Wogan-Browne, *Saints' Lives,* 123–50.

34. Jocelyn Wogan-Browne, "'Clerc u la, muïne u dame': Women and Anglo-Norman Hagiography in the Twelfth and Thirteenth Centuries," in *Women and Literature in Britain, c. 1150–1500,* ed. Carol M. Meale (Cambridge: Cambridge University Press, 1993), 61–85, at 64.

35. Brian Woledge and Ian Short, "Liste provisoire de manuscrits du XIIe siècle contenant des Textes en langue française," *Romania* 102, no. 405 (1981): 1–17; Sarah Kay, *Courtly Contradictions* (Stanford: Stanford University Press, 2001), 78–215; *Le Gracial* (Ottawa, Canada: Editions de l'Université d'Ottawa, 1982. See Duncan Robertson, "The Anglo-Norman Verse Life of 'St. Mary the Egyptian,'" *Romance Philology* 52, no. 1 (1998): 13–44, at 16. For the longer verse life, see also Peter Dembowski, *La Vie de Sainte Marie l'Égyptienne: Versions En Ancien et En Moyen Français* (Genève: Droz, 1977); Michèle Schiavone de Cruz-Sáenz, *The Life of Saint Mary of Egypt: An Edition and Study of the Medieval French and Spanish Verse Redactions* (Barcelona: Puvill, 1979).

the original vita about another Mary of Egypt who lives in chastity with her husband, a shepherd named Eucalist. They are approached by two men, who discover that the couple was living a modest life of unknown virtue. They labor by day to sustain themselves and provide hospitality and alms for the poor, while at night, they perform a daily practice of penance through wearing sackcloth. This brief tale frames the introduction of Audrey's own chaste marriage, emphasizing the possibility for spirituality within lay life in place of a flight into wilderness.

Female experience within the world becomes an asset to the management of religious community. This was a view also held by allies of female monasticism like Robert Abrissel, the founder of the Fontevrist order who preferred to elect *conversa laica,* women who had been married, to the office of abbess. In leading conventual institutions, this could involve managing large estates and defending rights and revenue from magnates, even bishops. His own vita by Andreas of Fontevrault reports that Robert asked a group of officials, when electing the first abbess, how a claustral virgin could handle their external affairs, declaring that chanting psalms would not produce the skilled tongue needed to engage with temporal authorities. His speech is then affirmed by an archpriest who reports that Urban II had not hesitated to elect a woman who had been married four times as abbess. The decision to elect a widow suggested that experience, sexual and otherwise, not only should be forgiven but was a particular strength.[36]

Marie emphasizes the married queen's ability to negotiate her responsibilities, including her successful management and disposal of dower property.[37] The lands of Ely are described as a gift from Audrey's first marriage to Tonbert, and her accomplishments in maintaining and building the abbey are attributed to her charismatic diplomacy. She is able to draw the dowers of daughters of nobility like Werburga; maintain relations with ecclesiastical friends like Wilfrid, who helps administer and provide for their needs; and finally successfully petition for tax exemptions from "des rois, de[s] ducs, de meint prudome" (line 1659), kings, dukes, and other noblemen, with her "cointise" (1657), ingenuity or astuteness. This realpolitik portrait of the saint sets this practical acumen alongside her private devotional practices for readerly emulation.

---

36. Bruce Venarde, *Robert of Arbrissel: Sex, Sin, and Salvation in the Middle Ages* (Washington, DC: Catholic University of America Press, 2003), 28–29; Dalarun, *Robert of Arbrissel,* 66–67.

37. Jocelyn Wogan-Browne, "Rerouting the Dower," in *Power of the Weak: Studies on Medieval Women,* ed. Jennifer Carpenter and Sally-Beth MacLean (Urbana: University of Illinois Press, 1995), 27–56, at 37.

Although her source praises the hierarchical superiority of monastic residents, Marie's poem celebrates the complementary nature of the active and contemplative lives often attributed to women. When Æthelthryth receives permission to take the veil and enter the convent at Coldingham, the *Liber Eliensis* celebrates her decision to abandon her former life, observing that "she delighted in being cut off from human relations for the sake of the sweetness of divine contemplation, so that she might live apparently like Martha, but devote herself utterly to the quietude of Mary (33)."[38] The passage cites the well-known account in Luke 10:38–42 of Christ's visit to the House of Martha and Mary, and his praise of Mary, the sister who sat at his feet, as having the "better part" in contrast to Martha, who is burdened with "many cares." In patristic writing, the biblical passage was often used to describe superiority of the contemplative life over the active life of good works, and was leveraged by religious writers for a stunning variety of polemical issues including feuds within religious houses.[39] In *La vie seinte Audree*, however, Marie makes the two sisters equal:

> Semblance out en la soue vie
> De deuz soreurs Marthe et Marie:
> Marthe ensuï de travaillier
> Et Marie de Deu prier. (lines 1229–32)

> Her life resembled
> the two sisters Martha and Mary:
> Martha pursued work,
> Mary chose to pray to God.

They are mentioned as a pair ("Marthe et Marie"), and, in poetic balance, each sister is accorded her own line.[40] The equity of her translation echoes the eleventh-century praise tradition that identified aristocratic women with both

---

38. Merito felix, merito gloriosa, probata obedientie glorificatur passione et sancte constituta discipline, tantum divinitatis cultus exercens, ob suavitatis divine contemplationis ab humanis cetibus delectabatur abiungi, ut sub specie Marthe resideret, quiete summopere vacaret Marie.

39. Giles Constable, *Three Studies in Medieval Religious and Social Thought* (Cambridge: Cambridge University Press, 1995).

40. Constable states that there was "almost no awareness of Martha and Mary distinctively as women," as they were employed as metaphors to describe the activities of male monastic communities. Yet consistently within his own account, women were particularly identified with both sisters. Constable, *Three Studies*, 39, 107.

Martha and Mary to praise them for their devotional spirituality and noble patronage. Even though Audrey retires to a life of prayer, she is compelled "as if she were abbess" to teach those who needed to learn how to perform good works like Martha (lines 1251–52). Marie is at pains, against the historical record, to suggest that Audrey is the acting leader at Coldingham before she founds Ely. While the monastery was officially under the charge of Ebba, aunt of Ecgfrith and sister of Oswald and Oswiu, Marie suggests that Audrey had the choice to be "haute abbesse" (1301) and "maistresse" (1249, 1302) over the religious house, refraining from taking the title out of humility. Where the *Liber Eliensis* takes rhetorical efforts to place the saint in a tradition of contemplative solitude severed from social relations, Marie's hagiography focuses on the saint's spiritual contributions through her communal obligations.

La vie seinte Audree further circumscribes the theme of *contemptus mundi* in its divine miracles. In the penultimate moment, the saint chooses life and companionship rather than perishing alone on the rocky summit surrounded by waves in flight from Egfrid's army. The author of the *Liber Eliensis* glides over her decision with all his rhetorical force, passing over her "bloodless martyrdom" with a vehement storm of hypotheticals and apologetic clauses:

> I hope most confidently and trust that she is entirely acceptable to those who have washed their garments in the blood of the Lamb [. . . .]. Because, if she had been permitted to fight her battle in those days, under Nero or Diocletian, it is unquestionable that she would have climbed up on to the torturers' rack of her own accord, would have thrown herself into the flames of her own accord, would never have been afraid to have her limbs severed by threshing-wheels or saw blades and would by now certainly have been standing unmoved, not recanting her acknowledgement of the Lord in the face of all the punishments and torments to which human weakness usually gives in, so that she would have laughed in the midst of any tortures whatsoever, happy in her sores, rejoicing in her agonies.

This passage is dramatically abbreviated in *Audree,* where the sublime is muted in favor of the relational. Instead of operatic descriptions of danger and the hypothetical tortures she might have endured, Marie focuses on the two handmaidens, Sewar and Oswen, who become refugees with her out of loyalty. In her prayers, Audrey remembers those on the rock with her and petitions for their lives. Instead of a singular martyrdom, Audrey later dies a more quotidian death in the presence of her companions, as she had always wanted and prayed it would be: "entre ses compaignes fina, / si com ençois le devisa, / Car ele avoit prié sovent / K'eles li fuessent en present" (lines 1997–2000). The hagiography celebrates living labor of a saint actively working within a female community instead of corporeal violence enacted on the virginal body.

In *La vie seint Audree,* to be an *amica dei* was first to be a friend to other women. Marie's work ultimately fulfills the monastic vision of spiritual friendship which strove to imitate the "unity and concord" of heaven through communal participation.[41] The purpose of human life in the Aelredian vision was to become attached and enmeshed in human bonds, even if they inflicted bitterness and grief.[42] In refutation of the Stoic argument that friendship produces an engagement with the world like Martha with "many cares" and causes one to be "afflicted with many bothersome matters," Aelred had suggested that virtue cannot be acquired without fear and sorrow.[43] For Marie's saint, the cares of friendship were not only trials of virtue; they were consolation for the fears and sorrow of martyrdom, as well as the means and reason to transcend them.

The miracles ultimately reaffirm acts of life and livelihood which, elsewhere in the hagiography, took the shape of patronage and institution-building. Yet the tenderest acts of friendship in the saint's life are perhaps portrayed through far more quotidian acts of intimacy and ritual courtesy. The women of Ely, for example, bathed as a community, and although Audrey is the abbess, she bathes last after the women in her care (lines 1737–38). She wishes to eat sparingly but partakes more on feast days in order to please others and lighten their abstinence:" "Ele haÿ come tempeste / Sorfait de manger, mes a feste / Mangoit pur les autres haiter / Et lur abstinence alegier" (1751–56). These minute details bespeak her humility, much closer to the married penitential practices of the nearly undiscovered Mary of Egypt than the demonstrative, even aggressive, asceticism modeled by her more popular incarnation and the desert fathers before her. The hagiography portrays a modest and communal practice of spiritual friendship that was conditioned into the daily life of religious houses yet were values and manners that could still be accessible to women outside those settings.

---

41. Aelred of Rievaulx, *The Liturgical Sermons: The First Clairvaux Collection, Sermons One-Twenty-Eight,* trans. Theodore Berkeley and M. Basil Pennington, Cistercian Fathers 58 (Kalamazoo, MI: Cistercian Publications, 2001), 270; Dutton, "The Sacramentality of Community in Aelred," 255–56.

42. Aelred of Rievaulx, *Spiritual Friendship,* 82.

43. Aelred of Rievaulx, *Spiritual Friendship,* 51–52.

LE FRESNE

In the *Lais,* the rituals of female friendship within religious communities are transferred into the language of courtly custom. The courtly gestures within these stories reveal inner virtue much like the conventions of *amicitia* exhibited in texts like the contemporary vitae of Thomas Becket, where the saint is frequently portrayed as the exemplar of courtly manners, which instruct the worldly figures that surround him. In one of the *Lives* written by Herbert of Bosham (1184–86), the archbishop travels incognito as a monk and is, nonetheless, recognized for his courtesy, eloquence in speech, and the 'exquisite shape of his hands' which betray him as 'some great man.' As Stephen Jaeger has suggested, the cultivation of spiritual nobility becomes manifest in an external culture of elegance, transferring ecclesiastical discipline into courtly society.[44] Such acts of translation were particularly relevant for women, who frequently lived at the intersection between court and cloister.

Le Fresne, in particular, enacts the translation of the monastic culture of friendship into the romance genre. The lay is framed through the spiritual re-education of her mother, who must learn to become a friend to other women through the example of her own daughter. After slandering a neighbor's wife, who gives birth to twins, for sexual infidelity, the mother had given birth to her own pair of daughters, forced to recognize that she had been her own judge when she spoke ill of all women: "car jeo meïsmes me jujai / de tutes femmes mesparlai" (lines 79–80). To avoid the consequences, she abandons one of her infants. The foundling is adopted by an abbess and named Le Fresne but eventually departs from the convent when she falls in love with a young lord named Gurun. At court, she is eventually reunited with her mother and performs an act of ritual courtesy and friendship that becomes the instructive miracle of the story.

Marie's courtly hagiography recasts the familiar figure of the eloping nun, which appears in a number of Marian miracle collections including those by Adgar (fl. 1150–1200), the theologian Jacques de Vitry (ca. 1160–1240), and Gautier de Coincy (1177–1236), an abbot, bishop, and chronicler.[45] In these analogous Old French and Latin versions, the nun's departure from her convent is prevented through miraculous interventions by the Virgin. The nun

---

44. C. Stephen Jaeger, *The Envy of Angels: Cathedral Schools and Social Ideals in Medieval Europe, 950–1200* (Philadelphia: University of Pennsylvania Press, 1994), 297.

45. Eileen Power, *Medieval English Nunneries, c. 1275 to 1535* (New York: Biblo and Tannen, 1964), 622–23. For the *Lais* and Adgar's *Le Gracial* that focuses on the role of the abject and the incestuous mother, see Kay, *Courtly Contradictions,* 179–215.

from Gautier de Coincy's *Miracles de Nostre Dame par Personnages* is rescued the night before her elopement when the Virgin sends her a vision of Hell and, persuaded by the message of chastity, sends away her lover in the morning.[46] Many later versions and miracle plays feature a blocked corridor, which physically prevents her from escaping the convent. In Jacques de Vitry's *Exempla*, for example, Mary's image hinders the runaway's passage through one door, but she escapes through another to her downfall.[47] These miracle stories serve to warn against female sexuality and disobedience. Such concerns may have only intensified with the proliferation of female religious communities and the scandal at Watton priory in Yorkshire, which brought the Gilbertines under regulatory scrutiny and resulted in Aelred's account of another Marian miracle in *De Sanctimoniali de Wattun* in 1160. In the story, a young girl's pregnancy is discovered before she can elope with her lover. Yet, before her affair can bring scandal and ill repute to her convent, all signs of her condition disappear overnight.[48]

Like these cautionary tales, *Le Fresne* confronts the social dangers and realities of the girl's decision to depart the religious life with her lover, which places her in a vulnerable position when he is forced to cast her aside to marry another. However, Marie rewrites the clerical conventions defining female religiosity exclusively through sexual identity, displacing the emphasis on the nun's inviolable body. In place of divine intervention or tragedy, the movement between these worlds instead produces a miracle that is ultimately human and ethical. Before his wedding night, Le Fresne replaces the old linens on the marriage bed with her sole possession of worth: the striped brocade from Constantinople that her mother left her swaddled in as an infant when she was placed on the doorstep of the abbey. This exertion of selfless humility toward her rival becomes the "grant merveille" (line 391) that produces wonder among the guests, demonstrating a model of *amicitia* for the women around her. Her act of friendship and service recalls the tale of patient Griselda, popularized by later medieval writers such as Chaucer, Petrarch, and

---

46. *Les Miracles de La Sainte Vierge Traduits et Mis En Vers Par Gautier de Coincy; Publiés Par m. l'abbé Poquet* (Paris: Parmantier, 1857), 474.

47. Jacques de Vitry, *Exempla Ex Sermonibus Vulgaribus Jacobi Vitriacensis*, ed. Thomas Frederick Crane (London, 1890), 24.

48. For a comparison of Adgar's version in the *Le Gracial* with Aelred and William of Malmesbury, see Emma Bérat, "The Authority of Diversity: Communal Patronage in Le Gracial," in *Barking Abbey and Medieval Literary Culture: Authorship and Authority in a Female Community*, ed. Jennifer Brown and Donna Alfano Bussell (Rochester, NY: York Medieval Press, 2012), 210–32.

Boccaccio, who performs a similar sacrificial gesture on the wedding night.[49] In Marie's version, the primary audience for this performance of virtue is not the husband but the mother, whose inner transformation becomes the lesson of the story. Although the woman arrives at the wedding scheming against Le Fresne and unaware that she is her daughter, the performance produces a transformation in her hardened heart:

> Sa mere l'a mult esguardee,
> en sun quer preisiee e amee.
> Pensa e dist, s'ele seüst
> La maniere e que ele fust,
> ja pur sa fille ne perdist
> ne sun seignur ne li tolist. (393–98)

[Her mother looked at her intently, and esteemed and loved her in her heart. She thought and said to herself that if she had known the kind of person she was, she would not have suffered harm because of her daughter, nor would her lord have been taken from her.]

This inner dialogue reinvents romance conventions for friendship. While the meeting between Gurun and Le Fresne is only briefly described, the awareness of an initial moment of love is instead dramatized as an encounter between two women. In the scenes that follow, she repeatedly calls Le Fresne *amie* (441, 451, 460). After the mother discovers the brocade, her heart trembles with feeling and she finally makes amends, confessing to her husband and reconciling with her daughter. This affection is ultimately a transition for the restoration of lost family and inheritance. However, the narrative demands that she learn to be a friend before becoming a mother.

The symmetry of the lay produces a poetic justice. The mother is punished for her act of female betrayal and discourtesy, for which the daughter's love atones. The selfless act is preceded by other female overtures of charity: Le Fresne is spared by her mother's maidservant, who persuades her mother not to kill her and bears the infant safely to the steps of the abbey, where she is nursed by the porter's wife. Afterward, Le Fresne is adopted by the abbess as her own niece and fostered in a monastic community of spiritual kinship. The lay begins with one crime which only seems to necessitate another, but

---

49. Sharon Kinoshita, "Two for the Price of One: Courtly Love and Serial Polygamy in the Lais of Marie de France," *Arthuriana* 8, no. 2 (1998): 33–55.

the tragic cycle is quickly staunched and redeemed by generous acts of women that create a multiplying spiritual economy. The vision of the rich fruitfulness of friendship is invited by the names of the two sisters, which contain arboreal metaphors. The abbess names Le Fresne for the ash where she was found, described in the poem as a luxuriant and many-boughed tree. When Gurun's subjects persuade him to trade Le Fresne for La Codre, the ash becomes a false symbol of infertility: they demand that their lord wed for political stability, implying that Le Fresne cannot bear him a legitimate heir like the hazel. Yet they misrepresent the ash, which was known within medieval literature to flower and fruit.[50] By the end of the lay, the ash becomes a symbol for the spiritual love of *amicitia,* which appears as a form of ascetic renunciation yet becomes a redemptive, proliferating force that overcomes betrayal founded on scarcity.

GUILDELÜEC AND GUILLIADUN

In the *Lais,* acts of *amicitia* between women become a more miraculous and spiritual expression of *fin'amur* than even the erotics of courtly love, which remain constrained by social and political bonds. As Karma Lochrie has observed, these spiritual possibilities are given their fullest articulation in *Eliduc,* or *Guildelüec and Guilliadun.*[51] Distinct from many female characters who are defined by the men who love them elsewhere in the *Lais* and other romances, the women become the truest practitioners of *amicitia.* The lay culminates in an act of sacrifice and loyalty that surpasses the pledges of romantic reciprocity that serve as bulwarks against shifting political allegiances and wavering loyalties within the genre.[52] The friendship between the two female characters becomes the founding occasion for female religious community, displacing the traditional romance narrative with a vision of a spiritual, bodiless, and expansive form of love consummated by epistolary exchange.

The lay contains a traditional courtship between Guilliadun and Eliduc, which is overshadowed with the knowledge, from the very beginning, that he already has a wife with whom he has explicitly promised to keep faith. Their restrained attraction and intimacy are framed by Eliduc's feudal obligations and grow alongside his military reputation. Their public relationship, while

---

50. Glyn Burgess, "Symbolism in Marie de France's *Laüstic* and *Le Fresne,*" *Bibliographic Bulletin of the International Arthurian Society* 33 (1981): 258–68.

51. Lochrie, "Between Women," 84.

52. For language of loyalty, see Usha Vishnuvajjala, "Adventure, Lealté, and Sympathy in Marie de France's Eliduc," *Texas Studies in Literature and Language* 59, no. 2 (2017): 162–81.

initially encouraged by her family, becomes haunted by a mounting sense of social judgment and surveillance from which they cannot escape and climaxes in a stormy scene aboard the ship, where a sailor accuses them of offending God and his law. Instead, their romance becomes a prelude to the otherworldly and solitary encounter between the two women. After discovering her lover's marriage, Guilliadun falls into a deathlike faint, and Eliduc bears her away to a deserted hermitage in the wilderness. It is at this spiritual site, once inhabited by a holy man, that Guildelüec meets her rival and eventually builds her abbey.

As in *Le Fresne*, Marie uses the language of *merveille* (line 1020) to describe Guildelüec's actions toward the interloper in her marriage. On the altar, she discovers 'a young girl who resembles a new rose' and, lifting the coverlet to her body, sees Guilliadun in a blazon reminiscent of love lyric, seeing the body so slender, the long arms, the white hands, the fingers, slim, long and full: "e vit le cors tant eschevi / les braz luns e blanches les meins / e les deiz grails, luns e pleins" (1011–16). Her physical delicacy and mannerist elegance evoke courtly conventions of *amicitia*, where manners and the 'exquisite shape of fingers' reveal the hidden nobility of strangers. Overwhelmed by the sacral beauty of this girl 'who resembles a gem,' Guildelüec begins to weep from her own wonder at her experience of a feeling she describes as indistinguishable from pity or love: "Tant par pitié, tant par amur / ja mes n'avrai joie nun jur" (1021–27).[53] The scene in the lay dilates this instinctive response toward all women, even strangers, as a natural act of friendship and sympathy. The inward transformation precipitates the miracle itself. Guildelüec wakens Guilliadun through the red flower that she sees revive a dead weasel; she reassures the girl that Eliduc suffers because he loves her and that her own heart grieves for his sorrow (1093–1100). After witnessing the tender reunion between the lovers, she decides to take the veil. Rather than a palinode of romance, to renounce the beloved for their own sake and to grieve for a stranger through their eyes becomes the most difficult act of courtly love, whose participants often risk their lives and patrimony.[54]

Like Aelred's notion of progression from carnal love as an ascent to more rarified forms of *caritas* or spiritual love, the turn to religious love emerges

---

53. Like Clemence of Barking's vita in the Campsey manuscript, the pité for the suffering of other women marks the capacity for friendship: "Bien en pout aver pité / Ki unkes vers femmes eust amisté" (lines 2351–53). See Catherine Batt, "Clemence of Barking's Transformations of Courtoisie in *La Vie de Sainte Cathérine d'Alexandrie*," *New Comparison: A Journal of Comparative and General Literary Studies*, no. 12 (1991): 102–23, at 112.

54. For themes of sacrifice, see Kinoshita, "Two for the Price of One," 51; Deborah Nelson, "The Implications of Love and Sacrifice in 'Fresne' and 'Eliduc,'" *The South Central Bulletin* 38, no. 4 (December 1, 1978): 153–55.

from human forms of affection. After Guildelüec's act of renunciation, Marie devotes only eight lines to the short-lived marriage between Eliduc and Guilliadun before announcing their own preparations for religious retirement in emulation of his former wife. The vows in the end of the lay contrast with his earlier, desperate desire to renounce living when he believes Guilliadun has died: "Le jur que jeo vus enforrai, / ordre de moigne recevrai; / sur vostre tumbe chescun jur / ferai refreindre ma dolur" (The day that I bury you I shall take holy orders. On your tomb every day I shall make my grief resound; 957–59). His funereal vision of the contemplative life is replaced by a conversion that emerges from the "parfite amur" (1150), much like Audrey's first marriage to Tonbert in *La vie seint Audree*. The two are described as having one body, one heart, and one desire between them spiritually: "Un cors, un cuer, et un talent / Heurent cist espiritelment" (361–62). Their mutual affection and purpose prefigure the fuller expression of elective harmony in the religious community Audrey builds at Ely:

> Une reule, un ordenement,
> Un corage, un cotivement
> Estoit entre eus de bien garder
> Cele maison et ordener. (1695–98)

> The house functioned well, for
> one rule, one order,
> one heart, one worship
> existed among them.

These passages draw on the Pauline language about the single heart and soul in Acts 4:32, which Aelred used to describe spiritual friendship.

In the lay, Guildelüec's experience of sacrificial love becomes the foundation for spiritual community, establishing her own order of thirty religious women and eventually receiving Guilliadun in her own convent. Within the communal religious life, the love triangle remains intact but accommodates the friendship between the two women and their mutual religious devotion to God:

> Deu preiouent pur lur ami
> qu'il li feïst bone merci,
> e il pur eles repreiot.
> Ses messages lur enveiot
> pur saveir cument lur estait

e cum chescune pur sei
de Deu amer par bone fei
e mult par firent bele fin,
la merci Deu, le veir devin! (1171–80)

[They prayed that God might show their beloved His sweet mercy and Eliduc in turn prayed for them, sending his messenger to see how they fared and how their spirits were. Each one strove to love God in good faith and they came to a good end thanks to God, the true divine.]

Their quadrangle echoes Aelred's description of "the most sacred bonds of friendship [*sacratissima foedera amicitiae*]" between the biblical figures of Martha, Mary, and Lazarus. The three are united by Christ's love and were intimately attached to him through "the special privilege of friendship [*specialis priuilegium amicitiae*]."[55] For Aelred, even spiritual friendship between individuals was, by definition, a love triangle, for "one who remains in friendship remains in God and God in him."[56] Marie invokes the subversive inclusivity of communal spiritual love in contrast to the felt intrusion of a third party in courtship, marriage, and even intimate friendships.

The letters they exchange become the ideal vehicle for divine love and friendship. As R. W. Southern wrote of monastic letter writers like Anselm, the ardent passion they described, even toward those never met in person, was an articulation of not only individual affection but universal divine love. The warmest intensity of expression was reserved for those who held the highest mutual dedication to the religious life.[57] This intimacy was public and conventional, even the occasion for virtuosic literary exchange to be read aloud or circulated within a religious community.[58] The letters collections of Baudri of Bourgueil, one of the biographers of Robert Abrissel, offers examples of these lively verse letters addressed to female religious on the subject of "loving friendship [*amor*] composed in Christ."[59] As Baudri wrote to one cor-

---

55. *De institutione inclusarum*, in *Aelredi Rievallensis Opera Omnia*, ed. A. Hoste and C. H. Talbot (Turnholt: Brepols, 1971), 31:667; *A Rule of Life for a Recluse*, trans. Mary Paul Macpherson, in *Treatises: The Pastoral Prayer, Works*, vol. 1, ed. David Knowles (Spencer, MA: Cistercian Publications, 1971), 85; Dutton, "The Sacramentality of Community in Aelred," 251–52.

56. *De Spiritali Amicitia*, in *Aelredi Rievallensis Opera Omnia*, 1.1:278–350 (Opera Omnia. Turnholt: Typographi Brepols, 1971), 301. Dutton, *Spiritual Friendship*, 69.

57. Southern, *St. Anselm*, 161–65. For the role of distant love in monastic and clerical letters, see Jaeger, *Ennobling Love*, 124–27.

58. See introduction to Giles Constable, *Letters and Letter-Collections* (Turnhout: Brepols, 1976).

59. Poem 138, lines 6–8.

respondent, this form of communion was ultimately predicated on distance, drawing on metaphors of Pauline community and marriage similar to those of *Audree*: "I do not want to be your husband, nor you to be my wife [...] Let our hearts be joined, but our bodies remain apart."[60] These fervent letters of love could take on a courtly, even Ovidian, character, which their authors playfully invoked to voice their dedication, while carefully displacing the erotic undertow to reaffirm the spiritual nature of that feeling. His affection, Baudri declares, was stirred not by a "filthy love [*foedus amor*]" or "lascivious love [*lasciuus amor*] or wanton love [*amor petulant amoris*]" but by "learned writing [*littera*]."[61] The genre saw *colloquium*, the mutual intellectual and spiritual edification of many, as Gerald Bond has described, the "culminating act of *amor*."[62] While Aelred had been wary of the erotic potential of such epistolary exchanges in the *De institutione inclusarum*, they articulate the passage from other carnal forms of love to spiritual friendship that he elsewhere described.

In Marie, the shift from courtly love lyric to spiritual friendship becomes a narrative event. Her works move across hagiography, Marian miracle tradition, and romance to articulate the new spiritual purpose of women whose lives had been defined by marriage. Spiritual friendship created a rich fictive space for imagining women, beyond their sexual roles and in relation to each other. Instead, female identity is expressed by acts of courtesy and service, more often performed by male figures in romance in situations that would demand enmity by other social and feudal values that the genre featured. The portrait of the *amica dei* described across these works was a charismatic female leader: a saintly figure who inspires loyal followers, yet remained self-renouncing, considerate, and tender in her private life. Her *amicitia* was ultimately an ethical model of virtue available to women in all phases of life through any number of major and minor forms, including quotidian chores and spiritual encouragement through letter-writing.

Marie celebrates the *merveille* of female friendship, which religious communities sought to make their founding principles, as well as habituate through their daily lives and literature. Much like the question of whether *fin'amur* was a living practice or literary phenomenon, the extent to which these ideals of female spiritual friendship were truly lived or emulated by readers is impossible to determine. Aelred was also skeptical of the classical accounts of friendship that nonetheless enraptured his imagination and influenced his conception of monastic life. Yet writing brought these ideals into

---

60. To Constance, a nun at Le Ronceray. See Bond, *The Loving Subject*, 173. Poem 200, lines 43–46.

61. Poem 200, lines 48–52.

62. Bond, *The Loving Subject*, 53.

the discursive realm of possibility and, moreover, was a public act of *amicitia*. As Marie states in the opening lines of *La vie seint Audree*, literary creation constituted good works, which earned both human and divine love: "An bon hovre e en bon propels / Devroit chasten user son tens / [. . .] Cil qui bien font sunt honuré / E de Dieu e del siecle amé" (1–8). The patronage, translation, reading, copying, and dissemination of vernacular literature for women were also belletristic acts of spiritual friendship. The Campsey Ash manuscript offers textual traces of these efforts to describe and enact *amicitia* by readers, who were enabled by historical networks and religious communities. The preservation of Marie's literary legacy is a testament to how these narratives must have resonated with medieval women, lay and religious, at various phases in their own spiritual quest to learn, discuss, and abide in friendship.

CHAPTER 3

Friendship and Resistance in the *Vitae* of Italian Holy Women

ANDREA BOFFA

CLARE OF RIMINI (d. 1346) might not have appeared to be on the path to sanctity during the first two and a half decades of her life. Her mother died when she was seven, and when her father remarried a widow, Clare—all of ten years of age—married her new stepmother's son.[1] Their time together was pleasurable but tragically brief, as soon Clare's young husband died, shortly followed by Clare's stepmother. Clare grew to be "excessively beautiful" and "full of lasciviousness." She had forgotten God, the hagiographer informs us, but not her own desires, and at twenty-four years of age, she chose for herself a new husband: a wealthy, politically connected man, "whom she had loved and desired over any good order, burning by the love she had for him not only because he pleased her, but also because he was rich of money and other riches, and powerful in the homeland of Rimini."[2] But one day, as Clare was visiting the church of Saint Francis in Rimini, the Virgin appeared to her and questioned her about the value of possessions and luxuries. After this experience, Clare underwent a complete conversion, and, although still married

---

1. The hagiographer moves quite quickly through this phase of Clare's life, so it is not clear whether this marriage immediately followed her father's marriage, or whether any time had passed.

2. Jacques Dalarun, *"Lapsus Linguae": La Légende de Claire de Rimini* (Spoleto: Centro Italiano di Studi sull'Alto Medioevo, 1994), 19. The translation is from Jacques Dalarun, "Gospel in Action: The Life of Clare of Rimini," *Franciscan Studies* 64 (2006): 179–215, at 185.

and living with her husband (chastely, of course), she adopted a penitential habit. Her husband did not interfere with her conversion, helpfully dying and leaving her a widow once again. After her conversion to the holy life, Clare increasingly gathered about her like-minded women, what Jacques Dalarun in his analysis of her *vita* describes as "a little circle of female solidarity."[3]

This essay examines the *vita* of Clare of Rimini along with those of two other lay holy women, Umiliana de' Cerchi (d. 1246) and Margaret of Cortona (d. 1297), who were recognized as saints by their communities. In their pursuit of an independent way of life, these women were already rejecting traditional forms of masculine authority, even as their hagiographers sought to present their paths as perfectly orthodox. In order to protect themselves and to enable them to devote themselves fully to their pious desires, these holy women turned to their female friends and networks of support. These experiences, like many in the *vitae* of these women, echo the lived experiences of the lay women who were the subject and context of these holy lives. There is something dismissive, unintentionally perhaps, in Dalarun's description of Clare's community as a "little circle of female solidarity." The use of the diminutive reflects the devaluation of women's relationships that we see in a wide swath of medieval—and not so medieval—sources. Yet, Dalarun's phrasing also reflects one possible function of relationships among women: a means of resistance in patriarchal society. Indeed, depictions of female friendship in medieval literature often present these relationships as a strategy of resistance, and the *vitae* of holy Italian women of the thirteenth and fourteenth centuries are no exception.

LAY HOLY WOMEN IN MEDIEVAL ITALY

The thirteenth and fourteenth centuries marked a period of proliferation of female saints, particularly noticeable in Italy, and to narrow that even further, the towns and cities of central and northern Italy.[4] Lay piety, and the appearance of lay female saints, was not restricted to Italy, but certain conditions within Italy contributed to the possibility of lay holy life, including the growth of urban centers and the presence of the mendicant orders within these centers. Many of these female saints were lay holy women who, like

---

3. Diana Webb, *Saints and Cities in Medieval Italy* (Manchester: Manchester University Press, 2007), 195.

4. For an analysis of the changing demographics of medieval and early modern sainthood, see Donald Weinstein and Rudolph M. Bell, *Saints and Society: The Two Worlds of Western Christendom, 1000–1700* (Chicago: University of Chicago Press, 1982).

Umiliana de' Cerchi, Margaret of Cortona, and Clare of Rimini, never took vows to join any of the monastic orders; others did take vows, but only after having some experience in the world, particularly getting married. Even while these women exhibited many of the standard saintly qualities, their *vitae* are also quite different from each other, suggesting a growing variety of experiences and actions that were perceived as pious. Many of the lay holy women are identified in modern texts by the ambiguous term *tertiary*, or part of the Third Order of the Franciscans or Dominicans: women who embarked on a life of penance under the guidance of the friars but who did so while remaining in the world, without the permanence of vows, and—perhaps even more alarming—with limited ecclesiastical oversight. But what is evident from the sources is that during this period, what the life of a tertiary was meant to look like was unclear. The variety of acts and lifestyles deemed pious (through their attribution to locally recognized holy persons) also reflects that this was a period of spiritual experimentation, and while such experimentation—particularly for lay women—would fall under increased scrutiny in the fifteenth century, for at least two centuries hagiographers grappled with how to present an independent, worldly woman as worthy of veneration.

The three women under examination in this essay are linked through their status as lay saints, but their individual experiences are unique.[5] Umiliana de' Cerchi was the daughter of a wealthy Florentine family. As is the case in many of the *vitae* of these lay holy women, her hagiographer, the Franciscan friar Vito of Cortona, skips over her childhood, instead beginning his account with her unhappy marriage, at the age of sixteen.[6] Umiliana gave birth to two daughters before her husband died, just over five years into their marriage. The young widow returned to her family home and devoted herself to charity, helping the poor and the lepers in her city of Florence. After renouncing her inheritance and dedicating herself to a life of chastity, she made an unsuccessful bid to join the Poor Clares, and instead lived the rest of her brief life in a tower attached to her family home, dying in 1246 at the age of twenty-seven.

Margaret of Cortona came from humbler beginnings than the other two women examined in this essay. Her conversion to the holy life is also the most dramatic. She was the daughter of a well-to-do farmer in Laviano, near Peru-

---

5. In this essay I use *saint* to identify any individual who was deemed so by their community, regardless of whether the individual has been formally recognized as a saint through the process of canonization.

6. Vitus Cortonensis, "*Vita Beatae Humilianae De Cherchis,*" in *Acta Sanctorum* (Antwerp: 1685). For an English translation, see "Umiliana De' Cerchi of Florence (D. 1246)," in Webb, *Saints and Cities in Medieval Italy*. In this chapter, all quotations are from Webb's translation.

gia. At the age of seventeen, Margaret ran away from her home with her lover. She lived with him for ten years, during which time they had a son together. However, when her lover was tragically murdered, she was left on her own. Rejected by both her own family and that of her lover, she turned to God, who led her to Cortona. Margaret's initial bid to become an official Franciscan penitent was rejected, but eventually her devotion was apparent to all, and Margaret moved into her own little house and adopted a penitential habit.[7]

Clare of Rimini, whose early life was described above, sought independence similar to Umiliana and Margaret, but eventually she founded a small, informal, community of like-minded women. Clare never matched the local fame of either Umiliana or Margaret of Cortona, although her cult was eventually recognized by the papacy, and she was beatified in 1782. Still, she hardly went unnoticed, inspiring a piece of art shortly after her death: a panel of a triptych depicts one of Clare's visions, painted by Francesco da Rimini sometime around 1333, now housed at the National Gallery.

Margaret of Cortona's confessor and hagiographer Fra Giunta Bevegnati was eager to stake a claim on Margaret for the city of Cortona and for the Franciscan friars there, even though she had moved out of their direct jurisdiction at the time of her death.[8] Perhaps this is why he was so rushed in putting together her *vita*, for which he apologizes in its prologue. Her body was entombed in a silver casket in a church that was built and dedicated to her just over thirty years after her death. Margaret was not canonized until 1728, but clearly her cult had a substantial following in the decades immediately after her death. Umiliana's hagiographer, her confessor Vito of Cortona, wanted his saint and her *vita* to help the Franciscans establish relationships with the women—and by extension the important families—of Florence. Umiliana was beatified in 1694 but never canonized. Her remains lie in a chapel in the Basilica Santa Croce in Florence.

FRIENDSHIP AND THE FEMALE SPACE

Anne M. Schuchman, in her analysis of the *vita* of Umiliana, examines the saint's life as an exemplum of female sanctity in the politically charged context

---

7. For a recent edited Latin version of Margaret of Cortona's *vita*, see Giunta Bevegnati, *Legenda de vita et miraculis Beatae Margaritae de Cortona* (Grottaferrata: Collegium Bonaventurae ad Claras Aquas, 1997). For an English translation of this edition, see *The Life and Miracles of Saint Margaret of Cortona*, trans. Thomas Renna (St. Bonaventure, NY: Franciscan Institute, 2012). Unless indicated, all translations from this *vita* are my own.

8. See the introduction to Renna, *Life and Miracles of Saint Margaret of Cortona*.

of thirteenth-century Florence. Schuchman also points out that while Umiliana's hagiographer, the Franciscan Vito of Cortona, asserted that Umiliana completely withdrew from society, the events in her *vita* demonstrate that she instead maintained close connections both with women in her family and with women in Florentine society and beyond; not only are all but three of her witnesses identified in the prologue to her *vita* women, but women made up the majority of the benefactors of her miracles. Schuchman suggests that Vito perhaps intended "society" to mean the political intrigues of Florence's male population from which he clearly wanted to separate his newfound saint.[9] For Vito, women's relationships with each other provided a loophole through which the Franciscans might be able to circumvent the factional nature of medieval urban society, particularly endemic in medieval Florence. This recalls the trivializing of female relationships implicit in Delarun's description of Clare of Rimini's "little circle of female solidarity" referenced above, a trivializing noted by numerous scholars of women's friendship. For example, in her classic analysis of the friendships between women in nineteenth-century America, Carroll Smith-Rosenberg rightfully chastises historians for the fact that friendship "is one aspect of the female experience which consciously or unconsciously we have chosen to ignore."[10] Fern L. Johnson and Elizabeth J. Aries, in their contemporary analysis of talk between female friends, acknowledge that "the slighting of female friendship is part, then, of the more general slighting and devaluation of those activities of women that go beyond their traditional connections to men and family."[11] This observation certainly reflects the view (or lack thereof) of the medieval hagiographer, Vito of Cortona. Indeed, the *vitae* include ample examples of female friendship, although the hagiographers simply do not acknowledge the relationships in those terms. Thus, on the one hand, female friendships are so unimportant that they often remain an aspect of women's experiences unacknowledged by both hagiographers and historians.[12]

On the other hand, women's relationships with other women might also be inherently dangerous. Karma Lochrie posits that within medieval society, the "official"—and patriarchal—perception of female fellowship was that no good could conceivably come of it. At the root of this perception was concern over

---

9. Anne M. Schuchman, "The Lives of Umiliana De' Cerchi: Representations of Female Sainthood in Thirteenth-Century Florence," *Essays in Medieval Studies* 14 (1997): n. pag.

10. Carroll Smith-Rosenberg, "The Female World of Love and Ritual: Relations between Women in Nineteenth-Century American," *Signs* 1, no. 1 (Autumn 1975): 1–29, at 1.

11. Fern L. Johnson and Elizabeth J. Aries, "The Talk of Women Friends," *Women's Studies International Forum* 6, no. 4 (1983): 353–61, at 354.

12. Although thankfully interest in the friendship between women, historical or otherwise, has been the subject of a growing body of scholarship that has increased significantly in the past few years, as this volume attests.

the grave danger of communication between women: that is, gossip, a failing to which women were particularly susceptible. Idle talk between women was a particular concern because of the presumption that when women talked to one another, the conversation would inevitably turn to sex. This "unbridled" sex talk between women was "inextricably bound up with their unrestrained licentiousness." Furthermore, women's speech constituted a site of resistance to male dominance.[13] The denigration of all women's speech to "gossip" must have intensified the potential dangers of women preaching, an issue that many hagiographers of lay saints had to navigate. While both Umiliana and Margaret of Cortona had sought a degree of solitude in their holy pursuits, Clare of Rimini initially opted for a life of active piety that drew the suspicion of the Papal Inquisition. So invigorated by her own conversion, Clare actively sought to encourage others to follow a penitential life. In this endeavor she reached out to both men and women. But it was her outreach to other women that drew the attention of the area's Franciscan inquisitors, who accused her of directly and purposefully undermining male authority through her relationships with other women. She was subject to direct questioning, but she also found herself being publicly preached against by the Franciscans. One particularly vehement preacher suggested that she was both a heretic and in league with the devil and specifically encouraged husbands to prohibit their wives from associating with her, publicly castigating her: "Gentlemen and gentlewomen and all you others, look to yourselves! This woman is a demon who deceives you under the pretense of humility, sometimes howling like a she-wolf, hissing like a serpent, and bellowing like a bull . . . Let your women keep no company with her!"[14] Notably, this preacher has nothing to say on the content of her words; he merely notes her presumption in using her voice so publicly. Indeed, according to this critic of the holy woman, the sounds that come from her mouth are animalistic; not even human. Perhaps it was experiences like this that led Clare to build her own community of women to whom she could "preach" in the privacy of their own residence.[15] Thus in a single

---

13. Karma Lochrie, "Between Women," in *The Cambridge Companion to Medieval Women's Writing*, ed. Carolyn Dinshaw and David Wallace (Cambridge: Cambridge University Press, 2003), 70–88, at 73.

14. *"Lapsus Linguae,"* 35.

15. Clare of Rimini is one of the few Italian female saints from this period who have been subject to such scrutiny, surprisingly so. Perhaps our other lay holy women—or their mendicant advisors and confessors—were better at ensuring that their activities did not cross into that dangerous category of preaching; for example, Vito of Cortona directly stated that Umiliana preached through her actions rather than her words. For a brief discussion of this necessary negotiation, see Beverly Mayne Kienzle, "Catherine of Siena, Preaching, and Hagiography in Renaissance Tuscany," in *A Companion to Catherine of Siena*, ed. Carolyn Muessig, George Ferzoco, and Beverly Kienzle (Leiden: Brill, 2012), 127–54.

text—the *vita* of Clare—we can observe the juxtaposition of female friendship as an acute threat but also a means of safety and security.

For women without the protection of men—whether husbands, fathers, or brothers, or the traditional patriarchal authority of the Church through the institution of the convent—other women could and did provide that security. For holy women who sought independence, female friends, companions, and acquaintances provided a space through which they could experiment spiritually. That protection provided by other women also allowed hagiographers to legitimize some rather remarkable female independence. Perhaps those accusations of heresy and illegal preaching are what eventually led her to form a little community, but Clare of Rimini was not initially interested in communal piety; rather, she sought a degree of solitude within her urban environment. In her widowhood, Clare took up residence in the home of her brother before moving into a small room of sorts (it lacked a roof) in the old Roman wall. Here Clare, who was so often public in her pious practice, had the privacy to loudly vocalize her desire for the divine, shouting "Lord, I can have you here!"[16] It was only later, when a neighbor offered to sell Clare his little house, and she had a vision encouraging her to establish a community for her sisters, that she moved to proper living quarters, although when craving solitude she often returned to her hole in the wall.[17]

Clare might have desired a space of her own, but her active and often noisy piety was purposefully on display throughout the city of Rimini, much to the chagrin of the local Franciscans. Noisy devotion is something of a trope in the lives of female saints, and lay women are no exception. For example, while in exile with her family in Urbino, Clare claimed a tower at the bishop's palace, although the canons of the cathedral complained about her nightly cries of anguish.[18] This appears to be why her hole in the old Roman wall was so appealing: no one could hear and complain about her sounds of anguished devotion. But during the day, her pious displays were purposefully public and dramatic, to boot! In addition, she annually performed a sort of "civic stations of the cross" on Good Friday, led around by two fellows (*ribaldi*) she hired for this purpose to various churches in Rimini, with a rope around her neck, dressed only in her undergarments.[19] Unsurprisingly, Clare was forced to stop this ritual, which left her miserable. In so many ways, Clare is often depicted by her hagiographer as revolutionary in her piety in a way that was

---

16. "*Lapsus Linguae*," 31.
17. "*Lapsus Linguae*," 39.
18. "*Lapsus Linguae*," 29. Clare's family, the Agolanti, was caught up in the continual conflict between the Guelfs and the Ghibellines of Rimini.
19. "*Lapsus Linguae*," 41.

incomprehensible to the male authorities in Rimini; even when she concedes to their demands, she does not accept the notion that her actions are wrong in the eyes of her Lord. Perhaps Clare's decision to convene an informal community of like-minded women was a concession of sorts to these troubled clerics, while at the same time her obligations to this community might have initiated some constraints in her public activities.[20]

As experiences mediated through texts, the pious ways of life for lay holy women were made legitimate through the creation and existence of the *vitae,* themselves composed by men who provided clerical authority to these spiritual experiments. Indeed, the hagiographers Vito of Cortona and Giunta Bevegnati were confessors to Margaret and Umiliana respectively, but their own intimate relationships with the holy women and their clerical authority were not enough to make these newfangled saints worthy of devotion, a challenge made more difficult by the imperfections of their subjects. Because their subjects continued to live in the world outside the confines and protection of convent walls, the hagiographers also had to demonstrate that the holy women were not sullied—at least not irrevocably—by association with the lay world in which they circulated. These were women whom the divine had raised above their lay family and neighbors, but whose sanctity was intimately associated with that same lay community. The holy women's integration within their communities of lay women was a way for the hagiographers to suggest the existence of boundaries within which they could safely and appropriately practice their piety. This was especially critical for the specific women under consideration here, who had limited—or, in the case of Margaret, no—familial oversite or connections. As an unmarried or widowed woman that the community needed to be female, a lay holy woman could only truly express her laity among other women.

Umiliana de' Cerchi is the earliest of the three women examined here, and her life is the least problematic, at least from the perspective of her path to piety. Unlike Margaret and Clare, and despite her married state, she did not have to overcome lust or other significant human flaws in order to partake in a holy way of life. Her piety was on display early in her life, when, as a young married woman, she risked the wrath of her husband by giving extensively to the poor. The wealth of her family, however unhappy they may have been when the young widow refused to remarry, allowed her security in her living arrangements, and she took to living humbly and semi-secluded in a tower attached to her family home. While demons might have assailed her and her

---

20. Perhaps Clare's reluctant decision to end this most public display of spirituality prevented an act of intervention.

own father might have stolen her dowry, her faith was not questioned by those around her.

During her brief life, Umiliana cultivated a few close friendships. One of these was with her sister-in-law Ravenna. Umiliana and Ravenna had found companionship through their unhappy marriages, and together the two women happily went against the wishes of their dominating husbands and distributed food to the poor. But as Umiliana turned from a life of active charity to inward mysticism, we hear less about Ravenna in the narrative, with the exception of one striking appearance that occurred in the second year of Umiliana's life as a recluse. It was Lent, and during this period Umiliana practiced devout silence. The devil, in an effort to tempt her to break her silence, produced the dead bodies of her kinfolk and tried to persuade Umiliana to speak with them, but she recognized them as illusions and ignored them. The devil took them away but reappeared with images of her (still living) two daughters, saying to her, "Do you say nothing to your daughters whom you see newly dead before you?" Umiliana was still not fooled. In a third attempt, the devil showed her the figures of Mary and the child Jesus, but still Umiliana refused to acknowledge his illusions. Finally, "After a little while, since she spurned this illusion, he produced the image of Monna Ravenna, saying 'Speak to your dear kinswoman, who has so faithfully visited you.'" Umiliana still would not take the bait, and so "the devil disappeared with his figments, striking her such a heavy blow in the kidneys that her teeth were violently clashed together."[21] This devil seemed to have upped the ante with each new illusion, yet the final temptation was not some holy figure but Umiliana's earthly friend! In what seems to have been a bout of loneliness, the person Umiliana most longed for was her sister-in-law, the woman who had been her closest companion in the dark days of her marriage. Ravenna, it should be noted, was very much alive at the time of this incident, for she appears among a list of thirty-four witnesses to Umiliana's sanctity that precedes her *vita*.

After enclosing herself in the tower attached to her father's home, Umiliana was less "out and about" in Florence, although her cell was not quite the prison one might imagine; she was by no means an anchorite. Umiliana might have cut down on her charitable activities, but she occasionally went out to visit her friends; further, she hosted many visitors in her cell. The most frequent was her confessor, and at times other Franciscans also visited Umiliana, but many of her visitors were women of Florence who came to pray with her. Two fellow religious penitents, Gisla and Sobilia, become important in this period of Umiliana's life. Neither woman was a Florentine: Mugello, where

---

21. Webb, *Saints and Cities in Medieval Italy,* 109.

Gisla lived, is an area about twenty miles north of Florence, and Sobilia lived about thirty-five miles southeast of Florence. Unfortunately, the *vita* provides no clues as to how Umiliana met these two women, but Umiliana journeys from her cell to visit both these women, and, likewise, they visit her. Alas, the hagiographer did not provide logistical details of such visits! While Umiliana circulated in a broad network of women, her friendships with Sobilia and Gisla, alongside that with Ravenna, certainly stand out in the text of Umiliana's *vita*.[22]

We see examples of an extended feminine network in the *vitae* of Margaret of Cortona and Clare of Rimini as well. The *vita* of Margaret provides glimpses of female community in the narrative that, at first glance, seems incidental to an argument for sanctity. As a woman with a dead lover in her past and saddled with an illegitimate child, Margaret's conversion to the penitential life was particularly dramatic, but it also meant a greater climb toward respectability than Umiliana or even the passionate Clare of Rimini. God, we are told by her hagiographer, led Margaret to Cortona after the death of her lover and placed her in the care of two well-to-do women, Marinaria and her daughter-in-law Raneria. Margaret desperately wanted to take on the habit of a Franciscan tertiary but was rebuffed by the friars. To help Margaret support herself during this period, her protectresses helped her establish herself as a midwife for the wealthy women of Cortona, work she left as soon as the local Franciscans permitted her to enter the penitential life. She also moved into her own little house with the desire to live a quiet and solitary life of contemplation. While the devil had attempted to draw Umiliana de Cerchi out of her pious contemplations with regular reminders of the life she had left behind, Margaret was regularly forced to confront the outside world. In her revelations, God constantly admonished her to withdraw from secular society, yet at the same time he forbade her from becoming a complete recluse. So, while she was compelled to leave her house daily to walk to church, she was supposed to avoid communicating with the people she encountered. For Margaret, this was a difficult task. It was not just that she was surrounded by others when out and about, as was the nature of urban life, she simply could not avoid interacting with her neighbors. For example, when she went to the church to pray, she found herself drawn into conversations about secular matters. Of course, medieval society—in small villages as well as in bustling cities—was no place for a person who desired to remain anonymous. It was by its nature intrusive. The church was as much a place to congregate for gossip and debate as it was

---

22. Notably, all three women appear in the list of witnesses; thus, it is possible that the accounts of their interactions with Umiliana were, at least in part, provided by the women themselves.

a place for prayer and worship. Such encounters would leave Margaret filled with considerable guilt and shame. Her *vita* recounts that she would attempt to avoid speaking or even gazing at anyone on her way to and from church, but "if it happened that during the day she heard or talked about worldly matters to secular people, she did not, during the night, dare to seek her usual comfort in prayer from Christ, but rather she would spend a sleepless night weeping in sorrow."[23]

Part of Margaret's problem was her own popularity; the women of Cortona could not seem to get enough of her. At church she found herself surrounded by women who, while devoted to her, could not seem to stop talking. In realization of her obvious weakness at avoiding the company of secular people, Margaret begged God to permit her to never leave her house, but he refused to ease this burden, ordering her to continue to go daily to church, and so Margaret had to continue to struggle with what seemed to be her natural instinct to communicate with others. Nor was her little house a place of refuge, as the women of Cortona were constantly outside her door, seeking advice, bringing her food, and—at least in their minds—protecting her privacy. In one instance where a group of local women were outside Margaret's cell, a woman who evidently considered herself a zealous defender of the saint attempted to drive the rest away. Someone took offense, and the resulting shouting match interrupted Margaret's prayers.[24] It took some effort for Margaret to smooth things out. This was no easy task since, according to the hagiographer, "when anger rages, particularly in women, all that is justly spoken is believed to be perverse."[25] Further, many times women—and it was always women—were drawn to her door by the sound of the holy woman's lamentations. Margaret was not a simple curiosity for them; rather, they were so moved by her devotion that they, too, ended up weeping and praying aloud. Margaret's sanctity was public, on display for all to see and hear, however much she might have desired the privacy enjoyed by Umiliana de Cerchi. While Umiliana's friendships were personal and intimate, Margaret was the center and focus of a rowdy community of women who sought to claim Margaret as their own and her sanctity as a reflection of what was possible for a lay woman. Unlike for the other two saints discussed in this essay, Margaret's social status rose with her conversion to the penitent life. Her acceptance into this well-to-do circle of women was only possible through her sponsors Marinaria and Raneria in a way that had not been possible through her noble lover, no matter how strong the love between the illicit couple.

---

23. Renna, *Life and Miracles of Saint Margaret of Cortona*, 54–55.
24. Bevegnati, *Legenda de vita et miraculis Beatae Margaritae de Cortona*, 250.
25. Renna, *Life and Miracles of Saint Margaret of Cortona*, 114.

The *vita* of Clare offers plenty of evidence that she circulated within a vast community of women that included both well-to-do lay women and religious sisters from different orders. It seems that all those public displays of extreme piety paid off; her hagiographer notes that a number of women were converted to the penitential life thanks to Clare. It is conceivable that her success rate contributed to the suspicions that surrounded her. For example, she converted to a penitential life a noble widow who could not find a new husband to suit her taste. After Clare visited her, the widowed countess rejected such earthy desires like passion and riches, much the way Clare did, and joined Clare's little community. Further, the countess's "brother and all his family from then on lived a life of honest virtue and comportment."[26] Another family was also diverted to a pious life when Clare converted the lord of the castle Mercatello, whose wife, mother, and sister all, like the countess, joined Clare's rapidly expanding community. In his analysis of these conversions, Jacques Delarun notes their exceptionalism. Commenting on the lord of Marcatello and family's conversion, Delarun comments: "Even when the main convert is a man, the female presence is often the more important in the legend."[27] Thus, through these conversions Clare's little community grew, and its existence and growth provided legitimacy for the radical acts of piety she had displayed before being reined in, largely by the very women with whom she had initially established her community. Had Clare wanted a more traditional model for a women's religious community, she had a number of examples on hand, and she counted among her network of friends at least two communities of religious sisters. For example, she often visited a community of religious women in the church of Santa Maria, whom Dalarun identifies as a group of exiled Cistercian nuns from Constantinople, in order to discuss such religious topics as fasting or the different saintly men and women, simply for the pleasure of the experience.[28] One might presume that if she could not partake in a life of solitary independence, at least her informal community was far less restrictive than any that would require life under a *Regula* regardless of her own position in such a house.

The significant differences in way of life and pious origin in the *vitae* of Umiliana, Clare, and Margaret is not unusual for lay holy women of this period. Their friendships with other women differ greatly from one another in quality but perhaps not in purpose. From the perspective of the hagiographers, these friendships were a way to anchor the holy woman to her lay community while insulating her from the corruptibility of worldly society. But

---

26. "*Lapsus Linguae*," 37.
27. Dalarun, "Gospel in Action," 200.
28. "*Lapsus Linguae*," 30.

while Care insisted on a public presence and Margaret had it foisted upon her by God, Umiliana appears to have had neither the inclination nor the expectation of public piety. Perhaps this made the job of her hagiographer a little easier, but her friendships with other lay holy women still established her own pursuits as valid and positive.

READING FRIENDSHIP AS RESISTANCE IN A PATRIARCHAL SOCIETY

Lay saints were the spiritual equivalent of the local girl (or boy) made good; these texts provide valuable insight into the daily lives and experiences of the lay women in whose same social class and context these saints were rooted, and the many instances of friendship depicted in the *vitae* demonstrate the importance and the ubiquity of such bonds between women in urban Italy. Yet the hagiographers, learned men as they often were, would not necessarily have identified these relationships as examples of classical *amicitia*. Whether these models were based on Stoicism, the works of Cicero, or those of Aristotle, friendship was a relationship based on equality in value and status of the friends and required of them commensurate reciprocity; the most perfect friendship existed but for the bond itself with nothing else gained.[29] A particularly Christian model of friendship also developed in the Middle Ages: spiritual friendship, a derivative of classical notions of educative love, through which a student was directed and guided by a master. This model was most fully articulated by the English Cistercian monk Aelred of Rievaulx (d. 1166), who asserted that a friendship of value and purpose could not be restricted to those without faults. Despite claiming Cicero as his source, Aelred turned the traditional philosophical notions of *amicitia* on their heads, arguing that friendship was not attained through perfection but rather the other way around. And as perfection of the soul is a mighty high bar to reach, that friendship was a way to seek perfection, not necessarily to attain it. Thus, in Aelred's model of spiritual friendship, goodness in intentions was the basis on which the relationship ought to be built rather than the perfect goodness of those involved in the relationship. Aelred explicitly rejected a notion of friendship based on human perfection because such a thing was unattainable within a Christian perspective. Spiritual friendship, unlike the models posited by Cicero or Aristotle, was a means of spiritual betterment, a tool for

---

29. See, for example, Reginald Hyatte, *The Arts of Friendship: The Idealization of Friendship in Medieval and Early Renaissance Literature* (Leiden: Brill); Julian Haseldine, ed., *Friendship in Medieval Europe* (Stroud: Sutton, 1999).

achieving perfection rather than a reward for its attainment. Unlike classical friendship, from which women were both implicitly and explicitly excluded, there are plenty of examples of cross- and same-gender spiritual friendships in the lives of medieval holy women. Jane Tibbets Schulenburg has outlined a number of examples of female friendships in the lives of early medieval holy women that include friendships between nuns in the same convent as well as long-distance relationships between nuns of different houses or between holy nuns and laywomen, notably queens or other significant benefactors. In these contexts, such relationships are often described in the language of intimate friendship. For example, in a discussion of the friendship between St. Leoba (d. 779) and Queen (and future saint) Hiltigard, the wife of Charlemagne, Schulberburg quotes this passage from the *vita* of Leoba: "Queen Hiltigard revered her [Leoba] with a chaste affection and loved her as her own soul."[30] Likewise, Ulrike Wiethaus compares the different natures of the female friendships of Hildegard of Bingen as expressed through letters. Like with the saints discussed by Schulenburg, Hildegard developed close relationships with women from other convents. These women, cloistered as they were, enjoyed friendships with both men and women; indeed, cross-gender spiritual friendships appear to be more frequent for holy women than same-gender friendships, even more so if we include the cross-gender friendships described in the *vitae* of holy men.[31]

The model of spiritual friendship is most clearly reflected in the *vita* of Umiliana and specifically her relationships with the two penitent women Gisla and Sobilia. For Gisla, in particular, Umiliana acted as advisor in her spiritual struggles, providing both practical and spiritual guidance. For example, poor Gisla was plagued with noisy neighbors who distracted her when she was at prayer. After she complained of this on one of Umiliana's visits, God ceased the disturbances because of Umiliana's intercession. Gisla was also tormented by the devil but was liberated when Umiliana once again interceded on her behalf. After Umiliana died, she appeared to Gisla while she slept, in order

---

30. Jane Tibbetts Schulenburg, *Forgetful of Their Sex, Female Sanctity and Society ca. 500–1100* (Chicago: University of Chicago Press, 1998), 357. The translation is from C. H. Talbot, *The Anglo-Saxon Missionaries in Germany* (London: Sheed and Ward, 1954). The chapter in which Schulenburg describes friendships of early medieval holy women also briefly describes the general proscriptions against special relationships in convents.

31. See, for example, Ruth Mazo Karras, "Friendship and Love in the Lives of Two Twelfth-Century English Saints," *Journal of Medieval History* 14, no. 4 (1988): 305–20; Blossom Stefaniw, "Spiritual Friendship and Bridal Mysticism in an Age of Affectivity," *Cistercian Studies Quarterly* 41, no. 1 (2006): 65–78; and the following articles included in Albrecht Classen's and Marilyn Sandidge's *Friendship in the Middle Ages and Early Modern Age*: Jennifer Constantine-Jackson, "On Rhetoric and Friendship in the Letters of Heloise and Abelard"; and David F. Tinsley, "The Spiritual Friendship of Henry Suso and Elisabeth Stagel."

to remind her not to neglect doing penance. Sobilia and Umiliana's relationship, meanwhile, can best be described as that of confidantes who were each other's spiritual companions on a shared pious journey. Sobilia first appeared in the *vita* when Umiliana cured her of a badly broken arm. Another time, when Umiliana was visiting her, the two women prayed together and Sobilia witnessed her companion being raised in the air. After Umiliana died, she also appeared to Sobilia in her cell, just as she had with Gisla, but with a different message: Sobilia asked her friend many things about her experiences after death, the details of which she would not reveal to the hagiographer. These postmortem visitations are particularly indicative of the different qualities of the relationships that Umiliana had with Gisla and Sobilia, the former as spiritual guide and the latter as spiritual partner; Gisla was left with a gentle scolding while the more spiritually advanced Sobilia was graced with revelations of the afterlife. Still, even if Umiliana and Sobilia's relationship was more equal, only one of these women was the subject of a hagiography.

The relationships of Clare and Margaret cannot be so tidily labeled spiritual friendship. As the leader and founder of a penitential community, clearly Clare of Rimini raised up her spiritual sisters, but as described above, her friends provided a check on Clare's instinctual drive toward radical and public displays of piety. Margaret's *vita* suggests both particular relationships and an extended community of women through which the holy woman circulated. Many of the women with whom Margaret interacts are unnamed, with the exceptions of Marinaria and Raneria, the two women who took Margaret in when she first arrived, destitute, in Cortona. Might their status in life have offered their own reputations some protection to take in and even promote a fallen woman such as Margaret? Exactly how Margaret came to their acquaintance is a mystery, but what is not is the real support they provided Margaret and her son at what must have been the worst of times. And that support was not just material. It was through their circle of well-to-do women that the pair managed to find Margaret work as a midwife, but through her friendship with Marinaria and Raneria and *their* friends, Margaret's social standing was raised significantly so that the local Franciscans were willing to take a chance on her. The relationship between Margaret and Marinaria and Raneria does not fit the typical dynamic of spiritual friendship; the aid and support two women provided Margaret are more directly personal than generally found in medieval notions of charity, which tend toward indifference. Beyond these two women, Margaret of Cortona's diverse relationships are reminiscent of the community of Margery of Kempe (d. 1438). What often stands out to modern readers in *The Book of Margery* are her conflicts with others who do not see or do not acknowledge her exemplary piety and devotion, but much like Margaret, the text often described Margery's daily interactions and connections within her female community. In her analysis of female friendship in *The Book of the City of Ladies* and *The Book of Margery Kempe,* Alexandra Verini describes both Margery's friendships with holy women long dead and her more earthly relationships. In reference to the latter, Verini describes the text as "radically imagin[ing] a dynamic web of female friends from all classes and degrees of religious dedication."[32] The diversity in status of Margery's relationships differs from those of Umiliana, Clare, and Margaret, whose circles of friendship remained within the social class of the saint, with the exception of Margaret herself, who was of a lower status than the women among whom she circulated in Cortona. Describing numerous instances when Margery is a recipient of some material kindness or the giver of some spiritual service (praying over a sick friend, for example), Verini argues that the friendships described in *The Book of Margery Kempe* reject the demand of reciprocity essential in classical models of friendship. In a statement that could just as easily describe Margaret and her circle of friends in Corona, Verini writes, "Women's acts of friendship seem, therefore, not to demand immediate or direct reciprocation but rather to balance out over time in a form of common reciprocity that benefits the larger community."[33]

This is particularly the case between Margaret of Cortona and her initial benefactors Marinaria and Raneria. The exact marital status of the two noble women of Cortona—that is, whether they have yet been widowed—is not indicated, but they clearly had sufficient autonomy to provide a place to stay and material support to a desperate fallen woman and her illegitimate son, who were strangers in Cortona. Evidently, they also had sufficient clout and respect within their own circles to promote Margaret's interests. Margaret might have been a saint in the making, but all those traditional forms of patriarchal security, including even the Franciscans who would one day claim her as their own, were unavailable to her. Presumably even the Brothers themselves could not see within Margaret the new Magdalene that she was. These noble women, because of their own status, could provide a space and opportunity for redemption while protecting what little respectability Margaret had left. With some exceptions, most lay female saints from this period were women of elite urban status, if not noble then certainly members of the upper echelons of urban society. As we can see with Umiliana and Clare, this allowed them some resources and protections that a fallen woman of low

---

32. Alexandra Verini, "Medieval Models of Female Friendship in Christine de Pizan's *The Book of the City of Ladies* and Margery Kempe's *The Book of Margery Kempe*," *Feminist Studies* 42, no. 2 (2016): 365–91, at 385.

33. Verini, "Medieval Models of Female Friendship," 387.

birth like Margaret simply did not have access to on her own. Marinaria and Raneria, as women, were able to raise Margaret up through her association with them and through their own circle of friends, in a way that a man—even a Franciscan—would not have been able to. While one should not read the nature of the friendships described in the *vitae* of Clare of Rimini and Margaret of Cortona as an intentional and explicit rejection of the classical models of *amicitia*, they provide a framework for understanding women's relationships in the context of medieval perspectives of the feminine space. The nature of these relationships reveals the ways in which female bonds provided a means of resistance and support.

While the *vitae* depicted the experiences of these holy women through the lens of male religious hagiographers, the variety of experiences and pious activities between the different *vitae* suggests that the hagiographers were seeking to mold the lives they witnessed into an acceptable expression of faith. But their source materials were indeed women who sought to create and navigate a way of life for which they had no map; indeed, these very women become the models of lay piety even during their own lifetimes, as we see within the accounts themselves. Because the hagiographers were writing these narratives so soon after the death of their subject and often drawing on the accounts of the saint's own community and network as well as their own memories and recollections, we can speculate that these *vitae* present a version of these women's lived experiences, even if mediated and molded to a certain extent. As central as they are to their own narratives, Umiliana de' Cerchi, Margaret of Cortona, and Clare of Rimini existed on the margins of their societies, sometimes literally so, as with Margaret, who eventually moved outside the walls of Cortona, and Clare, who at one point called an abandoned wall her home.[34] As much as this marginality allowed them significant autonomy to shape their lives and their pious practices, it also left them considerably more vulnerable than had they married or joined a convent. This is especially true for Margaret and Clare. By circumstance, Margaret did not have that physical protection available to Umiliana, who still inhabited the family home, albeit on its margins. Perhaps those neighborhood women whose constant presence so frustrated Margaret also afforded her some protection, be it from physical assault—a woman alone must have been an obvious target—or from rumor and suspicion. The latter might indeed have been the most essential given Margaret's sinful past. Clare, our most radical saint, could not seem to help

---

34. One cannot use that phrasing without referencing Natalie Zemon Davis's *Women on the Margins: Three Seventeenth-Century Lives* (Cambridge, MA: Harvard University Press, 1997), which examines the lives of women who also lived outside the traditional frameworks of patriarchal authority.

drawing suspicion and rumor to her—she was simply so purposefully *public* in her pious displays—and if the threat of the Inquisition could not persuade her to tone it down, the pleas of her friends could, albeit reluctantly. Clare's community of women whom she had herself inspired into the penitential life were her best protection against the saint's own impulses. And it is for the sake of these same women that Clare purchased her neighbor's house in order to establish a little community together for them all, even if she never quite gave up her roofless hole in the wall.

In her collection of the *vitae* of medieval Italian female saints, *Consolation of the Blessed,* Elizabeth Petroff stated that "almost every saint's life tells of a profound relationship with a woman friend."[35] Such friendships are evident in the *vitae* examined here, but the texts are also resplendent with passing or casual friendships that are no less important for the sanctity of the holy woman. The model of friendship we can find in the *vitae* of independent lay holy women is often practical but is born of the challenges of the way of life these women embarked on. Friendships between women within the penitential life or between women penitents and their extended female communities reflect the challenges women faced within the patriarchal structures of medieval Christian society. While their male hagiographers mediated their lives through texts in order to create a depiction of holy life that could be created outside the standard confines of traditional female religious experience, female friendships provided much-needed legitimacy and freedom for the holy woman to forge her own path to sanctity. Umiliana de' Cerchi's friendships are most closely aligned with the medieval model of spiritual friendship, but notably, at least in comparison to that of cloistered holy women, her *vita* lacks any evidence of similar friendships with men. While there is no evidence in the *vita* itself that Umiliana's virtue was questioned, the *vitae* of Margaret and Clare should be a reminder of her vulnerability in this context. Margaret's and Clare's paths to sanctity were considerably messier, and, whether by choice or divine command, both women led considerably more public lives than Umiliana. Female friendship is perhaps more urgent, as the stakes are higher. But while the hagiographers describe the relationships between the saints and their female friends in order to bolster the claim of an explicitly lay sanctity, these bonds of friendships also suggest that for these lay women, female friendships allowed them to remain in the world and largely independent from masculine authority.

---

35. Elizabeth Petroff, *Consolation of the Blessed* (Millerton, NY: Alta Gaia, 1980), 34.

CHAPTER 4

Sisters and Friends
The Medieval Nuns of Syon Abbey

ALEXANDRA VERINI

IN MARGARET CAVENDISH'S 1668 protofeminist utopian play, *The Convent of Pleasure*, Lady Happy's opening ambition to "live incloister'd" with other women who "are resolv'd to live a single life, and vow Virginity" frames the convent as a space composed of like-minded women in pursuit of a common goal: in other words, a community of friends.¹ Female friendship, never fully separable from the suggestion and subsequent foreclosure of female same-sex desire—what Valerie Traub has called the trope of *amor impossibilis*—is integral to this play's portrayal of convent life.² Indeed, the Princess (who later turns out to be a Prince) first persuades Lady Happy to kiss by invoking their bond as women friends: "Not any act more frequent amongst us Women-kind; nay it were a sin in friendship, should we not kiss: then let us not prove our selves Reprobates."³ Though the convent eventually dissolves after the Prince, his identity revealed, marries a silent Lady Happy, this initial friendship between women, which blurs the lines between spiritual and carnal love

---

1. Margaret Cavendish, *The Convent of Pleasure*, in *Paper Bodies: A Margaret Cavendish Reader*, ed. Sylvia Bowerbank and Sara Mendelson (Peterborough, ONT: Broadview, 2000), 101. A precedent for such a community, particularly given the convent's focus on pleasure, exists in Epicurus's garden, where friendships provide comfort and support. See John M. Rist, "Epicurus on Friendship," *Classical Philology* 75, no. 2 (1980): 121–29.

2. Valerie Traub, *The Renaissance of Lesbianism in Early Modern England* (Cambridge: Cambridge University, 2002), ch. 7.

3. Cavendish, *The Convent of Pleasure*, 118.

(as friendship so often does), offers a glimpse into an early modern woman writer's perception of the convent as a space in which women's affective bonds operate transgressively to resist patriarchal norms.

Given that monastic life in Cavendish's England belonged to the medieval past, we might then wonder: did possibilities for friendship exist in convents themselves, or were they confined to protofeminist utopian fantasies?[4] We assume that nuns had friends, but is there any evidence of such bonds? After an overview of scholarship on medieval nuns, the answer to these questions might well be a shrug. Though convents would seem particularly conducive to the development of women's friendships, there is little scholarship on the subject despite extensive consideration of friendship among medieval monks.[5] One reason for this neglect, particularly in England, may be the dearth of surviving texts attributed to nuns.[6] Another more insidious reason may be the omission of women from the classical friendship theories that both informed medieval views of friendship and shaped twentieth-century scholarship on the subject.[7] Because medieval women's bonds often defied the parameters set by classical theorists such as Aristotle and Cicero, they have not been recognized as friendships, necessitating Marilyn Sandidge's call, in one of very few edited volumes to include medieval women's friendship, to "look beyond male-centered language patterns and literary forms to recognize involvement of women."[8]

---

4. Cavendish would, however, have had direct experience of convent life during her exile in Antwerp. See Nicky Hallett, *The Senses in Religious Communities, 1600–1800: Early Modern "Convents of Pleasure"* (Farnham: Ashgate, 2013).

5. A notable exception to the dearth of scholarship on nuns' friendships is Ulrike Wiethaus, "In Search of Medieval Women's Friendships: Hildegard of Bingen's Letters to Her Female Contemporaries," in *Maps of Flesh and Light: The Religious Experience of Medieval Women Mystics* (Syracuse, NY: Syracuse University Press, 1993), 93–111. Karma Lochrie also brings to light many multiple examples of possible friendships between religious women in "Between Women," in *The Cambridge Companion to Medieval Women's Writing*, ed. Carolyn Dinshaw and David Wallace (Cambridge: Cambridge University Press, 2003), 70–90. For an extensive consideration of male monastic friendship, see Brian Patrick McGuire, *Friendship and Community: The Monastic Experience, 350–1250* (Ithaca, NY: Cornell University Press, 2010).

6. Diane Watt's recent book excitingly complicates the notion that writings from medieval nuns do not survive as it examines early medieval women's literary engagement in monasteries such as Ely, Whitby, Barking, and Wilton Abbey. Diane Watt, *Women, Writing and Religion in England and Beyond, 650–1100* (London: Bloomsbury, 2019).

7. Alan Bray excluded women from the medieval sections of his seminal study of friendship, writing that before the seventeenth century, he did not find evidence for a public, "objective character" of female friendship, and that women only make themselves heard "as the troubling silence between the lines." Alan Bray, *The Friend* (Chicago: University of Chicago Press, 2003), 11, 10.

8. Marilyn Sandidge, "Women and Friendship," in *Friendship in the Middle Ages and Early Modern Age: Explorations of a Fundamental Ethical Discourse*, ed. Albrecht Classen and Mari-

To locate women's friendship in medieval texts is to work both within and outside of canonical, androcentric theories. Thinkers from Plato to Aristotle to Cicero defined friendship as a virtuous, reciprocal relationship between identical male equals. For Aristotle, as for later philosophers, women's perceived inability to make rational decisions meant that they lacked the virtue required for the highest form of friendship.[9] Christian theologians, such as Augustine, Aquinas, Anselm, and Aelred, who absorbed and reconfigured these classical frameworks to include God, similarly excluded women from spiritual friendship. Indeed, medieval women's lives might well have precluded them from the friendships between exact equals that these male authors envision, since, in the medieval household, women would have been more likely to form close bonds with female family members or with women of different social ranks—medieval romances, for instance, often foreground the bond between a maid and a noblewoman. Medieval women's friendships, moreover, might often have been formed through networks that defied the limited number of friendships that classical thinkers like Plutarch insist on.[10] Indeed, in this volume, Jennifer N. Brown offers examples of how women's spiritual friendships function differently from Aelred of Rievaulx's vision of male monastic friendship, suggesting how frequently women's bonds offer models that differ from those of their male contemporaries.

While women's friendships may have exceeded androcentric classical theories, recognizing the tropes of classical friendship within medieval women's bonds reveals how relationships that do not at first look like friendships might still have fit within this category. Greek *philia* included a much wider range of relationships than those described by the word *friendship* today. Of particular relevance to convents, *philia* emphasizes above all a "thorough-going likeness in characters, feelings, language, pursuits, and dispositions."[11] Beyond such identicality, friendship involves goodwill (wishing the other good) that is reciprocated and recognized.[12] Epicurus, in particular, although his writ-

---

lyn Sandidge (Berlin: de Gruyter, 2011), 93. In my own work, I have attempted to show how medieval women's friendship exceeds the identicality and exact reciprocity demanded by thinkers like Cicero. See Alexandra Verini, "Models of Medieval Female Friendship in Christine de Pizan's *The Book of the City of Ladies* and *The Book of Margery Kempe*," *Feminist Studies* 42, no. 2 (2016): 365–91.

9. Aristotle does allow for other forms of friendship advantage and pleasure in which women might more easily partake, but the highest form of friendship, virtue friendship, excludes women. Aristotle, *Nichomachean Ethics Books VIII and IX,* trans. Michael Pakaluk (Oxford: Clarendon Press, 1998).

10. Plutarch, "On Having Many Friends," in *Plutarch's Moralia,* vol. 1, trans. F. C. Babbitt, Loeb Classical Library (Cambridge, MA: Harvard University Press, 1927).

11. Plutarch, 96F–97D, 69.

12. Aristotle, 1155b28–1156a6.

ings were not available in the Middle Ages, provides a source for thinking about friendships in convent settings since the Epicurean Garden shares with Christian monastic communities a desire to be set apart from the wider culture and an aspiration for salvation through the imitation of a divine man.[13] Epicurean communities in their retreat from the public, masculine space of political life, unlike other models of friendship, also included women.[14] An Epicurean notion of friendship is relevant to convent life not just because it portrayed friendship as crucial to freedom from pain and anxiety but also because it linked friendship to the absorption of philosophical truth. Friends within the community were expected to use "frank speech" (*parrhêsia*) to help one another in emulation of their chosen sage.[15] An Epicurean view of friendship, more than an Aristotelian or Ciceronian one, thus anticipates the kinds of bonds that might have developed in cloistered female communities in which, as I show, women collectively worked through theological questions. And if we understand friendship as an alliance of like-minded people who are joined in goodwill and reciprocally sharpen each other's virtue through philosophical conversations, we might more readily find examples of such bonds in convents. Only by recalibrating our understandings of friendship and working within and outside of traditional theories will we find what Karma Lochrie has called "the tracery of female relationships."[16] As the essays in this volume by Stella Wang, Jennifer N. Brown, and Andrea Boffa attest, women's spiritual life is a particularly generative site at which to locate such tracery.

In this essay, I explore the records of medieval Syon Abbey as an exemplary site of women's spiritual friendship. The only English house of the Bridgettine Order, which had been established by Saint Bridget of Sweden (c. 1303–73), Syon was founded by Henry V in 1415 at Twickenham in Middlesex (it later moved to Isleworth).[17] In accordance with the Bridgettine rule,

---

13. On friendship in Epicurus, see Attila Németh, *Epicurus on the Self: Issues in Ancient Philosophy* (New York: Routledge, 2017), esp. ch. 5. Understandings of Epicurus in the Middle Ages come from Cicero, not Diogenes Laertius, and he tended to be understood as heretical.

14. See Jane McIntosh Snyder, *The Woman and the Lyre: Women Writers in Classical Greece and Rome* (Carbondale: Southern Illinois University Press, 1989), 101–5.

15. Martha Nussbaum, *The Therapy of Desire* (Princeton, NJ: Princeton University Press, 1994), 134–37. The fragmentary remains of *On Frank Criticism* by the Epicurean philosopher Philodemus (c. 110–35 BCE) are explicit about the therapeutic role of candor. See Dirk Baltzly and Nick Eliopoulus, "The Classical Ideals of Friendship," in *Friendship, a History*, ed. Barbara Caine (London: Equinox, 2009), 39–41.

16. Lochrie, "Between Women," 86.

17. G. J. Aungier, *The History and Antiquities of Syon Monastery, the Parish of Isleworth and the Chapelry of Hounslow* (London, 1840), is still the standard history of Syon. See also John Rory Fletcher, *The Story of the English Bridgettines of Syon Abbey* (South Brent, Devon: Syon Abbey, 1933).

Syon had both men and women—sixty sisters and twenty-five religious men (thirteen priests, four deacons, and eight lay brothers)—who lived separately but were co-governed by an abbess and a confessor. While early scholarship on the abbey focused on the smaller but more extensively documented group of men, recent accounts have increasingly turned to the sisters, whose lives are glimpsed through a range of liturgical manuscripts written for them by male clerics at Syon. These texts, like *The Convent of Pleasure,* reveal the subversive potential of women's friendships, as, by going to lengths to negate bonds between nuns, male clerical authors reveal the vitality and transgressive potential of such bonds. The latent force of friendship between sisters is confirmed both in a range of performance scripts from the medieval abbey and in a later manuscript possibly written by an early modern nun at Syon's relocated foundation in Lisbon.

WOMEN'S FRIENDSHIP AS ABSENT PRESENCE AT SYON

Friendship emerges as a vital source of female agency at Syon ironically through the efforts of male-authored liturgical guides to repress it. The best known of these guides is *The Myroure of Oure Ladye,* a fifteenth-century Middle English translation and explication, possibly by Thomas Fishbourne, of the fourteenth-century Latin Bridgettine office, which was written in honor of the Virgin and based on Bridget's visions.[18] This office validated the abbey's female community in particular since the brothers did not have their own unique counterpart but rather recited the office according to diocesan use.[19] A second crucial text for understanding the experiences of Syon's sisters is the Middle English *Additions,* a document composed around 1425 to supplement Bridget's

---

18. No complete manuscript of this text survives: it is split between MS Aberdeen University W. P. R.4.18 and Oxford Bodleian MS Rawlinson C. 941, which are composed in a hand from the late fifteenth century or early sixteenth century (though the composition of the text is generally dated to 1420–50). John Henry Blunt's edition is based on the printed text (STC 17542, Fawkes, 1530), which first appeared in 1530. Seven other partial manuscript copies exist, only three of which have the third part bound with them. Blunt tentatively attributed the work to Thomas Gascoigne, Chancellor of Oxford (1442–45), but this attribution has since been discredited and the work is now associated with either Thomas Fishbourne, the first confessor-general of Syon, or Syon deacon Clement Maydeston. For an overview of the text, see Ann Hutchison, "Devotional Reading in the Monastery and the Medieval Household," in *De Cella in Seculum: Religious and Secular Life and Devotion in Late Medieval England,* ed. M. G. Sargent (Cambridge: Cambridge University Press, 1989), 215–27.

19. See Katherine Zieman, "Playing Doctor: St. Birgitta, Ritual Reading, and Ecclesiastical Authority," in *Voices in Dialogue: Reading Women in the Middle Ages,* ed. Linda Olsen and Kathryn Kerby-Fulton (Notre Dame, IN: University of Notre Dame Press, 2005), 309.

Rule of Seynt Saviour and adapt it to the new foundation in England.[20] While the Bridgettine order at its core foregrounds female community through imitation of the Virgin Mary and Saint Bridget, these guides go to great lengths to suppress any personal relationships or affinities between sisters.[21]

One way these texts implicitly discourage friendships is by promulgating an idealized uniform identity at the expense of particular bonds between sisters. As the *Myroure*'s title suggests and its prologue instructs, the Bridgettine sisters were intended to be mirrors of Bridget and the Virgin Mary. The narrator foregrounds their status as undifferentiated copies by likening them to wax impressions identically "reformed to the lykenesse of God" and to "pennies" that are "impressed" with the "the image of the kynge" (98).[22] For their part, the *Additions* emphasize uniformity of action: "In the quyer, all schall be as angels, enclynge togyder, rysynge togyder, knelying togyder, stondynge, turnynge and syttng togyder, all after oo forme, goynge and comynge togyder" (102). This identicality would have been visually signified by the sisters' habits with their distinctive crowns bearing five red pieces of cloth to signify Christ's wounds, which imitated Bridget's own.[23] Any deviation from this uniform identity was to be censured: the *Additions*, for instance, threatens punishment "[i]f any come to dyuyne seruyse, or to Indulgete, seuen psalmes, confession, procession, conynge, chapter, De profundis, or collacion or generally to any conuentual acte vsed in the monastery without her holle habit" (2).

While identicality itself is not antithetical to friendship, these descriptions of sisterly community lack the reciprocity that often accompanies friendship.

---

20. Bridget had specified that new additions be drawn up for each new foundation. The additional rules for the sisters are grouped together in fifty-nine chapters and contain elaborate directions not only about the occupation, behavior, and special duties of the sisters but for exigencies of every kind. The Syon sisters' additions have been edited by James Hogg, in *The Rewyll of Seynt Sauioure*, vol. 4, *The Syon Additions for the Sisters from the British Library MS Arundel 146* (Salzburg, Austria: Institut Für Anglistik und Amerikanistik Universitat Salzburg, 1980).

21. Julia Mortimer has noted similar efforts of erasure of Bridget's persona itself both in the Latin versions of her texts and in their Middle English successors. Julia Mortimer, "Reflections in the Myroure of Oure Ladye: The Translation of a Desiring Body," *Mystics Quarterly* 27, no. 2 (2001): 58–76.

22. *The Myroure of oure Ladye, containing a Devotional Treatise on Divine Service. With a Translation of the Offices used by the Sisters of the Brigittine Monastery of Syon, at Isleworth, during the Fifteenth and Sixteenth Centuries*, ed. John Henry Blunt, Early English Text Society, ES 19 (London: N. Trübner, 1873). Quotations from this edition are cited parenthetically within the text.

23. In *The Rule of Our Saviour*, Bridget says that Christ had prescribed the habit of her order: "upon the veyle must be sett a crowne of whyte lynen cloth, to the which must be sowyd five smale partyes of redde cloth, as five dropys." From *The Rule of our Savior*, in *Women's Writing in Middle English*, ed. Alexandra Barratt (New York: Routledge, 1992), 97.

For Cicero, "When a man thinks of a true friend, he is looking at himself in the mirror," but friendship is "complete identity of feeling about all things divine and human strengthened by mutual goodwill and affection."[24] Even friendships of a kind more flexible than Cicero's model include some form of mutuality. The *Myroure* narrator's emphasis on uniform identity, however, results ironically in solitary and separate selves who do not, in his account, display affection or even interest in each other. In his discourse on reading, for instance, he instructs them, "rede by your self alone" (67). The construction of each sister as a solitary among many is a common trope in monastic life, but this Bridgettine guide takes the trope to a greater extreme, disallowing smaller groupings and intimacies that other rules more tacitly permit.[25] As Rebecca Krug writes, "Bridgettine communities although composed of 'daughters' were to be little concerned with relations among siblings: the aim of Bridgettine communal reading was to establish a collective, visual identity, but that identity was in singular presence before God."[26]

However, when the *Myroure* and *Additions* move from an implicit omission of personal relationships to active discouragement of female bonds, they a ring a bit of "thou dost protest too much." For instance, when the *Additions* warns, "In the dortour none schal beholde other, nor make synge to other withoute a resonable cause: but all schal there kepe hygh silence" (140), we wonder whether this might be a regulatory response to chatter within the sister's dormitory. The mandate that silence "is to be kepte in the lybrary, whyls any suster is there alone in recordying of redynge" (*Additions*, chapter 14, 72) suggests that the sisters might in fact have found opportunities to speak to each other when they were intended to be reading alone. Friendships from outside the abbey were also discouraged and regulated, as the *Additions* dictates, "If any sustres frendes, desire to se her, þe abbes schal not lyʒtly graunte thys but seldom in the ʒere" and recommends that "the abbes take counsell of the general confessour and know by hym whan she schal open þe wyndowe . . ." (75). These discouragements of the nuns' friendships, however, draw

---

24. Cicero, "De Amicitia," in *Cicero de Senectute, De Amicitia, De Divinatione*, trans. William Armistead Falconer (Cambridge, MA: Harvard University Press, 2001), 194, 187.

25. McGuire notes that even while rules for monks like that of St. Benedict also display wariness of sexual contact between young monks and are relatively silent on monastic friendship, they still afforded some space for relationships between monks and resulted in spaces that cultivated a form of classically based friendship (*Friendship and Community* 83).

26. Rebecca Krug, *Reading Families: Women's Literate Practice in Late Medieval England* (Ithaca, NY: Cornell University Press, 2002), 182. Elizabeth Schirmer comes to similar conclusions in her analysis of the *Myroure of Oure Ladye*. See Schirmer, "Reading Lessons at Syon Abbey: The Myoure of Oure Ladye and the Mandates of Vernacular Theology," in *Voices in Dialogue: Reading Women in the Middle Ages*, ed. Linda Olsen and Kathryn Kerby-Fulton (Notre Dame, IN: University of Notre Dame Press, 2005), 345–76, esp. 355.

attention to their prevalence in the abbey and invest them with a disruptive potential.

A more extended example of bonds between sisters whose presence is felt through their repression occurs in the *Myroure*'s chapter 8, *On Divine Service*. In an exemplum that warns against talking during service, the difference between the *Myroure* and its source text is revealing. In the story's source, borrowed from Caesarius of Heisterbach's (c. 1180–1240) *Dialogus miraculorum*, Gertrude, a ten-year-old girl, appears as a ghost to another girl of the same age to make amends for whispering "half words" during service, essentially for engaging in the kind of intimate encounter against which the *Myroure* warns.[27] At the opening of Caesarius's account, the narrator says that he has heard this story directly from the abbess of the monastery, a detail that privileges female narrative authority. The subsequent story reports how this abbess instructs the young novice who has seen Gertrude to say "Benedicite" when Gertrude returns and to ask where Gertrude comes from and what she is seeking. These words cause Gertrude's ghost to retreat: "For in the sight of her friend she proceeded towards the cemetery, passing over the wall by a miracle." The *Myroure* narrator reproduces this story but omits both the central role that Caesarius afforded the abbess and the description of the novice as a friend. The *Myroure* instead concludes more dogmatically with the admonishment "take ye hede" since "this younge mayde ten yere of age was punysshed so for half words; what shall they suffer that are of greater age for hole words spoken" during the time of silence (47). This omission and refashioning of the story suggest the ways in which Syon's clerical authorities may have seen women's intimacy as threatening. In this instance, the *Myroure* replicates what Lochrie calls the "official view" of the Middle Ages, a point Andrea Boffa also notes in her discussion of Clare of Rimini: "when women get together in deliberate acts of female fellowship, corruption ensues."[28] However, as is the case in other medieval religious works, clerical discomfort with female intimacy draws attention to the disruptive potential of such bonds and, thereby, invests same-sex female relationships with authority.

Despite these efforts by Syon's clerical authors to suppress female collusion, the reality of life at Syon brought women together, often resulting in

---

27. Caesarius of Heisterbach, *The Dialogue on Miracles*, vol. 1, ed. G. G. Coulton and Eileen Power (New York: Harcourt, Brace, 1929), 344–45.

28. Lochrie, "Between Women," 71. Mary Erler also illustrates what she calls "a sustrum of unacknowledged yet powerful unease with such female groupings" by pointing to medieval interpretations of the story of Dinah (Genesis 34:1–2), some of which attribute Dinah's rape to her desire for female companionship. Mary Erler, *Women, Reading, and Piety in Late Medieval England* (Cambridge: Cambridge University Press, 2002), 8.

forms of collective agency. For one thing, recruitment within families appears to have been common at Syon, which meant that the women in the abbey might have had prior personal relationships with one another, which they might have further as they lived their life in close quarters.[29] For another, women constituted the majority in the abbey, and their image was thus foundational to the order's identity. This kind of collective identity differs from the *Myroure* narrator's enforcement of uniform obedience, as it instead frames the sisters' community as a group devoted to achieving a common purpose, something similar to what we see in Cavendish's convent. Though this kind of collectivity does not readily present itself as friendship, it contains the kind of political authority that friendship often brings. We see this, for instance, in a passage that the *Myroure* narrator adds to the Latin office in his explanation of the Sunday service as he writes "we ar closed in thys holy Monastery as knyghtes in a castell where we ar beseged wyth greate multytude of fendes that nyght and daye laboure to gette gentre and pocessyon in oure soules . . ." (72). The nuns' singing, he continues, will act as a "longe spere of fervente desyre of oure hartes stryeng up to god" to draw out "the sharpe swerde of the worde of god" (72). Unlike the descriptions of the sisters as pennies or wax impressions, which framed collectivity as passive imitation, this comparison of the sisters to knights defending a castle foregrounds their collective strength. Though they are not here described as friends, if we recall that pacts of friendship between medieval knights encouraged them to regard themselves as members of a community united by a common purpose, we might then understand the sisters' alliances as containing the political strength that was found in medieval friendship.[30]

The paradoxical commitment to solitude and community that we find at Syon is endemic to monastic life itself and present in a wide range of rules, but the vehemence with which Syon's rules discourage women's friendship may have a historical root. The Bridgettine order because it was started by a woman had, from its beginnings, been beset by efforts to regulate female authority.[31] While Bridget's original rule mandated that the abbess as mother

---

29. Krug notes that there were at least three families represented at Syon in 1428 (*Reading Families* 183).

30. Antonella Liuzzo Scorpo, *Friendship in Medieval Iberia: Historical, Legal and Literary Perspectives* (Burlington, VT: Ashgate, 2014), 106.

31. See Hans Cnattingius, *Studies in the Order of St Bridget of Sweden*, vol. 1, *The Crisis in the 1420s*, Acta Universitatis Stockholmiensis, Stockholm Studies in History 7 (Stockholm: Almqvist & Wisk, 1963), 22–25. Mortimer notes other changes such as the shift from the first-person narrative of the original, in which the voice of Christ articulates the structure of the Order, to the third person, which eliminates the exchange between Christ and Bridget ("Reflections in the Myroure of Oure Ladye," 68).

be head of both brothers and sisters, Pope Urban V insisted that the rule be revised to omit the dominance of a woman over men.[32] Syon's foundational charter of 1415 reverted to Bridget's initial vision and declared the abbess head of both spiritual and temporal affairs. This assertion enabled Syon's first abbess, Matilda Newton, to demand obedience from the general confessor and the brothers of the abbey as "hede and lady of the monastery."[33] The sisters supported Matilda's position, but, in 1416, after a meeting arranged by Henry V and a council of clerics, Matilda was removed from the abbey. If, as C. Stephen Jaeger argues, love and friendship acted as "alternate and higher forms of governing" in the Middle Ages, then the attempts of the *Myroure* and the *Additions*, written shortly after Matilda's dismissal, to stifle friendship among nuns might have been aimed at delimiting the sisters' political agency.[34] However, in these very efforts, as we have seen, they unwittingly draw attention to the powerful current of women's bonds within the abbey.

FRIENDSHIP AT THE ROOT OF THE BRIDGETTINE ORDER

Syon's liturgical guides make women's friendships visible primarily through their omission of it, but *The Life of St Bridget*, which is attached to the *Myroure* manuscript, brings these bonds further to the fore. As Boffa's essay in this volume indicates, women's *vitae* are rich sites for the study of female friendship. Based on the vita of St. Birgitta compiled by Bishop Alfonso of Jæn and Petrus Olavi and written in Latin by Archbishop Birger Gregersson of Uppsala and Nicholas Hermanni, Bishop of Linköping, Bridget's Life is no exception.[35] The Middle English translator at Syon, possibly the same as the *Myroure* author, interpolated Bridget's vita with episodes from the Life of her daugh-

---

32. *Rewyll*, fol. 56r–56v, cited in Nancy Warren, *Spiritual Economies: Female Monasticism in Later Medieval England* (Philadelphia: University of Pennsylvania Press, 2001), 11.

33. *Additions for the Sisters*, 198. See Warren's discussion of this historical moment (*Spiritual Economies* 11).

34. C. Stephen Jaeger, *Ennobling Love: In Search of a Lost Sensibility* (Philadelphia: University of Pennsylvania Press, 1999), x.

35. Birger Gregersson, *Vita S. Birgittae in Scriptores rerum svecicarum medii aevi*, 3 (Uppsala: Edvardus Berling, 1876); Birgerus Gregorii, *Legenda S. Birgitte*, ed. Isak Collijn (Uppsala: Almquist and Wiksells, 1946). A version of Bridget's life also appears in *Acta Sanctorum*, Oct. 4, 50:377. Early sources attribute this life to Thomas Gascoigne based on a marginal note in Oxford, Bodleian Library, Digby 172B, fol. 27, in which Gascoigne mentions compiling the life of Saint Birgitta (*Dictionary of National Biography* 43). However, since Gascoigne's authorship of the *Myroure* has been discounted, the authorship of this life is likely by a different author. The *Myoure*'s Middle English version of the Life was printed by Thomas Pynson in 1516.

ter Catherine, which was likely written by Johannes Johannis Kalmarnenensis.[36] Through its omissions and additions, this composite Life, which prefaces the *Myroure*'s religious rule, at once displays anxiety about the transgressive potential of female friendships and shows how relationships between women were integral to Bridget's order.

The Life begins by emphasizing the ways in which female bonding can lead to trouble. Moving more quickly to an example that the Latin life places later, the *Myroure* Life opens with an account of how a nun from the "Monastery of Shoo" berates Bridget's grandmother for "the great pryde that she aduiged to be in hir" (xlvii). Such animosity from women continues in Bridget's own life. When Bridget is twelve, her aunt finds her out of bed at night praying and, suspecting "the lyghtnesse of the virgin" (xlviii), beats her with a rod that miraculously breaks into pieces, proving Bridget's holiness. Strikingly, the aunt assumes that a woman has led Bridget astray, exclaiming, "hath nat some women taught the some fals prayers" (xlviii). This comment is clarified by an episode from the *Myroure* manuscript, which describes how Bridget receives divine help with her sewing from an unknown maiden whom her aunt catches sitting with Bridget on her bed.[37] This episode, which the *Myroure* translator omits, might account for the aunt's assumption that a woman has taught Bridget and suggests anxiety about intimacy between girls. A similar fear about female companionship is expressed in a subsequent story that relates how the devil appears to Bridget while she is "playing with Maydens of lyke age" (xlviii). By omitting the story about the young girl who helps Bridget and focusing instead on the animosity that women direct toward Bridget's grandmother and to Bridget herself, the *Myroure*'s Life foregrounds the saint's exemplarity rather than her bonds with other women.

Though this text is wary of intimacy between female peers, it more readily foregrounds Bridget's generative bonds with women in the spiritual realm. Such vertical friendships, as opposed to horizontal ones, might have supported the *Myroure* author's interest in enforcing imitative obedience among the sisters, but they nonetheless foreground the power of women's intimacy more broadly. An example of such vertical spiritual friendship occurs during Bridget's childhood when a "Lady syttynge in bright clothynge" (xlvii) puts a crown on the young girl's head, signifying divine feminine support. Bridget also develops a close relationship with the Virgin Mary, who appears to her in early childhood and during a life-threatening childbirth. While such bonds are not named as friendships and might seem to defy what we expect

---

36. Catherine's life appears in Oxford, Bodleian Library, MS Digby 172B, ff. 36–36v.

37. *Birgitta of Sweden: Life and Selected Revelations*, ed. Marguerite Tjader Harris and trans. Albert Ryle Kezel (New York: Paulist Press, 1990), 73.

from friendship, the Virgin's role as Bridget's instructor, intercessor, and guide models a caring and intimacy akin to that of friendship. This affection may have offered an imitative example for the nuns of Syon, who were themselves encouraged to emulate the Virgin.

The *Myroure* Life, moreover, emphasizes friendly bonds between Bridget and her biological daughters. This vita, for instance, describes the saint's attachment to her daughters, showing her distress when her daughter Ingeburgis, who was a nun at Rysburga, dies (not because her daughter is dead but because Bridget fears she did not provide adequate moral instruction) (li). Moreover, the episodes interpolated from the Life of Bridget's daughter Katherine further emphasize bonds between women. Describing Bridget's second daughter, the Life says that "after the deth of heir husband she was always with heir moder seint Birget & lyued in the estate of wydowhod al hir lyfe" (l). Katherine later becomes a posthumous extension of her mother's mission as she forms a community of virtuous women: "bycause she was feruent in deuocion . . . & lyued a blessyd lyfe to gyue other example of good lyving the most honest woman of Rome loued to be in hir company" (l). The value of this female community is confirmed by a miracle that occurs when Katherine is in their presence:

> And when she was on a tyme desired by the moste noble matrons of the Cytie of Rome to walke with them for recreacyon without the Walles of the Cytie as they walked here & there amonge many clusters of grapes. They desired that the sayd blessyd virgyne Katheryn bycause she was of Eligant staute wold gather them to the sayd grapes/ & as she stretched vp hir armes to the grapes it semyd as thoughe hir armes had been apperelled with shyng cloth of golde.[38]

Here, in a reversal of Dinah's story, in which a woman's desire to leave the city to commune with other women was exegetically connected with her rape during the Middle Ages, women's collectivity and movement outside the city (in a manner not dissimilar to convent life) results in visible signs from God.[39] Bridget's relationship with her daughters might not immediately read as friendship in modern terms, which tend to classify friendships as nonfamilial, but at Syon, where the nuns were often addressed as "sisters and daughters," such familial intimacies might have registered as models for the sisters'

---

38. This scene is illuminated with a drawing of two hands in sleeves plucking a bunch of grapes (Oxford, Bodleian Library, MS Digby 172B, fols. 36–36v).

39. Mary Erler discusses interpretations of the story of Dinah in *Women, Reading, and Piety in Late Medieval England*, 2.

own bonds within their spiritual family. While relationships between women in different spiritual stations might seem only to support the efforts of the *Myroure* to render the sisters as passive and obedient, as these familial bonds then extend to create larger supportive communities of women, as they also do in the sisterboooks in Brown's essay, they come to evoke the mutual support and comfort provided by medieval friendship.

The *Myroure*'s Life of Bridget, like the Italian saints' lives that Boffa examines in this volume, further demonstrates the generative nature of same-sex female bonds after the saint's death through the miraculous cures of the women who visit her shrine. For instance, a woman from Rome named Agnes, who "fro hyr burthe had a greate grosse throte moche foule & dyfformyd," is cured when she touches Bridget's hand with a girdle that she then binds around her neck (lvi). In another episode that might have been particularly relevant for the female community at Syon, a nun from Saint Lawrence, who is "famylyer" with Bridget, is cured of "febleness and great sykenes that she had in her stomake" after she prays to Bridget "that she myght with hyr Susters be at deuyne seruyce and that she myght when nede shulde requyre goo aboute the moanstery withoute helpe" (lvii). This nun's longing to return to the company of her fellow sisters foregrounds the spiritual value of women's community, while her familiarity with Bridget, as with the other cured women, foregrounds a special spiritual connection with the saint. Such intimacy might seem hierarchal, but there also exists an element of reciprocity: just as Bridget offers cures to her female devotees, they provide evidence of her saintliness, performing the mutual benefits that friendship is thought to include both in classical theory and today.

Although the Life begins by highlighting the dangers of female companionship, it concludes with a rich testament to the power of female intimacy. Such ambivalence is evidence of the complexity of women's friendships within the abbey: while clerical voices may have sought to suppress women's bonds, such relationships would have been inescapable as women lived and prayed together in a confined space. As Eileen Power observed in her still canonical work on nunneries, the inhabitants of Syon, like those in any convent, "spent almost the whole of their time together. They prayed together in the choir, worked together in the cloister, ate together in the frater, and slept together in the dorter."[40] The relationships they developed through this constant contact might well have afforded them comfort and collective authority similar to that which relationships between women provide in Bridget's Life.

---

40. Eileen Power, *Medieval English Nunneries c. 1275 to 1535* (New York: Biblo and Tannen, 1964), 315.

FRIENDSHIP PERFORMED

The palpable presence of women's intimacies within the abbey would have also been visible in the ceremonies they collectively performed. In describing the office, the *Myroure* narrator, despite his instruction that the sisters read by themselves alone, also recommends that they rely on each other to understand the Latin text during religious rituals: "yf ye cannot vnderstone what ye rede. Aske of other that can teche you. And they that can oughte not to be lothe to teche other" (67). Such collaboration is equally encouraged in liturgical ceremonies themselves. While the *Additions* includes debasing punishment for the sisters in the mandate that a sister perform penance by lying prostrate on the church door and asking her fellow sisters to pray for her (26–27), they also include more generative interactions. For instance, before Evensong, the *Myroure* instructs the nuns to ask forgiveness from each other: "For yt is sayd in the name of all and therfore it byndethe all whether they saye yt or saye yt not and whether they be there or thense" (152). The sisters are exhorted to say "I forgyue & forgyue me" "in the name of all & in unyte of all" (152). While this ritual, on the one hand, imagines a collective self, the performance of this self relies on dialogue between sisters and necessitates interpersonal interactions that are absent from the *Myroure*'s and *Addition*'s vision of a uniform, undifferentiated community. Moreover, as the sisters here rely on each other for mutual forgiveness, they foreground their own collective agency rather than that of a priest.

Syon's processionals further convey the ways in which the sisters would have participated in interpersonal exchanges as well as the authority these exchanges afforded them.[41] St John's College Cambridge MS 139, which has red English rubrics to clarify the Latin script for the sisters, particularly demonstrates the ways in which the sisters were brought into intimate contact and gives the nuns a determining role in the performance of their liturgy.[42] It does this through rubrics that put the sisters into smaller groupings:

> Uppon ester day at procession too sustris the two chauntresses or too othir that the cheef chauntresse allignyth shal in the myddes of the quere bygynne this procession. *Salue festa dies*. And ther stondyng ful shal synge the said

---

41. These include Additional MS 8885 (1460–80); Diurnale of Syon, Magdalene College MS F.4.1; and St John's College Cambridge 139; EUL MS 262/1 Processionale Book.

42. This manuscript may be in the hand of Thomas Raille. Christopher de Hamel, "The Medieval Manuscripts of Syon Abbey and Their Dispersal," in *Syon Abbey: The Library of the Bridgettine Nuns and Their Peregrinations after the Reformation* (Otley: Roxburghe Club, 1991), 48–133.

> use unto the ende whiche use the quere than first goynge forthe and not afor shal repete the two sustres that bygan goynge in the myddis of the processions and then too aloon shal synge euery vuse of the processsion and rest at eu[er]y use eeude and the quere shal at eu[ery] use cende [*sic*]. Shal repete the first use. *Salue festa dies*. And this forme is to be kept. (My transcription)

Similarly, on Saint Mark's Day, "The too chauntrelles in the myddes of the quetre or othir too at the chief chauntresse assignment shal begyn." While we cannot assume that the "too sustris" in these cases would have been friends in the way we understand the term now, such instructions reveal that the sisters were not always an undifferentiated homogenous group: they would have collaborated in smaller groupings and so might have understood themselves as allies, united in a common mission to serve God. These instructions also reveal that the sisters, despite the demand that "this forme is to be kept," had a determining power in the performance of their religious ceremonies since the chantress could choose which sisters would play crucial roles in the service.

Syon's performance texts thus reveal the ways in which, despite depersonalizing descriptions of the community, the nuns would, in fact, have been brought into intimate interpersonal contact on a regular basis. We cannot verify that such contact always resulted in friendship (enmity and indifference are also possibilities), but it did create the circumstances in which such bonds might be encouraged and thrive. As in Cavendish's play, the bonds that might have resulted from Syon's liturgical performances retain power precisely because they cannot fully be named or seen and because they leave no tangible trace. The tracery of their presence, however, suggests that such performances may have liberated the sisters from the uniform and singular identity that the male clerics in the wake of Matilda's insubordination had prescribed for them. The liturgy the sisters performed, which was at the heart of the abbey's spirituality, suggest that the sisters of Syon Abbey may have seen themselves as allies working toward a mutually beneficial cause and, thus, as friends.

EPILOGUE: FRIENDSHIPS IN EARLY MODERN SYON

The vitality of women's friendships at Syon is confirmed in the abbey's later history. After the dissolution of the monasteries, Syon was forced out of England and, after many years of wandering, resettled in Lisbon in 1594 (they remained there until 1861, when the order was finally permitted to return to England). In addition to "The Life and Good End of Sister Marie," which Brown analyzes in this volume, relationships between the sisters during their time in exile become visible through inscriptions in books that bear more than one woman's name.[43] An unpublished liturgical manuscript dated to 1657 and titled *Discourse or Entertainment for the Sacred time of Advent* makes female spiritual friendship even more explicit.[44] Hitherto unmentioned in accounts of Syon's nuns, this discourse consists of a dialogue between an abbess and several allegorical nuns as they prepare for Christ's birth during Advent. As the opening of the manuscript outlines:

> In this discourse the lady abbesse desirous her Nunnes should entertaine well ye saviorue at his birth enjoynes Placidda to adourne ye poor pores on Cribb wherein he is to be bourne, Lucilla to provide the babes Shirt, Esperanca ye Infants cloths. Serena his swaddling bands, Candida his cradle and cradle cloth and let Symplicia's office bee to worke ye Cradle. The Abbesse [con]cludes with a survay of the whole weeke, and in ye first place or weeke Humility is pratised in the second Faith in ye Third Hope in ye fourth charity in ye fifth Recollection, in ye sixth, Love of our Neighbour is explained commended and peacified and the seventh weeke is spent a reiteration of all former Exercises. (Preface, my transcription)

The subsequent dialogue between these allegorical sisters, who cast lots to decide which role each will play in the preparations for Christ's birth, may have been used as a script for performance, or it may simply have been read silently as a guide to devotion. In either case, given that there are no male speakers and that manuscript was produced at a time when there were very few brothers in the community, it seems likely that a nun at Syon composed the work (though neither the order nor Saint Bridget is mentioned).

In these dialogues, the abbess and the sisters develop a notion of spiritual friendship that trumps its worldly counterpart. The abbess argues that in "worldly friendship," "communication is diminished" (18) and instead advocates for a higher form of human affection: "the good wee wish to o[u]r neighbour soe much more wee gain to ourselves and by how much more

---

43. For example, on a blank page at end of an English translation of Lucas Pinelli's *The Mirror of Religious Perfection* (1618) is written "Sister Agatha her Book given her by sister Theresa Bosswell God rest her soul amen." On another copy of this text, "Lucy Smith" is written at bottom of the title page, and "Mary Lidd" on the last page. Christopher Fonseca's *A Discourse of Holy Love, by which the Soul is united unto God* has on its title page the names of "ms Sor. Constantia Thers. De Jesus" and "n Amanda Sorrell."

44. This manuscript has not been edited or, to my knowledge, mentioned in previous scholarship. The date is based on a signature at the end of the manuscript. There are three copies of this text in the Exeter University Special Collections: EUL MS 262/add2/4; EUL MS 262/add2/5; EUL MS 262/add2/6.

wee reconcise and contract friendship with them, soe much more foresight an union of souls are joyned to Almighty God" (18–19). In this description, friendship is construed not as preferential affection toward a particular person but as mutually beneficial goodwill that leads to union with God. Symplicia exemplifies this understanding when she describes her "good friends" in Purgatory whom she wishes to liberate and exhorts her fellow sisters to pray to God for "those which are in mortall sinn . . . and to desire with all earnestnesse that they may be received into his [God's] friendship" (188). This view of friendship as a triangulated relationship between God and humans accords with the writings of Christian theologians, for whom "love for a friend symbolized love for God."[45] However, in this case, it places the sisters rather than male theologians in the pivotal position of initiating this spiritual love.

Indeed, the text, as a whole, privileges women as collective producers of spiritual knowledge. As in the *Myroure,* the sisters are encouraged to imitate the Virgin Mary but in a way that gives them more determining agency. When the abbess describes "how the soul spiritually [con]ceaves Christ o[u]r Lord and how it imitates in this his most Holy Mother" (5), she foregrounds female biological reproduction as a vehicle for generating spiritual understanding, thus giving women a privileged role in this process. The form of the work itself emphasizes the benefits of dialogue and mutual instruction between women in a manner that recalls Epicurus's "frank speech." Candida, for instance, asks for clarification of Serena's words about the spiritual significance of choosing "the better part," saying "hold a little sister, here is a doubt that may not be deferred and perhaps it will help you the better to declare what you are to say . . ." (107–8). Here, she tactfully implies that her fellow sister's explanation needs to be expressed more clearly and hopes that her question will help sharpen Serena's ideas. Later, Esperance confesses to Serena, "it hath always beene very difficult to my poore understandi[n]g to apprehend how this can possibly be that God should conforme his will to the creatures . . . if they have no will at all?" (117–18). In moments like these, as an expression of confusion results in a further explanation and sharpening of theological points, the text enacts the *Myroure*'s call to the sisters two hundred years earlier to explain the liturgy to each other, but it does so in a way that generates spiritual knowledge collaboratively between women. In their conversations, the nuns display the kind of friendship that their theoretical discussions envision, one that promises to bring them closer to God.

---

45. H. M. Canatella, "Friendship in Anselm of Canterbury's Correspondence: Ideals and Experience," *Viator* 38, no. 2 (2007): 351–68, at 366.

Just as the ambiguous friendship between women was subsumed in the marriage between Lady Happy and the Prince in Cavendish's play, women's friendships at Syon were erased by the medieval clerical authors. And yet, the tracery of such bonds survives both in the discomfort that Syon's documents show with female groupings and in the emphasis on women's alliances in texts more closely connected with Bridget herself such as her Life and her liturgy. The strength of these bonds was later confirmed in the early modern liturgical text from Syon likely written by a nun. The relationships that emerge in this range of documents are not all explicitly identified as friendships, but they exhibit the intimacy, goodwill, and mutual benefits that friendships provide. Including these bonds between the sisters of Syon within the framework of friendship evades the passive uniform identity that clerical authors sought to promulgate and resists the androcentric language patterns by which friendship studies have been limited. Moreover, reading nuns' relationships through the lens of friendship reinserts medieval religious women's bonds into a nexus of politics and intimacy from which they have long been absent. The records of Syon Abbey reveal that religious women may indeed have participated in the kinds of friendships that Cavendish's play imagines: because they were presumed to be impossible but also clearly existed, women's friendships at Syon Abbey, as at the Convent of Pleasure, even in the process of being erased, had the power to unsettle patriarchal norms and offer women direct access to higher truths.

PART 2

~

Feminine Space, Feminine Voices

CHAPTER 5

"Amonge maydenes moo"
Gender-Based Community, Racial Thinking, and Aristocratic Women's Work in Emaré

LYDIA YAITSKY KERTZ

THE RELATIVELY SHORT anonymous Middle English poem *Emaré* has confounded readers for centuries, presenting them with an image of a white Christian princess, whose identity is intimately linked with that of an elite Muslim woman through an intricately wrought Islamicate silk cloth.[1] Informed by the global turn in medieval studies, this essay takes the decorative cloth and the narrative impulse to establish connections outside one's community of origin as an entryway into a complex world of medieval luxury textile production, envisioned in the poem as specialized knowledge shared "amonge maydenes moo" (line 60). Both Emaré and the Emir's daughter are introduced to us as aristocratic women who are proficient at working silk, sharing a skill that connects them across the geographic and confessional divide. The unnamed Emir's daughter had decorated the cloth with birds and flowers, gems and precious stones, and portraits of lovers, weaving her own love story into the fabric. Throughout the poem, Emaré wears the cloth even though it was never meant for her. The shine of the cloth establishes Emaré's new identity and governs her interactions with the residents of distant Galys and Rome. All

---

1. *Emaré*, in *The Middle English Breton Lays*, ed. Anne Laskaya and Eve Salisbury, TEAMS Middle English Text Series (Kalamazoo, MI: Medieval Institute Publications, 2001), 145–99, also available at https://d.lib.rochester.edu/teams/text/laskaya-and-salisbury-middle-english-breton-lays-emare. Quotations are from Laskaya and Salisbury's edition of the poem, cited parenthetically by line numbers.

the while, Emaré's ability "to sewe and marke / All maner of sylkyn werke" (376–77) becomes her contribution to her new communities and her route to acceptance on foreign shores. In teaching other women how to sew and embroider, Emaré participates in and perpetuates a multigenerational, skill-based, transnational female community that begins with Emaré's late mother Dame Erayne, Lady Abro, and presumably the Emir's wife (the mother of the woman who made the cloth); it continues with the Emir's daughter, Emaré, and Lady Abro's bower of maidens (Emaré's childhood companions); and it promises to be carried on by Emaré's unnamed female apprentices.

In looking closely at these communities, in which skills are learned, taught, and passed on by women and among women, this essay builds on the scholarly work of Karma Lochrie, who encourages us to read into the silences of the medieval record to find a variety of female friendships: "Only by reading between the women will the tracery of female relationships begin to emerge in medieval culture—those 'things' that she and she might have practised in the interstices of cultural formations of romantic and filial relationship, as well as those 'things' that signal cultural anxiety about female fellowship."[2] In a more recent project, Alexandra Verini pointedly critiques the androcentrism of friendship studies by showcasing two radically different female models of friendship in fifteenth-century literary works.[3] Countering the classical definitions of *amicitia*, which insist on sameness as foundation of male friendship, Christine de Pizan's network of women in *The Book of the City of Ladies* aims to build community while preserving and celebrating difference; conversely, in *The Book of Margery Kempe*, Margery forms spiritual bonds with holy women who are long dead and receives support from women in vastly different social circumstances from herself. Lochrie and Verini both showcase a vast spectrum of female experience, including but not limited to "women who lived in circumstances that allowed them to nurture and support other women."[4] The anonymous romance *Emaré* centers on a young motherless woman who strives to establish alternative connections to other women through skill-based knowledge, education, mentorship, association, and other forms of female fellowship.

---

2. Karma Lochrie, "Between Women," in *The Cambridge Companion to Medieval Women's Writing*, ed. Carolyn Dinshaw and David Wallace (New York: Cambridge University Press, 2003), 70–88, at 86.

3. Alexandra Verini, "Medieval Models of Female Friendship in Christine de Pizan's *The Book of the City of Ladies* and Margery Kempe's *The Book of Margery Kempe*," *Feminist Studies* 42, no. 2 (2016): 365–91.

4. Lochrie, "Between Women," 71.

The storyline of *Emaré* follows the Constance-saga narrative arc, most familiar to English readers from Geoffrey Chaucer's *Man of Law's Tale* and John Gower's *Confessio Amantis*. In these stories, a pious Christian woman escapes the incestuous desires of her father through expulsion from her community of origin and establishes new connections elsewhere through exomagous marriage.[5] In this particular story, Emaré's mother, Dame Erayne, dies before the young girl learns how to speak or walk. The mother's absence haunts the narrative, as the daughter is frequently compared to the woman she grows up to replace both in physical appearance and in aristocratic womanly virtues. Lady Abro takes over Emaré's education, placing young Emaré among unnamed maidens in her care. Performing the work of the absent mother, Lady Abro teaches young Emaré courtesy and the elite skill of silk embroidery. Upon her return to her father's court, Emaré becomes the target of his inappropriate desire and relies on her Christian faith to stand firm against his attempt to marry her. Like in many of these Constance narratives, narrow escape from incest and false accusations of sexual impropriety are followed by the casting adrift of the heroine in a rudderless boat, leaving the judgment on whether she deserves to live or die to providence.[6] Emaré is cast adrift twice, and she survives both times. First, her lecherous father, Emperor Artyus, exiles Emaré for refusing to give in to his incestuous desires, and later her wicked mother-in-law manages to banish Emaré together with her newborn son Segramour while her husband is away on a crusading mission.[7] While in Chaucer's version, the heroine's ability to learn multiple languages aids her in establishing new connections and gaining new Christian converts, in *Emaré* the young woman has no trouble communicating with strangers,

---

5. Both Chaucer's and Gower's poems are late fourteenth-century Middle English iterations of the Constance story type, which makes them rough contemporaries of *Emaré* in date of composition. Other such tales circulated in England, including *Vita Offae Primi* (twelfth-century Latin text written in England), Nicholas Trivet's *Anglo-Norman Chronicle* (c. 1335), and *Gesta Romanorum* (c. 1350). On the continent, we find the Constance-saga in Old French *La Belle Helene de Constantinople,* Phillipe de Beaumanoir's *La Manekine,* and Middle High German *Mai und Beaflor*. This grouping of tales includes a wide range of genres, including chronicles, exempla, and romance. Anne Laskaya and Eve Salisbury, "*Emaré*: Introduction," in *Middle English Breton Lays,* 145–46, also available at https://d.lib.rochester.edu/teams/text/laskaya-and-salisbury-middle-english-breton-lays-emare-introduction.

6. Helen Cooper, "Providence and the Sea: 'No tackle, sail, nor mast,'" in *The English Romance in Time: Transforming Motifs from Geoffrey of Monmouth to the Death of Shakespeare* (Oxford; New York: Oxford University Press, 2004), 106–36.

7. For a discussion of *Emaré's* complicity in the project of Christian imperialism, which includes crusading and the literary memory of crusading, see Amy Burge and Lydia Yaitsky Kertz, "Fabricated Muslim Identity, Female Agency, and Cultural Complicity: The Imperial Project of *Emaré,*" *Medieval Feminist Forum* 56, no. 1 (2020): 38–69.

and the communities she lands in are already Christian.⁸ It is through her knowledge of silk work that Emaré is able to establish a life-long connection to other women in these various locales, both as a disciple and as a teacher.

The poem tells us that soon after her mother Dame Erayne passes, Emaré is sent away to be raised and educated by Lady Abro:

> The chyld, that was fayr and gent,
> To a lady was hyt sente,
> That men kalled Abro.
> She thawghth hyt curtesye and thewe,
> Golde and sylke for to sewe,
> Amonge maydenes moo. (lines 55–60)

Thus, from an unspecified young age, Emaré is ensconced in a female community, where she learns from and alongside other women. Her education includes courtesy, manners, as well as the ability to sew and embroider gold cloth and silk. Emaré benefits immensely from the skills she gains in Lady Abro's bower among the countless and nameless maidens, who spend their days and nights in female fellowship. From the scant information provided in the poem, it appears that this community is multigenerational: "She [Emaré] was curtays in all thynge, / Bothe to olde and to yynge" (lines 64–65). From a young age, Emaré not only learns but practices the courtly skills of courtesy, applying them to her sociality with both older and younger women. In return, these women show respect and love toward the young girl: "All her loved that her sye, / Wyth menske and mychyl honour" (68–69). This community nurtures young Emaré and instills in her the value of reciprocal love and companionship. All those who see her, presumably other young and old women, love her in a proper way, with honor and propriety being stressed twice in one line. Quite tellingly, the plot of the romance hinges on sight and the way characters respond either with or without honor to the visual presence of Emaré as well as to Emaré dressed in the cloth woven and decorated by the Emir's daughter. Outside the all-female multigenerational community, Emaré finds herself at the mercy of various onlookers, including her own father, whose licentious and incestual gazes propel her initial expulsion.

---

8. Jonathan Hsy, *Trading Tongues: Merchants, Multilingualism, and Medieval Literature* (Columbus: The Ohio State University Press, 2013), 65–73; Shayne Aaron Legassie, "Among Other Possible Things: The Cosmopolitanisms of Chaucer's 'Man of Law's Tale,'" in *Cosmopolitanism and the Middle Ages*, ed. John M. Ganim and Shayne Aaron Legassie (New York: Palgrave Macmillan, 2013), 181–205.

Emaré enjoys a sense of security among her female friends and teachers and strives to re-establish similar environments throughout her travels. Her trials and tribulations begin immediately after her father recalls her back to his court, thus physically separating her from her female fellowship. Emaré establishes a similar female community in Galicia: in the household of Sir Kadore she takes on the role of Lady Abro and teaches a new group of countless and nameless maidens how to sew and embroider silk. These female spaces of learning provide a sense of security and perpetuation of specialized knowledge, as presumably by learning together and from each other these women carry the potential to commune with other women through the shared knowledge of the silk-craft. Overlaying these physical spaces of female fellowship is the spiritual or associative relationship between the unnamed Muslim woman who makes and decorates the cloth and the eponymous character of Emaré who wears it. This affiliation between the two women who never meet is built on their sameness as elite aristocratic women who are proficient at silk-craft while preserving their differences as members of the larger Muslim and Christian communities.

Following her repeated expulsions, Emaré traverses the seas in her little boat, landing first on the shores of Galys, and the second time in Rome. Emaré's second journey is rather more perilous than the first, as it would require her rudderless boat to pass through the Straits of Gibraltar and into the Mediterranean, which is the traditional seascape for the Constance narratives. Emaré's two journeys reverse the traditional *translatio studii et imperii* trajectory, which starts out in Mesopotamia, then moves westward to Greece and Rome, and from Rome disperses into the various European states.[9] At the same time, Emaré's travels, guided as they are by Christian providence, replicate traditional pilgrimage routes, first to the shrine of Santiago de Compostela in Galicia, and second to the seat of papal authority in Rome. Throughout her journeys, Emaré wears the magnificent robe, woven and decorated by an elite Muslim woman, racially marked in the Middle English poem as "Saracen"; the brightness of the gold thread, studded with gems and precious stones, aids Emaré in her multiple discoveries on strange shores but also marks her as "unearthly." The iridescence of the metallic gold thread and precious stones renders the visual narrative unreadable to various characters who can only see the luxurious surface as an otherworldly marvel. As such, the cloth remains a foreign object, fully signifying its alterity, and at times imparting it onto the

---

9. Sharon Kinoshita, "'In the Beginning Was the Road': *Floire et Blancheflor* in the Medieval Mediterranean," in *Medieval Boundaries: Rethinking Difference in Old French Literature* (Philadelphia: University of Pennsylvania Press, 2006), 77–104.

abject white Christian heroine, thereby exposing the racial hierarchy within the narrative economy of Middle English romance.[10]

In contrast to Emaré's geographic peregrinations, the cloth from which this robe is made replicates the *translatio* route. Moving from Babylon (Old Cairo) to Sicily and eventually to a Christian court in Northern Europe or Britain, this imaginative cloth follows the established mercantile routes along which highly prized fabrics were brought to European markets. We do not get to hear much about the Emir's daughter; in fact, we do not even learn her name. Reading into these silences at the urging of Lochrie we may discover yet another nameless woman from whom she had learned this elite female craft: her mother, or yet another stand-in for a maternal figure, for this specialized knowledge is passed on from one generation to the next from woman to woman. What we do know is that the Emir's daughter first embroidered and decorated the cloth for her lover, the son of the Babylonian Sultan. The father of the King of Sicily then took the cloth from the Sultan by military force, most likely through crusading action, and gave it to his son, Sir Tergaunte, who brought it to Emaré's father, Emperor Artyus, as a demonstration of fealty, or possibly as a betrothal gift.[11] A woman's love and time-consuming labor are thus nearly eclipsed by the political, military, and lecherous actions of men. It has taken the Emir's daughter seven years to complete the intricate weaving and decorating process, the description of which takes up one hundred lines of verse and constitutes about 10 percent of the entire poem. Meanwhile, it takes the Christian Emperor all of two lines to order the cloth to be refashioned into a wedding robe for his daughter Emaré. To marry his own daughter, the Emperor requests and receives papal dispensation from Rome, which enables him to circumvent the incest taboo.[12] With the text and the textile at his disposal, the Emperor is enraged when Emaré refuses to consent to this unchristian marriage. He thus disposes of her disobedient body, newly

---

10. Robert Bartlett, "Medieval and Modern Concepts of Race and Ethnicity," *Journal of Medieval and Early Modern Studies* 31, no. 1 (2001): 39–56; Geraldine Heng, "The Invention of Race in the European Middle Ages I: Race Studies, Modernity, and the Middle Ages," *Literature Compass* 8, no. 5 (2011): 315–31; "The Invention of Race in the European Middle Ages II: Locations of Medieval Race," *Literature Compass* 8, no. 5 (2011): 332–50; and *The Invention of Race in the European Middle Ages* (New York: Cambridge University Press, 2018); for a crowdsourced bibliography on the subject of race in the Middle Ages, see Jonathan Hsy and Julie Orlemanski, "Race and Medieval Studies: A Partial Bibliography," *postmedieval: a journal of medieval cultural studies* 8 (2017): 500–531.

11. Elizabeth Scala, "The Texture of *Emaré*," *Philological Quarterly* 85, no. 3-4 (2006): 223–46, at 232.

12. On the role of documentary culture in Emaré, see Joo Ok Yoon, "Medieval Documentary Semiotics and Forged Letters in the Late Middle English *Emaré*," *English Studies: A Journal of English Language and Literature* 100, no. 4 (2019): 371–86.

clad in the dazzling Islamicate silk robe. This confusing history of unnamed lovers, fathers and sons, absent mothers and talented daughters, rivals and allies, Christians and Muslims, ends with a conferral of the cloth onto Emaré, connecting the Emir's daughter to the Emperor's daughter through a textile surface upon which the Emir's daughter's image and love story are inscribed. Thus, at her most vulnerable moment, Emaré finds solace and protection in a gift from a woman whom she has never met and which was never intended for her. But the gift also lends insight into the complex racial politics of the period as Emaré in her surrogate skin experiences a transfer of racialized identity. Traversing the medieval Mediterranean in a rudderless boat, with her body enclosed beneath the luxuriously decorated Islamicate cloth, Emaré learns that aristocratic privilege can be bestowed and denied, and that even a white Christian princess is not immune to racially charged aggression.

The luxurious construction of the cloth in *Emaré* is emphasized through a literal ekphrasis,[13] which focuses on the details of the making process, including technique, materials used, and the impressive time investment of seven years. The cloth is of "ryche golde and asowr" (line 113), is "wordylye wroght" (83) and "rychyly dyght" (88), and it is "Full of stones ther hyt was pyght" (89). Working the gold and blue threads and decorating them with precious stones over the course of seven years, the Emir's daughter weaves her love story into a romance tapestry, presenting her love for the Sultan's son using the maiden with the unicorn iconography and casting it as a tale worthy of comparing to those of Amadas and Ydoine, Tristan and Isolde, and Floris and Blancheflour. The three romance couples are praised as examples of true and honorable loving, which glosses over the extramarital nature of their relationships with an emphasis on loyalty to one's lover rather than to one's spouse. This romance iconography provides a glimpse of yet another female fellowship—that of literary heroines whose troubles and tribulations in love unite them as much as the visual proximity does. Gems and stones of various colors accompany each set of lovers, and together with birds and flowers create a unifying decorative motif for the figural embroidery, connecting the cloth-maker to her literary sisters in visual fellowship.

Emaré enters this unusual fellowship when she wears the cloth as clothing. Through the rhetorical trope of *effictio*, a detailed description of garments and

---

13. I distinguish between literal and literary ekphrasis in "Literal and Literary Ekphrasis: A Medieval Poetics," *Medievalia et Humanistica* 45 (2019): 75–99, at 75: "Literal ekphrasis is most commonly used to describe the making process of an object, providing cues for visualizing the image and the action in the mind of the reader and/or listener, while the object itself is generally described using literary ekphrasis, a discursive description that does not adhere to the structures of visuality."

jewelry, the luxurious Islamicate cloth and the responses to it from various onlookers transform Emaré into an otherworldly creature. Once the decorative cloth is refashioned into a robe for Emaré, the new garment becomes a membrane that encloses the white royal body beneath it and simultaneously marks the woman as otherworldly: "And when hyt was don her upon, / She semed non erthely wommon, / That marked was of molde" (lines 244–46). Romance construction of identity for knightly heroes and aristocratic heroines often hinges on such material externalization of nobility, conflating the noble body with its luxurious clothing.[14] This transformation occurs at a threshold moment in the narrative, right before Emaré is cast adrift for the first time.[15] Before she can be discarded into the sea, her social privilege, marked outwardly by the color of her skin and her public performance of Christian piety, is symbolically covered by a robe woven by the Emir's daughter, thus initiating a transfer of racialized identity. And yet, it is Emaré's religious and racial identity as the pious white Christian princess that guarantees her safe passage not only across the dangerous waters but also among strangers on strange shores, who nonetheless see her as "unearthly."

Yet the separation between the body and the "wede" (clothing) in which it is enclosed creates a rift between external and internal signifiers, which undergird the trope of *effictio*. There are at least ten references in the poem to the body underneath the decorative cloth. Insisting on separating the flesh from the textile, seven of these refer to Emaré's female body, and three refer to the young male body of her seven-year-old son Segramour:

"Was godely unthur gare" (line 198)	Emaré
"Then sayde that wordy unthur wede" (250)	Emaré
"For that comely unthur kelle" (303)	Emaré
"That worthy unthur wede" (366)	Emaré
"That semely unthur serke" (501)	Emaré
"For that worthy unthur wede" (612)	Emaré
"He was worthy unthur wede" (736)	Segramour
"That lufsumme wer unthur lyne" (864)	Segramour
"Of that lady, goodly unthur gore" (938)	Emaré
"The chyld was worthy unthur wede" (988)	Segramour

---

14. Andrea Denny-Brown, *Fashioning Change: The Trope of Clothing in High- and Late-Medieval England* (Columbus: The Ohio State University Press, 2012); Nicole D. Smith, *Sartorial Strategies: Outfitting Aristocrats and Fashioning Conduct in Late Medieval Literature* (Notre Dame, IN: University of Notre Dame Press, 2012); Susan Crane, *The Performance of Self: Ritual, Clothing, and Identity during the Hundred Years War* (Philadelphia: University of Pennsylvania Press, 2002).

15. On the transformative power of clothing during moments of transition from one state of being into another, see Denny-Brown, *Fashioning Change*.

The Middle English adjective *worthy* generally refers to the noble status of the person described. Thus, five of the ten references to the body under the clothing recognize its inherent nobility. The other five adjectives recognize the beauty of this noble body: *godely/goodly, comely, semely,* and *lufsumme.* Insisting on separating the flesh from the textile, seven of these refer to Emaré's female body, and three refer to the young male body of her son. The preposition *unthur* (*MED* "under"),[16] repeated ten times in this context, acts as a violent undressing, insistently directing readerly gazes to what lies below the intricate fabric surface.

Within the codes of European aristocratic vestimentary culture, the cloth constitutes a social skin, externally available for interpretation: as such, this Islamicate figural embroidery becomes Emaré's second skin, borrowed or otherwise received from the Emir's daughter. Thus, the cloth simultaneously delineates the outer extremity of Emaré's body and associates it with the absent Emir's daughter's body, whose image is incorporated into the figural embroidery. And yet, the poem's preoccupation with the white aristocratic body beneath the foreign clothing—the repetition of the epithet *worthy unthur wede* [noble under clothing] and its various permutations—calls attention to the very site of cultural contact between the woman who made the cloth and the woman who wore it. The insistent and voyeuristic preposition *unthur* thus reveals the poem's primary narrative tension: a privileged white female Christian body racialized as "otherworldly" through the Islamicate silk cloth.

The racial tension becomes even more significant because it constitutes a radical departure from the romance convention in which "Saracen silk" is generally viewed as a marker of quality, costliness, and status. As E. Jane Burns has convincingly argued:

> The textile geography mapped by women's silk work in Old French [courtly] narratives effectively revalues the term "Saracen" and the concept of "foreign women" along with it, by staging Saracen silk and Saracen work as desirous and coveted while also positioning female protagonists as highly skilled creators and manipulators of the medieval Mediterranean's most lucrative commodity.[17]

In its valorization of luxury, the romance genre tends to subsume the East/West divide to the point that Islamicate silks become second skin for West-

---

16. The *Middle English Dictionary* (*MED*) lists "unther" and "unþur" as variants of "under." *MED*, s.v. "under" (prep.), Regents of the University of Michigan, 2014, https://quod.lib.umich.edu/cgi/m/mec/med-idx?type=id&id=MED48177.

17. E. Jane Burns, *Sea of Silk: Textile Geography of Women's Work in Medieval French Literature* (Philadelphia: University of Pennsylvania Press, 2010), 12.

ern aristocratic bodies. In Middle English romances such as *Sir Gawain and the Green Knight*, courtly heroes and heroines like Gawain and Guinevere are arrayed in fine silks and jewels both of European production and imported from distant lands; their representation as aristocratic models also serves as testament to the far-reaching imperial power of Christian courts like King Arthur's. In focusing on the cloth as a marker of alterity rather than high status, the Middle English *Emaré* is reverting to the exoticism of travel narratives[18] and the demonization of foreign luxury associated with sexual impropriety and other corporeal sins as found in classical and clerical treatises. The wicked mother-in-law views Emaré as a foreign threat, deemed "nonearthly." She essentializes Emaré's difference by falsely accusing her of bestiality, thereby transferring Emaré's alterity onto the new generation. Emaré as a foreign refugee in Galys is disparaged, bereft of humanity, and cast adrift for the second time, this time expelled from her marital home together with her newborn son Segramour. And yet, Emaré's very survival hinges upon a tacit recognition that her white aristocratic Christian body will be preserved by providence and restored to its proper position within the social and spiritual hierarchy of Middle English romance. But until such resolution can be achieved, her body remains enclosed in the decorated cloth, both inviting and refusing sight.

Even the men who respond with charity and proper love to the sight of Emaré in this robe describe the encounter as overpowering and otherworldly: Sir Kadore sees a "glysteryng thyng" (line 350); the King of Galys (Emaré's eventual husband) is captivated by the light, "The cloth upon her shone so bryghth / When she was theryn ydyghth, / She semed non erthly thing" (lines 394–96); and the merchant Jurdan similarly sees her as a "non erthyly wyght" because of the "glysteryng of that wede" (701, 699). No one is able to read the cloth except for Sir Tergaunte, the King of Sicily, who, like his place of origin in Sicily, functions as an intermediary between Islamic strongholds and the Byzantine Empire in the East, and the Latin Christian kingdoms in the West.[19] He brings the cloth to the Emperor's court and recounts its beauty and provenance. This privileged position allows Sir Tergaunte to translate between faiths and cultures as he converts the cloth from a visual to a textual object. For everyone else, the cloth is a thing, an aesthetic encounter that both mesmerizes and repels. The Emperor, among many others, claims that he cannot see it:

---

18. Elizabeth Sklar, "'Stuffed wyth Ymagerye': Emaré's Robe and the Construction of Desire," *Medieval Perspectives* 22 (2007): 145–56.

19. Sarah Davis-Secord, *Where Three Worlds Met: Sicily in the Early Medieval Mediterranean* (Ithaca, NY: Cornell University Press, 2017).

> The cloth was dysplayed sone;
> The Emperour lokede therupone
> And myght hyt not se,
> For glysteryng of the ryche ston;
> Redy syght had he non. (97–101)

The iridescence of the gem-encrusted surface refuses sight, denying access to the visual narrative. As an object introduced into the narrative via literary ekphrasis, the cloth refuses to function as a legible garment, particularly for those who lack the cross-cultural competency of the King of Sicily.

And not incidentally, for Sicily had played an important role in the lucrative trade of exported silk textiles as well as in the development of European silk manufacture. Evidence of domestic sericulture in al-Andalus, adapted from Chinese practices by Arab settlers from Syria and the Maghreb, dates as early as the eighth or ninth centuries; and the quality of silk cloth produced in Almería maintained international acclaim well into the twelfth century.[20] The second half of the twelfth century witnessed a rapid expansion of the silk industry in Norman Sicily at Palermo. By the thirteenth century, Northern Italy became an important site of European textile production, much of which relied on importation of raw fiber, including a booming cotton industry in Milan, the refining of Iberian-sourced merino wool in Florence, and the weaving of silk in Lucca and Siena.[21] At the same time, Genoa and Fabriano became the sites of the first Italian textile paper mills.[22] In the last quarter of the thirteenth century, relocated silk workers from the Mediterranean regions, including Italy, the Iberian Peninsula, Cyprus, and Acre, turned Paris into the first Northern European site of industrialized silk production.[23] This migrant population included large numbers of skilled women artisans, who brought with them generations of specialized knowledge.

Recent studies on the development of various European silk industries stress the role of such dislocated workers. More frequently than not, these

---

20. David Jacoby, "Silk Economics and Cross-Cultural Artistic Interaction: Byzantium, the Muslim World, and the Christian West," *Dumbarton Oaks Papers* 58 (2004): 197–240, at 199 and 217; Sharon Kinoshita, "Almería Silk and the French Feudal Imaginary: Towards a 'Material' History of the Medieval Mediterranean," in *Medieval Fabrications: Dress, Textiles, Clothwork, and Other Cultural Imaginings*, ed. E. Jane Burns (New York: Palgrave Macmillan, 2004), 165–76.

21. Susan Mosher Stuard, *Gilding the Market: Luxury and Fashion in Fourteenth-Century Italy* (Philadelphia: University of Pennsylvania Press, 2006), 23.

22. Lucien Febvre and Henri-Jean Martin, *The Coming of the Book: The Impact of Printing, 1450–1800*, trans. David Gerard, Foundations of History Library (London: N.L.B., 1976), 29–32.

23. Sharon Farmer, *The Silk Industries of Medieval Paris: Artisanal Migration, Technological Innovation, and Gendered Experience* (Philadelphia: University of Pennsylvania Press, 2017).

artisans migrated under duress.²⁴ While many traveled in response to economic incentives, still more moved under political and military coercion. In Northern Italy, Siena and Lucca began as prominent centers of silk production, thereby incurring the envy of neighboring towns. As a result, their wealth was pillaged through frequent raids and their skilled labor force was poached by rival towns.²⁵ Lucchese silk merchants and artisans migrated as far north as Paris, where they contributed to the establishment of local silk workshops. The silk industry in Palermo benefited from the coerced migration of Greek and Jewish silk workers, after King Roger II of Sicily pillaged the towns of Thebes, Corinth, and Athens, all of which had thriving silk factories.²⁶ As medieval Iberia and Italy became major players in textile and cloth-based paper production and exportation, the same traders were often imbricated in the cross-confessional slave trade.²⁷

The textual preoccupation with the fluidity of borders in *Emaré*, between the corporeal and the sartorial, points to the luxury textile industry as an important point of cross-cultural contact. Emaré, as a skilled migrant silk worker, whose journeys reverse the traditional labor migration from the Mediterranean regions, relies on her specialized knowledge of textile production to establish herself in new locales. The Islamicate cloth in all its alterity establishes Emaré's first interactions with residents on distant shores to positive and negative ends. Sir Kadore in Galys and merchant Jurdan in Rome find Emaré in her beached rudderless boat and take pity on a creature they deem otherworldly based on their visual assessment of the cloth in which she is wrapped. In Sir Kadore's household, Emaré takes on the role first performed by Lady Abro, instructing unnamed maidens in the castle in courtesy and teaching them "All maner of sylkyn werke" (line 377). Emaré thrives in this role, regains her health, and eventually establishes a marital union with the king of Galys, who takes notice of her beauty and courtesy. When describing Emaré to his king, Sir Kadore remarks on her worth:

"Hyt ys an erles thowghtur of ferre londe,
That semely ys to sene.
I sente aftur her certeynlye

---

24. Farmer, *The Silk Industries of Medieval Paris*, 101.
25. Stuard, *Gilding the Market*, 3.
26. Jacoby, "Silk Economics and Cross-Cultural Artistic Interaction," 223–25.
27. Steven A. Epstein, *Speaking of Slavery: Color, Ethnicity, and Human Bondage in Italy* (Ithaca, NY: Cornell University Press, 2001); Olivia Remie Constable, *Trade and Traders in Muslim Spain: The Commercial Realignment of the Medieval Iberian Peninsula, 900–1500* (Cambridge; New York: Cambridge University Press, 1994); Hannah Barker, *That Most Precious Merchandise: The Mediterranean Trade in Black Sea Slaves, 1260–1500* (Philadelphia: University of Pennsylvania Press, 2019).

To teche my chylderen curtesye,
In chambur wyth hem to bene.
She ys the konnyngest wommon,
I trowe, that be yn Crystendom,
Of werke that y have sene." (422–29)

Despite hiding her identity in foreign lands, Emaré displays her noble status through her courtesy, recognized by another member of the nobility as a marker of high status. The skill of embroidering and sewing silks adds to her image as a clever aristocratic woman. Quite tellingly, Emaré does not impart this knowledge in the household of merchant Jurdan. In this new abode in Rome, Emaré devotes her attention to the education and upbringing of her son, whose very existence is predicated on his mother's high status and her performance of this status through silk work and courtesy.[28] Performance of both skills enables Emaré to repair her family and establish new connections on distant shores.

And yet, working in tandem with the narrative impulse toward repair and suturing of fractured and geographically dispersed communities is the poem's divisive ideology of religion-as-race, which compels the reader to separate the Christian white protagonist from the non-Christian luxury cloth and by extension from its unnamed Muslim female maker. The luxury cloth, as a product of the Islamic world, becomes an aesthetic marvel when it crosses the boundary into Christendom, both envisioned in territorial terms, and is deemed otherworldly. This otherworldliness, when attached to a luxury object like the cloth, emphasizes its unstable point of origin, a geographic unknown located somewhere far away, which carries the potential to increase its value. When the same qualities, however, are transferred to the women associated with it, the racialized alterity of "elsewhere" tends to inspire wonder, admiration, and fear alike and presents them as potentially inhuman. When the Emperor exclaims, "'Sertes, thys ys a fayry, / Or ellys a vanyté!'" (lines 104–5), suggesting fairy magic, illusion, or enchantment as possible explanations for the cloth's otherworldly qualities, he casts aspersions upon the Emir's daughter, the unnamed maker of the cloth.[29] As mentioned earlier, Emaré in this

---

28. Amy Vines, "'Who-so wylle of nurtur lere': Domestic Foundations for Social Success in the Middle English *Emaré*," *The Chaucer Review* 53, no. 1 (2018): 82–101.

29. *MED* provides a connection between our modern sense of "vanity" as pursuit of frivolous or transitory desires and frivolity, illusion, transience of things. *MED*, s.v. "vanitę̄" (n.), Regents of the University of Michigan, 2014, https://quod.lib.umich.edu/cgi/m/mec/med-idx?type=id&id=MED50725. For more on the fairy connection, see Andrzej Wicher, "The Fairy Needlewoman Emaré: A Study of the Middle English Romance Emaré in the Context of the Tale of Magic," in *Evur happie & glorious, ffor I hafe at will grete riches*, ed. Liliana Sikorska and Marcin Krygier (New York: Peter Lang, 2013), 145–53.

dazzling robe is described as a "non erthely wommon" (245), a "non erthly thyng" (396), a "non erthyly wyght" (701), and even a "fende" (446)—though the last one is by a jealous mother-in-law. By reinforcing the cloth's Islamicate origins and using racially charged language to distinguish between the maker and the wearer of the cloth, the poem participates in the medieval religion-as-race social politics.

The internal evidence of the poem together with the conversion plots that we find in the related Constance-saga narratives such as Chaucer's *Man of Law's Tale* participate in late medieval faith-as-race social dynamics. Geraldine Heng (among others) urges us to apply the methodologies of critical race theory to the study of medieval literature and culture to investigate how race-based formations were constituted to uphold hierarchical systems of power:

> *"Race" is one of the primary names we have—a name we retain for the strategic, epistemological, and political commitments it recognizes—that is attached to a repeating tendency, of the gravest import, to demarcate human beings through differences among humans that are selectively essentialized as absolute and fundamental, in order to distribute positions and powers differentially to human groups.* [. . . As such,] *race is a structural relationship for the articulation and management of human differences, rather than a substantive content.*[30]

In the medieval period, religion was one of these totalizing mechanisms of race-formation, a system that stratified the social order based on faith affiliation.[31] Racial distinctions along confessional alignments were codified in Europe in 1215, in Canon 68 of the Fourth Lateran Council, which required Jewish and Muslim subjects residing in Christian territories to be visually distinguished from their Christian neighbors. In England, Canon 68 initiated multiple sartorial legislations regarding the badge worn by Jewish residents and contributed to their eventual expulsion in 1290.[32]

In line with the proscriptions of Canon 68, medieval literature contributed to the cultural conflation of adherents of Islam of various ethnicities into a singular, unified, faith-based enemy, figured in the European literary imaginary

---

30. Heng, *Invention of Race*, 27; emphasis in original.

31. Robert Bartlett addresses the conflation between race, ethnicity, and faith-based identity in "Medieval and Modern Concepts of Race and Ethnicity"; additionally, for Bartlett's position on Christianity as ethnic identity, see *The Making of Europe: Conquest, Colonization, and Cultural Change, 950–1350* (Princeton, NJ: Princeton University Press, 1993), 197–242.

32. Heng, *Invention of Race*, 15.

as "the Saracens" or "heathens."[33] Despite the continued economic, political, and military contact between Christians and Muslims, many European writers imagined "Christian" and "Saracen" as categorically different from each other, painting Muslim bodies as black, exceedingly tall, and overly sexual, often with inhuman features.[34] The ultimate level of faith-based racial polarization, however, was established via human trafficking, a practice simultaneously decried by religious leaders on both sides of the confessional divide, but which nonetheless continued, possibly enabled by cultural differences; the prohibitions against enslavement of co-religionists contributed to dehumanizing members of the competing faith. Thus, Christian and Muslim bodies were bought and sold as chattel, crossing the medieval Mediterranean often on the same ships as did the bales of luxury fabrics and cloth-based paper, as the primary slave trade was between Genoa and Egypt.[35] Skin color played an important role in the cross-confessional slave trade: the bodies of white men and women from Southern Europe and the Caucasus garnered higher prices, while black and dark-skinned peoples were sold at lower prices at both European and Near Eastern markets.[36] Moreover, Greek and Roman sources connect the ancient knowledge of silk production to an imaginary dark-skinned peoples known as the Seres, whose mysterious land lies far to the east, variously identified as a Scythian region, the Caucasus, North Africa, or Ethiopia;[37] their blackness was often emphasized as a negative trait in polemical writings against the dangers of foreign luxuries such as silk, which were seen as inducements to moral weakness, excess, and overindulgence, particularly by Roman standards.

Medieval romances deploy what Heng refers to as "the politics of the epidermis"[38] to reify the equivalence of whiteness with Christianity. The fig-

---

33. Heng defines "Saracen" as "a word of Greco-Roman origin that in late antiquity referred to pre-Islamic Arabs" and notes that "from the late eleventh and the twelfth century onward *Saracens* streamlined a panorama of diverse peoples and populations into a single demographic entity defined by their adherence to the Islamic religion" (*Invention of Race* 111). Also see Jeffrey Jerome Cohen, "On Saracen Enjoyment: Some Fantasies of Race in Late Medieval France and England," *Journal of Medieval and Early Modern Studies* 31, no. 1 (2001): 113–46, at 137n5; Suzanne Conklin Akbari, "The Saracen Body," in *Idols in the East: European Representations of Islam and the Orient, 1100–1450* (Ithaca, NY: Cornell University Press, 2009), 155–99.

34. Heng, *Invention of Race,* 187.

35. Heng, *Invention of Race,* 149–50, 158; Epstein, *Speaking of Slavery*; William D. Phillips Jr., *Slavery from Roman Times to the Early Transatlantic Trade* (Minneapolis: University of Minnesota Press, 1985), and *Slavery in Medieval and Early Modern Iberia* (Philadelphia: University of Pennsylvania Press, 2014); Barker, *That Most Precious Merchandise.*

36. Epstein, *Speaking of Slavery*; Phillips, *Slavery from Roman Times to the Early Transatlantic Trade* and *Slavery in Medieval and Early Modern Iberia.*

37. Burns, *Sea of Silk,* 7–9.

38. Heng, *Invention of Race,* 42.

ure of the "good Saracen," or the "reformed Saracen" who is open to eventual conversion to Christianity, was often depicted as already white or eventually becoming white. Examples include lily-white Muslim princesses of Old French epics and romances, who end up marrying Christian knights and converting. Elite Muslim men like Saladin and Floris are often portrayed as indistinguishable in appearance from their Christian companions in order to mark their exceptional goodness and to prepare the reader for a potential conversion to Christianity (or to bemoan a lack thereof, as we frequently see with Saladin). In Middle English conversion narratives such as *The King of Tars*, the transformation is visibly marked on the body as the Muslim king sheds his black skin and emerges through baptism in the form of a white Christian nobleman.[39] In Chaucer's version of the Constance saga, the *Man of Law's Tale*, the heroine's first husband is a Muslim sultan who converts to Christianity to marry her and is eventually martyred for his abdication of Islam.

Unlike the above-mentioned conversion narratives, however, the confessional and cultural alignments in *Emaré* remain intact throughout the romance while maintaining the faith-as-race connection between Christianity and whiteness of skin. From the moment Emaré is introduced, she is described through the physical attributes of her complexion, which in the aggregate emphasize the whiteness of her skin. On more than a dozen occasions, both Emaré and her mother Dame Erayne are described as "fayr." The descriptor *fayr* also appears in the superlative form *fayrest* three times: "fayrest creature borne" (line 50), "The fayrest wommon on lyfe" (222), the "fayrest thyng" (560). While the adjective *fayr* is not specific enough on its own, the various epithets and the familial association between consecutive generations along the axis of "fairness" become significant, as they also become linked to whiteness. When *fayr* is dropped as a descriptor, it is rather methodically replaced with *whyte*, suggesting that the two may be used interchangeably. Emaré is "whyte as lylye flour" (66, 205, 946) and "whyte as [sea] fome" (497, 818). Her mother is "Whyte as whales bone" (33), a local substrate that often served as a replacement for imported elephant ivory. Emaré's son Segramour is also described as "fayr" and "whyte" like his mother: "A fayr man-chylde" (521), "fayrest chyld on lyfe" (728), and "Whyte as flour" (729). His destiny as future king and emperor is inscribed on his newborn skin in the form of a double king's mark: "Thyll ther was of her body / A fayr chyld borne and

---

39. Cord J. Whitaker, "Black Metaphors in the *King of Tars*," *Journal of English and Germanic Philology* 112, no. 2 (2013): 169–93; Jamie Friedman, "Making Whiteness Matter: *The King of Tars*," *postmedieval: a journal of medieval cultural studies* 6 (2015): 52–63; Sierra Lomuto, "The Mongol Princess of Tars: Global Relations and Racial Formation in *The King of Tars*, c. 1330," *Exemplaria* 31, no. 3 (2019): 171–92.

a godele; Hadde a dowbyll kyngus marke" (502–4). This emphasis on readable skin presents whiteness as a marker of genealogical, royal, and Christian identity. For, as Geraldine Heng reminds us, "Elite human beings of the 14th century have a hue, and it is white."[40]

While Emaré experiences racially based aggression as a result of negative responses to the Islamicate cloth, her abjection is still very much part of the Christian theological hermeneutic which accompanies one's journey to salvation (from most abject to most rewarded). The centering of Emaré's experience serves in direct contrast to the marginalization and the silencing of the unnamed elite Muslim woman, whose love story and ultimate fate remain untold despite its inclusion in the visual program of the cloth. In this silence, the poem tells us about the privilege of having the cloth serve as a second skin for its eponymous heroine, social rather than epidermal, for presumably the Emir's daughter could never shed her markers of racialized difference the way Emaré could remove the decorated robe and reveal the white aristocratic body underneath. In this narrative economy, the Muslim woman ultimately disappears while the Christian woman is reintegrated into the larger program of Christian imperialism.

---

40. Heng, "Invention of Race in the European Middle Ages I," 318, and *Invention of Race,* 16.

CHAPTER 6

Women's Communities and the Possibility of Friendship in the Stanzaic *Morte Arthur*

USHA VISHNUVAJJALA

ONE CHALLENGE of teaching Arthurian literature is confronting the preconceptions students have about this body of literature. A persistent belief among students—and indeed scholars—is that of Guinevere's immorality or malice. More than one student has informed me at the start of a semester that Guinevere is a "cheater." Scholars, too, frequently refer to the "adultery" of Lancelot and Guinevere.[1] The romance novelist Nora Roberts once had a character refer to Guinevere as a "weak-moraled round heel [who] boffed her husband's best friend."[2] At the same time, we rarely encounter students or colleagues who casually refer to Gawain as a rapist, to Arthur as a child-murderer, or to Uther as a sexual predator. This hesitation to see Guinevere as an emotionally complex or sympathetic character persists among both casual consumers of Arthurian media and those whose life's work includes studying and teaching medieval Arthurian texts.

This essay is dedicated to the memory of my friend and colleague Fiona Tolhurst, without whose friendship and scholarship I would never have been able to write it.

1. For more on scholarly treatment of Guinevere, see Amy S. Kaufman, "Guinevere Burning," *Arthuriana* 20, no. 1 (Spring 2010): 76–94.

2. Nora Roberts, *Finding the Dream* (New York: Jove Books, 1997), 152.

• 114 •

This may explain why we hesitate to read Guinevere's interactions with other women as friendly or sympathetic.[3] Revisiting one such encounter through the lens of women's friendship, however, can help us see that Middle English Arthurian literature does not dismiss Guinevere's relationships with, or sympathy for, other women as completely as we are inclined to do in the twenty-first century. Although my reading of the Stanzaic *Morte Arthur* does not go so far as to suggest that what Guinevere (Gaynor in this poem) feels for her supposed rival, the (unnamed) Maid of Ascolot, is what we would call friendship, I do argue that she feels a complicated sympathy and empathy for her, which in turn frees her to express her own often-repressed emotions in a way she had previously only been able to do in the company of her ladies in her chamber.

The briefly mentioned and often-silent groups and communities of women who populate the background of many Arthurian romances—the maidens who revive Chrétien de Troyes's *Yvain* with an ointment from Morgan le Fay, the maidens living in Gawain's grandmother's castle at the end of Chrétien's *Conte del Graal*, the ladies at court at the beginning of *Sir Gawain and the Green Knight*, the queens at the end of Malory's *Morte*, and many others—rarely play a significant role in the narratives in which they appear, and are therefore rarely considered in scholarship. This essay examines literary representations of women's friendship by asking what a community of supportive women can make possible for a female character. Going beyond the intimacy between two women friends, I consider what a space populated by women might allow, particularly with respect to the expression of emotion and the experience of bodily affect. Arthurian romances abound with masculine spaces in which male characters are free to weep, swoon, and embrace each other. Female spaces, in contrast, are quite rare, and female characters in many of these romances must negotiate complex gendered social codes that keep them from freely expressing their emotions. This essay argues that the ability to access such a space, largely free from the gaze of the court's public areas and populated with a group of sympathetic women, is what allows the Stanzaic *Morte*'s Gaynor to access her emotions, and ultimately to feel a sympathetic connection to the woman the text frames as her rival. As we do the work of recuperating long-ignored women's friendships in premodern texts,

---

3. For more on the difficult relationship between Guinevere and popular feminism, see Amy S. Kaufman, "Liberating Guinevere: Female Desire on Film," in *Medieval Women on Film*, ed. Kevin J. Harty (Jefferson, NC: McFarland, 2020).

we should not discount the importance of such communities, which can be as powerful as intimate one-on-one friendships.[4]

In the Stanzaic *Morte*, Gaynor's "ladies," whom readers encounter only in her chamber in the background of scenes, make her chamber a space where Gaynor is able to succumb to her emotions, both by giving voice to them and by letting them manifest in bodily symptoms such as weeping.[5] In a text so invested in both the narration of emotion and affect and the delineation of different types of public and private spaces, it is the presence of the ladies, not the space of the chamber, that creates a private space—a women's space—for Gaynor in times of emotional difficulty. I argue here that such a space is also what Gaynor experiences when she is in proximity to the Maid's body and learns of the Maid's death and letter. Gaynor has never met the Maid in person, but her proximity to and awareness of the Maid's pain and grief creates a space in which Gaynor—despite being away from her chamber and her ladies and in the company of a male knight (Gawain)—is able to stop repressing her emotions and give voice to them, as well as to allow her body to be affected by them. In addition, reading this passage as one in which Gaynor is freed by the Maid's presence to emote and feel embodied empathy for the Maid opens up suggestive possibilities about the contents of the missing leaf of the poem immediately after this passage. Specifically, it should lead us to consider that the missing lines might include a more direct description of Gaynor's sympathy for the Maid than the poem's source, the *Mort Artu* from the French series of texts known as the Vulgate Cycle.[6] The invisibility of women's friendship in premodern literary studies has often closed off the possibilities for how readers interpret ambiguous texts or passages. Reading this poem with a focus on women's friendships in the background of the narrative and on Gaynor's sympathy for the Maid can perform a recuperation of the text's women at a time when scholars are working to recuperate this text from a long history of

---

4. As Lydia Yaitsky Kertz demonstrates in her essay in this volume, the role of a community of women in the background of the Middle English romance *Emaré* is instrumental to the development of Emaré's character and association with the magical cloth.

5. Although this is an oversimplification, I refer to both emotion and affect here to encompass both the personal cognitive experience of emotion and the bodily response to events or information, sometimes described as precognitive, that is usually called affect, and which is dependent on physical and social space. For more on the application of affect theory to medieval Arthurian literature, and the distinction between emotion and affect, see Frank Brandsma, Carolyne Larrington, and Corinne Saunders's introduction to *Emotions in Medieval Arthurian Literature: Body, Mind, Voice*, ed. Brandsma, Larrington, and Saunders (Woodbridge: D. S. Brewer, 2015), 1–12.

6. Later authors, including Sir Thomas Malory in his fifteenth-century *Morte Darthur* and T. H. White in his twentieth-century *The Once and Future King*, do depict Guinevere's explicit sympathy for the Maid.

negative scholarship. Such a reading can counter popular and scholarly bias against Guinevere figures and against this poem, which focuses far more on her than most Arthurian texts do and is in part considered a lesser work of Arthurian literature for this reason.

THE STANZAIC *MORTE*

The Stanzaic *Morte Arthur*, a fourteenth-century Middle English romance focused on the relationship between Lancelot and Guinevere, served as a source for Thomas Malory's influential fifteenth-century *Morte Arthur*. It is concerned more with domestic space, interpersonal relationships, and characters' interiority than the other English texts that share its title, Malory's *Morte* and the fourteenth-century Alliterative *Morte Arthur*. Although Malory's *Morte* has been translated into modern English several times, and the Alliterative *Morte* was recently translated by Simon Armitage, the Stanzaic remains accessible primarily in the TEAMS Middle English Texts Series, and therefore is slightly more difficult to teach to undergraduates not training as medievalists.[7] It is sometimes described as a less serious text, or less of an artistic achievement, than other fourteenth-century texts like the Alliterative *Morte* or *Sir Gawain and the Green Knight*. One reason for this might be its close focus on Guinevere, which is otherwise unusual in Middle English texts.[8] The antipathy for Guinevere that modern readers often bring to their reading of this and other medieval texts may impede our ability to read Guinevere as a figure whose conflicted emotions here include sympathy for her rival, the Maid of Ascolot.

Some critics, especially recently, have seen the poem's depiction of emotion as one of its strengths, while others have dismissed the poem's seriousness in part because of its close focus on emotion. As Fiona Tolhurst and K. S. Whetter write, although recent scholars display less open contempt for the poem than the scholarship of the mid-twentieth century did, "most of them

---

7. The only translation currently in print is that in Valerie Krishna's 1991 *Five Middle English Romances*, published by Routledge, a second edition of which was issued in 2015. Brian Stone's 1989 translation is out of print.

8. For example, although Morgan's contempt for her drives the plot of *Sir Gawain and the Green Knight*, Guinevere herself only appears in one scene. Although she is portrayed as a central part of the court in the opening narrative passage of *Ywain and Gawain*, she is absent from much of narrative after that. Similarly, although the *Awntyrs of Arthure* has a long passage about Guinevere's mother's ghost, who appears to warn Guinevere and the court, Guinevere herself is given very little narrative space. Unlike these texts and many others, the Stanzaic *Morte* devotes a good deal of space not only to her words and actions but also to her emotions.

either continue to treat this poem as a second-rate work of literature or . . . pronounce it a work whose success is of 'the simplest kind' because . . . it manages to have an emotional impact on readers despite the (supposed) artistic mediocrity of its author."[9] Tolhurst and Whetter identified in the *MLA International Bibliography* "a ratio of approximately one study of the Stanzaic *Morte* to every ten studies of its more well-regarded alliterative counterpart; even the more specialized *Arthurian Bibliography* has a ratio of one to four against the Stanzaic *Morte*."[10] Similarly, Marco Nievergelt recently wrote that "the *SMA* remains largely neglected in recent criticism" and "seems to have benefited very little from [the recent] recuperative turn towards cultural history in the study of Middle English romance, perhaps because it has no marvels, Saracens, princesses, monsters or otherwise exuberant plot developments to captivate its readers."[11] Nievergelt argues that the poem's often-derided elements are in fact what give the poem its emotional impact: "It seems then that somehow the *SMA* manages to achieve pathos not only *despite* its stylistic limitations but rather precisely *thanks to them*—and I would insist that this paradoxical effect is not due to incompetent versification, but to deliberate design."[12] The poem's achievements in both depicting emotions and potentially creating them in its readers can therefore be read as the result of those very qualities that some scholars read as the poem's supposed formal limits.

One of these qualities is the poem's use of space, although scholars often fall short of fully delineating the ways in which these spaces are gendered. The division between public and private space is central to the poem's depiction of the tension between the public and private lives and emotions of its characters. Nievergelt writes, "Space is used within the narrative to map the movements of the individual characters in a complex and dynamic social landscape, constantly shuttling back and forth between the demands of public and private, the chivalric and the domestic, community and subjectivity."[13] Similarly, Andrew Lynch writes that "location and emotion go closely together in the poem's episodes. Where and when the text's emotional life occurs matters strongly, and helps give its exchanges of feelings their particular color."[14] I go

---

9. Fiona Tolhurst and K. S. Whetter, "Standing Up for the Stanzaic-Poet: Artistry, Characterization, and Narration in the Stanzaic Morte Arthur," *Arthuriana* 28, no. 3 (Fall 2018): 86–113, at 86.

10. Tolhurst and Whetter, "Standing Up for the Stanzaic-Poet," 86.

11. Marco Nievergelt, "The Place of Emotion: Space, Silence, and Interiority in the Stanzaic Morte Arthur," *Arthurian Literature* 32 (2015): 31–58, at 31, 33.

12. Nievergelt, "The Place of Emotion," 34.

13. Nievergelt, "The Place of Emotion," 34.

14. Andrew Lynch, "Making Joy / Seeing Sorrow: Emotional and Affective Resources in the Stanzaic Morte Arthur," *Arthuriana* 28, no. 3 (Fall 2018): 33–50, at 38.

further than both Nievergelt and Lynch in parsing the ways in which spaces are treated as public or private in the poem by demonstrating that the space of Gaynor's chamber functions strangely in the poem as both a private one and, at times, a somewhat public one. She has a carefully guarded conversation with Launcelot there early in the poem, in which neither he nor the reader can access her emotions or her motives. But she also has private moments of sorrow there with her ladies, and later, a moment of grief and honesty with Launcelot, in the presence of those ladies. I argue that the privacy of her chamber—and of other spaces—for Gaynor seems to depend in part on the presence of other women. The spaces in which she operates are gendered by the presence or absence of women, even, eventually, the presence of the Maid of Ascolot through her posthumous letter.

The question of whose emotions are legible (and to whom) is often a fraught one in the study of medieval romance. Gaynor's emotions are only given voice, either in direct speech or in narration, in some of the passages in which she appears, even though the narrative suggests that she would be feeling strong emotions in many other passages. Nievergelt has argued that the poem's depiction of unspeakable emotion is one of the features that give it its emotional impact, and that critics' charges of emotional opacity in the Stanzaic *Morte*'s characters may be a form of presentism:

> from the point of view of strict psychological realism, individual characters in popular romances appear as rather underdeveloped, unfinished— and our reflex as readers conditioned by the cultural dominance of the nineteenth-century novel is to conclude that the characters are therefore uninteresting ... the reluctance of both characters and narrator to verbalise emotion directly—or, more accurately, to complete the transition from affect to emotion—does not necessarily reduce the pathos of the narrative or the complexity of the characters themselves. Instead, such lack of precision is employed by the poet as a rhetorical strategy to heighten the intensity of affect by leaving it unspoken and thus suggesting that it may be ultimately unspeakable.[15]

Much of what remains unspoken in the poem's first thousand lines is between Launcelot and Gaynor, and Gaynor's frequent silence or opacity might be part of what renders her so unlikeable to modern readers—not only in this poem but in medieval romances more generally. However, if we read her as guarding or even repressing emotions that may be too powerful, too difficult,

---

15. Nievergelt, "The Place of Emotion," 35.

or too dangerous to be voiced, we find that she subtly responds to the company around her, voicing her emotions only when she is not the only woman in a space, whether because she is surrounded by her sympathetic ladies or because the knights of the court have just read the Maid's letter.[16] Her inability to express emotion or experience affect when she is in the company of only men may lead to the types of silence or repression that have sometimes been read as the text's emotional opacity.

GAYNOR'S (LACK OF) AFFECT

In the first thousand lines of the poem, descriptions of characters' affective responses are fairly common, with the exception of Gaynor. Launcelot's facial and bodily reactions to his distress, his pain, and his inability to deal with his emotions are quite vivid, as are the Maid of Ascolot's facial, bodily, and vocal reactions to her feelings for Launcelot. Other characters, including Arthur and Gawain, are described as feeling certain emotions and at times reacting to events by sighing or embracing or kissing other knights. Andrew Lynch notes that the Stanzaic *Morte,* which is about a fifth of the length of its source, streamlines much of the narrative by cutting out episodes, but that the "emotion and affect—depicted as occurring within the fictional story, and presented as part of its own appeal to readers—actually receive a higher priority than in the French tale, and occupy more of the sum of narrative information."[17] Gaynor is very rarely narrated as reacting affectively or expressing emotion in this section of the text, however, despite the narration of lengthy scenes in which she speaks or acts. Gaynor's emotions seem the most obfuscated in this first thousand lines (this changes dramatically after the Maid of Ascolot's death), but it is not because the poem is not interested in them; rather, it is because she is only depicted as able to experience and express her emotions in specific company.

The poem's two opening scenes, which both take place in the ostensibly private spaces of bedrooms, depict a Gaynor whose emotions are hidden. Gaynor is narrated speaking or acting but not described as doing so with any specific emotions or motives; her emotions are not revealed to other characters within the poem, or to the reader. For example, in the opening passage, Gaynor suggests to Arthur that he revive the honor of his court by holding a tournament, and no words in the narration suggest motive, emotion, or affect: "Til on a time that it befell / The king in bed lay by the queen; / Of aunters

---

16. Similarly, Melissa Ridley Elmes argues in her chapter in this volume that Chaucer's Criseyde only expresses her emotions with tears when her friends try to cheer her up.
17. Lynch, "Making Joy / Seeing Sorrow," 34.

they began to tell, / Many that in that land had been:" is all that precedes her own words, and no more narration of the scene follows her words and Arthur's response; the narration cuts straight to the king having a tournament announced.[18] Less than two stanzas later, the narrator tells us that "Launcelot [was] left with the queen, / And seke he lay that ilke tide; / For love that was them between, / He made enchesoun for to abide" (lines 53–56). The close juxtaposition of these two passages makes it easy—perhaps too easy—to assign motive to Gaynor, but the narration itself does not mention any, nor does the poem narrate any emotion in her first diegetic encounter with Launcelot, even though her words suggest surprise and anxiety or fear:

"Launcelot, what dostou here with me?
The king is went and the court bydene;
I drede we shall discovered be
Of the love is us between.

"Sir Agravain at home is he;
Night and day he waites us two."
"Nay," he said, "my lady free,
I ne think not it shall be so" (69–76)

The emotions of all the characters remain inscrutable in this opening passage of the poem, but those of Gaynor, the character whose presence is a constant in these two connected scenes, seem particularly hidden from the reader. Beyond that, we are also denied any language of affect or any narratorial suggestion of motive. Here in these two bedrooms, which seem like private spaces, the text denies us any glimpse of these characters' emotions, affects, or motives, complicating the division of public and private space in the poem.

That changes once the narration moves away from court, leaving Gaynor behind, and the poem begins to suggest Launcelot's bodily affect before it explicitly narrates the emotions and motives of the unnamed Maid of Ascolot. The first suggestion of bodily affect we get is a description of Launcelot riding toward the tournament, the first time our gaze leaves the court where Gaynor remains: "With his shouldres gan he fold / And down hanged his hed full low, / As he ne might his limmes weld" (lines 99–101). Although this description of his body is framed as part of his attempts to hide his identity, it suggests a defensive posture, and perhaps the hiding of emotions as well as identity. When he reaches another domestic space, one with no Gaynor, we get a fuller

---

18. Larry D. Benson, ed., and Edward E. Foster, rev., *King Arthur's Death: The Middle English Stanzaic Morte Arthur and Alliterative Morte Arthure* (Kalamazoo, MI: Medieval Institute Publications, 1994), lines 17–20. Further citations to this version are parenthetical.

narration of characters' affects, emotions, and motives in the description of the Lord of Ascolot's daughter:

> Glad she was to sit him ner,
> The noble knight under sheld;
> Weeping was her moste cheer,
> So mikel on him her herte gan helde.
> Up then rose that maiden still,
> And to her chamber went she tho;
> Down upon her bed she fell,
> That nigh her herte brast in two.
> Launcelot wist what was her will,
> Well he knew by other mo;
> Her brother cleped he him til,
> And to her chamber gonne they go. (181–92)

This passage depicts a full picture of emotion and affect, as well as a narratorial explanation of that affect, in both the domestic space of the Maid's chamber and the more public spaces of her father's house. We also get a clear narration of Launcelot's motives in the following stanza:

> He sat him down for the maidens sake,
> Upon her bedde there she lay;
> Courtaisly to her he spake,
> For to comfort that faire may. (193–96)

Unlike the earlier passages in which readers are left to guess at the motives for both Gaynor's and Launcelot's actions, here the motivations of Launcelot and the Maid—who have very different aims—are made transparent. The Maid is motivated by love or lust for Launcelot, which leads to her weeping and her heart nearly bursting, and Launcelot seeks to comfort her and behave courteously to her without encouraging her affections. The poem continues to depict the emotions, affective responses, and motives of a number of characters, but only away from court, including Launcelot swooning and the Maid weeping as if she were mad (383–84).

When the poem first gestures toward a depiction of Gaynor as a character with an interiority, it is in a passage that has proved difficult to interpret. The first time Gaynor's nonverbal response to anything is narrated, in line 528, she "lough with herte free," echoing "Launcelot lough with herte free" in line 496. Benson glosses "free" differently in these two instances, first as "noble" for Launcelot, then as "relieved" for Gaynor, as she has just learned that Launcelot has been found alive and is expected to recover from his wounds. Although no narrative space has yet been devoted to her worry about Launcelot, we can infer her worry from her relief now that he has been found. But the different glosses here suggest that different categories or ranges of emotion are possible for these two characters, and it is hard not to read this as a gendered difference: Gaynor can be relieved but not noble; Launcelot can be noble, but perhaps not relieved. If we follow Benson and read Gaynor's laughter as relief, this is the closest she comes in the poem's first thousand lines to expressing emotion in a public place. But any way of reading these two instances of the same phrase differently reinforces the fact that Gaynor and Launcelot are operating in two different social frameworks here when it comes to where, how, and around whom it is safe to express emotion, and that those frameworks depend at least partly on gender. Launcelot's emotions are somewhat obfuscated by this gloss, but so is Gaynor's nobility and her participation in the community of knights.

It is notably in this sequence of events that Gaynor is first referred to by her name instead of just as "the queen": in line 421, when Arthur finds her without Launcelot at court ("To Camelot the king went there, / There as Queen Gaynor was; / He wend have found Launcelot there; / Away he was, withouten lees"; 420–23), and then in line 511, when Bors and Lionel return to court to tell her and the king that Launcelot is alive ("To the court the way they chese, / There as the Queen Gaynor lay"; 514–15). Before this, she is referred to as "the queen" with no name five times. This sequence of events, then—Launcelot's wounding, the court's awareness that he is missing, and then the discovery that he is alive and recovering—both gives Gaynor an identity separate from that as queen for the first time and narrates her expressing emotion for the first time.

Gaynor's ability to emote, to speak out loud about her sorrow, and to allow her body to respond to events with weeping and sickness seems to be in part something enabled by the female space of her chamber when it is inhabited only by women. Once the poem has begun narrating Gaynor's expressions of emotion and her affective responses, it continues to do so, but only in Launcelot's continued absence from the court, and in the privacy of her chamber, with her ladies around her, as we learn in line 656, but no men. When she learns that Launcelot has stayed away because he is with the Earl of Ascolot's daughter,

> The queen then said wordes no mo,
> But to her chamber soon she yede,
> And down upon her bed fell so
> That night of wit she wolde wede. (648–51)

Gaynor's ladies attempt to comfort her, to "let no man" see her distress, and put her to bed, but "Ever she wept as she were wode; / Of her they had full grete pitee" (662–63). Although the first narrated conversation between her and Launcelot took place in that same private chamber, that passage narrated no bodily affect and no expressions of emotion, only words spoken to each other that could be interpreted in numerous ways.

This scene of female companionship is juxtaposed with Lionel and Bors stopping in a forest "them to play," demonstrating the contrast between the two very different forms of homosocial bonding that take place in this poem. In fact, these two scenes are linked by appearing in the same sentence and stanza, although the knights' subsequent meeting with Launcelot is in a new sentence:

> So sore seke the queen lay,
> Of sorrow might she never let,
> Til it fell upon a day
> Sir Lionel and Ector yede
> Into the forest, them to play.
> That flowred was and braunched sweet,
> And as they wente by the way.
> With Launcelot gonne they meet. (lines 664–71)

This stanza furthers the plot by allowing Launcelot to ask Bors and Lionel about Gaynor ("How fares my lady bright?"), but the juxtaposition of the "blithe" meeting between these three male friends and the scene of female friends comforting a distressed Gaynor also highlights the different functions of these gendered communities of friends or companions in this text. While Bors and Lionel, even as they worry about Launcelot, spend their time together in the forest in enjoyment, Gaynor's community of women—which we might tentatively call something like friendship or sisterhood—functions primarily in a private domestic space and primarily as a means of consolation. Nevertheless, that community's role here, while easy to overlook, is significant when one considers that Gaynor's emotions remain hidden and her body remains devoid of any marked affect until she is in that space among them. Even her words of distress, which at first seem to be said only to herself, are said in their company:

> "Alas," she said, "and wele-a-wo,
>   That ever I ought life in lede!
> The beste body is lost me fro
>   That ever in stour bestrode steed." (652–55)

Although we do not learn of their presence until the line immediately following this (line 656 describes the ladies' presence), her words of distress, her bodily expressions of that distress, and narratorial descriptions of her emotions are all only enabled in the presence of her ladies. It might seem that this is merely about the division between domestic and private space and courtly and public space, but it is the same space—her chamber—in which she spoke to Launcelot at the beginning of the poem in a passage that contains none of these features.

Launcelot's meeting with Bors and Lionel, in contrast, suggests possible motivations and emotions, but, as in the poem's opening passages, the reader must guess at them by analyzing the dialogue in this scene, suggesting that Launcelot's community of male friends does not provide the same sort of safe space for emotions and affect that Gaynor's community of women does. Even the meeting's result, Launcelot's agreeing to return to court, only merits brief mentions that Lionel and Bors are "full blithe . . . with mikel pride" and that the king and court were also "blithe" when they heard of his coming (698–99; 702). When he returns to court—the place where he was earlier unable to express any emotion—we get the first real description of emotion and affect in the friendships between the king and knights:

> They ran as swithe as ever they might
>   Out at the gates him again;
> Was never tidandes to them so light;
>   The king him kissed and knight and swain. . . .
>   Ne dight him as himselfe wolde
> To make him both blithe and glad,
>   And sithe aunters he them told. (708–11; 717–19)

This scene of reunion takes place in the public spaces of the court, including standing on towers, but in it, the male characters, including Arthur, are narrated as experiencing bodily affect and emotion and acting in physically affectionate ways with Launcelot. This passage illustrates that the divide between spaces in which characters can express emotions and those in which they cannot is something other than a public/private distinction. While these celebrations are occurring in the public spaces of the court, however, Gaynor is in her chamber, where she mourns the fact that Launcelot will not come to speak with her:

> Three dayes in court he dwelled there
>   That he ne spake not with the queen,

> So muche press was ay them ner;
>   The king him led and court bydene.
> The lady, bright as blossom on brere,
>   Sore she longed him to sen;
> Weeping was her moste cheer,
>   Though she ne durst her to no man mene. (720–27)

This suggests that the privacy of her chamber might better accommodate so-called negative emotion and affect—grieving rather than joy—but also that the celebrations surrounding Launcelot's return are somehow inhospitable to her. That it is a celebration primarily by men might account for that inhospitality.

When Launcelot and Gaynor finally do see each other again, in that same chamber, the narrator tells us that her ladies are not only in attendance but weep with joy at his coming. The exchange between Launcelot and Gaynor here is very different from their conversation at the beginning of the poem—although it still involves some confusion and obfuscation, it also involves the open declaration of emotions and descriptions of affective responses, and the narration of the exchange also includes descriptions of their affective responses to each other:

> "Alas, Launcelot du Lake,
>   Sithe thou hast all my herte in wold,
> Th'erles doughter that thou wolde take
>   Of Ascolot, as men me told!
> Now thou levest for her sake
>   All thy deed of armes bold;
> I may wofully weep and wake
>   In clay til I be clongen cold!
>
> "But, Launcelot, I beseech thee here,
>   Sithe it needelinges shall be so,
> That thou never more diskere
>   The love that hath been betwix us two,
> Ne that she never be with thee so dere,
>   Deed of armes that thou be fro,
> That I may of thy body here,
>   Sithe I shall thus beleve in wo." (lines 744–59)

Only after Launcelot leaves court again do we see Gaynor openly expressing emotion in front of the rest of the court, in response to the death of the Scottish knight by poisoned apple. In addition to what seems like the appropriate displays of grief for a queen, she also expresses fear about the assumptions that others will make:

> "Wele-away," then said the queen,
>   "Jesu Crist, what may I sayn?
> Certes, now will all men ween
>   Myself that I the knight have slain." (860–63)

Even here, though, the text does not dwell on her words or her grief beyond the words "So grete sorrow the queen then wrought, / Grete dole it was to see and lithe" (868–69). Her fears, of course, are completely correct.

At this point in the poem, we have seen Gaynor seem to repress her emotions; we have seen her cautiously express relief by laughing at court; we have seen her openly express despair in the privacy of her chamber with her ladies; and we have seen her express emotion in Launcelot's presence (with her ladies present too), only to have him flee from court as a result. Not only can we understand that the text depicts Gaynor's emotions as potentially dangerous, we can also understand that her behavior is described in such a way that suggests that she is aware of this. So while others—Launcelot, Arthur, and even the Maid—are free to express their grief, their joy, and their worry openly, Gaynor must carefully control hers except when she is alone with her ladies in her chamber. Although her husband, her lover, and the court are all poor interlocutors for a Gaynor who is affected by what happens to and around her, her ladies provide a social space in which she is able to feel the effects of these happenings, to express her thoughts and emotions about them, and to be comforted rather than fled from. These first thousand lines of the poem establish which physical and social spaces are hostile to Gaynor's emotions and affect, and which are safe, creating a framework in which we can consider her reaction to the death and posthumous expressions of emotion by the Maid of Ascolot, her supposed rival whom she has never met.

THE MISSING LINES AND THE POSSIBILITY OF GAYNOR'S SYMPATHY FOR THE MAID

This framework for understanding Gaynor's emotions and affect should help us to understand how she responds to the death of the Maid of Ascolot. Although her reaction may seem like anger at Launcelot's affection for or time spent with the maid, or for the situation she finds herself in, partly as the result of Launcelot's absence from court, an examination of where—and in whose company—she is free to be affected and to express sorrow shows us that there are more circumstances at play here. Versions of this event appear in other English texts as well as the poem's French source, but the episode is given more space in the Stanzaic *Morte*. Moreover, the fact of a missing leaf from the sole surviving copy of the poem creates an opening for us to think hypothetically about the possibility of Gaynor's sympathy for the Maid—even in death—as the catalyst for the release of Gaynor's emotions. If she is affected by the Maid's body, by the Maid's suffering, and perhaps by the realization of the pain they share over Launcelot's rejection of them both, that affect may serve as a trigger for the release of the many emotions Gaynor has had to keep hidden or repress in order to navigate her role as queen. Elizabeth Archibald, in her study of the uses of direct speech in the Stanzaic *Morte* and Malory's *Morte*, writes that "the very selective direct articulation of emotion, often expressed in only one or two lines, gives considerable psychological insight into the main characters, not least when the direct speech is unexpected and breaks into a sentence of indirect narrative, as if the emotion expressed can no longer be contained."[19] Archibald notes that "three or more stanzas of continuous speech are quite rare in the poem" and that the passages in which it appears are "climactic moments in the plot."[20] One such moment is the passage in which Gaynor reacts to Gawain's speech after the discovery of the Maid's body and letter.

The missing lines at this point in the text likely depict at least some narration of Gaynor's grief over and sympathy for the Maid, along with more expressions of her own sorrow, made possible by her encounter, through the unwitting Gawain, with the contents of the Maid's letter. Although Benson notes that it is likely not more than ninety lines that are missing from the manuscript, he follows older conventions of line numbering in skipping from line 1181 to 1318, which means that the episode extends from about line 1128 ("To the queen then went Sir Gawain / And gan to tell her all the case") to somewhere in the missing leaf (lines 1182–1318), between 55 and 145 lines. When the text resumes at line 1318, Gaynor is no longer speaking about the Maid or Launcelot but about her ongoing legal predicament of needing a champion to fight on her behalf against those who accuse her of murdering the Scottish knight. Benson's note on the missing leaf includes this hypothesis based on the poem's source: "evidently it told of the burial of the Maid of Ascolot and

---

19. Elizabeth Archibald, "Some Uses of Direct Speech in the Stanzaic *Morte Arthur* and Malory," *Arthuriana* 28, no. 3 (Fall 2018): 66–85, at 66.

20. Archibald, "Some Uses of Direct Speech in the Stanzaic *Morte Arthur* and Malory," 78.

of the queen's distress, the material in chapters 74 and 78 of the French *Mort Artu*, our poet's source."[21] I offer a reading of Gaynor's words and the narrator's description of her movements and the sounds she makes, in order to suggest that one way to read lines 1128 through 1181 and the suggestive gap that follows them is to consider Gaynor's affective response to the Maid as a form of women's community enabled by the emotional community Gaynor has with her ladies. Although this may seem to be a violation of the poem's distribution of emotions in domestic and public spaces, Gaynor's expression or repression of emotion depends less on the physical space she is in than on who inhabits that space with her.

Gawain's words to Gaynor take the form of a confession for lying to Gaynor about Launcelot's feelings for the Maid before telling her that Launcelot's lack of feelings for the Maid is the reason for the Maid's death:

"Of Ascolot that maiden free
   I said you she was his leman;
That I so gabbed it reweth me,
   And all the sooth now tell I can;
He nolde her not, we mowe well see;
   For-thy dede is that white as swan;
This letter there-of warrant will be;
   She plaineth on Launcelot to eche man." (lines 1136–43)

Although the text does not specify whether Gawain tells Gaynor about the contents of the Maid's letter, which describes itself as a "plaint" addressed to Arthur and his knights (1056), it does say that he "gan to tell her all the case," in which the "gan" can be read either as a form "ginnen" (to begin; "he began to tell her the whole story"), as a tense marker ("he told her all the story"), or an intensifying auxiliary verb ("he did tell her the whole story"; 1129). If we consider that "all the case" might include not only Gawain's dialogue written in

---

21. The *Mort Artu* has almost no direct speech from Guinevere in this scene until after Gawain has left her. The passage that corresponds with the missing leaf of the English poem narrates more of Guinevere's distress, the burial of the Maid, and a lengthy passage describing Lancelot remaining at a hermit's lodging until a knight arrives to tell him of the queen's troubles and the poisoned apple. Only a single clause describes Guinevere's inability to find a champion, but this is the subject of one hundred lines in the Stanzaic *Morte*, narrated directly instead of in dialogue from a knight to Lancelot. See sections 73 and 74 of *La Mort le Roi Artu*, ed. Jean Frappier, 3rd ed. (Geneva and Paris: Textes Littéraires Francais, 1964), 92–94; or the translation that appears in *From Camelot to Joyous Guard: The Old French La Mort le roi Artu*, trans. J. Neale Carman, ed. Norris J. Lacy (Lawrence: University Press of Kansas, 1974), 62–64.

the text but also a summary or reading of the Maid's letter, we might consider Gaynor's reaction as partly a reaction to the Maid's words about her suffering:

> For no thing that I coude pray,
>   Kneeling ne weeping with rewful mone,
> To be my leman he said ever nay,
>   And said shortly he wolde have none.
> "Forthy, lordes, for his sake
>   I took to herte grete sorrow and care,
> So at the last deth gan me take,
>   So that I might live no more;
> For trewe loving had I such wrake
>   And was of bliss ybrought all bare;
> All was for Launcelot du Lake,
>   To wite wisely for whom it were." (1084–95)

The Maid's description of her weeping and bodily pain as the result of Launcelot's rejection echoes Gaynor's own pain and other bodily symptoms. Although readers have seen the similarities in their responses to their love for, and seeming rejection by, Launcelot, this is the first time in the narrative that Gaynor becomes aware of the Maid's suffering. Although Gaynor and the Maid never meet in person, this is the closest they come to doing so, and through learning of her suffering, Gaynor has some access to the Maid's humanity, her vulnerability, and her feelings for Launcelot. Even though Gawain acts as an intermediary, what we see here is something like communication from the Maid to Gaynor, who until now has only been able to express her sorrow or give in to her physical afflictions in the company of her ladies. Although the Maid is not one of her ladies, she is also a suffering woman, and one whose suffering is caused by the same thing—love for and rejection by Launcelot—as Gaynor's own suffering.

    It is possible to consider Gaynor's response to this news as not merely anger at Gawain for lying to her but also anger at Launcelot for his treatment of the Maid, which in turn revives her anger at Launcelot for his treatment of herself. Furthermore, it is possible to read Gaynor's ability to express her emotions verbally here as the result of the presence of the Maid through her letter, in the same way that the presence of her ladies allowed her to do so in her chamber. Gaynor's response to Gawain is three full stanzas long, the length that Archibald notes is rare for direct speech in this poem, which suggests a possible outpouring of suppressed emotions:

> The queen was wroth as wind,
>   And to Sir Gawain said she then:
> "For sooth, sir, thou were too unkind
>   To gabbe so upon any man,
> But thou haddest wiste the sooth in mind,
>   Whether that it were sooth or none;
> Thy courtaisy was all behind
>   When thou tho sawes first began.
>
> "Thy worship thou undidest gretlich,
>   Such wrong to wite that goode knight;
> I trow that he ne aguilt thee never much
>   Why that thou oughtest with no right
> To gabbe on him so vilainlich,
>   Thus behind him, out of his sight.
> And, sir, thou ne wost not right wiselich
>   What harm hath falle there-of and might.
>
> "I wend thou haddest be stable and trew
>   And full of all courtaisy,
> But now me think thy manners new;
>   They ben all turned to vilainy,
> Now thou on knightes makest thy glewe
>   To lie upon them for envy;
> Who that thee worshippeth, it may them rew;
>   Therefore, devoied my company!" (1144–67)

Her words emphasize Gawain's dishonesty ("gabbe," "sawes," "glewe,"), his motives ("for envy"), and the incompatibility of his behavior with his supposed honor ("thy worship thou undidest gretlich"). But she also mentions the harm that he failed to see would come of his gossip, without specifying what harm that is: "thou ne wost not right wiselich / What harm hath falle there-of and might."

Gawain's lies have caused harm to Gaynor, of course, by making her believe herself rejected. They have caused harm to Launcelot through Gaynor's anger at him and his subsequent self-banishment from court. They have caused further harm to Gaynor in the absence of a champion who can defend her against charges of poisoning the Scottish knight. But it is difficult to read her words here—both the content and the sheer length of this direct speech—in the aftermath of the discovery of the Maid's body and letter and before the missing passage containing the Maid's burial and Gaynor's further distress, as not including the Maid's pain and death among the harms Gawain is responsible for.

Through her awareness of and identification with the Maid's pain, Gaynor is able to acknowledge her own pain and to shift from feeling helpless in her pain, as she did in her chamber, to anger ("wroth as wind"). The fact that her three-stanza response to Gawain ends by ordering him to depart from her company takes on a slightly different meaning when we consider that the makeup of Gaynor's company influences whether she is free to feel and express her emotions, and in particular her pain. Just as she tries to shield her own emotions from his gaze and those of other male characters, we might also consider the possibility that she is moving to shield the Maid's emotions as well. Unlike Gaynor, the Maid has no community of women with whom she can safely feel and express her distress, and now in death has no agency over who reads her words or views her body, or how they interpret or appropriate those words. Perhaps Gaynor, who throughout the first quarter of the text has repeatedly sought both privacy and comfort in the company of her ladies, is attempting to extend a small part of that space to include the Maid.

The link between Gaynor and the Maid is, of course, too tenuous to be called friendship. However, reading it through the lens of women's friendship, and particularly the long history of premodern women's friendships being illegible to modern readers, shows us that there is a strong link between the Maid's suffering and death and Gaynor's own suffering. Not only does her posthumous presence prompt a release of emotion from Gaynor; it may also serve to foreshadow for Gaynor that her own death may result from her love for Launcelot, something she already fears as she awaits a champion to defend her against charges of killing the Scottish Knight. As K. S. Whetter writes, the link between Launcelot and Gaynor's affair and death comes to English Arthurian romances from French sources, but these English romances "do not use the association between love and death for the same moralistic purposes as do the great continental cycles."[22] Unlike some other romances, Whetter notes, "the stanzaic *Morte* reminds us that the various types of love can act simultaneously [and] contribute to death."[23] For Whetter, Gaynor's affection for the community of knights is as central to the text's depiction of death

---

22. K. S. Whetter, "Love and Death in Arthurian Romance," in *The Arthurian Way of Death*, ed. Karen Cherewatuk and K. S. Whetter (Cambridge: D. S. Brewer, 2009), 94–11, at 96.

23. Whetter, "Love and Death in Arthurian Romance," 104.

as her love for Launcelot.[24] For my own reading of the poem, the interplay between the barely visible community of women Gaynor belongs to and her love for Launcelot is also important: the support she gets from that community enables her to feel sympathy for the Maid of Ascolot, whose own death results directly from her rejection by Launcelot.

If we need not read these deaths as an indictment of the characters' love, whether for being selfish (the Maid's) or adulterous (Gaynor's), we can see some redemption for both characters in Gaynor's sympathy and identification with the Maid here. Although Benson has hypothesized the content of the missing leaf by both consulting the poem's main French source and deducing what must happen for the following narrative to make sense, a reading of Gaynor as sympathetic to the Maid and attempting to extend her circle of female friendship to include the Maid, even though she has died, allows us to imagine that the missing leaf might include Gaynor's thoughts about the Maid, her sympathy and sorrow for the Maid, or her thoughts on the similarity of their situations—including a fear that love for Launcelot will result in her own death.

CONCLUSION

The community of women in the background of the Stanzaic *Morte Arthur* is part of what constitutes a private domestic space in which Gaynor is able to feel, vocalize, and embody her emotions fully in the first quarter of the poem. Her ability to do so with Launcelot in that space seems to depend on their presence or absence, and her ability to do so outside her chamber is enabled by the presence of the Maid's words and expressions of her own emotions through her posthumous letter. Although the movement of characters through spaces that have varying degrees of privacy and exposure affects what emotions they express and how, and to whom those emotions are intelligible, Gaynor's experience of private space necessitates an extra factor: the presence of other women. In a largely masculine community of knights, which Gaynor is very much a part of, she needs the company—real or perceived—of other women in order to be free to succumb to affective responses to events and to vocalize her emotions. The space created by her ladies in her chamber eventually extends to the dead Maid of Ascolot too, in Gaynor's ability to express her anger and despair and her dismissal of Gawain from her presence as a way

---

24. Whetter, "Love and Death in Arthurian Romance," 104.

of shielding the Maid's grief from his gaze. A long history of scholarship on friendship in the Middle Ages excluding women has contributed to the ease with which we overlook these links between women in medieval texts, especially women like Gaynor and the Maid, who seem to exist only as rivals.[25] Even those of us who study this literature often find it far too easy to dismiss or overlook the sympathies or communities formed by these women. Considering the possibility of sympathy and friendship between women, and of such bonds influencing events in texts and the emotional connections between texts and their (especially female) readers, can begin to bring such relationships out of the background of texts and into the forefront of how we understand these texts' appeal and longevity.

---

25. See Judith Kegan Gardiner, "Review: Women's Friendships, Feminist Friendships," in "Women's Friendships," special issue, *Feminist Studies* 42, no. 2 (2016): 484–501.

CHAPTER 7

Female Friendship in Late Medieval English Literature
Cultural Translation in Chaucer, Gower, and Malory

MELISSA RIDLEY ELMES

PARTICIPATING IN what Ivy Schweitzer terms the "affective turn" in feminist studies,[1] medieval feminist historians have painstakingly mapped out the existence and theorized the significance of the social networks of secular women for whom historical records exist, including their friendships, kinships, and other various alliances brought about by marriage, childbearing and rearing, fostering, and patronage activities.[2] Scholars examining such women's patron-

---

1. Ivy Schweitzer, "Making Equals: Classical Philia and Women's Friendship," *Feminist Studies* 42, no. 2 (2016): 337–64, at 351–52. An earlier version of this chapter was delivered in the "Female Friendship I" session organized by Usha Vishnuvajjala at the 2017 International Congress on Medieval Studies. I am grateful to Usha, Karma Lochrie, Susanna Fein, David Raybin, and the session's audience for insightful and supportive comments that have improved my study; thanks also to Kat Tracy for helpful feedback on an earlier draft.

2. By "secular" I mean women living and working beyond cloisters and similar institutions. Much of this work mapping such women's networks has centered on queens and noblewomen; see, for example, Barbara A. Hanawalt's classic study, "Lady Honor Lisle's Networks of Influence," in *Women and Power in the Middle Ages,* ed. Mary Erler and Maryanne Kowaleski (Athens and London: University of Georgia Press, 1988), 188–212; Theresa Earenfight, *Queenship in Medieval Europe* (Basingstoke: Palgrave Macmillan, 2013); and Linda E. Mitchell, "Joan de Valence and Her Household: Domesticity, Management, and Organization in Transition from Wife to Widow," in *Royal and Elite Households in Medieval and Early Modern Europe,* ed. Theresa Earenfight (Leiden: Brill, 2018), 95–114. Representative studies on women's networks in the mercantile sphere include Barbara A. Hanawalt, *The Wealth of Wives: Women, Law, and Economy in Late-Medieval London* (New York: Oxford University Press, 2007), and Kathryn Ryerson, *Women's Networks in Medieval France: Gender and Community in Montpellier, 1300–*

age practices have demonstrated their influence on books and book-making and, more broadly, on material culture and its social influence throughout the medieval period.[3] Bringing these ideas of women's networks of influence and patronage into conversation with one another, this essay considers how representative late fourteenth- and fifteenth-century English authors working beyond the scholastic and religious traditions wrote in a sociohistorical milieu in which a profound cultural shift in women's visibility and significance was being realized through these avenues.[4] The audiences of such authors—namely, Geoffrey Chaucer, John Gower, and Sir Thomas Malory—included women who could wield influence over their reputation, their position, and their wealth. Subsequently, these writers needed to ensure that their work found favor with those audiences.[5]

Where earlier English writers sought to record, preserve, and disseminate a patristic worldview in service of their religion and were supported in this textual program by pious and literate women and men, later medieval authors writing for a secular audience within an ever-expanding cultural system that emphasized social over religious status were concerned with attracting, entertaining, and pleasing patrons. Earlier writers working within a more insular and religiously inflected sociocultural framework for a relatively finite and homogenous readership rarely strayed from a traditionally male-centric

---

1350 (New York: Palgrave Macmillan, 2016). Scholars including Judith Bennett have also located and theorized country and peasant women's experiences through manorial records; see "Public Power and Authority in the Medieval English Countryside," in Erler and Kowaleski, *Women and Power in the Middle Ages*, 18–36.

3. See, for example, Susan Groag Bell, "Medieval Women Book Owners: Arbiters of Lay Piety and Ambassadors of Culture" in Erler and Kowaleski, *Women and Power in the Middle Ages*, 149–87; Joan M. Ferrante, *To the Glory of Her Sex: Women's Roles in the Composition of Medieval Texts* (Bloomington: Indiana University Press, 1997); Karen K. Jambeck, "Patterns of Women's Literary Patronage: England 1200–ca. 1475," in *The Cultural Patronage of Medieval Women*, ed. June Hall McCash (Athens: University of Georgia Press, 1996), 228–65; Rebecca Krug, *Reading Families: Women's Literate Practices in Late Medieval England* (Ithaca, NY: Cornell University Press, 2002); and Jennifer R. Goodman, "'That wommen holde in ful greet reverence': Mothers and Daughters Reading Chivalric Romances," and Jennifer Summit, "William Caxton, Margaret Beaufort and the Romance of Female Patronage," in *Women, the Book, and the Worldly*, ed. Lesley Smith and Jane H. M. Taylor (Woodbridge: Boydell and Brewer, 1995), 25–30; 151–66. Lydia Yaitsky Kertz extends discussion of women's networks developed through material culture into the realm of sewing and embroidery in her study of Emaré's "skill-based transnational community" in this volume.

4. As Amy N. Vines documents in *Women's Power in Late Medieval Romance* (Cambridge: D. S. Brewer, 2011), 8–10.

5. As Larissa Tracy notes of Osbern Bokenham's *Legendys of Hooly Wummen*; see "Silence and Speech in the Female Lives of the *Gilte Legende* and Their Influence on the Lives of Ordinary Medieval Women," in *Women of the Gilte Legende: A Selection of Middle English Saints Lives*, ed. and trans. Tracy (Woodbridge: D. S. Brewer, 2003), 101–27, at 103–4.

worldview, a point attested by the relative scarcity of women's relationships in the early English literary corpus.[6] But late medieval English audiences were more diverse and expected greater variety in their choice of texts; indeed, as Alfred Thomas has shown, this expectation was heightened by the arrival of Richard II's wife Anne of Bohemia, who came from a tradition of highly educated women renowned for their piety and patronage and whom, per Thomas, Chaucer imagined as his ideal patron and reader.[7] Rather than faithful adherence to scholastic traditions, successful writing in this more cosmopolitan climate required the translation and adaptation of texts originally written in Latin or in continental vernacular languages into English, original invention, and circumspection on the part of writers concerning engagement with antagonistic materials like those involved in the ongoing *querelle des femmes,* or "woman question."[8] I argue that it is in their translations and adaptations that we can locate evidence for greater late medieval English authorial awareness of and attentiveness to their audiences' sociocultural experiences and interests, in a bid to attract the attention of possible patrons. Whether undertaking translation or adaptation work, or some combination of the two, these writers alter their source texts to revise misogynist language, offer scenes of women's networks not present in the original versions, and, within those scenes, expressly invent moments of women's friendship, appealing to the specific experiences of their female readership.

As case studies for this claim, I analyze scenes in which alteration of source materials to privilege women's friendship has been undertaken in texts by three of the later medieval period's most well-known English authors: Geoffrey Chaucer's *Troilus and Criseyde,* translated and adapted from Giovanni Boccaccio's Italian *Il Filostrato*; John Gower's *Albinus and Rosamund,* adapted into his *Confessio Amantis* from Paul the Deacon's Latin chronicle *Historia Langobardorum*; and portions of Sir Thomas Malory's *Le Morte Darthur* derived from his French sources. While all these texts include the classic Aris-

---

6. A phenomenon well documented in Old English literary scholarship, as noted in Clare Lees and Gillian Overing's essay in part 3 of this volume and examined by Alexandra Reider in "Ic ane geseah idese sittan: The Woman and Women Apart in Old English Poetry," *The Heroic Age: A Journal of Early Medieval Northwestern Europe* 19, August 13, 2019.

7. Alfred Thomas, *Reading Women in Late Medieval Europe: Anne of Bohemia and Chaucer's Female Audience* (New York: Palgrave Macmillan, 2015), 10.

8. For an overview of this debate, see David F. Hult, "The *Roman de la Rose,* Christine de Pizan, and the *querelle des femmes,*" in *The Cambridge Companion to Women's Writing,* ed. Carolyn Dinshaw and David Wallace (Cambridge: Cambridge University Press, 2003), 184–94; many of the essential texts are located in Christine McWebb, *Debating the Roman de la Rose: A Critical Anthology* (New York: Routledge, 2013). Carissa Harris's essay on alewife poems in part 3 of this volume addresses the extension of this misogynist literary tradition through the seventeenth century.

totelian and Ciceronian ideals of men's friendship grounded in the scholastic tradition in which these authors were educated,[9] the later English translations and adaptations also mediate the earlier texts' blatant misogyny. Their authors introduce and develop what can best be described in philosophical terms as communally supportive, epicurean friendship networks more in keeping with lived, observed, and recordable experiences of human, and more specifically women's, relationships than Aristotle's limited view of friendship as being between men of equal status, or Cicero's idealized view of friendship as being more than a practical and mutually beneficial relationship.[10] Thus, despite remaining steadfastly masculine in their point of view, Chaucer, Gower, and Malory inscribe women's friendship into their stories, recording a pivotal shift in English literature that stems from the cultural influence of women's literate activity.

TRANSLATION, ADAPTATION, AND INCORPORATION IN CHAUCER'S *TROILUS AND CRISEYDE* AND *FRANKLIN'S TALE*

Scholars have struggled to understand Chaucer's views on women. The tensions that arise between the antifeminist tradition surrounding the *Roman de la Rose*,[11] Chaucer, himself, both participating in the negative representa-

---

9. For texts and discussion of the classical tradition on friendship see: Aristotle, *Nichomachean Ethics Books VIII and IX*, ed. and trans. Michael Pakaluk (Oxford: Clarendon Press, 1998); Cicero, *Laelius, On Friendship and The Dream of Scipio*, ed. and trans. J. G. F. Powell (Liverpool: Liverpool University Press, 1990). Reginald Hyatte offers an overview of medieval understandings and representations of (male) friendship based in these classical ideals in *The Arts of Friendship: The Idealization of Friendship in Medieval and Early Renaissance Literature* (Leiden: Brill, 1994).

10. Alexandra Verini's essay on the nuns of Syon Abbey in part 1 of this volume also views women's friendship through an Epicurean lens, arguing that "an Epicurean view of friendship, more than an Aristotelian or Ciceronian one, [. . .] anticipates the kinds of bonds that might have developed in cloistered female communities." This view need not be constrained to cloistered women's experiences. As Tim O'Keefe notes, Epicurus and his followers understood friendship as "primarily communal, a network of support that included women and sometimes slaves more properly called 'fellowship.'" O'Keefe, *Epicureanism* (Berkeley: University of California Press, 2010), 148. Epicurean friendship is based in mutually pleasurable and beneficial networks, affiliations, and communities. In a January 23, 2020, conversation, my colleague Nicole Torbitsky pointed out that this model of friendship is far more realistic and represents people's, generally, and women's, specifically, experiences of relationships, corroborating that rather than a Ciceronian or godly ideal, this more mundane, epicurean friendship is what I see in the representations of women examined in this study. My thanks to Dr. Torbitsky for suggesting this philosophical framework.

11. Which Chaucer translated into Middle English as the *Romaunt of the Rose* sometime in the late 1360s to early 1370s, and which subsequently influenced many of his later texts; see

tions of women with his Wife of Bath modeled on La Vieille,[12] and berating himself for doing so in the Prologue of the *Legend of Good Women*;[13] the portrayals of women as lewd and adulterous figures in some of his *Tales*[14] juxtaposed with the admiring representation of secular women like Griselda[15] and saints like Cecilia[16] and Virginia,[17] and Pertelote's[18] and Prudence's[19] wisdom and support of their respective husbands; his abandonment mid-composition of the *Legend of Good Women*, ostensibly commissioned by Anne of Bohemia and unfulfilling to him as a male writer;[20] and his personal history of alleged sexual assault,[21] combine in a literary petri dish that thwarts efforts to view Chaucer either as proto-feminist or misogynist, as a champion of women or a rapist.

At this juncture, with appreciation for these earlier scholarly efforts at understanding Chaucer as a writer of women, I suggest returning to the texts themselves with an eye to where, and how, his inclusion of women's interactions yields important new insights, particularly where we can definitively claim that the presentation of women is his invention. This is possible for works that we know Chaucer translated and adapted, such as *Troilus and Criseyde*. While scholars of this text have written at length concerning the friend-

---

Larry D. Benson, "A Brief Chronology of Chaucer's Life and Times," *The Geoffrey Chaucer Page*, July 27, 2000, http://sites.fas.harvard.edu/~chaucer/special/varia/life_of_Ch/chrono.html.

12. See Ralph Hanna and Traugott Lawler, "The Wife of Bath's Prologue," in *Sources and Analogues of the Canterbury Tales II*, ed. Robert M. Correale and Mary Hamel (Cambridge: D. S. Brewer, 2009), 353; 367–78.

13. In the Prologue, Chaucer is confronted by the God of Love, who asks why he finds himself in the presence of a man who does not keep his laws (lines 237–60).

14. For example, Alisoun's adulterous affair in the *Miller's Tale*, and May's in the *Merchant's Tale*; see *The Miller's Tale*, 68–77, and *The Merchant's Tale*, 154–68, in *The Riverside Chaucer*, ed. Larry D. Benson (Boston: Houghton Mifflin, 1987).

15. See *The Clerk's Tale*, in *Riverside Chaucer*, 138–53.

16. See *The Second Nun's Tale*, in *Riverside Chaucer*, 264–69.

17. See *The Physician's Tale*, in *Riverside Chaucer*, 190–93.

18. See *The Nun's Priest's Tale*, in *Riverside Chaucer*, 253–61.

19. See *The Tale of Melibee*, in *Riverside Chaucer*, 217–39.

20. See Caroline Dinshaw, *Chaucer's Sexual Poetics* (Madison: University of Wisconsin Press, 1989), 87; Julia Boffey and A. S. G. Edwards, "The Legend of Good Women," in *The Cambridge Companion to Chaucer*, ed. Piero Boitani and Jill Mann (Cambridge: Cambridge University Press, 2003), 112–26.

21. See "Introduction" in Dinshaw, *Chaucer's Sexual Poetics*, esp. 11; Corinne J. Saunders, *Rape and Ravishment in the Literature of Medieval England* (Cambridge: D. S. Brewer, 2001), 266–67; Christopher Cannon, "Chaucer and Rape: Uncertainty's Certainties," in *Representing Rape in Medieval and Early Modern Literature*, ed. Elizabeth Robertson and Christine M. Rose (New York: Palgrave Macmillan, 2001), 255–79; and Kristin Bovaird-Abbo, "Is Geoffrey Chaucer's *Tale of Sir Thopas* a Rape Narrative? Reading Thopas in Light of the 1382 Statute of Rapes," *Quidditas* 35 (2014): 7–28.

ship between Troilus and Pandarus,[22] Criseyde is typically discussed in terms of her friendlessness. However, comparison of Chaucer's adaptation with Boccaccio's original reveals that the changes Chaucer makes to his source material both mediate Boccaccio's misogynistic tone and meaningfully alter the representation of the women surrounding Criseyde and her interactions with them. In Boccaccio's version, women are presented as ridiculous, annoying, and noisy, the narrator openly mocking them. In Chaucer's version, women are readily viewable as friends in the epicurean sense—their affiliation based on fellowship with beneficial intent—and their friendship is an important aspect of Criseyde's development as a sympathetic and psychologically complex character, rather than contributing, as in Boccaccio's version, to an ongoing program of narrative misogyny. Significantly, Boccaccio's text is dedicated to an unidentified, likely fictional woman (called *Filomena* to the narrator's *Filostrato*), whereas Chaucer dedicates his to two men, John Gower and Ralph Strode. That Boccaccio's text is dedicated to a woman yet is unself-consciously misogynist in tone, while Chaucer's is dedicated to men, yet diligently modifies that misogynist tone, indicates different audience expectations regarding representations of women.

In *Troilus and Criseyde*, composed sometime in the mid-1380s, Criseyde, widowed daughter of the prophet Calchas, who foretold the fall of Troy and subsequently fled into exile to avoid being charged with treason, fields suspicion and general ill will in the wake of her father's fall from favor.[23] Criseyde thus appears to be "friendless" according to the narrator's early description of her—"For bothe a widewe was she and allone / Of any frend to whom she dorste hir mone" (I.97–98)—and this line is Chaucerian, rather than stemming from his Boccaccian source, a point critics have discussed in making the claim that Chaucer paints her as friendless.[24] However, I suggest that this line has been misconstrued; it is not that Criseyde is wholly friendless but rather that she has no family members to advocate for her and also no friends

---

22. See John Hill, "Aristocratic Friendship in *Troilus and Criseyde*: Pandarus, Courtly Love and Ciceronian Brotherhood in Troy," in *New Readings of Chaucer's Poetry*, ed. Robert G. Benson and Susan J. Ridyard (Cambridge: D. S. Brewer, 2003), 165–82; Gretchen Mieszkowski, *Medieval Go-Betweens and Chaucer's Pandarus* (New York: Palgrave Macmillan, 2006), 139–42.

23. Geoffrey Chaucer, "Troilus and Criseyde," in *Riverside Chaucer*, 473–585: I.85–112. Hereafter, references are provided parenthetically in text.

24. Neil Cartlidge writes of Criseyde's friendless state, "Whereas both writers [Boccaccio and Chaucer] describe how Calchas left his widowed daughter in the lurch [. . .] and both emphasize that she was entirely innocent of any involvement in his treachery [. . .] it is only Chaucer who then chooses to focus on Criseyde's friendlessness," in "Criseyde's Absent Friends," *Chaucer Review* 44, no. 3 (2010): 227–45, at 228. Also, Alcuin Blamires, *Chaucer, Ethics and Gender* (Oxford: Oxford University Press, 2006), 36; Nicky Hallett, "Women," in *A Companion to Chaucer*, ed. Peter Brown (Oxford: Blackwell, 2000), 480–94, at 487.

to whom she can reveal her fears or express her emotions so that they are understood.[25] She certainly has women she knows from many years' acquaintance, who engage her in conversation and activities to pass the time and distract her from her troubles; what this line signifies is that she does not find among them someone to whom she dares open up entirely about her feelings, given the emotional environment of the city and general suspicion surrounding her father's recent actions. That she does not spill forth her innermost fears and desires to others is not automatically evidence of a friendless state, as the model of epicurean friendship alerts us. In the medieval era as today, the notion that only people to whom one's innermost soul can be bared count as real friends was recognized as an idealized view of friendship, and as Antonella Liuzzo Scorpo points out, "in different types of sources produced in Western Europe throughout the medieval period, the lexicon of friendship defined a wide and varied range of relationships," among these, friendships based on a shared sense of belonging to a community.[26] Criseyde does have this type of relationship—friendship brought about by the circumstances of where one lives and who one has to associate with, what we might term a "friendship of convenience"—with the townswomen (IV.680–735). Further, as evidence from medieval women's wills demonstrates, widows often enjoyed many significant friendships following their husbands' deaths.[27] Chaucer demonstrates awareness of this type of friendship, utilitarian and pleasurable in the Epicurean rather than idealized in the Ciceronian sense, in his characterization of Criseyde passing her time with other women in the absence of a husband and children.

These women's misunderstanding of Criseyde's tears, and Criseyde's growing tired of their company and wishing they would leave, has been presented as evidence that they are not truly friends, but this interpretation ignores that the narrator outright classifies them as such: "But as men seen in towne and

---

25. Per the *Middle English Dictionary*, "frend" can describe "a friend, comrade, an intimate" (definition 1) or a "kinsman" or "blood relative" (definition 4). I argue that Chaucer employs it here to convey both connotations. Chaucer's playful deployment of words in multiple of their meanings is well attested; for example, his use of two meanings of the single word *fals* to characterize the argument between Palamon and Arcite in the *Knight's Tale*, and his use of *queynte* as a double entendre in that same Tale.

26. Antonella Liuzzo Scorpo, "Friendship in the Middle Ages," *The History of Emotions Blog*, March 20, 2014.

27. For example, in her 2003 chapter "Widows," in Dinshaw and Wallace, *The Cambridge Companion to Medieval Women's Writing*, Barbara Hanawalt notes, "We must not assume that peasant widows lived lonely lives," citing evidence from widows' wills that include bequests to kin, servants, neighbors, friends, and clergy as proof of their often extensive networks (62–65). Chapter 2 of Kathryn Kelsey Staples's *Daughters of London: Inheriting Opportunity in the Late Middle Ages* (Leiden: Brill, 2011) also amasses evidence of women bequeathing items to friends.

al aboute / That wommen usen frendes to visite, / So to Criseyde of wommen com a route, / For piteous joie, and wenden her delite" (IV.680–83). This explicit use of the term *frendes* is not found in the source text. In *Il Filostrato*, this passage appears as "But as we see that it happeneth that one woman goeth to visit another at some new happening, if she bear her affection, thus many came to pass the day with Cressida, all full of piteous joy . . ."[28] Significantly as well, Chaucer smooths out the less flattering characterization of these ladies scattered throughout the *Filostrato*; he retains the description of them as "thilke fooles sittynge hire about" (IV.715) ["these stupid ladies, who encircled her" (70.84)] but omits, for instance, the description of their conversation as "a deal of foolish cackling, such as most women make" (70.86), demonstrating a more even hand in his characterization of women's conversation among themselves than does Boccaccio.

That Criseyde is preoccupied and does not want to participate in the small talk does not negate that these women visit her expressly to cheer her up, an act of friendship. In fact, it is their efforts to cheer her up that reduce her to tears, revealing her true emotional state to them: "[. . .] she felte almost hire herte dye / For wo and wery of that compaignie. / For which no lenger myghte she restreyne / Hir teeris, so they gonnen up to welle, / That yaven signes of the bittre penye / In which her spirit was [. . .]" (IV.706–11). When the women see her crying, they misconstrue the reason, believing she is sad to be leaving them. We are told that those who knew her earlier in life respond to her distress in kind: "they that hadde yknowen hire of yore / Seigh hire so wepe and thoughte it kyndnesse, / and ech of hem wepte ek for hire distresse" (IV.719–21). Despite their misunderstanding of her tears, the women feel an affective bond with Criseyde—a bond of friendship born over time in their community. They visit her not out of a sense of duty but in fellowship; they give their time and energy over to cheering her up; they weep with her when she is emotionally overwhelmed; and they comfort her by distracting her with small talk, even as they, themselves, feel sorrow in the face of her impending departure. The temptation to read this scene solely in terms of Criseyde's feelings is great, and certainly we are guided in that direction by the narrative. When we do so, we read this scene as one in which Criseyde is alone in a crowd, isolated and miserable in her lovesickness—and this is true from her perspective at the moment. But stepping back from a central focus on her point of view to consider everyone in the room, we are clearly observing a tableau of female friendship; Criseyde not wanting these women's company because she

---

28. *Boccaccio's Il Filostrato*, trans. Nathaniel Griffin and Arthur Myrick (Cambridge, ONT: In Parenthesis, 1999), 69.80. Hereafter, citations are provided parenthetically in text.

is pining for her lover doesn't erase its presence. In fact, the emotional crux of the scene, and the larger emotional program of the romance, hinges on her continued personal suffering from lovesickness even in the presence of such friendly support.

Alcuin Blamires's contentions that "Chaucer reveals little interest in projecting women engaging in strong friendships with each other";[29] that there are no "substantial personal alliances between women" in Chaucer's works;[30] and that "Chaucer [...] did not much represent women as women's friends"[31] are not technically wrong. However, in *Troilus and Criseyde* friendship between women is part of the social program of Chaucer's imagined world and, although it is filtered through his (male) gaze, he turns the same observant eye to it as he does to the rest of the social order. The narrative result of this effort at giving attention to women's lived experiences is greater emotional impact tied to the women's relationships with one another. No such effort is present in his source text, indicating that it is important for Chaucer's audience to see such relationships represented in ways that it was not for Boccaccio's. Chaucer does not make these crucial changes in how the women interact with one another solely in his adaptation of Boccaccio's *Il Filostrato*; he goes on to incorporate such scenes, and with a firmer touch, in later works as well.

In Chaucer's *Franklin's Tale*, one of the *Canterbury Tales* penned after *Troilus and Criseyde*, the relationship between Dorigen and her friends is similar in presentation to that between Criseyde and her friends. When her husband, Arveragus, "shoop hym to goon and dwelle a yeer or tweyne / In Engelond, that cleped was eek Briteyne, / To seke in armes worshipe and honour" (809–11), Dorigen grows heartsore; we are told that "For his absence wepeth she and siketh" and "she moorneth, wayleth, fasteth, pleyneth; / Desir of his presence hire so destreyneth / That al this wyde world she sette at noght" (817–21). Like Criseyde, Dorigen is presented as a woman heartsick over the absence of the man she loves. As with Criseyde, Dorigen's friends arrive on the scene to support her; however, this time, the friends are on the same page as she, well aware of Dorigen's situation, her thoughts and feelings, and why she is so distraught:

> Hire freendes, which that knewe hir hevy thoght,
> Conforten hire in al that ever they may.
> they prechen hire, they telle hire nyght and day
> That causelees she sleeth hirself, allas!

---

29. Alcuin Blamires, *Chaucer, Ethics and Gender* (Oxford: Oxford University Press, 2006), 36.
30. Blamires, *Chaucer, Ethics and Gender,* 37.
31. Blamires, *Chaucer, Ethics and Gender,* 37.

> And every confort possible in this cas
> They doon to hire with al hire bisynesse,
> Al for to make hir leve hire hevynesse. (822–29)

They convince her to go out for walks and seek to distract her (841–44), and, when walking by the seaside serves only to remind her of her woes, they take her to other locations and engage her in various pastimes, intent on helping her overcome her depression and fear that her husband is lost at sea:

> Hire freendes sawe that it was no disport
> To romen by the see, but disconfort,
> And shopen for to pleyen somwher elles.
> They leden hire by ryveres and by welles,
> And eek in othere places delitables;
> They dauncen and they pleyen at ches and tables. (895–900)

Ultimately, her friends' sustained efforts to cheer her up lead Dorigen to Aurelius, resulting in the tale's strange and amusing happily-ever-after denouement. Without her friends, Dorigen would have languished alone; and typically in medieval literature when a woman in love languishes alone, without some divine intervention she winds up dead, often by her own hand, as is the case with many of the women in Chaucer's earlier *Legend of Good Women*.[32] Chaucer avoids that deadly conclusion in the *Franklin's Tale* by surrounding Dorigen with friends who bring her solace and force her out of the house and back into the community she would so willingly set aside if left to her own devices.

Of all of Chaucer's tales, this is the one that showcases female friendship in its most conventionally recognizable form[33]—not simply a friendship born of convenience and proximity but one evincing clear and genuine affection for one another—yet scholars have historically neglected that aspect, focusing rather on the tale's "rash promise" motif, its role in the marriage debate, the possible sources of the tale and of the miracle of the vanishing rocks, and Chaucer's preoccupation (or not) with the ideas of *gentillesse* and *troth*.[34] It is worth noting that although *Decameron* 10.5 does feature a scene in which

---

32. Each of the Legends of Cleopatra, Thisbe, Dido, and Phyllis ends with the heroine's death following the abandonment or death of her lover. Indeed, Dorigen also contemplates suicide prior to her friends' intervention.

33. Karma Lochrie's essay in part 3 of this volume also examines various forms of female friendship in the *Man of Law's*, *Wife of Bath's*, and *Squire's Tales*.

34. See Joanne Rice, "The Franklin's Prologue and Tale," explanatory notes in *The Riverside Chaucer*, 895–96.

Madonna Dianora, a character potentially analogous to Dorigen, joins other city women walking in a garden,[35] none of this tale's currently known sources or analogues includes a similarly significant relationship between the woman at the center of the story and her friends,[36] suggesting either that there is a missing source with such scenes or that Chaucer developed this friendship for the tale. If it is original to Chaucer, then here he is paying more attention to women's friendships and writing them with more sensitivity to how women's communities function as systems of potentially life-saving emotional support than in any other of his works. Chaucer has moved from translating Boccaccio's *Il Filostrato* with an eye to adapting it for his audiences through the mediation of Boccaccio's misogyny and the establishment of a clearer sense of friendship between Criseyde and her friends to incorporating female friendship as an essential element in his narrative program. In a literary world where the patronage of their audiences dictated much of what was produced by writers, this evident shift would not have happened without audience approbation. Although Chaucer's dedicatees for *Troilus and Criseyde* were men, and we do not know for whom (if anyone) the *Canterbury Tales* were written, we do know that at least one of his patrons was a woman, that his audiences included women, and that women wielded increasing influence over literature and culture in his time, perhaps leading to this more intentional incorporation of such scenes of women's experiences of friendship into his writing as an effort to please his readership and attract patrons.

Thus far, I have argued that in translating and adapting Boccaccio's earlier misogynist text into one demonstrating sympathy for women's lived experiences and relationships with one another, and then incorporating similar instances of female friendship into his later texts, Chaucer's writing records a shift in audience expectations of the depiction of women from Boccaccio's time and place to his own. In what remains of this essay, I turn to the "Tale of Albinus and Rosamund" from John Gower's *Confessio Amantis*, a work contemporary to Chaucer's writing, and the exchange of letters between queens in Sir Thomas Malory's later *Morte Darthur*, to show that this sympathetic alteration of such relationships between women from source texts continues in vernacular writing produced throughout the later Middle English period. Because it is a phenomenon not unique to Chaucer's writing, it can be viewed as an audience-driven trend in late medieval English literary culture.

---

35. See Robert R. Edwards, "The Franklin's Tale," in *Sources and Analogues of the Canterbury Tales I*, ed. Robert M. Correale and Mary Hamel (Woodbridge: D. S. Brewer 2002), 211–65, at 240.

36. Edwards, "Franklin's Tale."

TRANSLATION, MEDIATION, AND ALTERATION IN JOHN GOWER'S "ALBINUS AND ROSAMUND"

In Paul the Deacon's Latin *Historia Langobardorum* (c. 720–99), which serves as the basis for John Gower's "Tale of Albinus and Rosemund," King Alboin is slain through a plot devised by his wife and two male co-conspirators:

> After [King Alboin] had ruled in Italy three years and six months, he was slain by the treachery of his wife [...] While he sat in merriment at a banquet in Verona [...] with the cup which he had made of the head of his father-in-law, Cunimund, he ordered it to be given to the queen to drink wine, and he invited her to drink merrily with her father [...] Then [Queen] Rosemund [...] burned to avenge the death of her father by the murder of her husband, and she formed a plan with Helmechis who was the king's squire [...] to kill the king, and he persuaded the queen that she ought to admit to this plot Peredeo,[37] who was a very strong man. As Peredeo would not give his consent to the queen when she advised so great a crime, she put herself at night in the bed of her dressing maid with whom Peredeo was accustomed to have intercourse, and then Peredeo, coming in ignorance, lay with the queen [...] Then he learned the evil thing he had done, and he who had been unwilling of his own accord assented, when forced in such a way, to the murder of the king [...] unfortunately alas! This most warlike and very brave man [Alboin] being helpless against his enemy, was slain as if he was one of no account, and he who was most famous in war through the overthrow of so many enemies, perished by the scheme of one little woman.[38]

This passage, written by a Benedictine monk and from the point of view of the Lombards, a Germanic people occupying the Italian peninsula between the late sixth and eighth centuries, demonstrates the clerical bias against women as dangerous and inherently untrustworthy found in many early medieval religious texts. In this chronicle version of the story, the facts of Alboin's death are

---

37. King Alboin's chamber guard; see Joaquin Martinez Pizarro, *Writing Ravenna: The Liber pontificalis of Andreas Agnellus* (Ann Arbor: University of Michigan Press, 1995), 128n58.

38. *History of the Langobards, by Paul the Deacon*, trans. William Dudley Foulke (Philadelphia: University of Pennsylvania, 1907), 81–83. The story as presented in Paul the Deacon's chronicle is repeated in the 1185 *Pantheon* or *Universalis libri qui chronici appellantur* of Godfrey of Viterbo (c. 1120–96), and Robert F. Yeager believes this later recension was the inspiration for John Gower's version of the tale. See Robert F. Yeager, *John Gower's Poetic: The Search for a New Arion* (Cambridge: D. S. Brewer, 1990), 145. For discussion of Paul the Deacon's sources and treatment of Alboin's death, see chapter 4 in Shami Gosh, *Writing the Barbarian Past: Studies in Early Medieval Historical Narrative* (Leiden: Brill, 2015).

laid out in straightforward fashion, with the author's bias against Rosemund on full display. While her maid is mentioned in passing, Rosemund is the sole executor of the plot to seduce and coerce Peredeo to aid in her revenge. There is no suggestion that she and her maid collude in this effort.

In his c. 1390 retelling of this story in Book 1 of the *Confessio Amantis* under the thematic rubric of Pride, John Gower significantly expands the narrative, including extended scenes featuring Rosemund and her maid, now named Glodeside, plotting Rosemund's revenge against King Albinus together following a more or less faithful translation of the feast scene. These extended scenes present Rosemund approaching "a maide which sche triste / So that non other wyht it wiste."[39] There is no explicit indication that this is Rosemund's personal maid and, therefore, a woman specifically beholden to her for her livelihood—this is "a" maid, not necessarily "her" maid—so that, rather than any hierarchic emphasis, the focus is on Rosemund's trust in this particular maid's discretion and willingness to help her. For Rosemund to trust this maid enough that she takes her into a plot to kill her husband, the king, their relationship must both be long-term and close. As with Chaucer's Criseyde and her townswomen, there is the sense that Rosemund and Glodeside have spent a great deal of time in one another's company and mutually benefited from this relationship enough that Rosemund turns to Glodeside in her hour of need. Glodeside does not disappoint; Gower's emphasis throughout their scenes together is on their shared goal:

> Thei felle in covenant,
> That thei acorden ate laste,
> With suche wiles as thei caste
> That thei wol gete of here acord
> Som orped knyht to sle this lord (lines 2586–90)

These women work together to accomplish Rosemund's aims, whereas in Paul the Deacon's chronicle the maid's role, if any, in aiding Rosemund is unspecified. Gower preserves the idea that their scheme is based in women's wiles, but beyond this, he mediates much of the misogynist tone of his source materials. In addition to expanding the amount of narrative space devoted to these women as co-conspirators, Gower conflates the characters of Helmechis and Peredeo into one figure and lessens Rosemund's guilt by erasing her affair with Helmechis, revising his material to bestow Helmechis's attentions instead to

---

39. John Gower, *Confessio Amantis*, book 1, ed. Russell A. Peck, TEAMS Middle English Text Series (Kalamazoo, MI: Medieval Institute, 2000), lines 2573–75. All citations of the text are from this edition; hereafter, line numbers are provided parenthetically.

her maid. Glodeside lures Helmechis—who, the narrator assures us, already loves and desires her: "Glodeside he loveth hote" (2595)—into her bed with promises of sexual satisfaction, gives him her body one night, then contrives for Rosemund to take her place on the second night (2596–604). After Helmechis and Rosemund conclude this tryst, she reveals her identity, telling him he either does her bidding in killing the king or suffers the consequences of having slept with the queen (2611–19).

Although it is not discussed explicitly, attentive readers are well aware that Helmechis has just (unwittingly) committed an act of high treason and faces death if this act is divulged; however, Glodeside has also committed an act of high treason, as has Rosemund herself. Glodeside and Rosemund are putting their lives on the line to achieve Rosemund's revenge on her husband the king. Unlike his predecessor's presentation of the story, which explicitly points to Rosemund as the female wrongdoer in comparison to Alboin's noble martyrdom at her hands, Gower does not comment on the women's actions as being treacherous. Rather, his focus throughout is on the sin of Pride: how Albinus's inability to control his arrogance catalyzes these events, leading to the deaths of himself and, ultimately, of Rosemund and Helmechis. Rosemund, too, acts out of pride—but she also goes to the person she trusts most, and they plot together to achieve her aims. This moment where they agree unhesitatingly to put their lives on the line characterizes them as more than queen and maid; it constitutes an act of true and loyal friendship.

That Gower has intentionally mediated his source materials to emphasize Rosemund's untenable situation and to mitigate her presentation as the villain in this tale is further underscored at the end of his version, where he emphasizes that Albinus met the fate of a man who is caught up in pride and omits entirely the final statement in Paul the Deacon's version that Alboin's fall was the fault of a woman's scheming. That Gower has intentionally invented this representation of these women's experience of friendship under duress and the lengths to which they go to help one another in the face of adversity and unfair treatment at the hands of their male counterparts is clear in the absence of any such scene in his source materials. Because versions of the *Confessio Amantis* were dedicated variously to King Richard II, Geoffrey Chaucer, and Henry of Lancaster,[40] this alteration of his source materials to incorporate scenes of women interacting with one another in this way is not at the behest of a female patron. However, Gower must have viewed these alterations not only as acceptable to, but somehow necessary for, the tale's positive reception

---

40. For discussion of these dedications, see Nigel Saul, "John Gower: Prophet or Turncoat?" in *John Gower, Trilingual Poet: Language, Translation, and Tradition*, ed. Elisabeth M. Dutton, John Hines, and Robert F. Yeager (Cambridge: D. S. Brewer, 2010), 85–97, at 87.

by his audience, as their incorporation alters the story but in no way affects the message behind his adaptation of it as a discussion of the sin of masculine pride. Where earlier audiences such as those for whom Paul the Deacon's works were penned expected women like Rosemund to be depicted as the villain in the stories of men's downfalls because of their inherent sinfulness and wickedness, Gower's audiences appear to have expected to see women interacting with one another in meaningful and supportive ways and to be treated with some degree of authorial sympathy, rather than straightforward and unmitigated misogyny. Like Chaucer, Gower understood himself as writing in a time and place where the representation of women's complex sociopolitical and public experiences, and of their positive and nurturing personal relationships with one another, mattered to his readership. Such an expectation could arise in a time and place that featured increased visibility of women's power as audiences and readers via the patronage system, to the extent that even when women were not directly involved in a text's production themselves, it allowed for women's influence and, thus, presence to be incorporated into literary works. Turning from Chaucer and Gower in the late fourteenth century to Sir Thomas Malory in the late fifteenth century, these early efforts at the incorporation of women's experiences to please audiences evolve into an integrated approach to narrative development, with women's relationships at the heart of the story and essential in successful world-building.

SIR THOMAS MALORY'S QUEENS: WORLD-BUILDING WITH WOMEN

Sir Thomas Malory's *Morte Darthur* (completed 1469–70; published 1485) is the culminating medieval text of the Arthurian legend, pulling material from the English chronicles and French romance cycles[41] together into a single, rambling narrative featuring Arthur's various knights and their deeds. It is easy to assign women a secondary place in this narrative, so focused is it on the masculine exploits of its knightly characters; yet, as I have shown elsewhere, women are present in essential ways and participate equally in the

---

41. See Edward Donald Kennedy, "Caxton, Malory, Arthurian Chronicles, and French Romances: Intertextual Complexities," in *And Gladly Wolde He Lerne and Gladly Teche: Essays on Medieval English Presented to Professor Matsuji Tajima on His Sixtieth Birthday*, ed. Yoko Iyeiri and Margaret Connolly (Tokyo: Kaibunsha, 2002), 217–36; and "Sir Thomas Malory's (French) Romance and (English) Chronicle," in *Arthurian Studies in Honor of P. J. C. Field*, ed. Bonnie Wheeler (Cambridge: D. S. Brewer, 2004), 223–34.

"gritty realism" of Malory's imagined world.[42] While women do not typically interact with other women in the *Morte Darthur*, embedded within the "First Book of Sir Tristram of Lyones" are two short but telling passages featuring direct interaction, albeit from a distance, between two queens, La Beale Isode and Guinevere. Scholars focusing on this interaction do so primarily regarding its role in the depiction of adultery in the *Morte Darthur*, and, while this is certainly one of the reasons for its inclusion, Isode and Guinevere are more than merely adulterous women sharing and glorying in their illicit conquests.[43] The way Malory represents their interactions suggests that they have known one another closely prior to and outside of the events described. Their interactions exhibit the characteristics of a female friendship characterized by scholars elsewhere as homosocial, born of shared social status and a shared female experience of the bad behaviors of beloved male counterparts that we see in, for example, the friendship between Canacee and the falcon in the *Squire's Tale*.[44] It is also epicurean, in the ways that these queens rely on their affiliations and networks to know one another socially and provide benefit to their communities and mutually aid one another through friendly support, advice, and encouragement.[45] Further, Malory demonstrably tones down and omits the misogynist language applied to women and especially to Guinevere in his source materials, focusing instead on the effects of their actions and experiences and on the networks in which they participate. These choices emphasize women's ultimate effect on the overall narrative rather than dwelling on their sinful wickedness as adulterers.[46] In Sir Thomas Malory's *Morte Darthur*, the

---

42. Melissa Ridley Elmes, "Public Displays of Affliction: Women's Wounds in Sir Thomas Malory's *Morte Darthur*," *Modern Philology* 116, no. 3 (2019): 187–210, at 190.

43. See, for example, Beverly Kennedy, "Adultery in Malory's *Le Morte Darthur*," *Arthuriana* 7, no. 4 (Winter 1997): 63–91. Usha Vishnuvajjala's essay on the *Stanzaic Morte Arthur* in this volume points out that modern audiences have received Guinevere as "a cheater" but that "revisiting [Guinevere's interactions with women] can help us see that Middle English Arthurian literature does not dismiss Guinevere's relationships with, or sympathy for, other women as completely as we are frequently inclined to do in the twenty-first century."

44. See Sara Deutch Schotland, "Talking Birds and Gentle Heart: Female Homosocial Bonding in Chaucer's 'Squire's Tale,'" in *Friendship in the Middle Ages and Early Modern Age*, ed. Albrecht Classen and Marilyn Sandidge (Berlin: De Gruyter, 2011), 525–42; and Melissa Ridley Elmes, "'Compassion and Benignytee': A Reassessment of the Relationship Between Canacee and the Falcon in Chaucer's 'Squire's Tale,'" *Medieval Feminist Forum* 54, no. 1 (2018): 50–64.

45. Kenneth Hodges likens Guinevere to real-life queens Margaret of Anjou and Elizabeth Woodville in terms of the network of influence she constructs through political and personal affinities, in "Guinevere's Politics in Malory's *Morte Darthur*," *Journal of English and Germanic Philology* 104, no. 4 (2005): 54–79.

46. As shown in Hodges, "Guinevere's Politics in Malory's *Morte Darthur*," 61–62; and Melissa Ridley Elmes, "Treason and the Feast in Sir Thomas Malory's *Morte Darthur*," in *Treason: Medieval and Early Modern Adultery, Betrayal, and Shame*, ed. Larissa Tracy (Leiden: Brill, 2019), 320–39.

literary program of translating and developing women's experiences from incidental or pointed meditations on their inferior and wicked nature into narratively meaningful scenes begun by earlier writers like Chaucer and Gower becomes even more clearly an effort to render visible the impact of women's relationships within the overarching social program of the imagined world. I view the interactions between Guinevere and Isode, and the way they ripple through the plot to affect the other characters, as evidence of a successful holistic integration of women's influence into literary invention, so that women's experiences and relationships become required elements in a believable and culturally resonant narrative.

The first of these interactions occurs directly after Tristram wins his battle with Palomedes for Isode's love; sending Palomedes into exile, Isode exhorts him to "take thy way [...] unto the court of Kynge Arthure, and there recommaunde me unto Quene Gwenyvere and tell her that I sende her worde that there be within this londe but foure lovers, and that is Sir Launcelot and Dame Gwenyvere, and Sir Trystrames and Quene Isode."[47] Although this message seems to come out of nowhere, it makes no sense that Isode would, having never before met her, suddenly think of Queen Guinevere, decide that her new relationship is on par with the well-known one between Guinevere and Lancelot, and send a strange knight to Arthur's kingdom to tell Guinevere that this other queen, far away in Cornwall, has determined that their loves are the greatest in the world. Isode requests that Palomedes recommend her to Guinevere, signaling prior acquaintance; the contents of the message are personal, suggesting more than general or passing familiarity. Isode reaches out to Guinevere in good-natured amity, not comparing their situations in some one-upwomanship concerning whose love is greater but conveying that she and Tristram have managed (however temporarily) to overcome their obstacles and come together in love. She is sending her happy news to a friend who she knows will appreciate it. That they have met and gotten to know one another in friendly fashion prior to this moment is not only possible but probable; after all, Isode is the daughter of the Irish king, and Sir Morhault, whom Tristram initially defeated to set into motion the events that have led to this point, was both her uncle and a knight of the Round Table (293.32–302.13). Malory does not make it explicit, but reading between the lines and with an awareness that Malory often drops narrative threads and significantly alters his source materials permits us to understand that Isode and Guinevere have developed a close prior bond.

---

47. Sir Thomas Malory, *Le Morte Darthur*, ed. P. J. C. Field (Cambridge; D. S. Brewer, 2017), 340.1–5. Hereafter, passages are cited parenthetically by page and line number(s).

The second of these queens' interactions occurs shortly after Tristram has seemingly abandoned Isode by wedding Isode le Blaunche Maynes. Inconsolable, La Beale Isode writes a letter to Guinevere, who responds in kind:

> [. . .] in this meane whyle La Beale Isode made a lettir unto Quene Gwenyvere complaynyng her of the untrouthe of Sir Trystrames, and how he had wedded the kynges doughter of Bretayne. So Quene Gwenyvere sente hir another letter and bade her be of good comforte, for she sholde have joy aftir sorow: for Sir Trystrames was so noble a knyght called that by craftes of sorsery ladyes wolde make such noble men to wedde them. "But the ende," Quene Genyvere seyde, "shulde be thus, that he shall hate her and love you bettir than ever he dud." (349.7–15)[48]

As with the message conveyed to Guinevere through Palomedes, it should seem to any critical reader absurd from both a psychological and a legal standpoint to imagine that Isode randomly sends Guinevere this single letter, out of the blue, detailing the failure of her adulterous affair with Tristram—information that would be viewed by unsympathetic eyes as shameful at best, treasonous at worst. Moreover, the contents of both letters suggest that the queens are familiar with the situation beyond this single discussion. While some scholars might claim an absence of evidence that Isode and Guinevere are friends, this letter and their prior interaction through Isode's message to Guinevere are clearly part of a larger program of interactions between them that, for whatever reason, has not made it into Malory's narrative. The nature of their interactions—Isode's playful initial message, her letter unburdening her broken heart to Guinevere, and Guinevere's compassionate, comforting response assuring her that obviously, only sorcery could wrest Tristram's affections from her, the other Isolde is a far lesser woman and lover than she, and it is only a matter of time before Tristram sees that—all exhibit the nature of friendship between women who share their deepest secrets and turn to one another for help and advice. Malory thus presents Guinevere and Isode as friends, however distant from one another geographically, and their friendship is the knot tying the Tristram materials into the larger pattern of networks and affinities developed in the *Morte Darthur*. While the knights are foregrounded

---

48. Isode is an inveterate writer of letters, generally for positive outcomes. As Siobhán M. Wyatt notes, "With the exception of Guinevere's unfounded accusation of sorcery against Isode le Blaunche Maynys, Malory's women write letters to heal rifts, console and, in Isode's case, to bring her love home, even with his new wife; their behaviour is exemplary, unlike that of the jealous knights who pervade the pages of 'The Boke of Syr Trystrams de Lyones.'" Siobhán M. Wyatt, *Women of Words in "Le Morte Darthur": The Autonomy of Speech in Malory's Female Characters* (New York: Palgrave Macmillan, 2016), 168.

throughout the narrative, these women's experiences—their social, political, and economic activities, and the friendships they develop through these activities—provide a framework for that narrative. Malory adapts and transforms his source materials to privilege women's roles in his imagined society, removing misogynist meditations and pointed criticism of women and developing their networks and affinities to showcase their influence in both private and public spheres, and, as Kenneth Hodges has shown, these alterations mirror the observable patronage networks of women in late medieval England.[49] Thus mirroring the effects of women's influence in observed reality, Malory's world-building in the *Morte Darthur* reflects the sociocultural milieu in which he is writing, as much as it does his preoccupation with chivalry and treason.

CONCLUSION

Patronage in all its forms was a powerful force in the medieval era, and where it comes to vernacular literary production, successful writers understood their audiences. Throughout the later medieval period in England, their networks of influence and patronage rendered women both more visible and more visibly influential in their communities. Corresponding with this rise in their visibility and influence, authors began incorporating more, and more meaningful, scenes featuring women's networks and affinities in their literary works. The evidence for this practice is clearest in texts that have been translated and adapted from other languages and earlier sources wherein women did not feature as prominently or in as positive a light. Geoffrey Chaucer's *Troilus and Criseyde* and *Franklin's Tale* offer a case study in how one author adapts a non-English source to mediate misogynist language and include scenes of women's friendship earlier in his writing career, before more concretely incorporating such scenes as meaningful aspects of the narrative in a later text. As does Chaucer's *Troilus and Criseyde,* John Gower's "Albinus and Rosemund" showcases the circumspection with which authors writing for an audience that included powerful and influential women had to approach translating and adapting source materials that included deeply misogynist and openly critical depictions of women; these writers opted out of the ongoing "women's question" in favor of quietly integrating sympathetic women's relationships into their texts to mirror their audiences' lived experiences and expectations. And Sir Thomas Malory closes the late medieval period in English literature with the *Morte Darthur,* a text that assumes the centrality of women's relationships,

---

49. See Hodges, "Guinevere's Politics in Malory's *Morte Darthur,*" passim.

and especially the friendship of two queens, to be essential in the overarching social program of his world-building. Their friendship is the crux from which ensue the networks and affinities that overlap and, ultimately, converge along the way to that text's denouement, in literary mimesis of the similar networks and affinities of the powerful women in England's ruling families.

The female friendships depicted within these later medieval texts adapted from earlier non-English sources demonstrate observable and realistic characteristics resonant with women's lived experiences; namely, they are all epicurean, emphasizing community and mutually beneficial activity over the more masculine, dyadic friendship privileged in classical and medieval philosophy. These authors shaped their female characters into literary versions of the women in their audiences, emphasizing their influence on one another and within their communities. The ways these authors translate and adapt their source materials to develop more, and more narratively significant, representations of women's experiences in tandem with a visible increase in women's influence in the sociocultural milieu in which they were writing offer a means by which we might better—because more clearly and accurately—understand women's friendship and thus, the representation of women's culture, in later English medieval vernacular literature.

PART 3

~

New Modes of Female Friendship

CHAPTER 8

Cultivating Cummarship

Female Friendship, Alcohol, and Pedagogical Community in the Alewife Poem

CARISSA M. HARRIS

WILLIAM DUNBAR'S *Tretis of the Tua Mariit Wemen and the Wedo* (c. 1507) features three female friends who gather on a summer evening to drink sweet wine, share candid narratives about their sex lives, and console one another with affectionate support and practical strategies for obtaining erotic satisfaction. Dunbar writes that the women "wauchtit at the wicht wyne and waris out wourdis" [emptied out the white wine and poured out words] (39), alliteratively linking their immoderate alcohol consumption to their verbal outpourings.[1] He characterizes their bond as marked by laughter, drinking, and obscene conversation:

Than all thai leuch apon loft with latis full mery
And raucht the cop round about, full off riche wynis,
And ralyeit lang, or thai wald rest, with ryatus speche (147–49)

[Then they all laughed loudly with full merry demeanors
And passed the cup around, full of rich wines,
And jested long, before they would rest, with licentious speech.]

---

1. William Dunbar, *The Tretis of the Tua Mariit Wemen and the Wedo* (*Digital Index of Middle English Verse* [henceforth *DIMEV*] 6134), in *The Poems of William Dunbar*, ed. Priscilla Bawcutt, 2 vols. (Glasgow: Association for Scottish Literary Studies, 1998), 1:41–55.

The women foment their merriment by drinking wine from the same cup and sharing "ryatus speche," licentious confessions that bind them together.² After these lines, the Maitland Folio's scribe writes, "*Hic bibent*" [here they drink], underscoring the communal drinking that accompanies the women's raucous conversation and inviting readers to imbibe along with them in a stage direction of sorts.³ The Maitland Folio was read by both men and women—including Helen Maitland, who wrote her name on one of its pages—thus leaving open the possibility that groups of women could have read this poem while drinking wine along with Dunbar's fictional ladies.⁴ The poem's three friends discuss their carnal experiences in a didactic framework modeled on scholarly disputation, illustrating how the feminized space of the late medieval alehouse facilitated edifying, affirming, and subversive same-sex communities.

Dunbar's *Tretis*, like numerous similar texts known as "alewife poems" or "gossips' songs" from the fifteenth through seventeenth centuries, depicts a model of female friendship in which women drink excessively, laugh merrily, encourage one another, share sexual knowledge, and speak candidly about their intimate experiences, humiliating their absent spouses with their blunt and bawdy sexual assessments.⁵ On one hand, this scenario reinforces misogynist stereotypes of women as drunken, duplicitous, idle, unruly, loose-tongued, and lascivious. It portrays them working together to undermine men, confirming a common medieval suspicion that women's bonds are socially disruptive and dangerous to men.⁶ As one popular proverb claims, "Quhair there is wyves, there are there words, quhair there is geiss, there are

---

2. *Dictionary of the Older Scottish Tongue* (henceforth *DOST*), s.v. "riot(o)us" (adj.), 2.

3. Cambridge, Magdalene College Library, MS Pepys 2553, p. 86. Similar directions occur on p. 88 ("*Nunc bibent*" [Now they drink]).

4. This note referring to "helyne m" appears on page 256 of the manuscript. Julia Boffey discusses the manuscript's female readership in "The Maitland Folio Manuscript as a Verse Anthology," in *William Dunbar, "The Nobill Poyet": Essays in Honour of Priscilla Bawcutt*, ed. Sally Mapstone (East Linton, UK: Tuckwell, 2001), 40–50.

5. Susan E. Phillips gives an overview of these texts in *Transforming Talk: The Problem with Gossip in Late Medieval England* (University Park: Pennsylvania State University Press, 2007), 148. For more on these poems, see Judith M. Bennett, *Ale, Beer, and Brewsters in England: Women's Work in a Changing World 1300–1600* (Oxford: Oxford University Press, 1996), 122–44; Carissa M. Harris, *Obscene Pedagogies: Transgressive Talk and Sexual Education in Late Medieval Britain* (Ithaca, NY: Cornell University Press, 2018), 177–82; Linda Woodbridge, *Women and the English Renaissance: Literature and the Nature of Womankind, 1540–1620* (Urbana: University of Illinois Press, 1984), 224–43; Sarah Annette McLoughlin, "Gender and Transgression in the Late Medieval English Household" (Ph.D. diss., University of York, 2013), 163–222.

6. Mary Wack, "Women, Work, and Plays in an English Medieval Town," in *Maids and Mistresses, Cousins and Queens: Women's Alliances in Early Modern England*, ed. Susan Frye

there tuirds" [Where there are women, there are words; where there are geese, there are turds]; here, women's fellowship is characterized by shared words that are as foul, plentiful, and worthless as goose excrement.[7] Another proverb declares that "glib'd tongued [garrulous] women seldom chast ar found," insisting that women's verbal and vaginal activities are connected and tying their excessive speech to their sexual transgressiveness.[8] But I argue that Dunbar's *Tretis*, and other poems like it, also probes the pedagogical and consolatory aspects of a historically specific model of female friendship known as *cummarship*, a term coined by Karma Lochrie that signifies "female intimacy that is both pedagogical and raucous."[9] Building on Mary Wack's claim that "[women's] drinking songs offer a model of community that challenges and inverts masculine marital and civic authority," I argue that these texts portray the alehouse as a merry all-female schoolhouse in which women affirm, listen to, and instruct one another using obscene speech.[10] At once convivial and educational, cummarship is produced within the framework of literary and cultural misogyny, including popular stereotypes of feminine deceitfulness, unruliness, and loquacity as well as male fears of what women talk about when no men are present. However, it nonetheless challenges that misogyny by portraying the alehouse as a supportive space for same-sex intimacy and edification and depicting marriage as both unsatisfying and unnecessary. After analyzing the genre's development over time from *Gilote e Johane*, its early fourteenth-century Anglo-Norman ancestor, to its sixteenth-century incarnations in print and manuscript, I discuss the model of cummarship central to alewife texts, outline its historical contexts, and point to its queer possibilities. I link these texts' representations of gendered bonds in feminized spaces where men are largely irrelevant to more recent examples of same-sex community in twentieth-century lesbian bar cultures, highlighting how medieval alehouses and lesbian bars are both spaces where women occupy leadership roles, exercise economic agency, and forge tight-knit communities.

---

and Karen Robertson (Oxford: Oxford University Press, 1999), 33–51. Wack notes how Chester mayor Henry Gee passed laws to curtail women-only childbed rituals in the 1530s (40).

7. M. L. Anderson, ed., *The James Carmichaell Collection of Proverbs in Scots* (Edinburgh: Edinburgh University Press, 1957), no. 1302.

8. Erskine Beveridge, ed., *Fergusson's Scottish Proverbs, from the Original Print of 1641, Together with a Larger Manuscript Collection of About the Same Period Hitherto Unpublished* (Edinburgh: William Blackwood and Sons for the Scottish Text Society, 1924), 124.

9. Karma Lochrie, response to "Female Friendship in Medieval Literature I" session at the 52nd International Congress on Medieval Studies, May 2017.

10. Wack, "Women, Work, and Plays," 35.

INTIMACY, PEDAGOGY, COMMUNITY: THE ALEWIFE POEM, C. 1300–1700

Alewife poems feature two or more female friends—typically wives or widows—who gather to share critiques of marriage, explicit sexual disclosures, transgressive instruction, and copious amounts of alcohol. These poems are multivocal, with two or more women sharing their perspectives and responding to their peers. Sometimes the friends enjoy food such as "soppe[s]" [bread soaked in wine], "bounes or maunchettes newe bake" [buns or freshly baked loaves of fine white bread], or "Gose or pigge or capons wynge, / Pastes of pigynnes [pigeon pies]," associating them with the deadly sin of gluttony in food as well as drink.[11] The women are often given popular names such as Sarah, Margaret, Margery, Eleanor, Cecily, Anne, Alice, and Joan. These naming conventions both render the characters as familiar figures whom one might encounter at any local alehouse and generate a sense of continuity across the different poems.

Purporting to share what happens among women when no men are present, alewife poems portray female friendship as a powerful social force. In her analysis of gossip in late medieval texts, Susan E. Phillips argues that "these intimate confessional exchanges ... transform relationships, for the characters who engage in them forge kinship through conversation," as "women swear alliance to one another at the expense of loyalty to their husbands."[12] These texts underscore the transgressiveness of women's alehouse conversations and vividly express the wives' anger at the institution of marriage, showing how homosocial fellowships foment women's collective rage over misogyny and lack of agency. They represent women as empathetic to one another's struggles, helping each other arrive at solutions by generating collective knowledge through bawdy personal disclosure. And as Phillips notes, many women in these texts "use their idle talk to teach" their friends.[13]

The alewife poem emerged in the second half of the fifteenth century with the staggeringly obscene *Talk of Ten Wives on Their Husbands' Ware* (1453–1500) and the popular *Good Gossip* carols (a. 1500), which survive in two different but related versions across four manuscripts.[14] These poems were followed in the first half of the sixteenth century by Dunbar's *Tretis* and *The*

---

11. Robert Copland, *The Seven Sorowes That Women Have When Theyr Husbondes Be Deade*, in *Robert Copland: Poems*, ed. Mary Carpenter Erler (Toronto: University of Toronto Press, 1993), lines 266, 236; *I shall you tell a full good sport*, in *The Early English Carols*, ed. Richard Leighton Greene, 2nd ed. (Oxford: Clarendon Press, 1977), 249–51, lines 35–36.

12. Phillips, *Transforming Talk*, 120–21.

13. Phillips, *Transforming Talk*, 165.

14. *Now shall youe her a tale fore youre dysport* and *I shall you tell a full good sport* (*DIMEV* 3795 and 2274), in Greene, *Early English Carols*, 249–53. For more on the textual history of

Twa Cummaris (c. 1507), John Skelton's *The Tunnyng of Elynour Rummynge* (c. 1521), "The Fyfth Sorowe" in Robert Copland's *The Seven Sorowes That Women Have When Theyr Husbandes Be Deade* (c. 1526), the "gossip's song" in the Chester *Deluge* play (added 1505-32), and the anonymous *Cryste crosse me spede* (1534?).[15] As Francis Lee Utley observes, the turn of the sixteenth century coincided with a rise in popular misogyny, and texts denigrating women become increasingly plentiful and virulent.[16] Tricia A. McElroy analyzes how Scots Protestant propagandist Robert Sempill drew on the genre to write *The Dialogue of the Twa Wyfeis* (c. 1570), a political poem in which female friends gather in an Edinburgh tavern to drink together and disparage Mary Queen of Scots's supporters.[17] The genre's popularity continued through the seventeenth century with printed broadside ballads such as Samuel Rowlands's *Tis Merrie When Gossips Meete* (1602) and *A Whole Crew of Kind Gossips, All Met to be Merry* (1609), and the anonymous *Fowre Wittie Gossips Disposed to be Merry* (c. 1632), *The Gossips Feast* (1635-36?), *The Seven Merry Wives of London* (1664-1703?), *The Merry Gossips Vindication* (1672-96?), and *The Gossips Meeting* (1674).[18]

---

these poems, which survive in four manuscripts, see Rossell Hope Robbins, "Good Gossips Reunited," *British Museum Quarterly* 27, no. 1/2 (1963): 12-15.

15. John Skelton, *The Tunnyng of Elynour Rummynge* (*DIMEV* 5126), in *The Complete English Poems of John Skelton*, rev. ed., ed. John Scattergood (Liverpool: Liverpool University Press, 2015), 186-200; R. M. Lumiansky and David Mills, eds., *The Chester Mystery Cycle*, 2 vols., Early English Text Society, SS 3 (London: Oxford University Press, 1974), 1:42-56. Two related texts featuring alewife poem conventions include Henry Watson's translation of *The Gospelles of Dystaves* (London: Wynkyn de Worde, 1510) and the anonymously translated *The Fyftene Joyes of Maryage* (London: Wynkyn de Worde, 1507). Phillips discusses these texts, which are both translated from Middle French sources, in *Transforming Talk*, 147-202.

16. In his index of misogynist literature until 1568, Francis Lee Utley notes that 250 of 400 pieces date from 1500 to 1568, as literary antifeminism gathered steam over the course of the fifteenth century before peaking at the turn of the sixteenth. Francis Lee Utley, *The Crooked Rib: An Analytical Index to the Argument about Women in English and Scots Literature to the End of the Year 1568* (Columbus: The Ohio State University Press, 1944; repr., New York: Octagon Books, 1970), 64.

17. Tricia A. McElroy, "The Uses of Genre and Gender in *The Dialogue of the Twa Wyfeis*," in *Premodern Scotland, Literature and Governance 1420-1587: Essays for Sally Mapstone*, ed. Joanna Martin and Emily Wingfield (Oxford: Oxford University Press, 2017), 198-210. A new edition of the *Dialogue* is forthcoming in McElroy's volume of Scottish satirical literature for the Scottish Text Society.

18. Samuel Rowlands, *Tis Merrie When Gossips Meete* (London: W. White, 1602); *A Whole Crew of Kind Gossips, All Met to be Merry* (London: W. Jaggard for John Deane, 1609); *Fowre Wittie Gossips Disposed to be Merry* (London: Printed for H. G., 1632); *The Gossips Feast: or, a merry meeting of women kinde each other greeting* (London: Printed for Thomas Lambert, 1635-36?); *The Seven Merry Wives of London: or, the Gossips' Complaint* (London: Printed for J. Blare, 1664-1703?); *The Merry Gossips Vindication* (London: Printed for P. Brooksby, 1672-96?); and *The Gossips Meeting, or the Merry Market-Women of Taunton* (London: Printed for F. Coles, T. Vere, J. Wright, and J. Clarke, 1674).

One ancestor of the alewife poem is the Anglo-Norman comic debate poem *Gilote e Johane*, performed at Winchester in 1301 and copied in London, British Library, MS Harley 2553 (1331–41).[19] While its titular speakers do not consume alcohol, the poem features other key elements of cummarship such as female friendship, bawdy confession, and peer education. In an overheard dialogue between two friends "talking about their lives" [*de lur vies entreparleyent*] (8), the pleasure-loving Gilote uses graphic sexual details to edify her friend Johane and convince her to forsake her life of chastity in favor of erotic enjoyment. Gilote critiques marriage as entailing confinement to the home, domestic violence, excessive childbearing, and lack of recourse to divorce (53–62). She frames her arguments as explicitly pedagogical when she commands Johane twice to "educate [her]self" [*Afeytez vous, file! Afeitez vous, fole!*] and "come to school" [*venez a l'escole*] (147–48). Johane follows her friend's teachings to the letter and affirms them as gospel. The two women then roam through Winchester together, with Gilote as "headmaster" [*chef mestre*], "preaching" [*precher*] their gospel to their peers (204–5). When a young wife seeks their instruction because her husband has "a prick / That's too pliant and too little" [*il ad un vit / Trop est il plyant e trop petit*] (230–31), Gilote teaches her how to take a lover and avoid punishment for adultery because her husband "can't fuck or fulfill her desire" [*Yl ne puet foutre ne fere talent*] (244; also 262). The wife follows "all the things that Gilote had taught her" [*totes choses qe Gilote la aprist*] (320). Here the Anglo-French term *counsail* [counsel, advice] repeatedly designates Gilote and Johane's carnal peer education (213, 218, 240).[20] The poem ends with Gilote, Johane, and their converts traversing England and Ireland to preach their gospel of feminine pleasure to all the women of the British Isles. In this poem, Gilote and Johane denounce marriage and draw on their corporeal experiences to teach their peers more enjoyable and livable alternatives. The poem frames itself as both entertaining and educational, at once "a jest to please the people" [*une bourde de reheyter la gent*] (342) and valuable "teaching" [*aprise*] (347).

After the Black Death decimated England's population during the period 1348–50, alcohol consumption rose and alehouses proliferated because of increased workers' wages, urbanization, and ale's reclassification as a dietary

---

19. *Gilote e Johane*, in *The Complete Harley 2253 Manuscript: Volume 2*, ed. Susanna Fein with David Raybin and Jan Ziolkowski (Kalamazoo, MI: Medieval Institute Publications, 2014), 156–73. I am grateful to Susanna Fein and David Raybin for bringing this poem to my attention.

20. *The Old French-English Dictionary* (henceforth *OFED*), ed. Alan Hindley, Frederick W. Langley, and Brian J. Levy (Cambridge: Cambridge University Press, 2000), s.v. "conseil" (n.).

staple.²¹ As Judith M. Bennett has shown, women brewed and served ale, ran alehouses, and employed other women, performing the domestic labors of brewing and hospitality on a larger scale outside the home.²² Because of increased employment opportunities in urban centers, adolescent women left their families in the countryside to work in the rapidly growing towns and cities, where they found jobs as servants and tapsters (barmaids) in alehouses or as tipplers (mobile ale-sellers) in the streets and marketplaces. Elizabeth Ewan demonstrates how brewing was similarly feminized in medieval Scotland, with urban women utilizing female friendship networks to sell their ale.²³ As a result of the rise in alehouse culture as well as its feminization, alewife poems began to emerge in the fifteenth century. Like *Gilote e Johane,* these texts center on female friendship and obscene conversation but feature a boozy twist with the addition of alcohol. They frame the alehouse as a physical space that is particularly conducive to fostering women's fellowship and affective expression, functioning similarly to Gaynor's private chamber in the Stanzaic *Morte Arthur* discussed by Usha Vishnuvajjala and Lady Arbo's bower of maidens in Lydia Yaitsky Kertz's essay on *Emaré*.

A Talk of Ten Wives on Their Husbands' Ware (1453–1500), copied in a Cheshire household miscellany in the latter half of the fifteenth century, is one of the earliest surviving alewife poems. In it, ten married women gather at their local alehouse to disparage their husbands' genitalia. The eavesdropping narrator promises to "tell yow a tale, / Howe ten wyffys satt at the nale [alehouse], / And no man hem amonge" (4–6), setting up the genre's foundational elements of entertainment, female fellowship, drinking, and men's ostensible exclusion. Over wine, the women amuse themselves by holding a storytelling competition to determine whose husband's penis is "most worthy ... Today to bere the bell [take the prize]" (11–12). However, the game quickly devolves into a contest over which penis is the worst. The first wife commands

---

21. James A. Galloway, "Driven by Drink? Ale Consumption and the Agrarian Economy of the London Region, c. 1300–1400," in *Food and Eating in Medieval Europe,* ed. Martha Carlin and Joel T. Rosenthal (London: Hambledon Press, 1998), 87–100.

22. Bennett, *Ale, Beer, and Brewsters*; Marjorie Keniston McIntosh, "Drink Work," in *Working Women in English Society 1300–1620* (Cambridge: Cambridge University Press, 2005), 140–81.

23. Elizabeth Ewan, "'For Whatever Ales Ye': Women as Producers and Consumers in Late Medieval Scottish Towns," in *Women in Scotland, c. 1100–c. 1750,* ed. Elizabeth Ewan and Maureen Meikle (East Linton, UK: Tuckwell Press, 1999), 125–35; also Ewan, "Mons Meg and Merchant Meg: Women in Later Medieval Edinburgh," in *Freedom and Authority: Scotland, c. 1050–c. 1650: Historical and Historiographical Essays Presented to Grant G. Simpson,* ed. David Ditchburn and Terry Brotherstone (East Linton, UK: Tuckwell Press, 2000), 131–42, esp. 136–38, 141–42.

her friends, "Talys lett us tell / Of owre hosbondes ware" (9–10), emphasizing the valences of "tale" as personal narrative, entertainment, and instruction.[24] This emphasis on "talys" shared among women also points to the genre's queer undertones: "tayl" was a popular term for the vulva, and their homophonous verbal and genital "talys" were often conflated with one another, as in Lady Mede's characterization as "tikel of hire tail, talewis of tonge" [lascivious of her vulva, talkative of tongue] in William Langland's *Piers Plowman* (c. 1380).[25] The women can thus be read as obtaining erotic pleasure from sharing "talys" with one another in the all-female alehouse space.

A Talk of Ten Wives underscores cummarship's physical and relational intimacy and stages its trademark obscene pedagogy. The narrator emphasizes the women's bond by describing them as "the floke" (43), a term denoting a group of people or a family, and "felowys" (56), which typically names close same-sex companions.[26] He points to the physical intimacy among the women ("The secund wyffe sett her nere," 19; "The ninth wyffe sett hem nyghe," 102) and highlights their affective responses to one another's bawdy disclosures. One wife is "full woo" [emphatically upset] (31) upon hearing about her friend's lack of pleasure. Another is "full fayn / When sche hard her felowys playn" (55–56), with "fayn" indicating that she is filled with either eagerness to share her experience or pleasure at knowing that she is not alone in her struggles.[27] The rhyming link between "fayn" and "playn" emphasizes the consolatory possibilities in shared complaint. The women repeatedly articulate the obscenities "pentyll" (35, 105) and "tarse" (58, 62, 94)—the most explicit terms for penises in Middle English—in their confessions, at once embodying misogynist stereotypes of women's transgressive speech and using the shock of obscenity to underscore the magnitude of their displeasure with marital monogamy. They direct animosity at their husbands with repeated curses, their anger contrasting sharply with the affection they show one another and illuminating how they view the all-female alehouse fellowship as a salutary substitute for the loneliness of marriage. The women use the first-person domestic plural to name their husbands and their penises, and their references to "owre syre" cast their individual experiences as a collective articulation of displeasure that can be read as critiquing the institution of marriage as a whole (34, 44, 61, 84,

---

24. *Middle English Dictionary* (henceforth *MED*), s.v. "tale" (n.), 1(a), 1(d), 3(d).

25. William Langland, *Piers Plowman: The B Version*, rev. ed., ed. George Kane and E. Talbot Donaldson (Berkeley: University of California Press, 1988), III.131; on "tail" as a genital term, see *MED*, s.v. "tail" (n.), 1b(c).

26. *MED*, s.v. "flok" (n.[1]), 2(a) and 2(b). On the homosocial valences of "felawe" for men, see Harris, *Obscene Pedagogies*, 31–36.

27. *MED*, s.v. "fain" (adj.), 1(a) and 2(a).

94). As I argue elsewhere, we can read obscene conversations in alewife poems as a form of feminist consciousness-raising, with each woman sharing her private experience in order to generate knowledge about deeply entrenched inequalities that affect them all.[28] The women also perform sexual education by sharing strategies for manipulating their husbands' members: one discloses, "I bow hym, I bend hym, / I stroke hym, I wend him . . . I torn hym twofold" (108–9, 112). Another relates, "I lyrke [squeeze] hym up with my hond" (72), telling her friends how she attempts to obtain pleasure. The women portray corporeal experience as a form of education: for example, the eighth wife is described as "well i-taghte" (90), which meant both "educated, learned, wise" and "experienced."[29] The wives generate mutual comfort through drinking together, with periodic calls to "fyll the wyne" (80) and references to alehouse furnishings ("the bynch," 78).

William Dunbar's *The Twa Cummaris*, surviving in four manuscripts, portrays women's friendship as both mutually affirming and dangerously subversive. It features two women drinking wine in front of a fire on the first day of Lent: "Drinkande the wyne sat cummaris tua. / The tane couthe to the tothir complene" [Two female friends sat drinking the wine. / The one began to complain to the other], we are told (2–3).[30] By naming them "the tane" and "the tothir," Dunbar portrays the women as inseparably paired. Their wine-fueled conversation is at once confessional, consolatory, and didactic. Emphasizing the closeness of their bond, they address each other as "cummar" [intimate female friend] a total of four times (9, 11, 16, 21). They share marital advice and encourage each other to break Lenten fasting rules, demonstrating how women's friendships were imagined to subvert both patriarchal and religious authority. One of the woman declares, "Cummar, be glaid baitht ewin and morrow . . . And lat your husband dre the sorrow" [Cummar, be joyful both evening and morning, And let your husband suffer the sorrow] (16, 19), offering encouragement and ordering her friend to enjoy herself while her spouse suffers for her transgressions. In response, her friend affirms her instruction and shares intimate details about her sex life:

"Your counsaile, commar, is gud," quod scho.
"Ale is to tene him that I do;
In bed he is nocht wortht ane bane.
File anis the glas and drink me to." (21–24)

---

28. Harris, *Obscene Pedagogies*, 177–78.
29. *MED*, s.v. "techen" (v.), 5a(e) and 6(b).
30. Dunbar, *Twa Cummaris* (*DIMEV* 4495), in Bawcutt, *William Dunbar*, 1:180–81.

["Your counsel, cummar, is good," she said.
"Everything I do is to make him suffer.
In bed he is not worth a bean.
Fill the glass once and drink to me."]

She confesses that her chief aim is to "tene" her husband, choosing a verb that means "to annoy, to afflict, to cause harm" and embodying antifeminist stereotypes of wifely shrewishness.[31] Like the women in *A Talk of Ten Wives on Their Husbands' Ware*, she disparages her spouse as worthless in bed and wishes him suffering as punishment for his failure to satisfy her. She links bawdy homosocial sex-talk with shared alcohol consumption by calling for a refill and encouraging her friend to drink with her. The poem closes with the two women drinking wine from a shared cup while plotting how to circumvent Lenten dietary restrictions. They consume "tua quartis" of "wyne out of ane chopin stoip" [a half-pint measure] (26–27), a feat requiring that the drinking vessel be filled at least eight times.

The incomplete *Cryste crosse me spede* does not even mention men, instead focusing solely on the merry solace created by women's drinking fellowship.[32] The poem names itself twice as *Cryste crosse me spede A. B. C.*, the addition of the pedagogical tag "A. B. C." echoing instructional texts aimed at young men such as the extremely popular *A. B. C. of Aristotle*.[33] In this text printed by Wynkyn de Worde, which is missing its middle pages, a group of women wielding domestic implements such as distaffs, reels, and bread peels descends upon their local alehouse like an army: "A grete company of gossyps garded on a route / Went to besyge an alehous rounde about," we are told. Martial terms such as "company," "garded," "route," and "besyge" suggest cummarship's militant possibilities and its capacity to engender social disruption through cummars banding together. Dame Molde the Greate commands, "Nowe give us drynke aboute," with the adverb "aboute" [to all, in a circular course] emphasizing the group's collectivity.[34] Her friend Joan responds, "Thou shalte

---

31. *DOST*, s.v. "tene" (v.).

32. *Cryste crosse me spede* (*DIMEV* 986) (London: Wynkyn de Worde, 1534?), now at Princeton University's Firestone Library (STC 14546.5); indexed in William A. Ringler Jr., *Bibliography and Index of English Verse Printed 1476–1558* (London: Mansell, 1988), no. 1741. This text was also copied from print to manuscript in the seventeenth century in Oxford, Bodleian Library, MS Eng.poet.e.97, 207–13.

33. *The A. B. C. of Aristotle* (*DIMEV* 6654), in *Early English Meals and Manners*, ed. Frederick J. Furnivall, Early English Text Society, OS 32 (London: Oxford University Press for the Early English Text Society, 1868), 260–61.

34. *MED*, s.v. "aboute(n" (adv.), 2(a), 5(d).

not drynke alone," portraying drinking together as a meaningful act of solidarity. The narrator casts the women's alehouse gathering as a form of alcohol-based kinship by closing with the declaration "Here endeth the kyndred of cuppe royall," centering the women's "kyndred" [family, closely knit group] on their sharing of the "cuppe."[35] This emphasis on fictive kinship generated by sharing drink in the alehouse posits cummarship as a queer family of chosen kinswomen. The narrator wishes that all readers might experience the joys of cummarship: "All ye be present, God sende you suche an ende / Ones to be gossip lyke or you hense wende," they declare in their closing benediction. This address to those who are "present" before they go "hense" points to how these texts themselves, when read or sung in alehouses, could engender cummarship among living bodies and with fictional figures through sharing drink and "game and gle" together.

"AND NO MAN HEM AMONGE": CREATING CUMMARSHIP

Cummarship, the model of female friendship central to alewife texts, comes from the Middle Scots term *cummar*, which designated "a female intimate, a woman gossip."[36] It originated from the Old French *comere*, meaning "godmother; (as friendly appellation) friend, neighbor."[37] As Gail McMurray Gibson observes, the requirement that godmothers be present at a godchild's birth generated intimate fellowships of women, since close female friends and relatives gathered to assist the laboring mother and share wine and food with one another.[38] *Cummar* is a fitting term for my analysis because it encompasses the generative, knowledge-building, and empowering, as well as the misogynist and disruptive, social valences of this female friendship model. On one hand, it is a term of gendered intimacy that women use to address each other. In Dunbar's *Tretis*, the women "carpit full cummerlik [chatted like sisters] with cop going round" (510), with the adverb *cummerlik* denoting a relational style of affectionate same-sex speech accompanied by drinking.[39] A popular Middle Scots dance song states, "Commer ga ye before, commer ga ye, / If ye wil

---

35. *MED*, s.v. "kinrede" (n.), 1(a), 2.
36. *DOST*, s.v. "cummer" (n.[2]).
37. *OFED*, s.v. "comere."
38. Gail McMurray Gibson, "Scene and Obscene: Seeing and Performing Late Medieval Childbirth," *Journal of Medieval and Early Modern Studies* 29, no. 1 (1999): 7–24.
39. Harris, *Obscene Pedagogies*, 181; Phillips, *Transforming Talk*, 143.

not ga before, commer let me."[40] Here, participants perform "cummarship" by dancing and singing together, the rhyming pronouns "ye" and "me" emphasizing their bond.

At the same time that it served as a positive designation of female fellowship, *cummar* also functioned as a term of misogynist abuse. In many texts, it links women to witchcraft and depicts them as violent, quarrelsome shrews. These connections to both sisterly intimacy and antifeminist stereotype illustrate how "cummarship" in these texts both portrays female friendship as a desirable alternative to marriage and denigrates it as deviant and disruptive. For example, in Alexander Montgomerie and Sir Patrick Hume of Polwarth's *The Flyting of Montgomerie and Polwart* (c. 1582), Montgomerie narrates Polwarth's supposed discovery as a foundling by a group of "wirdsisteris" [witches] (II.27). He names the witches repeatedly as "cummaris" (II.207, 209, 229, 278) who cast spells using "deid menis memberis" (II.178), associating the term *cummar* with witchcraft and castration. Dunbar and Walter Kennedy's *The Flyting of Dunbar and Kennedy* (c. 1505) features a conversation in which one woman warns her friend, "I reid yow, cummer, tak in your lynning clais" [I advise you, cummar, take your linen cloths inside (to protect them from theft)] (224). This text ties cummarship to pedagogy and domesticity with the instructional verb *reid* and the woman's concern for her friend's linens, while its disparaging designation of the women as "carlingis" [decrepit, lower-class old women] (221) aligns the term with popular misogyny directed at old women in particular.[41] Finally, *cummar* carried valences of collective female drunkenness, illustrated by Scottish Catholic controversialist John Hamilton's religious tract referring to "sipplers of guid sueit wyne" [imbibers of good sweet wine] who "tipple willinglie [eagerly] at their Comeres banquets."[42]

As illustrated by *cummar*'s rich and varied web of cultural associations—including witchcraft, drunkenness, shrewishness, intimate same-sex friendship, and support of vulnerable women who have just given birth—cummarship entails both unruliness and fiercely forged community. It aligns with Alice Walker's formulation of *womanist*, which signifies "a woman who loves other women, sexually and/or nonsexually" and designates "outrageous,

---

40. Anderson, *James Carmichaell Collection*, no. 429. David Calderwood's *History of the Kirk of Scotland* (1659) features a scene in which the devil sings these words to a mostly female group of witches, again tying the term *cummar* to witchcraft: "Playing to them upon a trumpe, [the devil] said, 'Cummer, goe ye before; cummer, goe yee,' and so they daunced." David Calderwood, *The History of the Kirk of Scotland Volume 5: 1589–1599*, ed. Rev. Thomas Thomson (Edinburgh: Printed for the Wodrow Society, 1844), 216.

41. *DOST*, s.v. "red(e" v., 1.

42. John Hamilton, *A facile traictise, contenand, first: ane infallible reul to discerne trew from fals religion* (Louvain: Laurence Kellam, 1600), 48.

audacious, courageous, or *willful* behavior."[43] Cummarship's collective feminine willfulness is united in staunch opposition to husbands and marriage as well as to religious and cultural rules governing feminine behavior. As Sara Ahmed notes, the communities created by cummarship illustrate "how a *we* can be brought forth by the willingness to go the wrong way."[44]

Same-sex pedagogy, particularly regarding erotic pleasure and marital relationships, is central to cummarship, since *cummar* was linked to peer instruction regarding spousal disobedience through its frequent alliterative pairing with *counsall* [counsel, advice].[45] These texts highlight cummarship's educational capacities by drawing on popular depictions of the alehouse as a perverse pedagogical space, such as *The Book of Vices and Virtues*'s assertion that "the taverne is the develes scole hous."[46] Sir David Lyndsay's *Ane Satyre of the Thrie Estaitis* (1552) depicts cummarly teaching between two friends, a shoemaker's wife and a tailor's wife, who repeatedly address each other as "cummar" while beating their husbands in an alehouse after they discover the men drinking with a strange woman.[47] By linking *cummar* with *counsall*, they tie their sisterly bond to peer instruction. When the tailor's wife expresses dismay at their husbands' behavior, her friend declares, "Cummar, this is my counsall, lo: / Ding ye the tane, and I the uther" [You strike the one man, and I the other] (1325–26).[48] Lyndsay imagines "cummar's counsall" as instructing wifely willfulness; here, women teach one another how to be shrews who defy their husbands. After they beat their men with distaffs, the women address each other as "cummar" while celebrating their marital violence and planning to enjoy good wine together:

---

43. Alice Walker, *In Search of Our Mothers' Gardens: Womanist Prose* (New York: Harcourt, 1983), xi.

44. Sara Ahmed, *Living a Feminist Life* (Durham, NC: Duke University Press, 2017), 82.

45. Dunbar's Wedo uses this pairing to illustrate how she taught her friends how to control their husbands: "Than said I to my cummaris in counsall about, / 'Se how I cabeld yone cout with a kene brydill'" [Then I said to my council of cummars, / "See how I secured that colt with a sharp bridle"] (353–54). See also Dunbar, *Twa Cummaris*, line 21, and "counsell" in *I shall you tell a full good sport*, line 82.

46. W. Nelson Francis, ed., *The Book of Vices and Virtues*, Early English Text Society, OS 217 (London: Oxford University Press for Early English Text Society, 1968), 54. *A Myrour to Lewede Men and Wymmen* similarly claims that "taverne may be cleped the develes scole," in Venetia Nelson, ed., *A Myrour to Lewede Men and Wymmen: A Prose Version of the 'Speculum vitae,'* Middle English Texts 14 (Heidelberg: Carl Winter, 1981), 210.

47. David Lyndsay, *Ane Satyre of the Thrie Estaitis*, ed. Roderick Lyall (Edinburgh: Canongate, 1989).

48. Lyndsay's women address each other as "cummar" during the alehouse beatings in lines 1364 and 1365.

Sowtars Wyfe: Sen of our cairls we have the victorie,
    Quhat is your counsell, cummer, that be done?
Taylours Wyfe: Send for gude wine and hald our selfis merie:
    I hauld this ay best, cummer, by Sanct Clone! (1376–79)[49]

[*Shoemaker's Wife*: Since we have the victory over our husbands,
    What is your advice, cummer, that we do?
Tailor's Wife: Send for good wine and keep ourselves merry;
    I consider this to be always best, cummer, by St. Clone!]

Once again, "cummer[s]" provide each other "counsell" that uplifts body as well as spirit, underscoring these texts' recurring connections between friendship, pedagogy, and drinking. An anonymous political broadside ballad titled *The Lamentatioun of Lady Scotland* (1572) similarly features a scene of "cummers" sharing transgressive "counsall" to undermine their husbands.[50] The allegorical female speaker warns men what their wives have been doing in secret: "ane yule evin your wyfes to counsall went" [one Yule evening your wives went to council] (301), she says, with the women's clandestine all-female "counsall" operating as a transgressive inversion of all-male meetings of secular or religious authorities. At this gathering, a lawyer's wife addresses the women as "cummers" (303, 315) and instructs them to entertain the sins of pride and envy in defiance of their virtuous husbands.[51] The women's spouses are "Burges, Craftis, & Merchand men, / And . . . Commounis, with . . . hynd yemen" [burgesses, craftsmen, and merchant men, and common men, with farmworker yeomen] (293–94). They come from the urban mercantile class as well as common and rural working social orders, portraying this "counsall" of "cummers" as facilitating bonds across class divisions. Cummars use their "counsall" to teach each other how to overcome and defy men, according to alehouse texts portraying female friendship as dangerous and disruptive to marriages. But we can also read these moments of "counsall" as women teaching each other how to navigate the abuses enabled by marital power imbalances and larger structural inequalities.

In addition to their portrayal of pedagogy among cummars, these texts perform another model of same-sex peer education, this one directed by the

---

49. "Cummer" also appears during this exchange in lines 1380 and 1392.

50. P. R., *The Lamentatioun of Lady Scotland, compylit by hir self, speiking in maner of ane Epistle, in the Moneth of Marche, the year of God 1572* (St. Andrews: Robert Lekpreuik, 1572), in *Satirical Poems of the Time of the Reformation*, ed. James Craunston, 4 vols. (Edinburgh: William Blackwood and Sons, 1890–93), 2:226–39.

51. "Cummers" additionally occurs in lines 322, 328, 329.

genre's eavesdropping male narrator to other men. He violates women's private spaces and reports back to his peers, teaching them what women do and say among themselves. One narrator highlights this model of man-to-man instruction when he informs his male listeners, "This is the thowght [frame of mind] that gossippis take" and purports to disclose their practices of habitual tavern-going and husband-deception.[52] Reflecting their framing by male speakers who teach other men about women's secret drunken revels, these texts were largely authored, copied, and printed by men, and they dramatize male fears that women's conversations are focused solely on mocking penises and strategizing how to overthrow men. But even though they are produced within a rotten misogynist framework, alewife poems nonetheless manage to portray the joys of cummarship as irresistible, as a source of "dysport" and "jest" for all who read them.[53] Rather than simply confirming tired stereotypes about women's collective depravity, these texts end up peering longingly through the alehouse window at the groups of women drinking and laughing raucously inside.

Cummarship entails a shared discourse connecting friendship, peer instruction, drinking, and mutual consolation. These texts feature intimate terms such as *cummar, sister,* and *gossip* (or *good gossip*) used by female friends to address one another, often coupled with *rede* or *counsall* to designate same-sex teaching. They depict women encouraging each other to "be glad" and generating "good chere" and "comfort" through fellowship, verbal solace, instruction, and drinking together, often with the vocabulary of alcohol consumption such as measures and drinking vessels ("pot," "cup," "quart," "galoun," "glas") and types of drink ("wyne," "muscadell" [sweet wine], "malwasy" [a type of wine], "good ale"). For example, Copland's *Seven Sorowes that Women Have When Theyr Husbondes Be Deade* features a recently bereaved widow who summons her "gossyps . . . her owne selfe for to chere" (225). The women arrive promptly to comfort their friend: "And whan the gossyppes assembled be, / 'What chere, goode gossip?' than sayeth she and she. / 'Be ye of good chere . . .'" (241–43). They attempt to lift the widow's spirits, with the designation "she and she" emphasizing their gendered collectivity. They share "a quart of Muscadel" (236) and encourage their friend: "'Alacke good woman, take it not so hevyly,' / sayth her gossyppes . . . Thus this wydowe they comfort every day" (273–74, 276). Dunbar's three women similarly link drinking with sisterly solace: "Thai drank and did away dule . . . Thai swapit of the sueit wyne" [They drank and chased away sadness . . . They quickly

---

52. *I shall you tell a full good sport*, line 124.
53. *Now shall youe her a tale for youre dysport*, line 1; *Cryste crosse me spede*, line 1.

downed the sweet wine] (242–43), we are told. By linking cummarship's foundational elements of sisterhood, pedagogy, and drinking and casting them as sources of merriment, these texts transform negative associations of women with drunkenness to positive portrayals of communal feminine drinking generating laughter and wisdom.

Finally, these texts' portrayals of same-sex bonds can be usefully analyzed through a queer interpretive framework, using Lochrie's claim that "'queer' cites a disruption of heteronormativity."[54] While the alehouse conversations in these texts are often (but not always) aggressively heterosexual—as my students always note, these poems do *not* pass the Bechdel test—they nonetheless critique heteronormativity by emphasizing the primacy of same-sex bonds, portraying all-female spaces from which men are ostensibly excluded, and depicting marriage as marked by violence, dissatisfaction, and lack of agency for women. The cummars in these poems do not seek their husbands' affection or express care for them. Instead, they teach one another how to resist men, as when they instruct each other to take circuitous routes to and from the alehouse in order to evade their suspicious spouses.[55] While these unruly wives embody derogatory stereotypes of women as conniving and disobedient, they are also women who see each other as the most important sources of love, intimacy, wisdom, and support. The sole example of a woman in an alehouse text who does *not* despise her husband is in Copland's *Seven Sorowes,* where her spouse is dead; here, the narrator suggests that he was "unto her unkynde" (217) and is beloved only because he is deceased. Sad that she now must dine alone, the widow calls her gossips and neighbors to join her, portraying her community of cummars as a superior replacement for marital companionship. In some alewife poems, women abandon their household duties to drink and make merry with each other, privileging cummarship's homosocial bonds over marital expectations.[56] Lochrie traces how medieval depictions of female fellowship with no men present are often shaped by the misogynist logic that women's natural carnal perversion renders them prone to sexual contact with one another.[57] She also notes how John Gower's rendering of Ovid's tale of same-sex love between Iphis and Ianthe in his *Confessio Amantis* (c. 1390) uses the designation "sche and sche" to characterize the women's erotic bond;

---

54. Karma Lochrie, "Preface," in *The Lesbian Premodern,* ed. Noreen Giffney, Michelle M. Sauer, and Diane Watt (New York: Palgrave Macmillan, 2011), xiii–xviii, at xiii.

55. *I shall you tell a full good sport,* lines 40–45, 118–19.

56. See the final stanzas of *Now shall youe her a tale fore youre dysport,* where the women forsake their domestic "werke" to pass out drunkenly instead.

57. Karma Lochrie, "Between Women," in *The Cambridge Companion to Medieval Women's Writing,* ed. Carolyn Dinshaw and David Wallace (Cambridge: Cambridge University Press, 2003), 70–88, at 79–81.

this same pronoun pairing appears in Copland's *Seven Sorowes* to name the women who arrive to console their widowed friend.[58] Alewife poems such as *Cryste crosse me spede* portray men as inconsequential by failing to mention them at all; instead, they emphasize the convivial pleasures of women drinking and making merry together.

CONTEMPORARY CONNECTIONS: "THE KYNDRED OF CUPPE ROYALE"

While the cummarship in these alehouse texts is culturally and historically specific, connected to social conditions arising in the aftermath of the Black Death, we can nonetheless identify more recent versions in order to explore its ongoing significance. One important transhistorical connection to premodern cummarship lies in twentieth-century lesbian bar cultures, where queer all-female communities formed beginning in the 1930s and 1940s.[59] The lesbian bar renders explicit the medieval alehouse's queer undertones of same-sex physical and relational intimacy as well as its political possibilities.[60] Lesbian bars have historically been owned, operated, and staffed by women, mirroring medieval alehouses in functioning as spaces where women held social and economic power and enabling their communities to be fostered by those who have a deep personal stake in them.[61] For example, Nancy Novak worked as a bartender at Attitudes, a lesbian bar in St. Louis, before opening her own now-shuttered lesbian bar Novak's, where I spent many merry weekends dancing with my roommates in the mid-aughts. The documentary *Last Call at Maud's*, which depicts the final night at a long-running lesbian bar in San Francisco, is narrated by Rikki Streicher, the bar's owner.[62] And in a recent list of lesbian bars still operating in the US, all were owned by women.[63] Because of their status as alehouse spaces run by women, typically with "no man hem amonge,"

---

58. John Gower, *Confessio Amantis: Volume 2*, ed. Russell A. Peck and trans. Andrew Galloway (Kalamazoo, MI: Medieval Institute Publications, 2013), IV.479; Lochrie, "Between Women," 82.

59. I am indebted to Steven Kruger for first suggesting this connection to me and encouraging me to read Joan Nestle, and to Colby Gordon for suggesting additional readings.

60. For a useful overview of scholarship on lesbian bar culture, see Kelly Hankin, *The Girls in the Back Room: Looking at the Lesbian Bar* (Minneapolis: University of Minnesota Press, 2002), esp. ix–xxv.

61. Nan Alamilla Boyd, *Wide-Open Town: A History of Queer San Francisco to 1965* (Berkeley: University of California Press, 2003), 82–83.

62. *Last Call at Maud's*, dir. Paris Poirier (Frameline, 1993).

63. Kristen Wong, "The Curious Disappearance of the Lesbian Bar," *The Story Exchange*, June 28, 2019.

lesbian bars created the conditions for community formation and marginalized group consciousness. At the same time, the lesbian bar's susceptibility to police intrusion echoed attempts by male medieval civic authorities to regulate medieval alewives by taxing their ale, testing their measures, and levying age restrictions on tapsters.[64]

Lesbian bars in cities across the US were integral for fostering shared identity, political solidarity, and collective action throughout the twentieth century. In their history of Buffalo's working-class lesbian community, Elizabeth Lapovsky Kennedy and Madeline D. Davis argue that "bars . . . and public house parties were central to twentieth-century lesbian resistance" because they facilitated both socializing and political consciousness.[65] They state that "bars were the only possible place for working-class lesbians to congregate outside private homes" during these decades, and they trace how Buffalo's lesbian bars were important spaces for drinking, dancing, friendship, erotic partnership, and community formation. Nan Alamilla Boyd argues in her history of lesbian bar culture in post–World War II San Francisco that "the heightened group consciousness that . . . lesbians secured in bars and taverns in the 1930s and 1940s enabled them to resist more forcefully the repressive policing and prosecution of the 1950s," illustrating cummarship's powerful political potential.[66] And Janet Kahn and Patricia A. Gozemba emphasize how lesbian bar culture in a working-class neighborhood bar near Boston generated strong friendships and love relationships and provided a means of psychic survival, much as alehouses in medieval texts furnished solace and generated survival strategies for the women who congregated there.[67]

The lesbian activist organization known as the Daughters of Bilitis powerfully illustrates the political possibilities of twentieth-century lesbian bar

---

64. Bennett, *Ale, Beer, and Brewsters*; Wack, "Women, Work, and Plays."

65. Elizabeth Lapovsky Kennedy and Madeline D. Davis, *Boots of Leather, Slippers of Gold: The History of a Lesbian Community*, 20th anniv. ed. (New York: Routledge, 2014), 29.

66. Boyd, *Wide-Open Town*, 101.

67. Janet Kahn and Patricia A. Gozemba, "In and around the Lighthouse: Working-Class Lesbian Bar Culture in the 1950s and 1960s," in *Gendered Domains: Rethinking Public and Private in Women's History*, ed. Dorothy O. Helly and Susan M. Reverby (Ithaca, NY: Cornell University Press, 1992), 90–106. See also Rochella Thorpe, "The Changing Face of Lesbian Bars in Detroit, 1938–1965," in *Creating a Place for Ourselves: Lesbian, Gay, and Bisexual Community Histories*, ed. Brett Beemyn (New York: Routledge, 1997), 165–81; Joan Nestle, *A Restricted Country*, 2nd ed. (San Francisco: Cleis Press, 2003), 26–28, 92–113. Audre Lorde traces how New York City's lesbian bar culture was the only place to find queer community in the 1950s and critiques its overwhelming whiteness and racism in *Zami: A New Spelling of My Name* (Freedom, CA: Crossing Press, 1982), 186–87, 220–26. Thorpe likewise highlights the Detroit lesbian bar scene's racism and discusses the importance of house parties for African American lesbians in "'A House Where Queers Go': African-American Lesbian Nightlife in Detroit, 1940–1975," in *Inventing Lesbian Cultures in America*, ed. Ellen Lewin (Boston: Beacon, 1996), 40–61.

cummarship and underscores how it, like premodern cummarship, can foster peer pedagogy that empowers and edifies its participants and provides them valuable knowledge to challenge their marginalized position. Founded in 1955, DOB was originally intended to be an exclusive social club serving as an alternative to San Francisco's lesbian bars, which were subject to police raids after California's Alcoholic Beverage Control agency was formed that same year.[68] The eight founders sought to create a community for friends and friends-of-friends to drink, talk, dance, and "mix socializing with social action."[69] Each new member had to apply for inclusion and needed to be "a gay girl of good moral character," at least twenty-one years old, and "interested in promoting an educational program on the subject of sex variation, and for sex variants."[70] DOB's statement of purpose outlined a commitment to educating its members as well as the public about lesbian rights. In order to facilitate this education, the organization established a library of lesbian fiction and nonfiction for members.[71] The Daughters of Bilitis illustrate how cummarship's combination of shared drinking, female fellowship, and peer pedagogy, which I have traced throughout this essay, became explicitly political and explicitly queer. While the raucous women's alehouse fellowships in the premodern texts are fictional—albeit grounded in the alehouse's real-life feminization—they nonetheless function as important precursors for imagining how the alehouse can be a place of inclusion, community-building, and conviviality that leads to necessary social change.

At the end of *Cryste crosse me spede,* the gossips' outspoken joy at creating cummarship together is transformed to bitter sadness when they must leave the alehouse: "To the ale they went with hey troly loly / But whan they came home theyr songe was not so / Theyr songe was of sorowe and most hatefull wo," reads the poem's title-page summary.[72] The poem's ending emphasizes the women's sorrow at leaving the company of cummars: "Forsothe thys partynge maketh theyr hertes to blede," notes the narrator. A similar sense of nostalgia for lost community pervades *Last Call at Maud's,* lamenting how the bar was forced to close in 1989 after the AIDS epidemic, declining business, and the owner's cancer diagnosis. The decline of lesbian bars in the US was accelerated by the COVID-19 pandemic, leading to the formation of a fundraising cam-

---

68. Marcia M. Gallo, *Different Daughters: A History of the Daughters of Bilitis and the Rise of the Lesbian Rights Movement* (Emeryville, CA: Seal Press, 2007), xliv.
69. Gallo, *Different Daughters,* 3–6.
70. Gallo, *Different Daughters,* 4, 7.
71. Gallo, *Different Daughters,* 10.
72. For more on this nostalgia associated with lesbian-produced film documentary portrayals of lesbian bars, see Hankin, *The Girls in the Back Room,* 114–56.

paign called the Lesbian Bar Project to preserve the fourteen establishments that remained across the country; they claimed that "without space, we lose power, validity, communal safety, and access to intergenerational dialogue."[73] This profound sorrow at leaving the alehouse space, with its intimate fellowship, raucous laughter, and free-flowing drinks, concludes many alewife poems, where the cummars disperse to homes where they do not feel supported and are in some cases subject to spousal violence.[74] But the survival of alewife poems, and the potential for communities of feminist medievalists to read them together and analyze them merrily over wine at academic conferences, means that the psychic space of the alehouse is always there, that the gossips do not need to part, that we can continue to make cummarship's energizing, illuminating, and convivial connections across space and time.

---

73. Sarah Marloff, "The Rise and Fall of America's Lesbian Bars," *Smithsonian Magazine*, January 21, 2021, https://www.smithsonianmag.com/travel/rise-and-fall-americas-lesbian-bars-180976801/; "The Lesbian Bar Project," https://www.lesbianbarproject.com/ (accessed May 13, 2021).

74. *I shall you tell a full good sport* and *Now shall youe her a tale fore youre dysport* both feature women who face abusive husbands when they return home from the alehouse.

CHAPTER 9

"All These Relationships between Women"

Chaucer and the Bechdel Test for Female Friendship

KARMA LOCHRIE

> All these relationships between women, I thought, rapidly recalling the splendid gallery of fictitious women, are too simple. So much has been left out, unattempted. And I tried to remember any case in the course of my reading where two women are represented as friends.
>
> —Virginia Woolf, *A Room of One's Own*[1]

> "I only go to a movie if it satisfies three basic requirements," she explains. "**One,** it has to have at least two women in it, who, **two,** talk to each other about, **three,** something besides a man."
>
> —Alison Bechdel, *Dykes to Watch Out For*[2]

THE FAMOUS GRAPHIC ARTIST and MacArthur genius-grant recipient Alison Bechdel attributes her idea for what is now popularly known as the Bechdel test for movies to her friend, Liz Wallace, who, in turn, "stole it herself from Virginia Woolf." Bechdel recounts the moment in book 5 of *A Room of One's Own* in which Woolf imagines a sentence by a fictitious female author in a fictitious book: "Chloe liked Olivia." This sentence inspires Woolf's reflection on the sheer anomaly of the fact that "Chloe liked Olivia perhaps for the first time in literature," and she contrasts this with Cleopatra's jealousy of Octavia and all the ways in which female friendship is "simplified, conventionalized, if one dared say it, absurdly."[3] Bechdel's 1985 translation of Woolf's observation into an indirect critique of the limited range of female relationships in movies leads

---

1. Virginia Woolf, *A Room of One's Own* (New York: Harcourt Brace & Co, 1981), 82.
2. Alison Bechdel, "The Rule," *Dykes to Watch Out For* (Ithaca, NY: Firebrand Books, 1985), 22.
3. Woolf, *Room of One's Own,* 82.

her to lay out the three criteria for a movie worth seeing—three criteria that seek to capture the spirit of Woolf's "Chloe liked Olivia." The triadic test aims to define as much as it indirectly critiques in contemporary cinema: the representation of female friendships and relationships that are not centered around men and heterosexual relationships. What is, perhaps, most telling about the Bechdel test is that it did not really become a "thing" until the 2000s, according to Bechdel herself. In 2021 it is widely and familiarly known to most college students, if my own experience is indicative, and this suggests that the critique remains largely relevant. In addition, there have been recent adaptations of the Bechdel test to include representations of people of color (the "DuVernay test") and calls for a higher bar for representing women in film.[4]

Like modern movies, medieval texts seem characterized less by "all these relationships between women" than they are by a paucity of female companionship. Either representations of female friendships in medieval texts are so rare that scholars have hardly addressed them at all, even during the heyday of feminist scholarship in the 1980s and 1990s, or we simply do not know how to recognize them when they do appear in medieval texts. Using the Bechdel test as a guide might not help, as it would more likely eliminate most literature that medievalists write about and teach. Chaucer's *Canterbury Tales,* for example, would probably fail the Bechdel test. Although it exceeds the two-women requirement easily, with three female pilgrims out of twenty-nine—the Wife of Bath, the Prioress, and the Second Nun—these figures do not speak to one another anywhere in the storytelling frame of the *Canterbury Tales.* Indeed, if the Bechdel test is applied to Chaucer's other works, it would shine an accusatory light on the *Legend of Good Women,* a work that, for all its professed enshrinement of the goodness of women, explicitly and relentlessly positions that goodness within the perfidy of men's faithlessness and untruth. Bechdel's test would also find fault with the story of Criseyde in that famous story of the "double sorwe of Troilus," in which, with the exception of the fleeting appearance of the female book club at the beginning of book 2, the heroine is isolated from peer women and even men to face Pandarus's manipulations and her own exile at the hands of her fellow Trojans alone. Two of three of Chaucer's dream poems entail the relegation of female characters offstage—to death, in the case of the *Book of the Duchess,* and to the final lines of the *Parliament of Fowles*—as the absent inspirations for masculine intimacy and performances of courtly love. "So much has been left out, unattempted," I can imagine Vir-

---

4. Manohla Dargis coins the former after filmmaker Ava DuVernay in "Sundance Fights Tide with Films like 'The Birth of a Nation,'" *New York Times* January 29, 2016. For calls for more rigorous standards for "women's stories," see Alyssa Rosenberg, "In 2019, It's Time to Move Beyond the Bechdel Test," *Washington Post,* December 21, 2018.

ginia Woolf saying of Chaucer's poetry, shaking her head in despair or, alternatively, concocting a hypothetical medieval Mary Carmichael.

In the case of medieval literature and culture, scholarship has mostly focused on spiritual friendships, such as those between mystics and their advisors, or between fellow nuns, mystics, and religious women.[5] In this volume, for example, Jennifer Brown extends the way we understand spiritual friendships among women in terms of collaboration, support, and community, while Alexandra Verini delineates a collective agency among women at Syon Abbey. Some studies of female friendship from the late 1990s and early 2000s, including my own, aimed at queering female friendships by invoking their erotic possibilities.[6] Studies of secular women's friendship as they emerge from historical documents and literary representations are still relatively nonexistent.[7] This is especially noticeable in Chaucer scholarship, where the study of medieval associational forms especially in *The Canterbury Tales* has loomed large since the publications of two important studies, Paul Strohm's *Social Chaucer* (1989) and David Wallace's *Chaucerian Polity* (1994).[8] Together but in differ-

---

5. For example, see Ulrike Wiethaus, "In Search of Medieval Women's Friendships: Hildegard of Bingen's Letters to Her Female Contemporaries, in *Maps of Flesh and Light: The Religious Experience of Medieval Women Mystics,* ed. Wiethaus (Syracuse, NY: Syracuse University Press, 1993), 93–111; E. Ann Matter, "'My Sister, My Spouse: Woman-Identified Women in Medieval Christianity," *Journal of Feminist Studies in Religion* 2 (1986): 81–93; John M. Jeep, "Among Friends? Early German Evidence of Friendship among Women," *Women in German Yearbook: Feminist Studies in German Literature & Culture* 14 (1999): 1–18.

6. Karma Lochrie, "Between Women," in *The Cambridge Companion to Women's Writing,* ed. Carolyn Dinshaw and David Wallace (Cambridge: Cambridge University Press, 2003), 70–88. See also Lisa M. C. Weston, "Virgin Desires: Reading a Homoerotics of Female Monastic Community," in *The Lesbian Premodern,* ed. Noreen Giffney, Michelle M. Sauer, and Diane Watt (New York: Palgrave Macmillan, 2011), 93–104; Susan Schibanoff, "Hildegard of Bingen and Richardis of Stade: The Discourse of Desire," in *Same-Sex Love and Desire among Women in the Middle Ages,* ed. Francesca Canadé Sautman and Pamela Sheinborn (New York: Palgrave, 2001), 49–84; and Robert Mills, "Gender, Sodomy, Friendship, and the Medieval Anchorhold," *Journal of Medieval Religious Cultures* 36, no. 1 (2010): 1–27.

7. One recent exception is Alexandra Verini, "Medieval Models of Female Friendship in Christine de Pizan's *The Book of the City of Ladies* and Margery Kempe's *The Book of Margery Kempe,*" *Feminist Studies* 42, no. 2 (2016): 365–91. Albrecht Classen and Marilyn Sandidge's volume of essays, *Friendship in the Middle Ages and the Early Modern Age: Explorations of a Fundamental Ethical Discourse* (Berlin: Gruyter, 2010), affords a range of studies on everything from monastic friendship to sworn brotherhood to Anglo-Saxon women's epistolary friendships.

8. Paul Strohm, *Social Chaucer* (Boston: Harvard University Press, 1989); David Wallace, *Chaucerian Polity: Absolutist Lineages and Associational Forms in England and Italy* (Stanford: Stanford University Press, 1994). See also Marion Turner's argument that an antagonistic, divisive, and fragmented version of community emerges from an era of political and social turbulence, in *Chaucerian Conflict: Languages of Antagonism in Late Fourteenth-Century London* (London: Oxford University Press, 2006), 4–5.

ent ways, these studies oriented the *Canterbury Tales* in particular around the larger social framework of the pilgrim community designated by the Middle English words *felaweshipe, compagnye,* and *communitas,* and those institutional associational forms of *universitates,* guilds, and confraternities. Women's fellowship, company, community, and friendship, however, are noticeably absent from scholarly perspectives of medieval fellowship in Chaucer's work. Indeed, the *Canterbury Tales* themselves seem to support such a one-sided, masculinist notion of fellowship. Although women might have participated in some medieval institutional forms of community and fellowship in Chaucer's time, fellowship among women in the Canterbury company and even within the tales seems to be singularly lacking. Even female rivalry and debate on the scale of some of the altercations among the male tale-tellers is missing from the interstices of the tales. A medieval version of the Bechdel test, therefore, seems destined to fault the entire Canterbury project for its failure to imagine friendships, rivalries, or frenemies among the female pilgrims, much less to conjure representations of female intimacy within the tales.

And yet. What exactly am I looking for in Chaucer's work when I claim that it is missing? In other words, to return to Bechdel, does female friendship become legible only when two women talk to one another about something other than men? As fond as I am of the three-part rubric for critiquing contemporary film, I also think it potentially skews the evidence of medieval texts: for example, I would not want to rule out the Wife of Bath's friendship with her gossip or any gossip based on the fact that their conversations are often about men and that such conversations bespeak an intimate community, shared pleasure, and transgressive potential, as Carissa Harris has so powerfully argued.[9] Female friendship in the *Canterbury Tales,* while it does involve two women, does not necessarily align with Bechdel's other requirements. Instead, as I will suggest, although female friendship is rare in the *Canterbury Tales,* it is neither absent nor insignificant. It emerges in three different forms, all of which exert pressure against the particular constraints in which the women find themselves: identity of feeling, *godsibbe* femininity, and cross-species empathy.[10]

---

9. Harris uses the term *pedagogy* to capture the mutual education that occurs in late medieval texts; see Carissa M. Harris, *Obscene Pedagogies: Transgressive Talk and Sexual Education in Late Medieval Britain* (Ithaca, NY: Cornell University Press, 2018); see also her essay in this volume on *cummar* culture.

10. "*Godsibbe* femininity" is a riff on Harris's term for the rape culture of the *Canterbury Tales,* which she terms *felawe masculinity.* Unlike the masculine intimacy that takes place under the sign of *japes* intended to demean and enact violence against women, *godsibbe femininity* offers women an intimate community that seeks its own pleasure, knowledge, and resistance to masculine culture in the company of women. See Harris, *Obscene Pedagogies,* 26–66.

"SHE IS A FRIEND OF MY MIND"[11]

Most readers of the *Canterbury Tales* might expect an essay on female friendship in that work to begin and end with the Wife of Bath's Prologue and Tale in fragment 3, but this one begins with the *Man of Law's Tale* in fragment 2, where the issue of female friendship and female community first emerges as a side effect in the fifth tale. While women's friendships do not appear in the tales that precede the *Man of Law's Tale,* the destruction of female community as a prerequisite of Thesean regnal politics does: the *Knight's Tale* begins with the conquest of the Amazon "regne of Femenye"[12] and the translation of Hippolyta and Emelye from Amazon royalty to wife and political pawn, respectively. This destruction of female community brings with it the domestication of Hippolyta as Theseus's wife and the isolation of Emelye to conduct her own devotions to May and dedicate herself to Diana the chaste. In a tale that disguises masculine friendship under a more conventional rivalry over a heterosexual love interest, the issue of female community is situated in Hippolyta's and Emelye's past as Amazon warriors.[13] Susan Crane is one of a few scholars to assert the "shadowed potential" of feminine community that erupts in the tale, first in the conquest of the Amazons, followed by the grieving Theban women and the women who intercede during the hunt to save Palamon and Arcite.[14] In the succeeding fabliaux of the *Miller's Tale,* the *Reeve's Tale,* and the *Cook's Fragment,* the potential for female friendship and community all but disappears as women in these tales negotiate male rivalries and their own desires without the benefit of female companionship.

The *Man of Law's Tale* reintroduces female friendship not as a "shadowed potential" but as a recurrent crisis in the tale of Custance's exile and conversion of pagan multitudes. A tale about a young Christian woman's serial exile from Rome, Syria, and, finally, Northumbria might seem to exemplify heroic

---

11. Toni Morrison, *Beloved* (New York: Knopf, 1987), 272.

12. Geoffrey Chaucer, *Knight's Tale,* in *The Norton Chaucer,* ed. David Lawton (New York: Norton, 2019), I.866. Further references to this edition are cited parenthetically in the text.

13. For a queering of the masculine friendship in the *Knight's Tale,* see Tison Pugh, "'For to be Sworne Brethren til They Deye': Satirizing Queer Brotherhood in the Chaucerian Corpus," *The Chaucer Review* 43, no. 3 (2009): 282–310. For other treatments of male friendship, homosociality, and/or erotic relations between men, see Alcuin Blamires, *Chaucer, Ethics, and Gender* (Oxford: Oxford University Press, 2006), 20–45; Robert Stretter, "Rewriting Perfect Friendship in Chaucer's 'Knight's Tale' and Lydgate's 'Fabula Duorum Mercatorum,'" *The Chaucer Review* 37, no. 3 (2003): 234–52; Richard E. Zeikowitz, *Homoeroticism and Chivalry: Discourses of Male Same-Sex Desire in the Fourteenth Century* (New York: Palgrave, 2003); and Susan Crane, *Gender and Romance in Chaucer's "Canterbury Tales"* (Princeton, NJ: Princeton University Press, 1994), 16–54.

14. Crane, *Gender and Romance,* 200.

female abjection rather than female alliance. Indeed, Custance spends more of the tale exiled from all human contact—familial, romantic, and cultural—than she does in the company of others, female or male. The Man of Law intensifies Custance's isolation rhetorically by structuring his tale around a feminine animus directed at her and polarizing the women who come into relationship to her. Donegild and the Sultaness are the two demonized women, both mothers of kings, who regard their sons' prospective marriages to Custance as threatening either to them or to their religious faith and power. The degree of narrative animus directed at these two characters is also noteworthy, as it signals the narrator's own affective investment in his tale—a misogynistic affect that erupts in over-the-top apostrophes addressed to each. The Man of Law calls out the Sultaness as the *roote of iniquitee*, a *virago*, a *serpent under feminitee*, and a *feined woman* (II.358, 359, 360, and 362). He imputes similar gender crimes to Donegild, including *malice, tyrannye, traitorye,* and mannishness (II.779, 783, and 782). Insubordination, treachery, treason, and underlying all these crimes, the perversion of masculinity in a woman—these are the implied horrors embodied by the two women. They are paganism, evil, and disorder personified, and they are determined to destroy innocent, virtuous, and submissive Custance, a figure of Christian femininity idealized.

By most modern standards of friendship, indeed, the *Man of Law's Tale* fails the Bechdel test for female friendship, according to classical definitions that were applied exclusively to men; however, there just might be a "shadowed potential" for friendship between Custance and the Sultaness. Cicero defines male friendship in *De amicitia* as "nothing else than an accord in all things, human and divine, conjoined with mutual goodwill and affection."[15] Aristotle's definition of friendship in the *Nicomachean Ethics* includes an equal "comradeship" that is based on "identity of feelings and character,"[16] an idea that is akin to Cicero's "accord in all things." In this respect (and minus the "mutual good will and affection"), Custance and the Sultaness share a kind of friendship that does not extend to a firm bond of affection. The "identity of feeling" that unites these two women otherwise divided by culture and

---

15. "Est enim amicitial nihil aliud nisi omnium divnarum humanarumque rerum benevolentia et caritate consensio." Cicero, *De amicitia*, in *Cicero de senectute, de amicitia, de divinatione,* trans. William Armisted Falconer (Cambridge, MA: Harvard University Press, 2014), 131 and 130. See Alexandra Verini's discussion of Cicero and Aristotle's idea of friendship as an "identity of feeling" in the context of Christine de Pizan, "Medieval Models of Female Friendship," esp. 365–66.

16. Aristotle, *The Nicomachean Ethics,* trans. H. Rackham, Loeb Classical Library, 2nd ed. (Cambridge, MA: Harvard University Press, 1934), VIII. xi.5, 495.

religion is their experience of male authorities trafficking in them and their beliefs. Even though they express their distress in different registers and act on that distress in vastly different ways, they both object to the way in which they have been coerced by male authorities to be instruments of masculine designs. On the day of her departure for Syria to marry the Sultan and convert the Muslims to Christianity, Custance delivers a muted protest to her father:

> Allas, unto the Barbre nacioun
> I moste anon, sin that it is youre wille. . . .
> I, wrecche womman, no fors thogh I spille:
> Wommen are born to thraldom and penaunce,
> And to been under mannes governaunce (II.281–87)

Although Custance seems to be accepting women's condition of suffering and slavery in this passage, her remarks actually serve as an unambiguous rebuke to her father, even as she complies with his request of her. By constellating *thraldom and penaunce* with being *under mannes governaunce,* she throws shade on the motives for her journey, namely, the "destruccioun of Maumetrye, / And . . . encrees of Cristes lawe deere" (II.236–37). Custance's use of the Middle English word *thraldom,* meaning "captivity, slavery, submission, and tyranny," is emphatically negative. If she were merely expressing the proper submission of women to men, she would have used a different word, such as *obesiaunce* or *submissioun. Suffering* and *slavery* are the coordinates of "man's governance" with respect to the effect of their governance *on women.* She accepts this condition, it is true, but not without a searing indictment of what her father, "the Pope, the Church and all chivalry" initiated "through treaty and diplomacy" (II.234–35 and 233).

The Man of Law's sympathies are aligned with Custance throughout his tale, but in this one case, those masculine feelings reinforce the criticism implied in Custance's complaint:

> Allas, what wonder is it though she wepte,
> That shal be sent to straunge nacioun
> Fro frendes that so tendrely hire kepte,
> And to be bounden under subjeccioun
> Of oon, she knoweth nat his condicioun?
> Housbondes been alle goode, and han been yore:
> That knowen wives—I dar saye you namore (II.267–73)

In one respect, the Man of Law's sympathies are of a piece with his sentimentalization of Custance's victimhood; however, in this passage he goes beyond his usual mawkish commentary to suggest an equivalence between Custance's exile to a strange, friendless land and her marriage to the Sultan. No wonder she wept, he remarks, because she was sent to a strange nation and "bound in subjection" to a husband she doesn't know. The narrator's sympathies seem to align with Custance's point of view insofar as they mirror her equation of female suffering and women's "subjection" to men, in the Man of Law's words. In the last two lines, his sympathies shift abruptly to misogynistic sarcasm. By asserting that "husbands are all good and have always been so, / Wives know this—I dare say no more," the narrator playfully contradicts himself. If this were true, Custance would have nothing to worry about. But the ostensible joke of these lines derives from the obvious fact that wives are the ones least likely to testify to the goodness of husbands. His parting "I dare say no more" invites a conspiratorial misogynistic smirk, since all the debates about marriage ventriloquize the evil of wives, as the Wife of Bath will point out. His gesture by way of making light of Custance's suffering only highlights the equation she and he make between marriage and slavery, or subjection.

The Sultaness is framed by the narrator as the antithesis of Custance's Christian femininity, but she also exhibits an uncanny "identity of feeling" with Custance's expressed despair over the thralldom and suffering that devolve to women under man's governance. The Man of Law's intense aversion to the Sultaness notwithstanding, the Sultaness speaks in language that explicitly echoes Custance's complaint in the context of religious conversion, not of forced marriage:

> What sholde us tiden of this newe lawe
> But thraldom to oure bodies and penaunce,
> And afterward in helle to be drawe
> For we renayed Mahoun oure creaunce? (II.337–40)

The *thraldom* and *penaunce* that Custance aligned with the condition of women are here expanded to include the condition of Muslims forced to convert to *this newe lawe* under the agreement between Rome and Syria for the Sultan's marriage to Custance. Unlike Custance, the Sultaness refuses this slavery and suffering due to women under men's laws, something the Man of Law, in his sputtering invectives for her, associates with mannishness and virility. For all of his narrative effort to claim the Sultaness as Custance's Other—that pagan woman who refuses men's governance in order to usurp it—nevertheless, her identity of feeling with Custance marks an uncanny affinity between these two women. Unlike Donegild, the Northumbrian mother of Alla who directs her animus toward Custance, the Sultaness directs her outrage not at the Christian woman on whose behalf the entire nation of Syria must convert to Islam but at the men behind the scheme.

What difference does this affinity that binds the Christian Custance with the Muslim Sultaness in the *Man of Law's Tale* make? An identity of feeling between two women works against the narrator's project of unifying and heroizing Christian identity against the religious Other in his tale. As Susan Schibanoff demonstrated, this tale chafes at the proximate threats to masculine, Christian identity, endeavoring to distance and oppose East and West, Christianity and Islam/paganism, and virtuous Christian woman and non-Christian virago.[17] The two women might share the position of "proximate Other" in the tale, but I also want to claim for them this affinity in their shared experience of slavery and suffering under men's governance. The Sultaness is not simply a version of Donegild, the jealous mother-in-law whose anger is directed at Custance. She is a "friend of her (Custance's) mind," one might say, in the sense of their shared experience of patriarchy, cultural differences notwithstanding. The irony of the Sultaness's decision to wipe out the Christians and exile Custance is that it alienates her from the one person who shares her experience and sense of injustice. The "friendship" of Custance and the Sultaness remains forever circumstantial and merely plausible insofar as their affinities are forever fractured by religious and cultural difference and patriarchy.

The other affinity between women of alien cultures in the *Man of Law's Tale* is marked not only by an identity of feelings but by intimacy and affection. When Custance washes up on the Northumbrian shore, she is taken in by the Constable and his wife, Hermengild. Although they are both pagans and Christianity has fled to Wales, according to the Man of Law, nevertheless Hermengild "loved [Custance] right as hir lif" (II.535) and eventually converts to Christianity. Because Christianity has been banished from England, Hermengild practices it with Custance in secret until the day on the beach when she performs a miracle in front of her husband at Custance's insistence (II.554–67). This moment on the beach is a powerful one, however brief, as Hermengild recoils in fear from the blind man before Custance encourages her and "made hire bold" to cure him (II.566). Ultimate credit for the miracle goes to the Christian God, of course, but this fact does not diminish the strength Hermengild draws from Custance's encouragement. Their friendship goes beyond shared beliefs as the two pray long hours into the night and

---

17. Susan Schibanoff, "Worlds Apart: Orientalism, Antifeminism, and Heresy in Chaucer's Man of Law's Tale," *Exemplaria* 8, no. 1 (1996): 59–96.

sleep together.[18] The murder of Hermengild ends this short friendship, but it is significant nonetheless because it is the only relationship in the tale—besides Custance's relationship with Christ and the Virgin Mary—that is intimate and unbound by the demands of men. When she later marries Alla, she "moste take pacience at night / Swich manere necessaries as been plesinges / To folk that han ywedded hem with ringes, / And laye a lite hir holinesse aside" (II.710–13). Custance in the marriage bed returns to man's governance, "laying . . . her holiness aside" in order to patiently endure that which is pleasing to her husband's desire.

Identity of feeling between women slips through the Man of Law's narrative strategy of opposing East to West, Christian to Muslim/pagan, and virtuous woman to evil virago. The friendship of Hermengild and Custance, while it partly serves the Man of Law's vision of Custance's conversion powers, also supplies an interlude apart from the grand Christian/heterosexual/Western triumphal narrative in the making. It might be worth pausing to consider what might have happened had Hermengild not been murdered—had Custance and she remained BFFs in Christ. It would have short-circuited the Man of Law's need for a Custance adrift with her baby—that "floating tableau of twinned human connection" and the "human community in miniature" on which that image depends, in the words of Geraldine Heng.[19] The tale of serial affinities between Custance and the Sultaness and Custance and Hermengild is not a story around which to build Christian identity and community. Female friendship, like female affinities through emotional identification, proves recalcitrant, if only briefly, to fantasies of heterosexual containment, empirical expansion, and religious conversion.

CHLOE GOSSIPED WITH OLIVIA

Chloe and Olivia "share a laboratory," which, for Woolf, "will make their friendship more varied and lasting because it will be less personal."[20] Woolf desires women's friendships to free themselves of that element of the personal historically associated with them. But there is more than one way for Chloe

---

18. I argue elsewhere that this relationship "represents the sole counter-voice to models of domestic and spiritual isolation of women found in most of the *Canterbury Tales.*" Karma Lochrie, "Between Women," in *The Cambridge Companion to Medieval Women's Writing,* ed. Carolyn Dinshaw and David Wallace (Cambridge: Cambridge University Press, 2003), 70–88, at 74.

19. Geraldine Heng, *Empire of Magic: Medieval Romance and the Politics of Cultural Fantasy* (New York: Columbia University Press, 2003), 182.

20. Woolf, *A Room of One's Own,* 84.

to "like Olivia." In medieval culture, gossip was chiefly a gendered language associated with women, and although it was regarded as a sin by the Church, as I have argued elsewhere, it also provided a transgressive oral community in which lay women formed friendships.[21] According to medieval conduct manuals for women, women's gossip entailed a specific kind of emasculation associated with betraying a husband's most embarrassing secrets. In the *Wife of Bath's Tale*, for example, the Wife digresses from her plot about the knight's search for what women most desire to retell the story of King Midas as an object lesson in women's indiscretion (with her key revisions to Ovid's version).[22] As I suggested earlier, I would like to redeploy the Middle English word for *gossip, godsibbe*, in its meaning of "close friend or companion," by way of designating a particular kind of female fellowship found mainly the Wife of Bath's *Prologue* and *Tale*,[23] and at the same time, offering a countercommunity to what Harris has termed "felawe masculinity." I do not mean to suggest that godsibbe femininity poses a binary with the masculine rape culture signified by Harris's term, so much as it might usefully delineate enclaves of feminine resistance to that community and spaces of collective conviviality and shared knowledge so prioritized by the Wife over marital intimacy. Like the fifteenth- and sixteenth-century *cummar* culture that Harris deftly documents in this volume, the Wife of Bath relies on the counsel and bawdy confidences of her godsibbe community. Ultimately, in using godsibbe femininity to designate the Wife of Bath's important rhetorical, psychological, and affective affiliation with a circle of women, I am interested in shifting the emphasis of the word from "gossip" as a dissolute activity of women to "gossip" as the *community* in which an important kind of female fellowship, intimacy, transgression, and knowledge transmission occurs. The Wife overtly tags this com-

21. Karma Lochrie, *Covert Operations: The Medieval Uses of Secrecy* (Philadelphia: University of Pennsylvania Press, 1999), 56–92. See also Susan E. Phillips, *Transforming Talk: The Problem with Gossip in Late Medieval England* (University Park: Pennsylvania State University Press, 2007); and Harris, *Obscene Pedagogies*.

22. The Wife of Bath riffs on the story in Ovid's *Metamorphosis* in which Midas is cursed with asses' ears hidden beneath his hair. Only his wife knows his secret, and she can't bear to keep it. So instead of telling another human, she goes down to a marsh and whispers the truth in the reeds. The Wife ends her story here, as an illustration of how women cannot keep any secret, but Ovid's story gives the revelation to a servant, not Midas's wife, and it ends with the reeds whispering the secret forevermore: *aures aselli*, "asses ears" (III.952–82). For an example from Caxton's English translation of Geoffrey de La Tour's instruction to his daughters (CE 1371), see William Caxton, *Book of the Knight of the Tower*, ed. M. Y. Offord, Early English Text Society, SS 217 (London: Oxford University Press, 1971), 191.

23. Although the *Middle English Dictionary* defines the word as a gender-neutral reference to a close friend or companion, there are no examples among its quotations of the word applied to men; see the *MED* entry for *god-sib(be)*: https://quod.lib.umich.edu/m/middle-english-dictionary/dictionary/MED18998/track?counte.

munity and its transgressive function in her preamble to the account of her fifth husband, Jankyn:

> He somtime was a clerk of Oxenforde,
> And hadde laft scole and wente at hom to borde
> With my gossib, dwelling in oure toun—
> God have hir soule!—hir name was Alisoun;
> She knew myn herte, and eek my privetee,
> Bet than oure parissh preest, as mote I thee.
> To hire biwreyed I my conseil al,
> For hadde myn housbonde pissed on a wal,
> Or doon a thing that sholde han cost his lif,
> To hire, and to another worthy wife,
> And to my nece which that I loved wel,
> I wolde han told his conseil everydel. (III.527–38)

Two seemingly ancillary details are worthy of note here: first, Jankyn's lodging with the Wife's gossip literally situates the object of her desire *within* her female community of gossips. The second detail is the indistinguishability of the Wife's and her favorite gossip's names—Alisoun, signaling the very alignment of perspective and solidarity she testifies to in this passage. Her gossip is, as the Wife boasts, privy to more of her secrets and her deepest attachments than is the parish priest: in the world of godsibbe femininity, gossip trumps confession as a source of truth, and no man's secret is safe. The Wife's brandishing of her indiscretion as a gossip is as much about her own intimacy and unfiltered "conseil" with her double, Alisoun, as it is about her revealing the most humiliating of her husband's secrets. His humiliation or even death poses no hindrance to the Wife's confidence in her fellow gossip. In using the Middle English word *conseil* twice in this passage, the Wife erects a firewall between the *confidence* and shared intimacy of her gossips and masculine *secrets* that she and her gossips traffic in. *Conseil*, it might be said, is an activity that binds the Wife and her circle in a nexus of intimacy, shared experience, and raucous irreverence of masculine vulnerability. As Harris in this volume suggests for later cummars, or gossips, this counsel assumes a pedagogical significance, too.

"Another worthy wife," "my dame," and a niece "whom I love very much" complete the Wife's tight-knit community of women who know each other's secrets, as well as her husband's most embarrassing confidences, "that made his face often reed and hoot / For verray shame" (III.541–42). The superiority of her loyalty to, and intimacy with, her gossips over her discretion for the sake of her husband haunts both Prologue and Tale such that the abiding theme of female sovereignty in marriage turns out to be a function of the fellowship of her feminine enclave, where gossip, loyalty, and betrayal thrive on the margins of heterosexuality. The limitations of Bechdel's condition for cinematic female friendship that women's conversations not be about men could find no more powerful counterargument than the Wife's gossiping cabal, which sustains and supports her, even as it provides her pleasure and the salutary sociality of storytelling. If readers are misled into thinking that the Wife is more allied with men than with women, they should attend to her scattered direct invocations to her imaginary audience: "ye wise wives" (III.225). She also reserves the collective pronoun "us" for herself and like-minded wives, again deploying godsibbe femininity to create a performative gossip circle replete with shared arcana, pleasures, and stratagems for women in a masculine culture and clerical narrative. The Wife's plural subject position within a community of like-minded wives is so constitutive of who she is that she ends her tale with a prayer not for herself but for herself and all wives: "And Jesu Crist us sende / Housbondes meeke, yonge, and fresshe abedde— / And grace t'overbide hem that we wedde" (III.1258–60). The community of gossips, like that of wives, shares men's secrets as well as those women's intimacies that they don't disclose to men. Their godsibbe friendship affords the Wife et al. that sovereignty that they do not otherwise enjoy in the culture at large in the form of transgressive speech. The Wife ultimately includes her reader in this rallying cry addressed to "us," thereby ushering us into that privy and penumbral place where gossips salaciously thrive and female friendship finds fervent expression.

It is not surprising, given the Wife's primary identification with a fellowship of women, that she populates her tale with analogous communities of women who know each other's most intimate desires. There are two female courts in the tale. The first is an Arthurian court composed of the queen and her entourage who intercede in the rapist knight's death sentence, convincing King Arthur to surrender the accused to their judgment and assigning him a quest to discover "what thing it is that wommen most desiren" (III.905). The other female court is a fairy one belonging to the Hag, who ultimately answers the riddle, saves the knight's life, and marries him as her reward. In addition to these formal female courts, there are extensive and diverse communities of women that the knight surveys in order to discover the answer to the question of what women most desire. Before the Hag provides him the answer, the knight "seeketh every hous and every place" (III.919), and the volume of answers he receives attests to the underworld of sundry desires that resides in female communities: "Some saiden wommen loven best richesse; / Some saide honour, some saide jolinesse" (III.925–26), the Wife recounts, using anaphora to concatenate the variety of answers and plurality of voices reporting them. The knight's visit to female communities across the realm is a fascinating example of what we might term *medieval gender slumming*, borrowing from the 1920s sense of that term to mean a dominant culture's visitation of and exposure to nondominant worlds they otherwise would not have known.[24] The difference here is that the women consulted by the knight are hardly representative of an exotic underground comparable to 1920s black voguing and gay clubs, and the knight who is doing his slumming is doing so under duress; it is instead a community of women that crosses class divisions and yields a puzzlingly diverse array of answers to the knight's question. His fruitless search provides an alternative answer to the queen's riddle—one based on the Wife's favorite discourse, the discourse of gossip—in the sense that the knight's forced initiation into female communities reveals to him *that* women desire and that they desire *many different things*. This comes as depressing news to him, since it does not answer the question in a way that will save his life, but it does, nevertheless, provide him a record of the vast and varied array of women's desires, and it predisposes him to pause before the dancing ladies in hopes of receiving any "wisdom" they might have. At this point, the knight is no longer that knight from the beginning of the tale, inflicting his own desire on women without regard for their consent; he is schooled in the communities of women—"every hous and every place" to register their desires and seek their wisdom. His life depends on it.

 The answer to the riddle, that women desire to have sovereignty and mastery over lovers and husbands, reprises what has already happened in the tale, namely the claiming of sovereignty by women, first by Arthur's female courtiers interceding in the knight's fate; second, by the knight's survey of all women's desires; and finally, by the knight's surrender to the Hag's wisdom. He does, of course, require one final bit of schooling in a husband's surrender of sovereignty, but the key role that feminine communities play in the knight's transformation should not be subsumed under the "happy ending" of the story. The contingent transformations—of Hag into young, fair wife—and of knight-rapist into obedient husband—depend on the whole of the knight's quest, not simply the Hag's lecture. The Wife narrator, for all her assertion of her own desires for sovereignty in marriage, also insists on the female community from which she derives her stratagems and to which she speaks in the first-person plural in her Prologue and at the end of her tale. While the reader

---

24. See Scott Herring, *Queering the Underworld: Slumming, Literature, and the Undoing of Lesbian and Gay History* (Chicago: University of Chicago Press, 2007).

is not treated to conversations between the Wife and her female community, we are reminded that she is both a product of and participant in female communities of wives, gossips, and the imaginary fellowships of court and forest in her tale—those collective—if not always visible—sources of wisdom that rival masculine *auctorite*.

CROSS-SPECIES FEMALE FRIENDSHIP

Female friendship in the *Canterbury Tales* is so far confined to the otherworldly terrains of romance in the *Wife of Bath's Tale* and the hybrid realm of saint's legend/romance in the *Man of Law's Tale*. It is also noteworthy that in both tales, female community is often consigned to the margins of society, either the "barbarie nacion" of Syria or pagan Northumbria in the *Man of Law's Tale*, or in the *Wife of Bath's Tale*, the forest beyond the Arthurian court. In the *Squire's Tale*, female affinity is rendered not spatially or geographically, but interspecially. Although the Bechdel test assumes female friendship to be a human bond, Chaucer's tale shifts the terrain entirely, rendering female friendship posthuman, magical, and otherworldly. Set in the Mongol-Tartar empire of the Caucasus, a place often associated with monstrous races in medieval *mappamundi*,[25] the tale "wraps itself in an aura of exotic alterity," according to Kathryn Lynch. Other scholars have focused less on the alterity of the Cambiuskan's court and more on its "sophistication and cosmopolitanism," as well as its marvelous gifts from the king of Arabia and India: the flying brass horse, a ring that allows its wearer to understand animals, a magical mirror that reveals enemies and adversities, and a sword that can kill and heal.[26] The tale is unfinished, making it difficult to tell how the four gifts might have figured in the Squire-narrator's story, but part 2 of the tale recounts the adventure of the princess Canacee and her gift, the ring that allows her not only to understand the language of birds but to speak to them "in his langage" (V.152). When she goes for a walk with her new ring, Canacee encounters a formel, a female falcon the narrator cannot identify. "A faucon peregrin thanne seemed she / Of fremde land" (V.428–29). The falcon is both from a "foreign" (*fremde*) land and a *peregrin*, or traveler, a visitor from an unknown place. The Squire tells

---

25. See Lawton's introduction to the tale, *Norton Chaucer*, 210–11.
26. Kathryn L. Lynch, "East Meets West in Chaucer's Squire's and Franklin's Tales," *Speculum* 70, no. 3 (July 1995): 530–51, at 531. Patricia Ingham reads the tale in terms of its disenchanted rationalism and enchanted wonder for gadgets and novelty: "Little Nothings: The Squire's Tale and the Ambition of Gadgets," *Studies in the Age of Chaucer* 31 (2009): 53–80. Scott Lightsey, too, examines the role of wonder and mirabilia in the tale in *Manmade Marvels in Medieval Culture and Literature* (New York: Palgrave, 2007), 58–59, 61–62, and 73–75.

us that Canacee not only understood the falcon's speech but was able to reply in falcon-speak under the ring's power.

The scene of friendship, however magical, is also one of shared sensibilities and cross-species empathy, as Susan Crane has observed.[27] Canacee's morning walk is distracted by the "pitous vois" (V.412) and the bloody avian body of the female falcon in distress. Canacee asks in fluent bird-ese what the cause of her woe is (V.447–62). It is her expression of compassion and a desire to help the falcon even before she knows the cause of its despair, however, that is suggestive of her cross-species affinity with it:

> I have of you so greet compassioun
> For Goddes love, com fro the tree adoun
> And as I am a kinges doghter trewe,
> If that I verraily the cause knewe
> Of youre disese, if it laye in my might,
> I wolde amende it er that it were night. (V.463–68)

As Crane also points out, Canacee's compassion and desire to help the bird occur without the benefit of the magic ring's decoding of bird speech.[28] The incomprehensible falcon shrieks are sufficient for Canacee to feel compassion for the bird and to seek to heal her self-inflicted wounds.

Speaking in her falcon idiom (*haukes ledene,* V.477), the falcon recognizes Canacee's nobility precisely because of her empathy. This recognition and testimony to Canacee's nobility from the perspective of an animal is both striking and significant insofar as such socialized cognition is usually reserved for human beings. The fact that the falcon recognizes human compassion and nobility without the benefit of a magical ring suggests that the capacity for cross-species empathy is mutual and that nobility is not confined to human beings. Their shared *gentil herte* affords not only empathy but a capacity for friendship:

---

27. Susan Crane, *Animal Encounters: Contacts and Concepts in Medieval Britain* (Philadelphia: University of Pennsylvania Press, 2012), 120–36. Sara Deutch Schotland views the friendship between bird and human as "female homosocial bonding" providing "protection in a dangerous world": "Talking Bird and Gentle Heart: Female Homosocial Bonding in the Squire's Tale," in *Friendship in the Middle Ages and Early Modern Age: Explorations of a Fundamental Ethical Discourse,* ed. Albrecht Classen and Marilyn Sandidge (Berlin: de Gruyter, 2010), 525–42, at 531.

28. Crane, *Animal Encounters,* 128.

"That pitee renneth soone in gentil herte,
Feeling his similitude in paines smerte,
Is preved alday as men may it see
As wel by work as by auctoritee;
For gentil herte kitheth gentilesse.
I see wel that ye han of my distresse
Compassioun, my faire Canacee,
Of verray wommanly benignitee
That nature in youre principles hath set" (V.479–87)

This is a remarkable passage for many reasons: first, the bird is quoting authorities and general received wisdom, as if birds and humans shared the same written traditions and emotional experience. The falcon also attributes Canacee's pity to a "similitude" shared by bird and human, that is, the gentle heart that allows one to feel compassion and recognize itself in the pain of others, even other nonhumans. Finally, the falcon assigns this compassion born of a gentle heart to Nature, who herself installs "womanly kindness" in Canacee as an innate characteristic ("in your principles"). The implication is that this very natural gendered compassion is shared by bird and human princess alike, and that the "similitude" of female benignity crosses species boundaries.

The intimacy already shared by Canacee and the falcon is deepened in the falcon's "confession" of her betrayal by a tercelet's wooing and abandonment of her. Her story recounts a stock courtly tale of his complaints and pledges to serve her with "heigh reverence" (V.545). The falcon faults her own excessive pity and innocence in her surrender to his love, which turned out to be nothing but doubleness, feigning, and sophistry (V.556, 554). She says that she loved him and surrendered her will to his while "keeping the boundes of my worshipe ever" (V.571). After a year or two he leaves her, promising to return; instead, he becomes enamored of a kite and abandons the falcon. The falcon attributes his infidelity to men's tendency to love *newfanglenesse*, or novelty. In the course of telling of the tercel's falseness, the falcon conflates his behavior with that of human men, blurring the behaviors of men and male birds. She ends her complaint with a strange comparison of men who love novelty and caged birds (as if she were a human whose relationship to birds was as pets), who would rather escape to the woods to eat worms than remain in the comfort of their cages. She ends her story by swooning in Canacee's lap. Before the tale cuts off, Canacee takes the falcon home, builds her a mew lined with blue velvet for women's troth and painted green outside to symbolize male infidelity, and places the mew at the head of her bed. She dedicates her life to healing the falcon by digging up and applying herbs to her wounds.

"The little mew Canacee constructs is a wonderfully complex attempt at hosting without taking hostage," argues Crane,[29] but I view the little coop and her own dedication to the bird as less a lesson in hospitality than a lesson in female friendship. The intimacy that inspired Canacee's compassion and identification with the formal is the basis on which Canacee takes the bird into her care. The mew of female companionship displaces the cage of male infidelity that the falcon alludes to in her confession. In contrast to the love of novelty, the two female creatures—one human, the other avian—are joined by a female bond based on identification, a gentle heart, empathy, and courtly manners. The "metonymy of gentle hearts"[30] uniting falcon and human not only erases the need for a magic ring's access to species difference but also grounds a friendship across species in a shared nature.

"In the face of a true friend we see, so to speak, a second self."[31] This claim of Cicero's in *De amicitia* captures the unusual dynamic between alien species, between the human Canacee and the female falcon, who perceive through compassion that second self in one another. The *Squire's Tale* is interrupted by the Franklin soon after this strange episode of female friendship across species, making it difficult to determine what role this friendship would have taken in the tale as a whole.[32] Perhaps it is fortunate that the Squire was not permitted to complete his tale, because within the fragments that are extant, the tale imagines cross-species female friendship based on empathy and compassion that reaches across difference and short-circuits an otherwise Orien-

---

29. Crane, *Animal Encounters*, 133.
30. Crane, *Animal Encounters*, 126.
31. "Verum etiam amicum qui intuetur, tamquam exemplar aliquod intuetur sui," Cicero, *De amicitia*, 132. My translation.
32. An ambiguous precis of the next part of the tale concerning Cambiuskan and Cambalo raises the specter of incest involving Canacee and her brother, Cambalus, a specter that would seem utterly to supersede and obscure the female cross-species friendship in the second part of the tale. The incest suggestion comes in these lines: "And after wol I speke of Cambalo, / That fought in listes with the bretheren two / For Canacee, er that he mighte hire winne" (V.667–69). As Lawton in the *Norton Chaucer* explains, the implication of incest here is based on two assumptions: first, that the Cambalo mentioned here is the same person as Cambalus, Canacee's brother mentioned earlier in the tale; second, that his possibly "winning" her means winning as his wife / love interest. John M. Fyler argues that incest as a theme serves up the romance genre's desire for the exotic: "Domesticating the Exotic in the *Squire's Tale*," *ELH* 55 (1988): 1–26. In Lynch's judgment, this possibility results from the Westernization of Eastern versions of this story, such that "the promised exotic ending is not just a horror; it is ludicrous": "East Meets West," 542. Elizabeth Scala has argued that "the incest narrative functions as a cipher for the narrative alterity it foregrounds": "Canacee and the Chaucer Canon: Incest and Other Unnarratables," *Chaucer Review* 30, no. 1 (1995): 15–39, at 31.

talist narrative taken up with exotic Eastern cultures, gifts, and foreignness. Female friendship of the avian–human variety, in other words, actually does quite a bit of work despite the tale's inconclusiveness—or rather, perhaps, precisely because of its inconclusiveness.

CHAUCER AND THE "VAST CHAMBER"

> For if Chloe likes Olivia and Mary Carmichael
> knows how to express it she will light a torch in the
> vast chamber where nobody has yet been.
> —WOOLF, *A ROOM OF ONE'S OWN*[33]

I wonder what Woolf would have thought of my analysis of female friendships in Chaucer, whether she would have considered them sufficiently luminous to begin to "light a torch in the vast chamber where nobody has yet been."[34] Insofar as Woolf reserved the representation of female friendship—of Chloe liking Olivia—for future female authors, I suspect she would be disappointed in the fleeting and even quirky moments of women's friendship that I have carved out of the predominantly male fellowship in the *Canterbury Tales*. Likewise, the Bechdel test, in its attempt to counteract the kinds of representation of female intimacy found in modern cinema, restricts the representation of women's intimacy to confidential conversations that don't involve men. The salutary effect of her test is that it brings its own torchlight to the striking absence of female intimacies in modern film, except where those intimacies are tandem to women's heterosexual relationships with men.

Female friendships in premodern texts, like Chaucer's *Canterbury Tales*, require a somewhat different corrective than those offered by Woolf and Bechdel. How might Chaucer's few fleeting examples of female friendship provide us with the "torch," so to speak, with which we might light the cavern of medieval representations of fellowship, friendship, and community more broadly? In other words, can we devise new parameters for "finding" and thinking about female friendship in medieval texts? Without claiming that Chaucer's *Canterbury Tales* constitutes a bar for measuring other literary representations of female friendship—the way Woolf's "Chloe liked Olivia" or Bechdel's test do—I would like to suggest a somewhat different, less aspi-

---

33. Woolf, *A Room of One's Own*, 84.
34. Elizabeth Abel uses this same passage from *A Room of One's Own* to focus on female friendships in contemporary literature: "(E)merging Identities: The Dynamics of Female Friendship in Contemporary Fiction," *Signs* 6, no. 3 (Spring 1981): 413–35.

rational, kind of rubric for thinking outside the usual parameters of female friendship in medieval texts. I will formulate this rubric as a series of questions in the spirit of Bechdel: What kinds of "identity of feeling" can be traced to reveal affinities between women—even those polarized by the text? What enclaves are afforded by misogynistic discourses surrounding women, such as their association with gossip? And finally, what surprises and resistances are possible in the mise-en-scène of female empathy? These questions derived from the three main examples of female friendship in the *Canterbury Tales* redirect our attention from what female friendships should look like and toward the kinds of things they are capable of doing. In the process, we are afforded an expanded understanding of female friendship both as a concept and as a historically specific phenomenon in premodern literary texts.

CHAPTER 10

The Politics of Virtual Friendship in Christine de Pizan's *Book of the City of Ladies*

CHRISTINE CHISM

> Surprisingly, even in the dark archaic Greek myths one can detect glimmers of other options. Traces of alternative story lines in vase paintings and fragments of Greek literature hint that peaceful interactions, even romance, might have been possible outcomes. In the Greek myths about Amazons that have come down to us, war always triumphs over love. But *outside* Greek mythology, and *beyond the Greek world*, women warriors and male warriors might make love and war together as equals—and even live happily ever after.
>
> —Adrienne Mayor, *The Amazons*[1]

LIKE ADRIENNE MAYOR, Christine de Pizan was fascinated by Amazons and by the ancient sources that described them.[2] However, as a late fifteenth-century writer striving to make her living in the courts of France, she only had the Greek-framed versions to go on. She could not point to the Scythian excavations of bodies and grave goods that bolster Mayor's account of historical warrior women who were admired rather than killed, or the Greek vase paintings that hint at other kinds of relations for them than war. But Christine de Pizan, like Mayor, could follow the "traces of alternative story lines" in her sources like an Ariadne thread to a vantage point *outside* and *beyond* classical misogynies, through a process of careful, multisourced, comparative research. In *Le livre de la cité des dames* (hereafter, *LCD*), she digs not just to enlarge the "glimmers of other options" but also to imbue them with urgent affective

---

1. Adrienne Mayor, *The Amazons: Lives and Legends of Warrior Women Across the Ancient World* (Princeton, NJ: Princeton University Press, 2016), 30.
2. This chapter is dedicated to the fellow scholars and researchers with whom I've enjoyed many conversations about Christine de Pizan over the past decade, but especially to Alexandra Verini and Lauren Rebecca King, whose work explores respectively the utopian tactics of feminine alliance and readerly identification as a protreptic allure.

and political power. In doing so, she recovers a history erased by authoritative Greeks and the Romans, hand in hand with the antique patristic writers and medieval clergy: a history of women's friendship in a staunch classical sense, where friendship is the bedrock of polity itself. De Pizan, like Mayor, had to look skeptically at the tragic or misogynist sources she received in order to re-trope and repurpose them toward an ideal of women's friendship—with other women, with men, and with society at large—that could compel loyalty, urge virtue, and enact friendship in the very act of reading, In *LCD* de Pizan enlarges "glimmers of other options" into full-blown visions of an alternate sociality that equalizes women as friends and as friendly rather than consuming them.

Christine de Pizan's *LCD* performs a medieval version of feminist fabulation.[3] It constructs a memory palace of historically separated exemplary women, thereby bringing about a new allegorically asynchronic polity of women.[4] De Pizan's City can, on the face of it, seem a singularly inert place, since its inhabitants are both the City's subjects and its building blocks, and none of the women who inhabit it, locked each within their own historical milieu, can become friends with each other. The City's siloed women thus structurally recapitulate the historical isolation of women under patriarchy. However, this allegorical isolation is tactical. By soliciting its readers' imaginative interlocution, the *Book* invites a sociality not depicted between characters but rather enacted by women readers who are imagined as equally isolated and disheartened as the *Book*'s disconsolate narrator, and as remote from each other as the City's exemplary women entrapped within separate histories. This chapter explores the politics of the City's virtual socialities, arguing that the City urges readers to perform idealized women's friendship as an imagined community across time, as powerful and galvanizing as the idealized masculinized friendships found in the medieval intertexts of Cicero's *De amicitia*.

The first section of this chapter explores the idea of women's virtuous friendship as a form of needful solidarity in a hostile world, foregrounding the crucial role of women's alliances materialized in[5] books: acts of reading

---

3. Feminist fabulation is a radical relationship with existing archives that foregrounds its own transgressive epistemologies. It draws attention to its own fictionalizing strategies, highlighting the relationship of the researcher-writer to the texts she receives as a zone of intense, intersubjective exchange that acknowledges and enjoys its own fictionality; see Holly Pester, "Archive Fanfiction: Experimental Archive Research Methodologies and Feminist Epistemological Tactics," *feminist review* 115 (2017): 114–29; Marleen S. Barr, *Feminist Fabulation: Space/Postmodern Fiction* (Iowa City: University of Iowa Press, 1992).

4. For de Pizan's memory-work, see Margarete Zimmerman, "Christine de Pizan: Memory's Architect," in *Christine de Pizan: A Casebook,* ed. Barbara K. Altmann and Deborah L. McGrady (New York and London: Routledge, 2003), 57–81.

5. Alexandra Verini shows how feminist alliance in Christine de Pizan meddles with the distinction between public and private spaces to create feminotopian communities. This chap-

become acts of friendship with and between women. The second section of this chapter examines the allegorical frame of the *LCD* as an act of historical redress possible only between virtuous women, energized but not imprisoned by their history of wrongs. I read the compact between the narrator, Reason, Rectitude, and Justice in the light of discourses of virtuous friendship between men, derived from Cicero's *De amicitia*, and deeply at play in one of de Pizan's chief sources and literary models, Dante. As in Dante's *Convivio* and *Divine Comedy*, friendship is mediated by the intimacies of vernacular language, which is concretized and personified into a fast friend all on its own, animated in readings and in writings. The third section of this chapter looks at the actual architecture of the *LCD*. I summarize the antique, pagan, and Christian women who fabricate it and are joined by it and analyze the ways that de Pizan performs friendship to each woman in the city by reframing their stories to reproportionalize their deeds and virtues and to reverse masculinist reductions. Finally, I argue that Christine's city functions most powerfully in the phenomenology of active reading and rewriting. Reading de Pizan's text actively, skeptically, and interestedly makes feminist reading itself into a performance of friendship between women, especially if readers test de Pizan's decisions and editing strategies, and thereby increase their own capacities for education and study. By reworlding women's history into testing grounds for women's readerly interpretation and interlocution, de Pizan offers her audiences a form of women's friendship that gains power through its very virtuality and irreality. It makes women not only into worthy objects of study but also into worthy and active students, and it converts masculinist histories to histories written "by women and for women, with love."[6] Thus, through the education of its female readers, *The LCD* undertakes the profoundest act of ennobling friendship of all.

WOMEN UNDER SIEGE

Alan Bray gives the silence on women's friendship a prominent, anxiety-provoking place in the introduction to his groundbreaking study of early modern friendship, an anxiety that energizes the ultimate conclusion of *The Friend*—to show that "there has never been a time when male intimacy was

---

ter owes thanks for her work and unpublished research by Becky King on the pedagogical force of reading in Christine de Pizan: Alexandra Verini, "Medieval Models of Female Friendship in Christine de Pizan's *The Book of the City of Ladies* and Margery Kempe's *The Book of Margery Kempe*," *Feminist Studies* 42, no. 2 (2016): 365–91.

6. Joanna Russ, *Magic Mommas, Trembling Sisters, Puritans, and Perverts* (New York: Crossing Press, 1985), 79.

possible in a space untouched by power and politics . . . For women it may have been different, in that silence between the lines."[7] This chapter follows the rest of this collection in asserting that for women, it is not different. Rather, the pressures of power and politics are intensified, and the silence between the lines is an effect of those powerful political pressures. This anxious silence has been a clarion call to scholars studying premodern women's friendship. Many scholars have found historical evidence as "formal and objective"[8] as any could please, for women's friendship, gatherings, culture, networks, and patronage, from letters and manuscript circulations, to Anglo-Saxon abbeys to fifteenth-century monastic architecture.[9] That is not my project, however; this chapter is more interested in the ways that literary cultural fantasy lays bare the stakes of that silencing as an effect of masculinist, androcentric ways of reading. Although de Pizan writes many histories, biographies, and treatises, her most memorable texts are fantastical allegories, even though they are culturally situated and leverage from a precise variety of social positions to intervene against the silencing induced by historical objectivism itself.[10] Christine de Pizan's (1364–1430) *Livre de la cité de dames* (1405) and its peritexts, *Le chemin de longue étude* (1403), *Livre de fais d'armes et de chevalerie* (1410), and the *Livre de paix* (1413), are genre-mixing compilations that bespeak complex literary genealogies even as they are driven by historical evidence and broad social experience. These texts do not even dwell on the word *friendship*, much less sworn friendship, though they do use oaths in various ways to exert power and declare commitment: they speak more of "alliance" and "citizens." Their focus on alliance rather than affective bonding hooks into discourses of masculine virtuous friendship that make it the basis of public, political life,[11] even as they respond to the limits of history by opening literary spaces for utopian social speculation.[12]

However, along with their political aims, de Pizan's works do dramatize emotionally/politically resonant affections both between women and between women and men. I argue that they address the vicious realities of medieval

---

7. Alan Bray, *The Friend* (Chicago: University of Chicago Press, 2003), 11.
8. Bray, *Friend*, 25.
9. For a starting place, see Roberta Gilchrist, *Gender and Material Culture: The Archaeology of Religious Women* (New York and London: Routledge, 1997); Jocelyn Wogan-Browne, *Saints' Lives and Women's Literary Culture: c. 1150–1300* (Oxford: Oxford University Press, 2001); Mary C. Erler, *Women, Reading, and Piety in Late Medieval England* (Cambridge: Cambridge University Press, 2006).
10. Michel-Rolph Trouillot, *Silencing the Past: Power and the Production of History* (Boston: Beacon Press, 1997).
11. Lochrie and Vishnuvajjala, "Introduction."
12. Verini, "Medieval Models," and in this volume, "Sisters and Friends."

women's oppression and isolation from other women by transforming reading itself into an act of friendship, inviting women readers into a community that is both virtuous rather than vicious, and asynchronically virtual rather than historically real.[13] In this, they poise themselves against androcentric socialities of reading, rooted particularly in classical and clerical misogynist traditions (which rely on equally asynchronous connections—say, between Eve or Jezebel and *all* women). Christine de Pizan's allegorical works thus seize the potentials for social re-engineering that reading, education, and reasoned argument represent, taking them from the hands of misogynist writers, and in an act of friendly alliance, placing them into the hands of women readers and writers.

By transforming reading into a process of virtual friendly alliance, Christine de Pizan's texts press hard against the line between the virtual and the "real," as they offer an emotional reality to readers. Instead of "hate speech" they viralize friendship, through the technology of the day, the circulation of books and manuscripts. And in so doing, Christine de Pizan's women-centered allegories open up a glimpse into the longer histories of womanly friendships that we are only now beginning to ratify through such historical and archaeological recovery projects as Adrienne Mayor's richly evidential account of ancient Scythian Amazons, and through the literature-focused chapters in the present volume.

COMBATTING MISOGYNISMS

In reconceiving polity as based on women-inclusive friendship, Christine de Pizan's texts have their work cut out for them. It is not for nothing that the *LCD* imagines a defensible city built on a strong foundation constructed of ancient powerful women (Amazons) twinned with sapient women (sibyls and goddesses). It requires impenetrable walls, studded with exemplars of female virtue culled from the androcentric histories of Virgil, Plutarch, Boccaccio, and Dante. It is roofed with the most formidable women saints that Christine de Pizan can muster, commanded by the Virgin Mary and including her own name-saint, St. Christina of Tyre, who is the fiercest of all. The resulting city is a time-crossing assemblage that mortars the ancient together with the contemporary to create a rugged, asynchronic fortress of honor.

---

13. For the affective force of asynchronic contact across time, see Carolyn Dinshaw, *How Soon Is Now? Medieval Texts, Actual Readers, and the Queerness of Time* (Durham, NC: Duke University Press, 2012).

Reminding readers how hostile are the surrounding masculinist reading cultures is a crucial part of the *LCD*'s structure. To that end, all three books of the *LCD* are driven by what I will call *misogynisms* that are drawn from St. Jerome and Theophrastus, Ovid and Virgil, Matheolus, Jean de Meun, and Boccaccio.[14] These are doxic, toxic truisms about women, and they pervade Christine de Pizan's text like a barrage of missiles whose equally relentless deflection comes to dramatize the City's strength. The suffix *ism* connotes imitation and also affiliation: "isms" take sides with what they append to; and these misogynies don't simply exfoliate like memes but also march together, actively and collaboratively. Thus, throughout the *LCD*, Christine the narrator voices misogynisms she has heard about women's inconstancy, weakness, proneness to sin, ineducability, passionate madness, bad counsel, general depravity, and deficiency, and they all aggregate into a loathsome conglomerate, so widely attested and persuasively composited that one can come to doubt the goodness of a God who willingly created it. In *LCD* Christine de Pizan depicts the invasive and demoralizing force of these misogynisms in her own thought by giving them to her homodiegetic narrator, Christine, to articulate. To Christine, these misogynisms glide through textual histories like predatory bats, always looking for a place to settle and sap the self-determination of women readers.

How do these misogynies work their harm?[15] Just as they gain a general power from their mutual affiliations, they are driven by an engine of exemplarization in which a single exemplar (say, Eve) or a skeletal constellation of them (say, Jezebel, Delilah, or Pasiphae) synecdochally come to stand for the entire species. The species in turn is concretized and energized by the specific historicity of the exemplar, thus gaining social credibility in a nightmare version of the process that Pierre Bourdieu describes as a mystery of ministry: "Group made man, he personifies a fictitious person, which he lifts out of the state of a simple aggregate of separate individuals, enabling them to act and speak, through him, 'like a single person.'"[16] Just as an elected representative substitutes for and receives the communal force of the group, creating it while incarnating it and becoming a fictitious person with redoubled social power,

---

14. Rosaline Brown-Grant usefully discusses de Pizan's address to medieval misogynist traditions in "Christine de Pizan as a Defender of Women," in Altmann and McGrady, *Casebook*, 81–100.

15. Carissa M. Harris, *Obscene Pedagogies: Transgressive Talk and Sexual Education in Late Medieval Britain* (Ithaca, NY: Cornell University Press, 2018), 1–26; R. Howard Bloch, *Medieval Misogyny and the Invention of Western Romantic Love* (Chicago: University of Chicago Press, 1991).

16. Pierre Bourdieu, *Language and Symbolic Power*, trans. Gino Raymond and Matthew Adamson (Cambridge, MA: Harvard University Press, 1991).

through a similar fictionalizing process the conscripted, slanderous representative casts an inculpating shadow over the whole group. When one chooses a single woman, say Eve or Jezebel, to represent all women, all women are reduced to a single, sin-originating face. Further, all subsequent individual women with flaws can be impressed as collaborators in a transhistorical sin-army, that becomes more credible the longer the list grows (hence the desire of misogynists to amass notebooks full of women).

The same synecdochic reduction can be applied to a single woman's eventful life story, allowing it to be entirely commandeered by one detail or flaw. To take one instance, Dido can be ripped from her own timeline, annexed to a Roman imperialist mythography featuring Aeneas, dragooned into a fit of passion (which figuratively alludes to its own belated insertion by being attributed to a motivating goddess), in a tragic rewriting that would climax with her unforgettable self-immolation. In the process of getting caught up with Dido's passion, we can disregard everything else in her history: her valiant escape from Phoenicia, her clever seizure of land-right in North Africa, her foundational success, her years of good leadership, her capacity for rule and self-governance: Queen Dido fades into tragic Dido, to inspire the horror and sympathy of men in a transhistorical affective "cosi fan tutti" that has reached tsunami force by the time Christine de Pizan encounters it.[17] This reductive synecdoche can be applied to every notable woman in history, so that Zenobia's long and successful sovereignty disappears behind the fictitious distaff she had to display in the Roman triumph that signaled her defeat, or Semiramis's regnal power dwindles behind her incest. For each woman's life, a historical or fictional flaw is enlarged to become the inescapable frame for the whole account (re-troped as tragedy or horror show), and thus she can be conscripted to join hands with her foremother, Eve, in a snowballing genealogy of evil that would make Benjamin's afflicted Angel of History weep yet again.

How can one deal with these multitudinous misogynisms—this army of fictionally collaborative bats? Christine's divine allegorical interlocutors, Reason, Rectitude, and Justice, refute these misogynisms promptly and judiciously, using a one-two punch of rational rebuttal followed by counterexamples, and each rebuttal thus creates a new focus for discussing the lives of the women who serve as counterexamples—a countergenealogy of feminine virtue, which snowballs into its own transhistorical force. In this way the *LCD* pins misogynisms down for the purposes of both logical and exemplary rebuttal, and then uses their own fictionalizing strategies of exemplarism, representation, and

---

17. Thomas Hahn, "Don't Cry for Me, Augustinus: Dido and the Dangers of Empathy," in *Truth and Tales: Cultural Mobility and Medieval Media*, ed. Fiona Somerset and Nicholas Watson (Columbus: The Ohio State University Press, 2015), 41–59.

alliance to confect a counterhistory on the side of truth. Some misogynisms are acknowledged as half-truths, others are lies, while others actually invert the truth. For instance, in terms of women's purported viciousness, de Pizan sees women as more intrinsically inclined to virtue than men—a situational essentialism she bases logically on women's historical disempowerment and thus remoteness from the temptations of tyranny.

Yet these misogynisms with their trailing notebooks full of evil women cannot simply be reasoned away one by one, since they gain power through pervasiveness of their collective reiteration. Accordingly, Christine de Pizan's defense becomes an almost statistical corrective: a refiguring of what counts as significant given sampling and ideological biases. First, de Pizan draws on a wider array of women than any of her sources to showcase the sheer diversity of feminine virtue. Second, her retellings reproportion and re-trope individual stories so that emplotments shift from provoking denigration or tragic defeat to reinforcing respect and assessing lasting gains.[18] In the process, significant flaws such as Semiramis's incest or Dido's passion dwindle from catalysts to singular details among many other details. De Pizan thus changes women's stories by writing, in Rachel Blau Duplessis's terms, "beyond the endings" that foreclose possibilities of historical significance: carrying the women's lives beyond marriage, defeat, or death, toward ongoing ennobling loves, virtuous service, and social utility.[19] In most stories she compiles different sources to enrich the details that show historical friendships between famous women and those they loved, their families, friends, husbands, and peoples, while underscoring that the whole picture is complicated, extensive, and irreducible.

A case in point is de Pizan's reframing of the story of the Sabine women, who are noted in many sources only for being the victims of rape by the settlers from Romulus's army. In Livy's account, which Christine works from and writes against, the women are endangered by their fathers, who had refused intermarriage rights to the Roman settlers. In response to this refusal, the rape becomes a successful Roman reproductive gambit, justified because the Roman men's dynastic urgencies are paramount. However, this outcome requires a horrific betrayal of hospitality rights. The Sabine families are invited to attend celebratory games at the new city of Rome, hosted by individual Romans in their houses, and then at a prearranged signal, their daughters are abducted by their hosts, with the most beautiful earmarked for the noblest

---

18. See Hayden White's "The Historical Text and Literary Artifact," in *Tropics of Discourse* (Baltimore and London: Johns Hopkins University Press, 1978), 81–199, for a discussion of the power of reframing and re-troping historical retellings and the generic shifts that result.

19. Rachel Blau Duplessis, *Writing Beyond the Ending: The Narrative Strategies of Twentieth-Century Women Writers* (Bloomington: Indiana University Press, 1985).

Roman patricians. The Sabine paterfamiliases are driven back, leaving the city in rage, while Romulus assures the daughters that they will be honorably married, share citizenship and property rights with their husbands, and be mothers to a new race of freemen (and what is better than to be free? the captives are asked, with some irony). But what really gains the Sabine women's assent is their individual captors "justifying their acts by their lust and love—the plea most moving of all to a woman's temper" [purgantium cupiditate atque amore, quae maxime ad muliebre ingenium efficaces preces sunt], as Livy, secure in his grasp of women's natures, assures us.[20] Their angry families then go to war and beat the Romans almost to a standstill. At that point, the women intervene to stop the two armies, apparently convinced by Romulus's argument and the interests of their children.

Christine de Pizan's interpolation takes us beyond the rape, underscoring instead how the women take charge of their circumstances and rewrite tragedy into triumph. They do this by organizing. Their story crystallizes the personal and political force of friendship that de Pizan envisions throughout her book. Hearing that their fathers and brothers are preparing to attack the settlers and take back their daughters, the queen of the Sabines addresses her fellow victims and proposes an act of what amounts to civil disobedience: to place their bodies and those of their children between the encroaching armies and plead for peace.

> "Honored Sabine ladies, my dear sisters and companions, you know how we were abducted by our husbands and how this caused our fathers and relatives to wage war on our husbands, and our husbands on them. There is no way whatsoever that this deadly conflict can be brought to an end or continue without it being to our detriment, no matter who wins... What is done is done and cannot be undone. That is why I think it would be a very good idea if we could find a way to end this war and reestablish peace. If you are willing to trust my advice, follow me, and do as I do, I am convinced that we can bring this matter to a good end."

> ["Dames honnourees de Sabine, mes chieres suers et compaignes, vous savez le ravissment qui fu fait de nous de noz maris, pour laquel cause nos peres et parens leur mainent guerre et noz maris a eulx. Sy ne puet de nulle part en nulle manière terminer ceste mortelle guerre ne estre maintenue, qui qu'en ait la vittoire que ce ne soit a nostre prejudice... ce qui est fait est fait et ne

---

20. Livy, *History of Rome*, I.9.16, in *Livy in XIV Volumes*, 1–2 (Cambridge MA: Harvard University Press; London: William Heineman, 1962), 37–38.

puet autrement estre. Et pour ce me semble que moult seroit grant bien se aucun conseil, par nous y povoit estre trouvé que paix fust mise en cestre guerre. Et se mon conseil en voulez croirre et me suivre et faire ce que je feray, je tiens que de ce vendrons nous bien a chief."][21]

In this speech (which is not present in Livy), the Queen of the Sabines not only organizes her fellow victims but models a kind of leadership that is antithetical to Livy's Romulus. She invites them to a political collaboration rather than an imperial rape. She addresses them as *Dames honnourees*, honorable rather than dishonored, as dear sisters and companions (*chieres suers et compaignes*) rather than dynastic conveniences. She acknowledges the rape as rape (*ravissment*) before going on to talk about the virtuous necessity that brought love for children and therefore husbands out of acts of violence at the cross-section of past and future families). Most of all, she places that rape in a past that should not continue to determine the women's lives. Rather, they should acknowledge that through no choice of their own, they now have deep affiliations not only with their Sabine families and kinfolk but also with the Romans. Whoever wins, either their children, or their fathers and kin, will suffer. She urges them to decline the roles of motivators for masculine action,[22] defined only by the crime done to them and its ramifications for the honor of their Sabine paterfamiliases. The women assent as a body, a moment of public consent, "elles obeyroyent tres voulentiers" (Curnow, *LCD* 867), that again counter-indicts the assumption of naturalized consent implicit in Livy. The queen's speech is a declaration of friendship, then, in at least three Ciceronian ways: (1) it restores honor and virtue to the women, (2) it invites them to a loving alliance in which they become equals in action, and (3) it rouses them to further acts of civic virtue. The women take their children and go with loose hair and bare feet to stand between the two armies, shouting to them in a public, political declaration of love, friendship, and double affiliation: "Beloved fathers and kinsmen, beloved husbands, for God's sake, make peace! If not, we are prepared to die under the hoofs of your horses." ["Pares et parens tres chiers, et seigneurs maris tres amez, pour Dieu faittes paix! Ou

---

21. Christine de Pizan, *The Book of the City of Ladies and Other Writings*, ed. Sophie de Bourgault and Rebecca Kingston, trans. Ineke Harde (Indianapolis: Hackett, 2018), 136; Christine de Pizan, *The Livre de la cité des dames of Christine de Pisan: A Critical Edition*, ed. Maureen Curnow (Ann Arbor MI: UMI Dissertation Information Service, 1975), 866–67. I use these editions throughout for text and translation of *LCD*. Subsequent citations appear in parentheses in the text.

22. Gail Simone, "Women in Refrigerators," https://www.lby3.com/wir/ (accessed January 29, 2020).

se ce nom, yoy toutes voulons mourir soubs les piez de voz chevaulx!"] (de Bourgault and Kingston, *LCD* 137; Curnow, *LCD* 867).

The brashness and self-sacrifice of the women's stratagem is a seizure of gendered discourse itself. It troubles categorical distinctions between men and women by simultaneously seizing control of a masculinized public space (the battlefield) and making a feminized affective plea (they strategically dress like victims, hair uncovered, kneeling, and in tears).[23] This act startles the men on both sides into a new relationship with each other:

> The husbands, who saw their wives and children before them in tears, were shocked and certainly most unwilling to run at them. The fathers were equally moved by seeing their daughters in tears. Touched by the women's humble plea, the two sides looked at each other and their rage faded, replaced by the filial piety sons feel for their fathers. Both sides felt compelled to throw down their weapons, embrace each other, and make peace. Romulus led the king of the Sabines, his father-in-law, into the city and welcomed him and all his company with great honor. That is how the good sense and moral courage of the queen and her ladies saved the Romans and the Sabines from destruction.
>
> [Les maris qui la virent plourans leurs femmes et leurs enffans moult furent esmerveilliez et bien enuiz—n'est pas doubte courussent parmy eulx. Semblablement appitoya et attendry moult les cuers aux peres d'ainsi vecir leurs filles. Parquoy, regardant les uns les autres pour la pitié des dames qui si humblement les prioyent, tourna felonnie en amoureuse pitié comme de filz a peres tant que ilz furent contrains a gitter just leurs armes d'ambedeux pars et d'aler embracier les une les autres et de faire paix. Romulus mena le roy de Sabins, son sire, en sa cite et grandement l'onnoura et toute la compagnie. A ainsi par le scens et vertu de celle royne et de dames furent gardéz les Rommains et les Sabins d'estre destruiz.] (de Bourgault, *LCD* 137; Curnow 867–68)

De Pizan's account of this intervention shows how the women deliberately adopt the semiotics of victimhood (the very victimhood that Livy's account attempts first to instrumentalize and then to smooth over) because they know that that is what their husbands and kin expect from women. And sure enough, it's their tears that the men read and their humility that shocks and

---

23. For other uses of gendered space in *LCD*, see Judith L. Kellogg, "*Le Livre de la cité des dames*: Reconfiguring Knowledge and Reimagining Gendered Space," in Altmann and McGrady, *Casebook*, 126–46.

arrests both their kin and their lord-husbands (*seigneurs maris*—de Pizan never lets us forget the coercion implicit in their marriages). However, to the reader, this feminine humility has already been framed by a feminine political alliance based in pragmatism and daring. Transplanting feminine tears into the hypermasculinized center of the battlefield rather than its decorous margins effectively regenders war as central to women's concerns.

And yet the appeal that exerts the most effective alchemy on the men is not the implicit gender trouble of the women's intervention but the double love they declare, which transforms the two army's zero-sum homosocial conflict into something else. These doubly affiliated women choose to inhabit a place that could be read by one army as accession to their rape and by the other as continued affiliation despite rape and overcoming it. As though the pressure of this double vision were a catalyst, suddenly and miraculously the men look at each other and *see each other as the women see them*—as kin. The women's act of friendship with each other catalyzes the armies' mutual hate into filial love (*tourna felonnie en amoureuse pitié comme de filz a peres*), compelling the men (*ilz furent contrains*) to abandon their contest over masculine honor and to see with women's eyes: the eyes of friendship and familiarity. The patriotic gains are immediate, as de Pizan presses home. The provocative virtue enacted in this theater of loving victimhood will enable both the Sabines and the Romans to survive. The new invitation of the Sabines into Rome, with all honor, redresses the horrific breach in hospitality that the previous rapes had inflicted.

By focusing on this moment of feminine alliance, rather than Livy's rape, or his imperatives of empire, or his staging of honor and revenge, or his recourse to the women's susceptibility to male passion which comes from their natures, Christine de Pizan unwrites Livy. She takes the story beyond the triumphalist zero-sum logic of Roman imperial colonialism to a new zone of collaborative alliance. These women become politically significant by bringing women's perspectives into masculine public spaces, to serve virtuously their own needs and those of their countries.

This anecdote is just one of the most forceful of many such throughout the *LCD*. By publicly dramatizing women's virtue as rational, heartfelt, and above all politically beneficial, de Pizan shows how friendly love and alliance between women extends the profile for Ciceronian civic friendship beyond men, to the betterment of both men and women and the lands they inhabit. The drama of these detournements casts light on the twofold tactics of *LCD*'s battle with misogynisms: both critical (rational point-by-point rebuttal) and countervisionary (affective narrative cruxes). The high-walled, enduring city of ladies, with its call to unite women readers in friendly citizenship, promises to do this visionary work. The *LCD* envisions a defensible city that combines the military prowess of Amazonia with the liberating luster and sempiternity of the celestial Jerusalem itself.

> My dear ladies . . . you have good reason . . . to rejoice in God and virtuousness at seeing this new city completed. It will not only serve as a refuge for all of you virtuous women but also as a bastion from which to defend yourself against your enemies and assailants, provided you guard it well. You can see that the material used in its construction is pure virtue, shining so brightly that you may see your reflection in it.

> [Mes tres chieres dames . . . si avez cause orendroit . . . de vous esjouyr vertueusement en Dieu et bonnes meurs par ceste nouvelle cite voir, parfette, qui puet ester non mie seullement le reffuge de vou toutes, c'est a entendre de vertueuses, mais aussi la deffense et garde contre voz annemis et assaillans, si bien la gardez. Car vous povez veoir que la matière dont elle est faitte est toute de vertu, voire, si reluysant que toutes vous y povez mirer.] (de Bourgault 219; Curnow 1031–32).

Reflected in the city thus are not only the virtuous women of the past but the virtuous woman readers to come, who can see themselves in its heavenly mirror. The iconography of an ethical heaven is offered to all who need such a refuge, so long as they ally with it and take up virtuous arms to guard it.

That vigilance makes friendship a political act, an act of defense against war, even as it draws on feminized, spiritual tropes, such as mirroring. In subsequent treatises, such as the *Book of Deeds and Chivalry* and the *Book of Peace*, Christine refined the political work of friendship or amity as a national virtue that could resist the centrifugal forces of masculinist elite warfare she saw tearing turn-of-the-century France apart. The *LCD* at its most aspirational imagines a powerful role for women themselves as sowers of a defensible peace. They are invited to become like the Sabine women, ravaged by androcentric histories, but working together in ways that benefit man and women alike, to enact a national-scaled politics of friendship. In this time-crossing feminist alliance, reading is transformed from androcentric gaslighting into a virtual alliance of women who can write forward in their turn.

INVISIBLE CITIES: READING FOR FRIENDSHIP

The experience of reading in de Pizan's works is intimate, always imagined as an intersubjective exchange, for good or ill, even when allegorical personification is not involved (as it often is in de Pizan's texts) to embody the intercourse. For instance, when de Pizan reads Jean le Fèvre de Resson's recent French translation of Mathieu of Boulogne's *Liber lamentationum Matheoluli*, a misogynist treatise against marriage, Matheolus worms his way into her consciousness like a sapper undermining her morale from within, until she is sick at heart and cursing herself and God for allowing her to be born into the body of a woman.

As de Pizan dramatizes how books infiltrate readerly consciousness, she also experiments with how books are activated in readers through a reader's idiolectic processes of meaning-making and frustration. Frequently books gain bodies in the process and become physically interactive as mentors and friends (or detractors and enemies such as Matheolus). For instance, in books 3 and 4 of *Le Livre des faits d'armes et de chevalerie* (1410), the act of shifting to a new source becomes a personal conversation with the author of that source. As Christine de Pizan proceeds to engage at length with Honoré de Bouvet's *Arbre des batailles*'s granular treatments of military legality and best practice, she dramatizes this as a visionary visit from Honoré de Bouvet himself: in the form of a "solemn man in clerical garb" ["tres solempnel d'abit de friere"] who addresses her as "Dear Friend, Christine" ["Chere amy, Christine"].[24] De Bouvet addresses de Pizan as an old friend, and he consents to be her mentor for her current project. De Pizan references a history of past textual liaisons:

> "O worthy Master, I know that you are one whose work I admire greatly and have admired as long as I can recall; your haunting and virtuous presence has already helped me, thanks be to God, to bring to a successful conclusion many fine undertakings. Certainly I am very glad to have your company."

> [O digne maistre, je congnois que tu es celluy estude que j'ame et tant ay amé que plus de riens ne me souvient et par laquelle vertu et frequentation ay, la Dieu grace achevée maintes belles entreprises. Certes de ta compaignie suis tres joyeuse ... BNF 1183 f. 49.].

The collaborative compact between de Pizan and de Bouvet references a longer relationship of continual revisitation and endowment, more like a long-term collaboration. Textual friendship is enacted in active, ongoing iterations of reading and usage that deepen over time. Further, while textual friendships

---

24. Christine de Pizan, *The Book of Deeds of Arms and Chivalry*, trans. Sumner Willard, ed. Charity Cannon Willard (State College: Pennsylvania State University Press, 1999). Transcription from BNF 1183, f. 49.

endear writers to readers, they can also empower them to become better writers on their own and reach other readers in turn.

By creating friendships with other texts, Pizan models for her own readers the power to be gained by compiling old books into new collaborations, to get needful work done. De Pizan thus repurposes even the most androcentric literary histories and strategies: Livian empire-building, Boethian protrepsis, Dante's *comedic* world-making. Even Jean de Meun's debates in the *Roman de la rose* (which she publicly critiqued for their misogynist content) modeled forensic flexibilities that helped her turn the genre of dream vision allegory toward her own needful interventions.

So if books can be friends with writers and readers, how is textual friendship transformative? In *LCD* de Pizan dramatizes how books can become friendly catalysts for virtuous knowledge, morale, and solidarity in two ways. The first is diegetic: faculty allegories can model women mentoring other women, even as they intermesh allegorical characters with the reader's internal thoughts, feelings, and urgencies. The second way is extradiegetic: by rewriting historical characters in such a way that they can step out of the worlds of the textual past and emerge affectively into the reader's present everyday life. Just as biblical drama allowed the re-presenting of remote scriptural truths with medieval contemporary worlds, reading Christine de Pizan's composite histories (whether those of virtuous women, literary knowledge systems, or French national history) provoke not only an aesthetic reading but also what Louise Rosenblatt calls an efferent one (from Latin *efferre*: to carry away, produce, elevate): something readers carry away with them.[25] This is not so much a lesson or a message as a set of new ways of engaging in the world. Efferent readings galvanize social, political, ethical action. Christine de Pizan's allegorical journeys can arrest readers with their vividness, fluidity, and strangeness, and energize their own world-building alliance-schemes. This means that most crucial friendships for Christine's projects are not those she depicts within her vision-texts but rather those that her books provoke readers to enact.

Thus, the most vivid diegetic models of de Pizan's seizure and detournement of the modes of Ciceronian friendship are the relationships between her narrators and her mentors, who are at once her idealized doubles gleaned from her reading of other texts and intimately reimagined, and the divine, profoundly illustrious, and remote daughters of God.[26] In *Chemin de longue*

---

25. Louise Rosenblatt, *The Reader, The Text, The Poem: The Transactional Theory of the Literary Work* (Carbondale: Southern Illinois University, 1978), 22-47.

26. Though they differ from the remoter goddesses of Nature and Fortune in de Pizan's work, precisely because they do become her friends: for the unnerving ambiguities of Nature

étude, we find the sibyl Almathea; in *LCD,* Reason, Rectitude, and Justice; and in the *Avision,* the princess who is simultaneously the human capacity for divine insight, the holy church, and the nation of France. All are gendered female, and all occupy a richly mixed space between subject and object, text and reader, past and present, self and larger world, because reading is exactly the intersubjective space where such liaisons can happen. In modeling these textual friendships, Christine grasps the fully transactional nature of reading and the active, emotional, multifaceted, ultimately political activity the reader performs.

This transactionality is underscored through the composite mentors of *LCD*: the alliance of Reason (with her mirror), Rectitude (with her ruler), and Justice (with her measuring cup) as they work together to guide, correct, and energize Christine. The very homeliness of their insignia, as tools any woman might use around the house, actualizes their ability to translate divine reflection and ethical assessment into productive action. Justice declares that they work in tandem and that their cooperative division of labor makes them supremely effective: "And we, the three ladies you see before you, are all one: we could not function without each other. What the first one decides, the second one puts into effect, while I, the third one, ensure that it is brought to fruition." As they restore moral vision to Christine, their alliance makes friendship operational. Once the *LCD* is finished, it can become a replicant mentor and go out into the world to comfort, teach, support, and inspire other women, by showing them that they are not alone. In this way *LCD* mobilizes Ciceronian models of friendship by building virtue into its transmission, but it flouts those models by making it elective, promiscuous, diverse, inclusive, and textually reproductive. Where Cicero considered true male–male virtuous love to be rare almost to extinction, de Pizan shows that women's virtuous love can be electively transacted across the generations, through efferent reading and inspired re-creation.

Christine de Pizan goes out of her way to stress the heterogeneity of women's virtue across history, offering her readers a huge variety of possible identifications, carefully allocated the parts of the city de Pizan considers best for them.[27] The three parts of the *LCD* divide into three books which describe different levels of construction: (1) foundations and ramparts, (2) walls and buildings, and (3) rooftops and towers. At the foundations are ancient pagan

---

and Fortune in Christine's writings, see Barbara Newman, *God and the Goddesses: Vision, Poetry, and Belief in the Middle Ages* (Philadelphia: University of Pennsylvania Press, 2003), 115–22.

27. I am grateful to the insights of Lauren Rebecca King, whose promising dissertation on identification and interventional reading in Christine de Pizan and Geoffrey Chaucer has been a guide to my own thinking.

illustrious women, whom de Pizan salvages from androcentric histories that have exceptionalized, vilified, or fetishized them. In the process, she permutes their histories to capitalize on their virtuous friendship not only to other women but to their families, countries, and allies. There are two groups of women at the City's foundations: (1) women of power, equal to the best of men in both battle and governance; and (2) women of knowledge. Sovereign women include Semiramis, the Amazons, including their founding queens Lampheto and Marpasia, Thamaris, Menalyppe and Hippolita; and then Penthesilea (who demonstrated her virtuous friendship for Hector by dying to avenge him), Zenobia, Artemisia, Lilia, Fredegund of France, who fought with her sons in her arms, Camilla, and Berenice. The final exemplar, Cloelia, gives us a powerful figure for de Pizan's own feminist salvage project. Cloelia was a seemingly helpless virgin among many taken hostage and imprisoned by a Roman adversary. She broke her fellow hostages out of prison with the help of a single horse to carry them one by one across a river, an accomplishment that wrung reluctant admiration even out of the Romans. De Pizan's salvage project performs a similar service to the woman captured in masculinist narratives, extracting them and working them one by one into the fabric of the City.

The second group of knowledgeable women at the foundations of de Pizan's City includes poets and writers (such as Cornificia, Proba, and Sappho), oracles and magicians (such as Manto, Medea, and Circe), sibyls (such as Nicostrata), and inventors (including some euhemerized goddesses like Minerva, Ceres, and Isis, whom de Pizan humanizes into very accomplished women who innovated new technologies). An account of ancient painters—Thamaris, Irene, and Marcia—prompts Christine to leap forward in time and praise one of her own scribal collaborators, a fifteenth-century Parisian illuminator named Anastasia. Finally, we get prudential women who showcase the ethical utilities of knowledge: Gaia Cyrilla, Dido of Carthage (now a figure of good governance rather than passion), Ops of Crete, and Lavinia of Latinum. Placing a varied consortium of antique pagan power, knowledge, and wisdom at the bedrock of the city allows Christine to initiate a variety of virtuous genealogies that the next level of the city can ramify forward in time.

The second book of *LCD* gives us the buildings of the city—its middle stratum. At this level, figures from different times and traditions mingle freely and promiscuously in defiance of the temporal and religious segregation maintained in de Pizan's central sources, particularly Boccaccio's *De mulieribus claris*.[28] This middle stratum of the city is the most asynchronous and

---

28. Boccaccio uses the first hundred of his biographies upon notable ancient pagan women, and then moves to Christian and medieval times with the last six: Pope Joan, Irene of Constantinople, Gualdrada, Constance, Camiola, and Joanna, queen of Jerusalem: Boccaccio, *Famous Women*, trans. Virginia Brown (Cambridge, MA: Harvard University Press, 2003).

mixed space in the *LCD*, weaving from the ancient to the contemporary; from queens to peasant girls; from history to legend to romance and literature. We can see how women operate beneficially within a huge range of social relationships, both with other women and with men. Their loving virtue is made visible as the social adhesive that preserves dynasties and civilizations. Their fidelity to men at all costs parts company with many contemporary feminisms, but this is precisely where Christine de Pizan touches most insistently on the power of women's friendship to pervade the lives of those it touches in ennobling Ciceronian ways.

Rectitude is the genia loci for this central stratum. Thus, this level devotes itself to rectifying particularly insidious misogynisms: those that desocialize women by making them monsters who corrode human relationships. Rectitude combats these misogynisms by showing women as faithful protectors of the ties that bind families and societies together. Throughout the book, women work as powerful, kindly mediators, enacting the power of friendly intercession by weaving peace amid hate. The book begins with prophets and emissaries who mediate God's word to the world: the ten sibyls and other oracles. It goes on to dutiful daughters (Drypetina, Hypsipyle, Claudine, Griselda); meritorious wives (Hyspsicratea, Triaria, Artemisia, Argia, Agrippina, Julia, Tertia Aemilia, etc.); wives faithful to clerical husbands (Xanthippe, Pompeia), to old husbands (Sulpicia); to lepers (contemporary women); women who keep their husband's secrets at all costs (Portia, Curia); good advisors to husbands (Antonia, Roxanne); and social benefactors of many kinds: rescuers of good men (Thermutis) or dispatchers of bad ones (Judith); culminating with women who save whole nations (Esther, Deborah, and the Sabine women, discussed above, Veturia, Clotilde, the women who sheltered the first apostles, and Catulla, who kept St. Denis's body for France). Guided by Rectitude, Christine moves from women who augment social good to those who repay gratefully the social goods they are given, such as education: Hortensia of Rome (ancient) and Novella of Bologna (contemporary). Other women repay a good marriage by remaining chaste (various biblical, pagan, and Jewish women) or exhibit great beauty while remaining chaste (Mariamne, Antonia). Then we find the women who repay great wrong with virtue: victims of rape who requite dishonor on their own terms (Lucrecia, wife of King Ortiagon of Galatia, Hippo, Virginia); victims of abuse who persist, survive, and do good (Griselda, Florence of Rome, Sicurano); and women faithful in love unto death (Dido, Medea, Thisbe, Hero, Ghismoda, Lisabetta, Dame de Fayel, the Chatelaine of Vergie, Isolde, Deianera). Then come a group of women misunderstood or appropriated, who became famous by chance or because of men's desire for them, usually to their own detriment (Juno, Europa, Jocasta, Medusa, Helen, Polyxena), and women who like elegant fashion and shouldn't be denigrated as mantraps since not everything is about men (Claudine, Lucretia, and Queen Blanche mother of St. Louis)—a section that targets the androcentrism of de Pizan's sources. A final group stresses women's friendship and generous giving to the unfortunate when charity benefits everyone (Busa of Apulia, Marguerite de la Riviere, Isabeau of Bavaria [the current queen of France], the Duchess of Berry, the Duchess of Orleans, and even more contemporary figures, commoners as well as the elite). From the ancient women who mediate God's wisdom and foresight to the world, to the contemporary women whose charitable giving enacts God's love in the world, women are presented as donors and keepers of the troths of love and friendship that bind society together.

The third and final level of the city is the roofs and towers, under the administration of lady Justice, and it contains only Christian saints from across history. Here Christine welcomes the queen of Heaven, Mary herself, into the city, in a formal triumph grandiose enough to ensure that Ave replaces Eva as the delegate of womankind. Mary illuminates the renovated dialectical mystery of ministry of the female sex by descending willingly to be written into the fabric of the city, a citizen among others, but its most paramount representative.

The hagiographies and martyrologies that follow, like the stories of the ancient Amazons at the city's foundations, underscore women's absolute indomitability, showing that what Amazon warriors begin, saintly Christian women can finish (and often with even more ferocity). This is particularly evident in the melodrama of St. Christine of Tyre, Christine de Pizan's own name-saint. The story opens an allegorical window onto one of Christine de Pizan's favorite tropes: how misfortune can be turned into new opportunity. When Christine of Tyr adopts Christianity, her pagan father Urban imprisons and tortures her, and finally throws her into the sea. Christine prays to Christ himself to baptize her in the Mediterranean, since she's there already, turning the instrument of execution into the means of regeneration, and he obliges. Crowned with a star by Christ himself, the newly baptized Christine gains a lethal power over those who oppose her: the power to reflect their own hatred back upon themselves. That night the father who tortured and tried to kill her is tortured and killed by a devil. Arraigned before a tribunal, Christine tames snakes and raises the dead, while two prosecuting judges die in trying to dispatch her. The last judge, Julian, tears her breasts off (thereby giving her a double Amazon insignia), but she bleeds milk rather than blood—replacing loss of lifeblood with gift of nurture. She preaches and he tears out most of her tongue, but rather than silencing her, this paradoxically invests her speech with even more force and clarity. Julian has a final dig at the remains of her tongue, but she spits the last piece out—into his eye, where it blinds him—and continues to speak: "Do you really think, you tyrant, that cutting out my tongue will stop me from blessing God, when my soul will eternally bless Him and yours will be damned forever? You failed to heed my words, so it is only fair that my tongue has blinded you" [Tirant, que te vault avoir couppee ma langue adfin que elle ne beneysse Dieu, quant mon esperit a tousjours le beneystra et le tien demourera perpetual en maleysson? Et pource que tu ne congnois ma parole, c'est bien raison que ma langue t'ait aveuglé] (de Bourgault 207; Curnow 1009). Ultimately, only distance weapons—two arrows—can take her down, and, instantly arrowlike, she flies up to God.

This story that bears Christine's name suggests that although Christine de Pizan passionately believes in the cause of peace, patience, and social cohesion and seizes the tropes of friendship to intimate these causes in heartfelt ways, sometimes peace is not enough. Those who attack women need to be met with a reflection of their own force. In book 3, driven by the sigils of Justice, the fervor of Christian witness, and violent strictures of martyrology, a ferocious anger bursts forth. The sheer rage of St. Christine's story as it alchemizes death into new life, silence into speech, and speech into a blinding weapon against those who will not see is the hostile face that the hospitable City must turn to its detractors. In that face, virtue becomes not only a shield to mirror women's virtue but a sword against those who decry it.

The three levels of the city compound so many stories of so many genres and types that readers may pick and choose; this variety is tactical. De Pizan makes the structural logic so clear that one can skim, and thus some things will stand out at one reading and others at subsequent ones. The diversity of the *LCD*'s allegorical and historical characters refuses to provide ideal models for emulation—that would risk reducing readerly agency and thus losing readerly love. Rather, these historical women appeal not through likeness, or ideality, but through unlikeness and historicity. They do not model female virtue so much as measure the wider latitudes of virtuous femininity itself, across time and cultural difference.

Readers who have already read some of these stories from other sources will find another insight as well. When de Pizan retells familiar tales differently, she exemplifies feminist reframing practices. She offers women readers a toolbox for actively reading to demonstrate virtuous friendship toward notable women who are all too often rolled, like Chaucer's poor Criseyde, upon many a tongue. In sum, the *LCD* not only represents but performs a feminist intervention against the imaginative strictures of androcentric narrative cultures. De Pizan enacts friendship with women readers by (1) critiquing misogynisms as they occur in a thoroughgoing attempt at feminist reprogramming,

(2) offering a variety of imaginative affiliations with other historical women across time to many kinds of readers, and (3) revivifying possibilities of new writing and thinking by modeling how narratives can be reproportionalized and redressed so that the complexity of woman's lives, multiple affiliations, and political service can become visible.

As its more than two hundred manuscripts show, de Pizan's book was an invitation to creative collaboration that many subsequent readers, artists, and scholars have been eager to take up. These include texts owned by Anne de Beaujeu, Gabrielle de Bourbon, Marguerite de Navarre, Georgette de Montenay, and Margaret of Austria.[29] It jumps media from architectural allegory and plain text to illuminated text to painting to tapestry. Queen Elizabeth I herself owned a six-section tapestry of the City of Ladies, each section extending eight by five meters; she could literally walk the City across fifty square meters of her house.[30] The *LCD*'s complicated and very rich reception history attests at once to its affective power, its creative invasiveness across media, and the fear it induced in those who tried to appropriate or control it.[31] The *Book of the City of Ladies* ultimately works because the City escapes de Pizan's book and becomes an open-ended mobile assemblage, spawning a thousand new cities in the process of reading. To be sure, de Pizan's Ciceronian focus on public virtue at whatever social level limits her congeniality to many of the socially denigrated women treated in this volume, from Harris's obscene and educative gossips and cummars, to Lochrie's excavation of a half-occluded likeness of feeling in Chaucer's Sultaness or Wife of Bath, to Vishnuvajjala's beautifully complicated Gaynor. However, the text's virtuous elitism itself can be discarded and critiqued by its readers, even as they adopt its writerly strategies. In the end, *LCD* models a form of feminist fabulation that could be seized upon by women who needed it and taken anywhere—in public or in private—through reading, which itself muddles public and private boundaries in both diegetic and extradiegetic ways[32] to extend a politics of women's friendship across the ages.

Reading a book as a collaboration with a friend is to perform friendship at a distance, while also realizing it is as intimate as a personification of one's

---

29. Zimmerman, "Memory's," 57; James Laidlaw, "Christine and the Manuscript Tradition, in *Casebook*, 231–51; Nadia Margolis, "Modern Editions: Makers of the Christinian Corpus," in *Casebook*, 251–70; Susan Groag Bell, *The Lost Tapestries of the City of Ladies: Christine de Pizan's Renaissance Legacies* (Berkeley: University of California Press, 2004).

30. Bell, *Lost Tapestries*, 6–7.

31. Orlanda Soei Han Lie, *Christine de Pizan in Bruges: Le Livre de la Cite de Dames as Het Bouc van de Stede der Vrauwen*, London, British Library, Add. 20698 (Hilversum: Verloren, 2015).

32. This volume, Verini, "Sisters and Friends."

own thoughts. As Anderson argues in her afterword, this paradox of intimacy and remoteness is at the heart of this volume.[33] The afterlife of de Pizan's City resurges in the networks of women who declared their friendship to the City through manuscript exchange and tapestry creation, material support, and notional affiliation. Similar traceworks of friendly women have been made visible by archivists both careful and transgressive, in this volume and, it is to be hoped, many others to come. The Amazons are still out there, waiting to be heard.

---

33. This volume, Anderson, "Afterword."

CHAPTER 11

Prosthetic Friendship and the Theater of Fraternity

LAURIE A. FINKE

I USED to practice yoga in a studio located in a disused Oddfellows Lodge on the Main Street of a small rural town in northeastern Ohio.[1] In the US (or at least in rural Ohio towns), yoga studios are spaces frequented almost exclusively by women. How might it signify that a space once dedicated to male friendship through ritual and conviviality had been transformed (with few changes to the décor) into a space where women gathered to perform their friendship rituals, often in the very same formations in which men practiced theirs? This essay explores the ritual space of fraternal initiation as a mechanism for creating and sustaining what David Wills in "Full Dorsal" calls prosthetic friendship, "friendship artificially conceived or produced."[2] I investigate the ways in which spaces, institutions, and rituals that have supported institutionalized homosociality for men can, over time, create opportunities for female and even feminist camaraderie. Members of fraternal orders used the Middle Ages to enact certain performances of masculinity as a means of

---

My thanks to Karma Lochrie and Usha Vishnuvajjala for their friendship, understanding, and practical advice.

    1. The Oddfellows is a fraternal organization for men; its roots go back to eighteenth-century England.

    2. David Wills, "Full Dorsal: Derrida's Politics of Friendship," *Postmodern Culture* 15, no. 3 (2005), https://doi.org/10.1353/pmc.2005.0032.

instantiating "friendship as a union of virtuous souls."[3] These organizations not only drew upon but claimed an unbroken line of descent from medieval guilds and chivalric orders, associations that promoted prosthetic friendship in the Middle Ages and provided models for later rituals. Belief that the Middle Ages survive well into the modern period in fraternal organizations ameliorated the anxieties of modernity, particularly the alienating individualism fostered by capitalism.[4] At least for men.

In *The Politics of Friendship*, Derrida remarks on "the double exclusion of the feminine, the exclusion of friendship between a man and a woman and the exclusion of friendship between women" in the philosophical literature on friendship.[5] In this literature, Ivy Schweitzer notes, "friendship was characterized as ethical, public, exclusively masculine and elite."[6] Marc D. Schachter, however, challenges this characterization of women's exclusion from the philosophic tradition of friendship: "The danger of Derrida's analysis as it stands is that it risks erasing moments of insurrection against the friendship tradition that might further develop fissures within it."[7] Because he concludes with women's exclusion from friendship rather than beginning with it, he argues, Derrida invests the philosophical tradition with more power than it already has, the power to obliterate dissent within the tradition. Women's place in the history of friendship might, Schachter argues, be "rescripted as a series of inclusions and erasures available for analysis rather than a continual, emphatic absence."[8] This essay on women's friendships in initiatic societies constitutes one intervention into that tradition that attempts to make visible what has been erased: women's participation in organizations promoting prosthetic friendship by remediating medieval histories.

Wills's essay on *The Politics of Friendship* describes prosthetic friendship as a "friendship against nature": "a concept of friendship that did not suppose it to issue from a beating heart, or some seat of emotion." He does so to counter the tendency to idealize friendship in the history of philosophy. He continues:

---

3. Janet M. Burke, "Freemasonry, Friendship and Noblewomen: The Role of the Secret Society in Bringing Enlightenment Thought to Pre-revolutionary Women Elites," *History of European Ideas* 10, no. 3 (1989): 283–93, at 284.

4. T. J. Jackson Lears, *No Place of Grace: Antimodernism and the Transformation of American Culture, 1880–1920* (Chicago: University of Chicago Press, 1994).

5. Jacques Derrida, *The Politics of Friendship*, trans. George Collins (New York: Verso, 1997), 290.

6. Ivy Schweitzer, "Making Equals: Classical *Philia* and Women's Friendship," *Feminist Studies* 42, no. 2 (2016): 337–64, at 337.

7. Marc D. Schachter, *Voluntary Servitude and the Erotics of Friendship: From Classical Antiquity to Early Modern France* (Aldershot: Ashgate, 2008), 164.

8. Schachter, *Voluntary Servitude*, 164.

A friendship that is also a politics has in some way been *impersonalized* if not *depersonalized*. It has gone public or become something like a business relationship in a way that exceeds or acts in competition with what we naïvely understand friendship to be.[9]

Fraternal organizations like the Freemasons and Oddfellows, that gained popularity and prestige in the eighteenth and nineteenth centuries, provide a distinctive example of this concept of artificial friendship. According to one Masonic commentator, "our Fraternity is a Brotherhood, or sacred band of Brothers, committed to mutual support, understanding, and affection."[10] Fraternal friendships were forged in the spaces of the lodge, a home away from home planted firmly in the public sphere.

What if the figure of the witch, so regularly coming back on stage, to paraphrase Derrida, with the features of the friend, offers a glimpse into a less androcentric configuration of prosthetic friendship?[11] Like Carissa Harris, I want to tease out a possible hidden history of female friendship, of what she, following Karma Lochrie, calls *cummarship,* by considering the emergence of pagan witchcraft in the middle of the twentieth century.[12] Rescuing witchcraft from the sixteenth- and seventeenth-century witch trials, which, as Sylvia Federici argues, attempted to quash female solidarity,[13] practitioners of Wicca describe their history as an unbroken line of oral transmission of occult knowledge from pagan times to the Middle Ages and through to the modern era; it is a form of medievalism, a desire to harness the authority of ancient knowledges supposed to have survived into the modern world, even if only secretly. Wicca reclaims the oldest recorded form in English of the word *witch* from its mostly derogatory meanings to rewrite (or re-rite, as Kristy S. Coleman aptly puts it) women into Western esotericism.[14] As an origin myth, its narrative is no more fanciful than those of most religions. While there are many accounts of witches in folklore, anthropology, literature, and his-

---

9. Wills, "Full Dorsal." Wills's deconstruction of friendship reveals the artificiality at the heart of all friendship.

10. "The Five Points of Fellowship," *The Masonic Trowel*, last modified March 22, 2014, http://www.themasonictrowel.com/Articles/degrees/degree_3rd_files/the_five_points_of_fellowship_gltx.htm (accessed May 9, 2021).

11. Derrida, *Politics of Friendship*, viii.

12. Harris explores the link between witches and cummarship in her discussion of Alexander Montgomerie and Sir Patrick Hume of Polwarth's *The Flyting of Montgomerie and Polwart* (c. 1582), p. 168.

13. Sylvia Federici, *Caliban and the Witch: Women, the Body and Primitive Accumulation* (Brooklyn, NY: Atonomedia, 2014), esp. 163–206.

14. Kristy S. Coleman, *Re-riting Women: Dianic Wicca and the Feminine Divine* (Lanham, MD: Alta Mira Press, 2009).

tory, the documentary history of Wicca can only be told through sources that trace its roots back no more than about one hundred years before its founding in the mid-twentieth century. This chapter traces a genealogy describing the emergence of Wicca in the mid-twentieth century out of a number of esoteric fraternal societies.

One of the most prolific sources of ritual for initiatic societies has been Western esotericism, which also staked its claims on an uninterrupted line of descent from the Middle Ages. Esotericism draws on knowledge that has been "consigned to the dustbin of history by Enlightenment ideologues and their intellectual heirs up to the present, because it is considered incompatible with normative conceptions of religion, rationality and science."[15] This chapter, then, charts a genealogy directly from the esoteric degrees of Freemasonry, through the occult Hermetic Order of the Golden Dawn to Aleister Crowley and Gerald Gardner, the founders of modern Wicca, and finally to new-age versions of Wicca. A practice today mostly (though not exclusively) espoused by women, Wicca has been connected to the radical feminism of Mary Daly, Starhawk, and Zsuzsanna Budapest. Although tracking the mechanisms of transmission through these groups is not particularly original, these connections allow me to theorize the emergence of institutional structures that encouraged new forms of female friendship.

The esoteric interests of the organizations I track have spawned a long, complex, and diffuse body of esoteric lore, which, except for a brief introduction, I intend to ignore in favor of a focus on the dramatic and performative elements of initiation that instantiate prosthetic friendship. The *Oxford English Dictionary* characterizes the esoteric as "philosophical doctrines, . . . designed for, or appropriate to, an inner circle of advanced or privileged disciples; communicated to, or intelligible by, the initiated exclusively."[16] Its most important features, then, are secrecy, initiation, and the division between initiates and the profane;[17] its content, cribbed from often wildly unrelated texts, is secondary. While all forms of esotericism claim to possess lost and secret knowledge passed on from master to acolyte for millennia, historical research demonstrates that most are of recent vintage. Western esotericism braids together strands of medieval theology, philosophy, art, science, and culture. The roots of esotericism, a transcultural phenomenon, can be found in the theology of Bernardus Silvestris, Alain de Lille, and Hildegard of Bingen; the philosophy of Averroes; the summae of Bartholomaeus Anglicus, Joachim de Fiore, and

---

15. Ethan Doyle White, *Wicca: History, Belief, and Community in Modern Pagan Witchcraft* (Brighton: Sussex Academic Press, 2016), 17.

16. *OED Online*, s.v. "esoteric" (adj., n.), Oxford University Press. December 2019.

17. Antoine Faivre, *Western Esotericism: A Concise History*, trans. Christine Rhone (Albany: State University of New York Press, 2010), 9.

Nicholas of Cusa; the astrology of Ramon Llull; alchemy, as it was reintroduced to Europe from Islamic Spain; the Jewish Kabbalah, which arrived in Spain in the form of the *Sepher ha-Zohar* shortly after 1275; the rituals of initiatic societies such as medieval guilds and chivalric orders from the Knights Templar to the Order of the Garter; and the courtly romances of Arthurian literature.[18]

Scholars of esotericism, such as Faivre, render its history sequentially, with Neoplatonic and Pythagorean philosophies in the ancient world giving way to medieval theology, alchemy, astrology, and the appropriation for Christian ends of the Kabbalah, culminating in the Renaissance with the works of Giordano Bruno and John Dee.[19] These threads, then, were gathered up and elaborated by the Rosicrucian manifestos[20] in the early decades of the seventeenth century and codified as a secret society in the early eighteenth by the Freemasons. I am less interested in this narrative of continuity than in understanding how initiatic societies pick and choose from diverse texts to claim unbroken ancient descent, syncretizing them to create rituals that foster new forms of friendship, even friendships that can include women.

Most fraternities, however, excluded women, whose primary relationships were forged in the domestic sphere of the family. Masonic apologists offered myriad reasons for this exclusion: because women can't keep secrets; because their presence would sexualize the proceedings; because Masonic knowledge exceeds women's capabilities; because women's exclusion is required by "ancient manners and customs," "transmitted to us by our forefathers"; and, of course, because women cannot be friends in the philosophical sense. At the same time, however, there are notable exceptions, at once visible and erased. Perhaps the most important evidence for women's friendships can be found in the early Masonic "lodges of adoption." By about 1725, Masonry had migrated from England to France; the first female lodge appeared in 1737. *Maçonnerie des dames* was officially recognized by the governing body of French Masonry, in 1774.[21] These lodges afforded elite women access to the community of

---

18. Faivre, *Western Esotericism*, 27–33.
19. The latter two were contemporary with the execution of witches throughout Christendom.
20. Rosicrucianism emerged out of a series of German texts that invent a *Fraternity of the Rosy Cross* supposed to possessed secret philosophies. There is no evidence that any such fraternity ever existed, but several subsequent fraternal orders claimed descent from it. On esotericism's history, see Henrik Bogdan, *Western Esotericism and Rituals of Initiation* (Albany: State University of New York Press, 2007), 1–26.
21. Burke, "Freemasonry, Friendship, and Noblewomen," 283; see also Janet M. Burke and Margaret Jacob, "French Freemasonry, Women, and Feminist Scholarship," *Journal of Modern History* 68, no. 3 (1996): 513–49; and Alexandra Heidle and Jan A. M. Snoek, *Women's Agency and Rituals in Mixed and Female Masonic Orders* (Leiden: Brill, 2008), esp. 89–217.

friends that their Masonic brothers enjoyed: "powerful rituals, the emotional bonds of sisterhood, the assertiveness of their incipient feminism and the novel feelings of friendship as a union of virtuous souls," prosthetic friendships free from personal and emotional affinity.[22] Most Masonic women either were executed or went into exile during the Revolution, however, and the lodges disbanded, along with those of their male counterparts. After the Revolution, the lodges of adoption returned, but they had been reduced to women's auxiliaries, focusing on charitable works rather than initiation or friendship and promoting the traditional values of proper wives and mothers. They died out about two decades after the Revolution.

While the history of women's involvement in fraternal organizations has largely been told through women's auxiliaries, such as the Eastern Star,[23] a different narrative of women's prosthetic friendship emerges from an examination of the esoteric rituals of initiation characteristic of male fraternal organizations. Virtually all scholars of Wicca point to Freemasonry, not women's auxiliaries, as Wicca's precursor, primarily because the creators of Masonic rituals were the most significant architects of Western esotericism as a secret lore that bonds initiates. Freemasonry organized the patchwork of ancient, medieval, and Renaissance texts that Faivre describes into a system of initiations that, while highly innovative at the time, claimed ancient origins. I use the term *system* advisedly, since the higher degrees of Freemasonry are largely a jumble of side degrees and rites, each insisting that it is "the sole custodian of what was claimed to be *the* secret of masonry."[24] Perhaps this incoherence is integral to the secrecy that marks esotericism; Babel-like, lost knowledges have been fragmented and scattered.

Freemasonry has to be at the center of any analysis of Western esotericism, but Masonic esotericism should figure in the study of friendship as well. If fraternal rituals of initiation are designed to inculcate moral lessons and reveal secret wisdom, they are also performances designed to produce friendship, to bond individuals. As Ronald Hutton notes, "The actual religious element in [Masonic initiations] was always superficial, their rituals being intended as acts of incorporation and sociability rather than of worship; which did not make them any the less powerful."[25] In 1897 W. S. Harwood captured the attractions of fraternal ritual:

---

22. Burke, "Freemasonry, Friendship, and Noblewomen," 285. See also Karma Lochrie in chapter 9 of this volume.

23. Perhaps the best-known women's auxiliary. A Masonic organization, it is open to both men and women. To join, men must be Master Masons and women must be related to a Mason.

24. Bogdan, *Western Esotericism*, 95.

25. Ronald Hutton, *Triumph of the Moon: A History of Modern Pagan Witchcraft* (Oxford: Oxford University Press, 1999), 61.

> There is a peculiar fascination in the unreality of the initiation, an allurement about fine "team" work, a charm of deep potency in the unrestricted, out-of-the-world atmosphere which surrounds the scenes where men are knit together by the closest ties, bound by the most solemn obligations to maintain secrecy as to the events which transpire within their walls.[26]

Initiation into the Masonic Craft degrees of Entered Apprentice, Fellow Craft, and Master Mason (the basis of all Freemasonry) is modeled on the tools and skills of operative masonry and thus on the mysteries of the medieval guild, remediating medieval labor, shaping it into an intellectual enterprise, through rituals that allegorically re-enact the building of Solomon's Temple (1 Kings and 2 Chronicles). The Five Points of Fellowship, a posture used in the third degree of Master Mason to convey the secret Masonic word, illustrates how initiations both produce and mark prosthetic friendship. At the climax of this initiation, the Worshipful Master and the initiate embrace one another foot to foot, knee to knee, breast to breast, hand to back, and mouth to ear.[27] However, bonding rituals like this one are generally not prominent in the initiation rituals of women's auxiliaries. Bayliss J. Camp and Orit Kent, who investigated the initiation rituals of eight American fraternities and their auxiliaries, discovered that women's auxiliaries did not attempt to "inculcate strong bonds between female members" through elaborate rituals: "a woman's primary allegiance was, by implication, that which tied her to the husband, father, and so on whose membership in the male order made her own membership in the auxiliary possible."[28]

I turn to the initiation for Master Mason, the highest of the three Craft degrees, to parse out the essential ingredients of esoteric initiation, the main features of which will be replicated in all subsequent initiation rituals, including Wiccan rituals. This initiation is based on an apocryphal story recounting the murder of Hiram Abif, the master mason who is supposed (by Masons) to have built Solomon's temple. In the course of the initiation, the candidate, who takes the role of Hiram, is murdered by three "ruffians" in an attempt to wrest from him the master mason's secret word. I am interested in the ways in which the embodied performance of this initiation bonds initiates to the group, creating new prosthetic friendships. Initiations include all the generic features of drama. The lodge is the theater, the initiation room the stage; there

---

26. W. S. Harwood, "Secret Societies in America," *North American Review* 164 (1897): 617–24, at 621.
27. Bogdan, *Western Esotericism*, 79.
28. Bayliss J. Camp and Orit Kent, "'What a Mighty Power We Can Be': Individual and Collective Identity in African American and White Fraternal Initiation Rituals," *Social Science History* 28, no. 3 (2004): 439–83, at 446.

are sets, scenery, props, and actors; movements are choreographed and lines memorized. But initiations into secret societies differ from the theater in two important features. First, rituals have no author. To claim authorship would vitiate the claim to ancient origin. Second, initiation rituals have no audience. The purpose of the initiation is not catharsis but transformation. The candidate, by participating in the ritual and learning the secrets, takes on a new social identity, created through the collaborative efforts of the fraternity. Drawing on Camp and Kent's analysis of fraternal initiations, I examine the constitutive features through which fraternal rituals not only set the initiate apart from outsiders or "cowans" but, just as important, bind its members in friendship. Camp and Kemp isolate four key components of initiation: hierarchy and equality, boundedness, hazing, and movement.[29] These are not easily isolated from one another, as they are braided together throughout a ritual that climaxes in an oath and the revelation of secrets.

The first mechanism—boundedness—isolates the initiate and articulates the hierarchies within the fraternity. Masonic rituals take place in a lodge, set aside for the fraternity, that excludes nonmembers. The room in which the initiation for Master Mason takes place, which represents King Solomon's Temple, further excludes members of the lodge who are not initiates of this degree. The Tyler (a kind of sentry) must "keep off all cowans and eavesdroppers, and not . . . pass or repass any but such as are duly qualified."[30] The opening of the Lodge sets the "sacred space" of initiation off from all other spaces: the Worshipful Master asks whether the lodge is properly guarded and whether all present are Master Masons. Those present indicate their membership by wearing the appropriate regalia and giving the secret sign.

Meanwhile, the initiate is isolated and prepared by the Junior Deacon and two stewards, who

> [divest him] of all wearing apparel, except his shirt and drawers, and if he has not the latter, he is furnished with a pair by the brethren preparing him. The drawers are rolled up just above the candidate's knees, and both arms are taken out of his shirt-sleeves, leaving his legs and breast bare. A rope, technically called, by Masons, a cable-tow, is wound around his body three times, and a bandage, or hoodwink, is tied very closely over his eyes.[31]

---

29. Camp and Kent, "'What a Mighty Power,'" 448–49.

30. "Entered Apprentice or First Degree," Malcom C. Duncan, *Duncan's Masonic Ritual and Monitor*, https://www.sacred-texts.com/mas/dun/dun02.htm#fr_2 (accessed May 9, 2021).

31. "Master Mason or Third Degree," *Duncan's Masonic Ritual and Monitor* [1866], https://www.sacred-texts.com/mas/dun/dun04.htm (accessed May 9, 2021).

These preparations begin the second mechanism, the hazing, which might include "blindfolding, binding hands or feet, making loud noises during a ceremony, or testing an initiate's courage or pain threshold."[32] Hazing not only "proves" the candidate worthy of membership; it bonds members of the group through a common experience by setting them apart from all others who have not undergone such testing.

Movement is the third mechanism of initiation. The candidate is led blindfolded three times around the lodge at four key moments. These circumambulations are ritualistic, distinct from routine movements in the Lodge. Camp and Kent note that "by marching a candidate in a circle around the lodge room—typically while blindfolded—the assembled membership gained a first glimpse of the initiate and gauged whether the person was worthy of membership."[33] But more importantly this movement marks "the liminal moment at which the initiate crosses over from being an outsider to a member."[34] His worthiness having been established through ordeal and ritual perambulation, the candidate kneels before the Worshipful Master to take the oath. He swears an elaborate oath which is accompanied by a recital of the lavishly gruesome punishments awaiting the man who breaks the oath. As I note elsewhere, "Secrecy creates social networks, forging bonds that coagulate around the oscillation between withholding and revealing."[35]

At this point the initiate is allowed to believe that the ritual has concluded and that the Worshipful Master will close the lodge. But the candidate must undergo further hazing because the brethren "require a more satisfactory proof of your fidelity to your trust, before they are willing to intrust [sic] you with the more valuable secrets of this Degree."[36] This second hazing re-enacts the murder of Hiram Abif with the candidate, still blindfolded, as victim. He is knocked down with "a large setting maul,"[37] carried around the room three times in a canvas, buried, and then resurrected. Only after this ritualistic death and rebirth is the initiate given "more valuable secrets of this Degree" and the five points of fellowship. After a recital of the meaning of the ordeal, the lodge is closed in a ceremony that echoes the opening.

---

32. Camp and Kent, "'What a Mighty Power,'" 447.
33. Camp and Kent, "'What a Mighty Power,'" 447.
34. Camp and Kent, "'What a Mighty Power,'" 447.
35. Laurie Finke, "Fraternal Conspiracy and the Subject of Feminism," *Women's Studies* 47, no. 5 (2018): 485–503, at 490. Here I examine in detail the punishments set out for betraying Masonic secrets, 491–92.
36. "Master Mason," *Duncan's Monitor*.
37. The text reassures readers that the candidate is not intentionally injured in this scenario.

The appendant or higher degrees of Freemasonry that promise esoteric knowledge provided the structure and content for later occult orders. Since its inception in the early decades of the eighteenth century, Freemasonry has proliferated thousands of appendant or side degrees beyond the initial three Craft Degrees; most of these have not survived, but today there are still a significant number of appendant degrees. "These rites, which include elements of chivalric, Christian, alchemical, kabbalistic, Rosicrucian, and various other esoteric traditions, competed with each other to serve as the sole custodian of what was claimed to be *the* secret of masonry."[38] The most popular in the US is the *Ancient and Accepted Scottish Rite,* which offers twenty-nine degrees beyond Master Mason.

By the late nineteenth century, Masons involved in some of the more obscure appendant orders began to create organizations and rituals of their own outside of official Masonry. These new esoteric orders, which dabbled in occultism, theosophy, spiritualism, Tarot, Kabbalah, and various forms of magic, tested the limits of the friendships formed within Masonry; at the same time, they encouraged the participation of individuals who had previously been excluded, most notably women. One of the best known and most important for the development of esoteric rituals was the Hermetic Order of the Golden Dawn. "The crowning glory of the occult revival in the nineteenth century," it "synthesized into a coherent whole a vast body of disconnected and widely scattered material and welded it into a practical and effective system."[39]

Combining the ritual glamor of Freemasonry with the mass appeal of Madame Blavatsky's theosophy, the Hermetic Order of the Golden Dawn was founded in 1888 by three fellow Masons, William Wynn Westcott, S. Liddell Mathers and William Robert Woodman. All three were members of the *Societas Rosicruciana in Anglia,* an appendant order of Freemasonry, whose membership was restricted to high-ranking Masons who "gathered for the purpose of studying the cabbala, the hermetic texts, and other arcane wisdom of the ancient and medieval world."[40] Woodman was its Supreme Magus. Westcott claimed he had come into possession of certain documents, written in cipher, containing "pseudo-masonic rituals of a Rosicrucian provenance." Westcott and Mathers deciphered the rituals. Among the papers

> was an address to a certain Fräulein Anna Sprengel in Germany, . . . who was supposed to be a Rosicrucian adept and member of "Die Goldene Dämmerung," that is, the Golden Dawn. After a brief correspondence with her,

---

38. Bogdan, *Western Esotericism,* 95
39. Gerald York, cited in Bogdan, *Western Esotericism,* 122.
40. Hutton, *Triumph of the Moon,* 72–73.

Westcott was chartered to open a Temple of the Golden Dawn, which was to be ruled by a triumvirate: Westscott, Woodman, and Mathers.[41]

This narrative gave legitimacy to the new society, allowing the three friends to claim ancient descent for the order as well as a link to an established initiatic body. None of it, of course, was true. The documents were likely written by another high-ranking Mason, Kenneth Mackenzie, and lifted almost verbatim from the initiations of the *Societas Rosicruciana in Anglia*.[42] Though it lasted only a dozen years before it was torn apart by internal conflicts, Golden Dawn Temples were established in London, Weston-super-Mare, Bradford, Edinburgh, and Paris. One of the order's innovations was that it admitted women on equal terms with men. The order's rituals invoke "the Fratres and Sorores of the Order of the Golden Dawn."[43] Women were prominent among the leadership. Among its illustrious members it counted William Butler Yeats; the actress and Irish revolutionary Maud Gonne; Constance Mary Wilde, Oscar Wilde's wife; Sir Arthur Conan Doyle; and Florence Farr, an actress, women's rights advocate, and journalist who became the order's Chief Adept in Anglia.[44]

The degree structure of the order exactly mirrored that of the *Societas Rosicruciana in Anglia*. The first of its three orders, designed by Westcott and Mathers, was called the Outer Order; it was divided into four grades, each based on one of the four elements: earth, air, water, and fire. Candidates ascended through the levels by passing a written examination on each element. The second level, the Inner Order, was designed and ruled by Mathers alone. Its members "would begin learning practical magic such as astral travel, alchemy, and scrying (attaining otherworldly visions with the aid of objects such as crystals and mirrors)."[45] The third level consisted of the "secret chiefs": "alchemists whose practices were part of an unbroken hermetic tradition going back to ancient Egypt," though no one ever knew whether these secret chiefs were actual people, myths, or symbols. The order's rituals were never published while the order was operating; they circulated among members only

---

41. Bogdan, *Western Esotericism*, 124.
42. Bogdan, *Western Esotericism*, 124. This British rite still exists.
43. Israel Regardie, *Outer Order Rituals and Commentaries*, vol. 6 of *The Complete Golden Dawn System of Magic*, ed. David Cherubim (Phoenix, AZ: New Falcon Publications, 2014), 415 (ebook).
44. Mary K. Greer's *Women of the Golden Dawn: Rebels and Priestesses* (Rochester, VT: Park Street Press, 1995) attests to the importance of women in the order.
45. Dennis Denisoff, "The Hermetic Order of the Golden Dawn, 1888–1901," in *BRANCH: Britain, Representation and Nineteenth-Century History*, ed. Dino Franco Felluga, *Extension of Romanticism and Victorianism on the Net*. http://www.branchcollective.org/?ps_articles=dennis-denisoff-the-hermetic-order-of-the-golden-dawn-1888-1901 (accessed May 9, 2021).

in manuscript form. Long after its demise, Israel Regardie began publishing versions of Golden Dawn rituals.[46]

In the Golden Dawn, women were able to experience firsthand the same initiation rituals that high-ranking Masonic men enjoyed; they could become members of the Inner Order and even officiate rituals. The initiation for the Neophyte grade, because it was the very first, was the most elaborate.[47] All the elements that create prosthetic friendship are present: boundedness, hierarchy, movement, and hazing. The boundedness of ritual space and hierarchies are marked by the opening and closing of the order, separating the sacred space of the temple from the mundane world. A Sentinel, "armed with a sword to keep out intruders,"[48] ensures that the temple is properly guarded and that all present are initiates, wearing proper regalia, who can give the secret sign. The officers, robed in black, white, and red and carrying the symbols of their offices, correspond precisely to the officers in Masonic rituals, as does their placement in each of the four directions, which correspond to the four elements, and the four humors.[49] The candidate is isolated both from the mundane world and from members of the order, dressed in a black gown, red shoes, and sash, blindfolded and bound three times around the waist with a rope. As in Masonic initiation, "mystic circumambulations" of the Hall are repeated at regular intervals in the ceremony. Officiants purify the candidate with water by making the sign of the cross on her forehead and fire by censing her.[50] She takes the oath of secrecy. As usual, the candidate pledges never to reveal any secrets of the order, its members, or its teaching. The element of fraternal friendship is clearly marked in the candidate's pledge "to maintain a kind and benevolent relation with all the Fratres and Sorores of the Order" (loc. 11469–98).

---

46. An earlier work from the late 1930s, *The Golden Dawn: An Account of the Teachings, Rites and Ceremonies of the Order of the Golden Dawn*, printed the rituals of one of the offshoots of the order, *Stella Matutina*. *The Outer Order Rituals and Commentaries*, vol. 6 of *The Complete Golden Dawn System of Magic*, replaces these with rituals found in the original manuscripts held in the Gerald Yorke Collection, Warburg Institute, University of London (Bogdan, *Western Esotericism*, 127–28).

47. Even though the Golden Dawn rituals map easily onto the rituals of high Masonry, the explanation of the symbols varies (Bogdan, *Western Esotericism*, 137).

48. Regardie, *The Outer Order Rituals and Commentaries*, loc.11340. Subsequent quotations from this text are noted by location number parenthetically in the text.

49. Correspondences in nature are a major feature of esotericism; see Faivre, *Western Esotericism*, 12, and Bogdan, *Western Esotericism*, 10–11.

50. Although the ritual in *The Outer Order Rituals and Commentaries* consistently uses the generic singular masculine, to remind my readers of women's presence, I occasionally use the feminine singular pronoun.

There are some interesting features in the oath that reflect Golden Dawn's occult interests. The candidate pledges never to use her powers for evil purposes, and that "I will not suffer myself to be hypnotized, or mesmerized, nor will I place myself in such a passive state that any uninitiated person, power, or being may cause me to lose control of my thoughts, words or actions" (loc. 11498). The punishment for breaking the oath reflects a shift from esoterica to magic. Punishments are dealt not by human hands but by occult forces, the initiate swearing "under the awful penalty of voluntarily submitting myself to a deadly and hostile current of will set in motion by the chiefs of our Order, by which I shall fall slain and paralyzed without visible weapon as if slain by the lightning flash." After the oath is complete, an official instructs the candidate in "the secret signs, grip, grand word and present password of the Neophyte Grade of the Order of the Golden Dawn in the Outer" (loc. 11579), removes the rope around the candidate's waist, and "invest[s] him with the distinguishing badge of the grade" (loc. 11607). The ritual ends with the closing of the Hall in a briefer recapitulation of the opening, moving the celebrants from sacred back to profane space.

At its height, the Golden Dawn numbered nearly four hundred members, of whom roughly 150 were women.[51] More important than its numbers, however, the Order challenged the exclusivity of fraternity, opening the world of fraternal rituals and friendships to women in an unprecedented way. Other associations were opening their lodge doors to women at the same time. Women were prominent in the Theosophical Society founded by Madame Blavatsky, while Co-Masonry, which admitted both men and women, emerged in the 1890s. One of the Theosophical Society's members, Annie Besant, established the first overseas lodge of Co-Masonry, *Le Droit Humain*, in London. Participation in group rituals allowed women to collaborate in the creation of new public social identities outside the domestic sphere of the family. To be sure, most of the women associated with these fraternal, esoteric, and occult organizations did not fit the stereotypical "angel in the house," the Victorian ideal of the submissive and devoted wife and mother made popular by Coventry Patmore's novel of the same name.[52] They were on the whole an accomplished group of independent, educated career women, revolutionaries, journalists, women's rights advocates, actresses, writers, mystics, and art-

---

51. Henrik Bogdan, "Women and the Hermetic Order of the Golden Dawn: Nineteenth-Century Occultistic Initiation from a Gender Perspective," in Heidle and Snoek, *Women's Agency and Rituals*, 253–54.

52. In "Professions for Women," Virginia Woolf writes, "Killing the Angel in the House was part of the occupation of a woman writer": "Professions for Women," in *The Death of the Moth and Other Essays* (London: Hogarth, 1942), 151.

ists, exemplars of the "new woman" ideal of the nineteenth century. But such women could seem like oddities. By participating in institutionalized homosociality, these women could escape the singularity of their accomplishments and form intellectual friendships with both accomplished men and women.

At the same time, the history of the Golden Dawn and its breakdown illustrates the fragility, even transience, of friendship. By 1891 Woodman had died. If nothing else, death ends even the best of friendships, and that knowledge, as Geoffrey Bennington has written, is constitutive of friendship, which "is marked by the knowledge that we will *not* die together, that one of us will survive the other, will *see the other die,* and will live on in mourning and memory of *the* other."[53] By 1896 Westcott had been forced out of the organization and had cut all ties with the group, leaving Mathers as sole Chief of the Order. As Mathers became more despotic and erratic, dissension broke out among members of the Inner Order, much of it caused by clashes of ego. By 1900 that dissent became outright revolt. In February of that year, Mathers sent a letter to Florence Farr, who was governing the Order in England, in which he justified his leadership by denouncing his former friend as a fraud. Westcott "has NEVER been *at any time* either in personal, or in written communication with the Secret Chiefs of the Order, he having *either himself forged or procured to be forged* the professed correspondence between him and them."[54] Only their friendship, the "Oath of Secrecy" Mathers swore to Westcott, had prevented him from speaking up sooner. The dispute fatally fractured the order, which soon died out, though splinter groups operated well into midcentury, and there are still organizations today that claim descent from the "genuine" Golden Dawn.

I need to address the end of friendship at this moment because the events leading up to the creation of modern Wicca are characterized by this alternation of friendship and friendship's end in recrimination, conflict, and dissolution. Confronting this question prevents us from overidealizing friendship, prevents us from asking too much of it. In the ironically titled "Forever Friends," Bennington, quoting Derrida, allows for "the friend who is no longer or who is not yet."[55] He invokes "a certain complex co-implication of friendship and enmity."[56] As Derrideans deconstruct the discourse of idealized friendship, they move the philosophic discourse closer to descriptions of women's (non)friendships. As Judith Taylor notes, "Friendship among women

---

53. Geoffrey Bennington, "Forever Friends," in *Interrupting Derrida*, ed. Bennington (London: Routledge, 2000), 113; emphasis in original.
54. Bogdan, *Western Esotericism*, 126.
55. Derrida, *Politics of Friendship*, 150.
56. Bennington, "Forever Friends," 112, 122.

is necessary for their survival and political hopes, but friendship disappointment, heartbreak, and anger pervade feminist cultural production."[57]

Much of the dissension in Golden Dawn resulted from clashes of ego. Those egos were stoked by the shift from the study of esotericism to the practice of magic, which tended to refocus occult groups away from group formation and maintenance (initiation) and toward individual growth and achievement. Magic is characterized by its commitment to Victorian values of individualism and progress. Magic's goals were

> to develop or release the latent spiritual and mental abilities of humans by using the framework of traditional ritual magic. The object and centre of each operation was now the magician, and its aim was to bring him or her closer to spiritual maturity and potency, by inflaming the imagination, providing access to altered states of consciousness, and strengthening and focusing will-power.[58]

No better example of the kind of havoc wreaked on friendships by privileged egos unchecked exists than the case of Aleister Crowley. The end of Golden Dawn was surely hastened by Mathers's friendship with his acolyte, whom he sent to London in a desperate attempt to salvage his leadership. "Crowley only managed to worsen the conflict even more if indeed that were possible."[59] Mathers initiated Crowley into the Order in 1898 and was his patron until 1903, when they quarreled. Hutton describes Crowley as "a self-indulgent and flamboyant young man empowered by the inheritance of a substantial inherited fortune, which allowed him to pursue his enthusiasm at will and to set about a deliberate flouting and provocation of social and religious norms."[60] He created his own religion, Thelema, inscribing in its foundational text, the 1904 *Book of the Law*, his own egotism: "Do what thou wilt shall be the whole of the law." After the demise of Golden Dawn, he created a successor organization, which he called A∴A∴ (1907), and in 1912 he was initiated into the German *Ordo Templi Orientis*. Crowley's ego, however, was simply too big to be contained by such groups.

---

57. Judith Taylor, "Beyond 'Obligatory Camaraderie': Girls' Friendships in Zadie Smith's *NW* and Jillian and Mariko Tamaki's *Skim*," *Feminist Studies* 42, no. 2 (2016): 445–68, at 448.
58. Hutton, *Triumph of the Moon*, 82; Bogdan, "Women and the Order of the Golden Dawn," 246.
59. Bogdan, *Western Esotericism*, 127.
60. Hutton, *Triumph of the Moon*, 172. After he squandered his fortune, he was left in old age dependent on the charity of the few friends he hadn't alienated.

I treat Crowley here as a transitional figure between fraternity and Wicca because of his influence on the individual whom most consider to be the founder of Wicca, Gerald Gardner. Before turning to Wiccan friendships, however, I must debunk two widely repeated stories about Gardner's role in founding the movement, both of which provided Wicca the necessary ancient lineage. The first concerns the so-called New Forest coven. Gardner claims that while he was living in the New Forest, he encountered a coven of witches, a survival of an ancient religion, run by an elderly lady, "Old Dorothy." He was initiated into the coven in 1939, and this coven provided the basis for Wiccan rituals. In this account, Gardner does not claim that he founded Wicca but rather that he discovered an ancient and continuous lineage of practicing witches. In *Triumph of the Moon*, Ronald Hutton exhaustively investigates this story, even though "no academic historian has ever taken seriously Gardner's claim to have discovered a genuine survival of ancient religion"; he finds no evidence to support it.[61] He identifies a more likely precursor in Gardner's friendship with a woman he called Dafo, who was the leading lady and stage director of a local group called the Rosicrucian Theatre. This theatre was founded by G. A. Sullivan, who, together with Mabel Besant-Scott, daughter of Annie Besant (one of the founders of Co-Masonry), established their own quasi-Masonic group called the Rosicrucian Fellowship of Crotona. This documented connection ties Wicca much more closely to nineteenth-century esoteric fraternities than to a continuous folkloric tradition of witchcraft. Dorothy's coven, however, provided a legitimating figure connecting the new organization to an old initiatory descent, as Anna Sprengel had done for the Golden Dawn.

The second myth that needs debunking is the claim that Crowley wrote the Wiccan initiation rituals for Gardner. The two men met only once, when Gardner visited Crowley in 1946, and Crowley was dead by 1947, making this claim unlikely. Analysis of Gardner's rituals reveals that Crowley's published works were among the many sources found in his rituals,[62] but the initiation rituals of the Masonic Craft Degrees are far more pervasive. In 1984 Janet and Stewart Farrar published the Gardnerian rituals of initiation, which initially circulated only in a manuscript called *The Book of Shadows*.[63] They distinguish

---

61. Hutton, *Triumph of the Moon*, 206; see 207–16.

62. Roger Dearnaley examines these borrowings in detail in "The Influence of Aleister Crowley upon 'Ye Bok of ye Art Magical,'" http://geraldgardner.com/dearnaley.php
(accessed May 9, 2021); for Gardner's acquaintance with Crowley, see Hutton, *Triumph of the Moon*, 216–23.

63. Janet Farrar and Stewart Farrar, *The Witches' Way: Principles, Ritual and Belief in Modern Witchcraft* (Custer, WA: Phoenix, 1986).

three distinct texts. The *A Text* contains "Gardner's original rituals as copied down from the New Forest coven which had initiated him, and amended, expanded or annotated by himself."[64] The *B Text* dates to 1953; the *C Text* was written in collaboration with Doreen Valiente. In this version, Crowley's contributions were largely eliminated and replaced by new material written by Valiente.[65]

In fact, the initiations for the three Wiccan degrees resemble nothing so much as the initiations for the Masonic Craft Degrees.[66] The ritual separation of the sacred space from mundane space is accomplished through "The Casting of the Circle." Because Wiccan covens generally lack the economic resources of Freemasons, initiations take place in ad hoc spaces rather than bespoke temples, either outdoors or indoors. As in Masonic initiation, hazing begins as the candidate, isolated outside the circle, is prepared by a member of the opposite sex by "having [her] wrists tied together behind [her] back, a cord tied around the right ankle, and another above the right knee."[67] As the candidate enters the circle, she is accosted by the initiator, who places the tip of a sword or athame against her heart, a feature taken directly from the Masonic ritual for Entered Apprentice. The initiation proceeds with hazing and ritual movement. After the ordeal, the candidate swears an oath reminiscent of Masonic oaths. The new witch is then anointed with oil and receives the secrets of the degree and its "working tools." Gardnerian Wicca uses a Masonic vocabulary. Like Freemasons, members call Wicca "the Craft," outsiders are "cowans," and members possess "tools" they use to "work," that is, to perform, rituals.[68]

Two features unique to Wiccan hazings include taking the candidate's "measure" and a ritual scourging. In the first,

> the initiator "takes the measure" of the postulant by tying knots in a cord which indicate the various dimensions of her or his body. This is regarded as to some extent capturing them, so that the initiator can then either keep the cord in order to ensure that the initiate holds to the oath of secrecy (on

---

64. Farrar and Farrar, *The Witches' Way*, 3.
65. Bogdan, *Western Esotericism*, 154.
66. Hutton, in *Triumph of the Moon*, writes "that is true (as should be plain by now) of most initiation rituals in English secret societies since the eighteenth century," 229.
67. Bogdan, *Western Esotericism*, 157.
68. For Wicca these include the athame, knife, wand, cup, pentacle, cauldron, censer, and scourge; Bogdan, *Western Esotericism*, 159.

pain of having destructive magic worked with the measure) or return it to the initiate as a sign of trust.[69]

This ritual embodies the vague threat of magical punishments should the candidate break her oath of secrecy. Hutton argues that the scourging, in which the candidate's "ankles and knees are bound together" and forty strokes are given, far from being "flagellant fiction," or, as Aidan Kelly claims, intended to produce sexual excitement (235), was meant to induce an "ecstatic trance."[70] Although practices vary among covens and individuals, the Wiccan attitude toward sexuality is on the whole positive. Janet and Stewart Farrar write:

> Sex is holy—a manifestation of that essential polarity which pervades and activates the whole universe, . . . and without which the universe would be inert and static—in other words, would not exist.[71]

But sexuality was introduced into the esoteric tradition as soon as women were included in its rites. Earlier occult societies, like the *Ordo Templi Orientis,* practiced forms of sex magic, claiming to

> possess the Key which opens up all Masonic and Hermetic secrets, namely, the teaching of sexual magic, and this teaching explains, without exception, all the secrets of Nature, all the symbolism of Freemasonry and all systems of religion.[72]

Crowley was famous for his experiments with sex magic, and Gardner may have been influenced by him to include a sexual union between the initiator and initiate in his Third Degree.

Gardnerian Wicca, however, differs from these esoteric fraternities in that its main goal seems to be to promote fertility as much as friendship, to balance the sexes based on heterosexual pairing. A woman is always initiated and taught magic by a man, and a man by a woman. While this feature does not preclude homosocial bonding and prosthetic friendship, it does introduce an element of sexuality. The Five Points of Fellowship, which I described earlier, becomes in Wicca the Five-Fold Kiss, "an adoration and celebration of the

---

69. Bogdan, *Western Esotericism*, 158.
70. Hutton, *Triumph of the Moon*, 235; Bogdan, *Western Esotericism*, 158–59. Jo Pearson, "Embracing the Lash: Pain and Ritual as Spiritual Tools," *Scripta Instituti Donneriani Aboensis* 23 (2011): 351–63, https://doi.org/10.30674/scripta.67394.
71. Farrar and Farrar, *The Witches' Way*, 48.
72. Bogdan, *Western Esotericism*, 152.

whole human body as a sacred vessel, made by woman to man and man to woman."[73] The High Priestess (or Priest) kisses each part of the body—feet, knees, womb/phallus, breast, and lips, while reciting

> Blessed be thy feet, that have brought thee in these ways.
> Blessed be thy knees, that shall kneel at the sacred altar.
> Blessed be thy [womb/phallus], without which we would not be
> Blessed be thy breasts/chest, formed in [beauty/strength]
> Blessed be thy lips, that shall utter the Sacred Names.[74]

In this ritual, a compulsory heterosexuality replaces the homosocial prosthetic connection of Masonic initiation.

"Gardner's witch religion emerged into public view in the early 1950s. By 1950 he was circulating news of its existence within the London occult community, and it was announced to the national press in the summer of 1951," following the repeal of the Witchcraft and Vagrancy Acts.[75] Whether we consider it a religion or an occult society, Wicca expanded women's participation in esoteric communities, reproducing the lodge room as a coven, a female space that reverenced both a Goddess and God, femininity and masculinity on equal terms, in ceremonies presided over by a High Priestess. Women have outnumbered men in Wiccan covens in the US, UK, Canada, and Australia by more than two to one.[76] In *The Spiral Dance,* Starhawk argues that while the Craft offers women "a model of female strength and creative power" as well as female camaraderie, it may hold less attraction for men, as they are required to renounce traditional forms of power and interact with "strong empowered women who do not pretend to be anything less than what they are."[77]

By the 1970s Wicca had gained a foothold in the US, where it thrived, particularly among feminists seeking a woman-centered spirituality. Wicca connected to the strain of feminism Alice Echols identifies as "cultural feminism,"[78] which, like Wicca, asserted the primacy of matriarchy and the essential differences between the sexes, often advocating separatism. In 1971 Zsuzsanna Budapest, a Hungarian refugee transplanted to California, founded

---

73. Hutton, *Triumph of the Moon,* 230.
74. Bogdan, *Western Esotericism,* 156.
75. Hutton, *Triumph of the Moon,* 237.
76. Statistics are difficult to track, as, unlike Freemasonry or the Episcopalian church, there is no "official" organization to join.
77. Starhawk, *The Spiral Dance: A Rebirth of the Ancient Religion of the Great Goddess* (New York: Harper, 1999), 127.
78. Alice Echols, *Daring to Be Bad: Radical Feminism in America, 1967–1975* (Minneapolis: University of Minnesota Press, 1989), 243–81.

a Wiccan coven, the Susan B. Anthony Coven No. 1, "that catered specifically for the needs of feminist women."[79] She rewrote the Gardnerian rituals for women only, eliminating the balancing of the sexes and the male God and rejecting the patriarchal values that allowed Gerald Gardner and Alex Sanders to overshadow female collaborators and High Priestesses like Doreen Valiente. Budapest "expressed the goals of seeking the female principle of the universe, gaining women power over their own souls, fighting patriarchal oppression, and restoring the lost golden age of prehistoric matriarchy."[80] In 1975 Budapest self-published her rituals in *The Feminist Book of Light and Shadows*, so that women who lacked access to a coven could still participate as lone practitioners. In the US, Wicca was transmitted primarily by text rather than through covens. The publication of countless books on the subject contributed to the democratization and massification of an esoteric tradition previously reserved for elites. Most participants today are self-initiated, lone practitioners, hedge witches.[81] Perhaps the best known and most popular do-it-yourself book of Wicca is Starhawk's *Spiral Dance: A Rebirth of the Ancient Religion of the Goddess*,[82] published in 1979. Unlike Budapest, Starhawk recognizes "the duotheism of Wicca,"[83] even as she reinforced the primacy of the goddess. She restored the polarity of male and female, arguing for the need to "reexamine questions of male and femaleness. For the definitions are no longer working. They are oppressive to women and confining to men."[84] For her, the coven serves as the training ground through which "women could be liberated, men re-educated, and new forms of human relationships explored which were free of the old gender stereotypes and power structures."[85]

Despite the popularity of her book among lone witches, Starhawk insists that Wicca is still an initiatic society, one that promotes what I have been calling prosthetic friendship.

---

79. White, *Wicca*, 59.

80. Hutton, *Triumph of the Moon*, 344–45. Budapest's version of Wicca is today known as Dianic Wicca; see Coleman, *Re-riting Woman*.

81. The internet has accelerated this trend; a version of Gardner's *Book of Shadows* has even been uploaded to the Internet Sacred Text Archive at https://www.sacred-texts.com/pag/gbos/index.htm (accessed May 9, 2021).

82. The spiral dance is an alternative to scourging as a means of inducing a trance. Starhawk's initiations draw on features from the Gardnerian first- and second-degree rituals (*Spiral Dance* 159–64).

83. Hutton, *Triumph of the Moon*, 346.

84. Starhawk, *The Spiral Dance*, 19. Men belong in Wicca, even if "what it offers men is more subtle and not always easy to comprehend" (127).

85. Hutton, *Triumph of the Moon*, 346.

Witchcraft is not a religion of masses—of any sort. Its structure is cellular, based on covens, small groups of up to thirteen members that allow for both communal sharing and individual independence.[86]

Covens are autonomous; unlike Freemasonry and other fraternal societies, there is no central governing body. Yet Starhawk insists that they are associational, recognizing the close connection between friendship and knowledge: "An initiation creates a strong emotional bond and a deep, astral tie between coven members, so be careful whom you initiate."[87] As she looks to the future, she expresses the hope that "we as a movement can become ever more inclusive, diverse, and accessible, that people of all backgrounds and ancestries will find a warm welcome in our communities and a deep understanding of the complex issues of race and class in our society," although Black Witch's takedown of a commenter who felt that Wicca should be reserved for white people suggests that work remains to be done.[88]

Let me conclude, then, by considering the intersections of race, prosthetic friendship, and the internet in Wicca today. One view might hold that the internet has disrupted Wicca's ability to facilitate prosthetic friendship, promoting individualism by encouraging the lone, self-initiated witch. But another might suggest that the internet encourages new forms of prosthetic friendship whereby people, and especially women of color, who may feel isolated in their Wiccan practice, can connect to others like them to build new traditions. The African American Wiccan Society offers a model. Its mission is "to reassure people of color that they are not alone in their quest for the spiritual self" and "to build membership and inform members about networks, merry meets, Pagan groups, workshops and celebrations that are important to them," charges that do not seem too far removed from those of Freemasonry. As syncretic as any esoteric association, the Society embraces "many Pagan religions and practices including Wicca, various Spiritualisms, various Witchcrafts, Ontology, Shamanism, Kemetics, and African Diasporic religions such as Ifa, Santeria, Candomble, Hoodoo,and Umbanda."[89] "Wicca is not just Celtic anymore," proclaims Jeanine de Oya, co-creator of the African

---

86. Starhawk, *Spiral Dance*, 38.
87. Starhawk, *Spiral Dance*, 97.
88. Starhawk, *Spiral Dance*, 20th anniv. ed., 10; "'Trolololo—She Rachet': Is Wicca Just for White Folks?" Afropunk, https://afropunk.com/2012/07/black-witch-trolololo-she-rachet-is-wicca-just-for-white-folks/ (accessed May 9, 2021).
89. The African American Wiccan Society, http://www.aawiccan.org/site/welcome.html (accessed May 9, 2021).

American Wiccan Society.[90] Indeed, I hope this chapter demonstrates that it never was just Celtic, just English, just European, or just for white people. The traditions on which its esoteric precursors have drawn have always been diverse and eclectic: not only Western forms of esotericism but also Asian, Middle Eastern, Jewish, Egyptian, African. In a 1964 speech, Doreen Valiente rephrased Aleister Crowley's rule of Thelema—"An it harm none, do what ye will," she says—recasting Crowley's egocentrism to consider the individual's actions in relationships—in friendships—with others. For early twenty-first-century African American witches, the last and final "Wiccan's Rede" is

> "Do these eight words if no others you fulfill:
> 'If yeh harm none, do what yeh will.'"

---

90. Jeanine de Oya, *Portal into the Light of Truth: The First Book of Wicca for African Americans and All Seekers* (Publish America, 2002).

CHAPTER 12

Conversations among Friends
Ælfflæd, Iurminburg, and the Arts of Storytelling

CLARE A. LEES AND GILLIAN R. OVERING

> There is no narrative in silence.
> —"After Life," Sara Maitland

> We are looking at Coquet Island in the long blue evening light.
> How awkward we are at Compline.
> We have no habits.
> The smell of the sea is in our hair yet, after supper.
> Our hearts are stranded here, transparent, lit
> Like jelly fish in the afternoon.
> How awkward it is to be at Compline in the long blue evening light
> With my old shoulder-bag lying there yet, at my feet.
> —"At the Friary at Alnmouth," Gillian Allnutt

> *gemæcce*: formal female friendship or partnership; one of a pair
> —*Hild*, Nicola Griffith

ABBESSES, ABBOTS, AND THE CONTEMPORARY MEDIEVAL

We would like to bring together strands of a conversation that imagines where female friendship, both medieval and modern, might begin and end. We face the long-standing challenge to feminist medievalists of the male-authored canon, which is our primary source of information—or indeed dearth of information—about women in general, and in particular their personal relationships. Evidence for friendship in early medieval England is predominantly about men, as is well known.¹ By contrast, we turn to writers of the contemporary medieval to help us imagine female friendships beyond the constraints of the historical record and the academy.²

We begin with two quotations from two modern British writers and a third from a British American writer. The first is by Sara Maitland, novelist, essayist, and writer of short stories, many of which rework myth, fantasy, faith, and history from a feminist perspective.³ The second is a short lyrical poem by Gillian Allnutt, an award-winning poet and writer established in the north of England, known for her rich sympathies for the people and stories of the past and her tightly wrought meditations on place, history, and faith.⁴ Both are associated with the creative energy and cultural power of British women in what is sometimes known as "second wave" feminism of, roughly speaking, the 1970s and '80s.⁵ Allnutt and Maitland are examples of contemporary writers who draw on early medieval materials, which brings us to Nicola Griffith. "Writer. Queer Cripple with a PhD. Seattle & Leeds," Griffith is a celebrated sci-fi author who is also well known for her historical novel *Hild*, about Abbess Hild of Whitby, perhaps the best-known woman in early medieval Britain.⁶ We take up Maitland's point that there is no narrative in silence to offer an account of a possible friendship between two early medieval women from

---

1. David Clark, *Between Medieval Men: Male Friendship and Desire in Early Medieval English Literature* (Oxford: Oxford University Press, 2009). See also the introduction to this volume.

2. Clare A. Lees and Gillian R. Overing, *The Contemporary Medieval in Practice* (London: UCL Press, 2019).

3. Sara Maitland, "After Life," in *Far North and Other Dark Tales* (London: Maia Books, 2008), 61–74, at 74.

4. Gillian Allnutt, "At the Friary in Alnmouth," for Marian Goodwin, in *How the Bicycle Shone: New & Selected Poems* (Tarset, Northumberland: Bloodaxe Books, 2007), 143. Allnutt was awarded the Queen's Medal for Poetry in 2016.

5. For an introduction, see Patricia Waugh, "Feminism and Writing: The Politics of Culture," in *The Cambridge History of Twentieth-Century Literature*, ed. Laura Marcus and Peter Nicholls (Cambridge: Cambridge University Press, 2005), 600–618.

6. https://nicolagriffith.com/ (accessed May 3, 2021). See also Nicola Griffith, *Hild* (London: Blackfriars, 2013), 620 (Glossary). We acknowledge with deep gratitude how Nicola's work has shaped our thinking about the early medieval period here and elsewhere. We explore other contemporary artists who draw on early medieval materials in *The Contemporary Medieval in Practice*. Griffith's *Ammonite* (New York: Ballantine Books, 1993) is perhaps her best-known sci-fi novel; for brief discussion, see Helen Merrick, "Gender in Science Fiction," in *The Cambridge Companion to Science Fiction*, ed. Edward James and Farah Mendlesohn (Cambridge: Cambridge University Press, 2003), 249–50. For Hild, see Alan Thacker, "Hild [St Hild, Hilda] (614–680), Abbess of Strensall–Whitby," *Oxford Dictionary of National Biography*, September 23, 2004, https://o-www-oxforddnb-com.catalogue.libraries.london.ac.uk/view/10.1093/ref:odnb/9780198614128.001.0001/odnb-9780198614128-e-13255 (accessed April 6, 2020).

seventh-century Northumbria not known to be associated with one another in the historical record: Ælfflæd, who followed Hild as Abbess of Whitby, and Queen Iurminburg, second wife of Ecgfrith of Northumbria.[7] Allnutt's "At the Friary at Alnmouth," a place also associated with Ælfflæd, and Griffith's *Hild* offer us the poetic and narrative space for our imagining.

Maitland's short story "After Life" reworks early medieval accounts of two better-known figures from early medieval Northumberland, Cuthbert and Wilfrid. Her modern story reimagines the medieval story of St Cuthbert's body and its long peregrination from Holy Island to, eventually, Durham Cathedral. Maitland brilliantly and humorously narrates the dilemma that Cuthbert finds himself in *after* death, in spite of his in-life intimations of mortality and prophecies. This is an afterlife that Cuthbert *failed* to predict and that the many medieval versions of his written *Life* record.[8] Each time a saintly life is reworked, it is rendered anew, contemporary, as historical circumstances change. In reworking Cuthbert's afterlife, Maitland's modern short story is testimony to the future of the past and to the importance of resisting silence. Maitland creates new ways to imagine and narrate relationship(s), inspiring us to rethink friendship, female and male.

"After Life" brings together the monastic recluse and abbot of Lindisfarne, Cuthbert, with the worldly abbot of Ripon, Wilfrid. These two men, the alliterative abbots of our subheader, are also bishops and saints, and the sources we have about them figure prominently in our discussion of the abbesses with whom they come into contact in the third section of this chapter. Like Ælfflæd and Iurminburg, Wilfrid and Cuthbert rarely feature in the same historical narratives, although there is a clear textual relationship between their two *Lives*.[9] Maitland's fictional pairing of these male saints connects two very dif-

---

7. Alan Thacker, "Ælfflæd [St Ælfflæd, Elfleda] (654–714), Abbess of Strensall-Whitby," *Oxford Dictionary of National Biography*, September 23, 2004, https://o-www-oxforddnb-com.catalogue.libraries.london.ac.uk/view/10.1093/ref:odnb/9780198614128.001.0001/odnb-9780198614128-e-8622 (accessed April 6, 2020). Iurminburg does not have an entry in the *Oxford Dictionary of National Biography*; see, however, Stephanie Hollis, *Anglo-Saxon Women and the Church* (Woodbridge: Boydell Press, 1992); references to Iurminburg (Hollis uses the spelling Jurmenburg, also cognate with West Saxon Eormenburh) are threaded throughout the book, but see especially 167–70,175–78, and 232–33.

8. Maitland offers a summary at the beginning of "After Life," 61–63. For the earlier, anonymous *Life of Cuthbert* and Bede's slightly later prose *Life*, see Bertram Colgrave, ed. and trans., *Two Lives of Saint Cuthbert* (Cambridge: Cambridge University Press, 1940, repr. 1985). For the *Life of Wilfrid* by Stephen of Ripon, see Bertram Colgrave, ed. and trans., *The Life of Bishop Wilfrid* (Cambridge: Cambridge University Press, 1927, repr. 1985). All references to the *Lives* of Cuthbert and Wilfrid are to these editions.

9. The preface to *The Life of Wilfrid* is borrowed from that of the earlier anonymous *Life of Cuthbert*; see Colgrave, ed. *Life of Wilfrid*, 150.

ferent ways of doing Christianity in the seventh century—that of the wild wonder-worker in the desert of the north and that of the cultured and urbane bishop with his eye on the Franks and on Rome. However, this is not the only homosocial coupling in "After Life." Another, mentioned in passing but no less interesting to us in terms of imagining friendships, is that of Cuthbert and Herefrith, in whose arms the Cuthbert of "After Life" dies ("After Life" 63). And a third associates Hild, Abbess of Whitby, with a much more difficult figure to understand, the "storm woman" (68).

The early medieval historian Bede is more eloquent and expansive than is Maitland about the spiritual friendship between Herefrith, a monk at Lindisfarne, to Cuthbert.[10] He offers a long account of Cuthbert's dying, apparently narrated in Herefrith's voice, spanning several chapters of his prose *Life of Cuthbert*. Maitland captures this affection economically in a single sentence that nevertheless puts Cuthbert in Herefrith's arms in a scene not described by Bede.[11] Bede also recounts another, deeper and more affecting same-sex spiritual bond between Hereberht, hermit of Derwent, and Cuthbert. It is to Hereberht that Cuthbert discloses his foreknowledge of his death, and, in fulfillment of his prayers and imprecations to Cuthbert, Hereberht dies at the same time as his beloved Cuthbert. Separated up to and including the moment of their deaths, the two souls of this loving couple are joined after life in Bede's narrative, but they are not included in Maitland's "After Life."[12]

"After Life" does, however, spend narrative time on two women in the story of Cuthbert and Wilfrid; the wise Abbess Hild, whose spiritual remoteness or distance, smile, and "detached hilarity" ("After Life" 67) from the ecclesiastical politics of the age Maitland's Cuthbert admires, and the "storm woman of the North" (68), a woman larger than life, more figural and prophetic than historic and actual. The "storm woman" is modeled in part on the apocalyptic woman of Revelations, but we also associate her with the northern gods, the sea, the Valkyries, and the Vikings. She is beyond organized religion, out there, a "wild Christ" to Cuthbert, "from a heroic people, crucified, harrowing hell, rejoicing on the far side of destruction" (69), as she "stands before the mast and the wind blows her hair towards him, plaited, interwoven as the pages of his lovely book, but alive and wild" (68). The "lovely book" referred to here is the Lindisfarne Gospels, dedicated to God and Cuthbert, but the "storm woman" contrasts dramatically with the words of God interlaced in

---

10. Bede's prose *Life of Cuthbert*, ed. Colgrave, cap. xxxvii–xxxix.
11. "He died quietly in the arms of his friend Herefrith" ("After Life," 63).
12. Bede's prose *Life of Cuthbert*, ed. Colgrave, cap. xxviii.

the Gospels.[13] Rather, she draws Cuthbert toward those fierce, violent, uncompromising pleasures of the spirit that are so antithetical, indeed incomprehensible to those of a monastic community. Cuthbert's divinity is female: "she is a wild Christ to him" (69). Using Hild and the "storm woman," and associating both with Cuthbert across the gendered, the human, and the divine, Maitland radically challenges the paradigmatic male-authored sources that dominate modern academic perceptions of the early medieval imaginary.

Allnutt's "At the Friary at Alnmouth" also opens up another perspective on the monastic environment, modern and medieval. The poem draws us in, as outsiders, as female onlookers on the past and the present. Indeed, time—and the time of day in particular—is used in two ways in this poem. It refers to the lengthening evening light observed by the two friends, and also to the liturgical hours of the day. One natural and social (the light of the day; two friends together), the other communal and religious (the liturgy that organizes the days of the friars). Compline, in line 2, is the last monastic hour or service of the day. Caught between the natural, the social or worldly, and the religious, we are reminded of Cuthbert's dual allegiance to the asceticism that the "storm woman" represents, on the one hand, and to the monastic community represented by Abbess Hild, on the other.

The Franciscan Friary at Alnmouth is a modern foundation of monastic brothers, though it welcomes guests of both sexes. It is also a place rich in associations with the life of Cuthbert and his meeting on Coquet Island with Abbess Ælfflæd, to which we return later in this essay. The modern visitors to the Friary in Allnutt's poem, however, are unsettled. Their sense of displacement is evident from the poem's startling combination of the lyrical with the discomforting. Line 2, "How awkward we are at Compline," is repeated in line 7. In line 7 the contrast is between the church service and the sheer beauty of looking out at Coquet Island "in the long blue evening light," which refers us back to line 1, "We are looking at Coquet Island in the long blue evening light." Medievalists familiar with Old English poetry will note this repetition and variation, with its interlaced lines reminiscent of the visual art of the Lindisfarne Gospels.[14]

The speaker in "At the Friary at Alnmouth" registers her awkwardness with these reflections on the diurnal, or habitual, and the religious. At the

---

13. References to the Lindisfarne Gospels and their "interfolded, intwining, intricate lines" frame "After Life" at the beginning and end, 61 and 74.

14. Allnutt's knowledge of Cuthbert is evident in "Arvo Pärt in Concert, Durham Cathedral, 1998," in *How the Bicycle Shone*, 112–13. Her interest in Old English poetry surfaces early in her career; see, for example, the reference to "The Wife's Lament" in "The Unmaking," *How the Bicycle Shone*, 45.

beginning of the poem, the friends have "no habits" in this place that seems to require them (of men, at least), but the woman at the end of the poem does have a handbag, which seems oddly out of place, awkward. The poem concludes, "How awkward it is to be at Compline in the long blue evening light / With my old shoulder-bag lying there yet, at my feet." Awkwardness here is a matter of propriety, of gender and spiritual practice (those "habits," that "old shoulder-bag"), and of place itself. The modern Friary looks out to sea, like Cuthbert's Inner Farne, his retreat from Lindisfarne. The friends are at Compline in a male foundation (one source of disorientation, perhaps), but their sense of place, their belonging links them with the sea, much as Cuthbert's ambivalence about collective worship in "After Life" is registered by his longing for the natural world and a place by the sea. Allnutt's friends have "the smell of the sea [. . .] in our hair" (line 4). Though they have no habits, the poem captures a moment of belonging: "our hearts are stranded here" and "transparent, lit / like jelly fish in the afternoon." Key to this line is "stranded," on the shore (the Old English word for "shore" is *strand*). Like "jelly fish," the friends in this poem are out of place, on the shore. Operating across the literal and the figurative, the diurnal and the spiritual, the poem offers us a glimpse into women's hearts and friendships.

That glimpse is more fully realized in Griffith's *Hild*. Indeed, the novel is a remarkable act of historical imagining. The novel tackles the lack of historical sources for Hild's early life before she became a nun, after which Bede's account of her life properly begins, by building a convincingly accurate seventh-century world in which the young Hild can live her life.[15] Central to that imagining is female friendship, for which Griffith adapts an Old English word, *gemæcce*, which she glosses as "formal female friendship; one of a pair."[16] Recorded uses of *gemæcce* are not gender-specific; if anything, the noun refers to cisgender partnerships or male friendships.[17] Griffith's appropriation of the Old English word is therefore a bold but necessary one, for, as she well knows, the female world of friendships and relationships is barely visible in the historical record. *Hild* peoples its seventh-century world with women and pairs them with an activity often associated with early medieval women, weaving: ". . . in their *gemæcce* pairs, old women with old, young with young, women who had woven and spun and carded together for yours,

---

15. *Bede's Ecclesiastical History of the English People* (Oxford: Clarendon Press, 1969), ed. and trans. Bertram Colgrave and R. A. B. Mynors, Book IV, cap. 23.

16. Griffith, *Hild*, 620 (Glossary); see also Griffith's blog post "Hild and Her Gemæcce," https://nicolagriffith.com/2012/06/20/hild-and-her-gemaecce/ (accessed May 3, 2021).

17. See the *Bosworth-Toller Anglo-Saxon Dictionary*, https://bosworthtoller.com/48772 (accessed December 4, 2021).

through first blood and marriage and babies" (*Hild* 57). Women establish these formal friendships at adolescence and they persist throughout life: "Hereswith and Mildburh, Breguswith and Onnen, Cwenburh and Teneshild, old Burgen and Æffe" (*Hild* 57) surround the young Hild until she is bonded with Begu, her own *gemæcce*.

The modern reimaginings of the seventh century by Griffith, Maitland, and Allnutt are examples of creative engagements with early medieval culture.[18] In this essay, we are interested in how our three women writers re-vision the past, its places and personae, their relationships, and their relationship to us in the present. By so doing, the contemporary medieval offers new models for the scholarly understanding of female friendship. To reiterate Maitland's point, without narrative there is only silence. This essay explores how modern scholars, like modern writers, might create narrative in the face of absence.

To this end, in the next section we look at some reported, literal and meta conversations in which our seventh-century women, Ælfflæd and Iurminburg, appear, and adopt the usual but perhaps not inevitable academic pose of listening at a distance to our male-authored sources even as we rehearse them. The introduction to this volume asks "where might women's friendship reside and under what cultural rubrics other than masculine virtue, political affinity, and civic polity might it be found . . . What are the conditions of its emergence . . . ?"[19] As we delve into the complicated political world in which Ælfflæd and Iurminburg lived, we too ask how to imagine a cultural rubric beyond a male-authored polity. Penelope Anderson calls attention to five chapters in this volume (Boffa, Chism, Harris, Lochrie, and Verini) that engage with varieties of "political friendship" and its conditions and drawbacks for women.[20] Alexandra Verini's essay "Sisters and Friends: The Medieval Nuns of Syon Abbey" resonates with our project. We also "assume that nuns had friends," and share her question "but is there any evidence of such bonds?"[21] However, we reframe the discovery of such "evidence" and expand the cultural rubric that gives it credence. We revisit those male-authored sources, sift through them, repeat and recap, following the intersections of our abbesses' presence and absence. We aim to create a nuanced picture as a context for a different conversation about women, and among women, and to provide the historical framework for our more speculative imaginings about female friendships that follow in section three of this essay.

---

18. Lees and Overing, *The Contemporary Medieval in Practice.*
19. "Introduction," 6.
20. "Afterword: Friendship at a Distance," 266.
21. Verini, 77.

OVERHEARD CONVERSATIONS FROM THE SEVENTH CENTURY

Most modern scholars would agree that to read for women in the early medieval Latin *Lives* of Cuthbert and Wilfrid is to read intransigent material awkwardly, often against narrative intent. The sources for women's lives and relationships are few and far between. Bede refers to a book recording the early history of the dual monastic foundation at Barking (later a famous female foundation), and to a *Life* of Æthelthryth, first wife of King Ecgfrith of Northumberland, Ælfflæd's brother. The modern case for a lost life of Hild has also been made. None of these narratives have survived, although it could be argued that Bede himself must have reworked them in composing his accounts of Barking and of Æthelthryth in his *History*.[22]

The absence of women's saint's lives contrasts strikingly with evidence for the three northern male saints from this same period, Cuthbert, Wilfrid, and Gregory, Apostle of the English. Episodes from the *Lives* of these saints have long enjoyed a potent "after life." That of Gregory the Great furnishes the account of the conversion of the kingdom of Kent to Christianity (together with the anecdote of Gregory seeing his angelic Angles in a Roman market). Cuthbert swims with seals or otters (thereby providing the British Isles with a precursor to the Italian St. Francis). Wilfrid furnishes a useful myth about northern independence from and conformity with the ruling family and with Rome as required, together with "another stonking great stone church" (as Maitland puts it; "After Life" 73), Ripon Cathedral.[23] The absence of early Latin *Lives* of women religious entails the loss of such iconic figures and stories, but we can reconstruct some women-oriented narratives out of this initially unpromising material. Women's history needs a better understanding of relations between secular and religious women in particular—between queens and abbesses like Ælfflæd and Iurminburg—to put alongside our understanding of the delicate and sensitive balance of power between abbesses, bish-

---

22. Bede, *Ecclesiastical History*, Book IV, cap. 10, 19; see also *The Ecclesiastical History of the English People*, ed. and trans. Judith McClure and Roger Collins (Oxford: Oxford University Press, 1994), 406, where the possibility of a lost *Life* of Æthelthryth is discussed. See further Clare A. Lees and Gillian R. Overing, "Women and the Origins of English Literature," in *The History of British Women's Writing*, vol. 1, ed. Elizabeth McAvoy and Diane Watt (New York: Palgrave Macmillan, 2013), 31–40. The evidence is most recently summarized by Diane Watt, *Women, Writing and Religion in England and Beyond, 650–1100* (London: Bloomsbury, 2019), ch. 1 and 2.

23. For an overview, see Clare A. Lees, "Gender and the Subjects of History in the Early Middle Ages," in *The Cambridge History of Historical Writing: Britain and Ireland, 500–1500*, ed. Emily Steiner, Jennifer Jahner, and Elizabeth Tyler (Cambridge: Cambridge University Press, 2019), 299–318, at 299–303.

ops, and kings in this period. The pioneering work of Lisa Weston on female friendships points in the right direction, but, as Weston also notes, in order to think about women's friendships and alliances with other women, we are going to have to develop innovative strategies for reading against and imaginatively the historical record. Speculation is sometimes the only way to go.[24]

The conversations we overhear in this section are about and between Ælfflæd and Cuthbert, and about and between Iurminburg and Cuthbert. Neither woman is mentioned in Maitland's "After Life," but both, we argue, are central in the early hagiographical tradition represented by the *Lives* of Cuthbert and Wilfrid. Ælfflæd, mentioned earlier in connection with Allnutt's poem, is referred to as Abbess and Holy Virgin in the *Lives* of Cuthbert and of Wilfrid and became Abbess of Whitby after Hild, as we have seen; sister to Ecgfrith of Northumbria, her mother was Eanflæd, wife of King Oswy. Iurminburg, queen and second wife of Ecgfrith, also appears in the *Lives* of Cuthbert and Wilfrid, albeit anonymously in the former and demonized in the latter. Ecgfrith's first wife was the celebrated virgin, St Æthelthryth. Iurminburg became a nun after Ecgfrith's death and ultimately an abbess as well.

Allnutt's reference to "looking at Coquet Island" in "At the Friary at Alnmouth" resonates for us with a much older meeting in 684 between Ælfflæd and Cuthbert. It was on Coquet Island that the Abbess persuaded the then hermit and monk to predict the destiny of her royal family and his ecclesiastical career. Alnmouth is where Cuthbert later reluctantly agreed to become bishop, fulfilling the prediction made at Ælfflæd's behest. Their recorded conversation in the earliest anonymous *Life* and in Bede's prose *Life* is one-sided.[25] Cuthbert does most of the talking, while her strategically tearful response to hearing his prediction of her brother Ecgfrith's death is sometimes narrated indirectly. In both accounts, however and notwithstanding the many tears she is shedding, Ælfflæd's voice is clearly and somewhat tersely heard in her demand to know who will succeed to her brother's throne. The fall of the Northumbrian royal house is prophesied a second time a year later, by Cuthbert in Carlisle, and in 685 Ælfflæd's brother, Ecgfrith, dies in battle and her half-brother, Aldfrith, inherits the kingdom.

In 685, according to the anonymous *Life of Cuthbert* and Bede's prose Latin *Life of Cuthbert,* Cuthbert traveled west to Carlisle to visit Queen Iurmin-

---

24. Lisa M. C. Weston, "Where Textual Bodies Meet: Anglo-Saxon Women's Epistolary Friendships," in *Friendship in the Middle Ages and Early Modern Age: Explorations of a Fundamental Ethical Discourse,* ed. Albrecht Classen and Marilyn Sandidge (Berlin: de Gruyter, 2010), 231–46.

25. The anonymous *Life of Cuthbert,* Book III, cap. xxvi, and Bede's prose *Life,* cap. xxiv; ed. Colgrave, *Two Lives of Saint Cuthbert.*

burg, Ecgfrith's second wife. She was in Carlisle apparently to await news of Ecgfrith's disastrous battle of Nechtansmere against the Picts. Bede adds the detail that Iurminburg was staying in her sister's minster or convent, though not who the sister was nor, just as frustratingly, any further information about the minster itself. The day after his arrival in Carlisle, Cuthbert was taken to see the city walls and—perhaps highlight of the tour—a "well formerly built in a wonderful manner by the Romans" (anonymous *Life*, Book IV, cap. viii) or a "marvelously constructed fountain [*fons*] of Roman workmanship" (Bede, prose *Life of Cuthbert*, cap. xxvii). Suddenly "troubled in spirit," Cuthbert leaned on his staff, looked to the ground and up to the heavens, sighed, and speculated in a whisper, "Perhaps even now the issue of the battle is decided" (Bede, prose *Life*, cap. xxvii). Bede includes the detail that Cuthbert hurried to the queen and urged her to leave Carlisle as soon as possible for the royal city of Bamburgh in the east of the kingdom, but does not report their conversation, unlike the one between Ælfflæd and Cuthbert at Coquet Island a year earlier. Ecgfrith died "on the very day and at the very hour" ("ipsa die eademque hora") that his death was revealed to Cuthbert.

And what of Iurminburg? For whatever reason, she returned to Bamburgh at Cuthbert's behest and subsequently entered holy orders, like so many early medieval royal women before and after her. Bede notes pointedly in the next chapter of the prose *Life* (cap. xxviii) that Cuthbert consecrated her in the convent at Carlisle. Iurminburg was Ecgfrith's second wife, we recall. His first—whose own story is threaded through Iurminburg's—was that virgin saint, Æthelthryth, much admired by Bede and a profound, material source of speculative fascination for us in the next section of this essay.[26] There seem to have been no children from either of the marriages: whence, perhaps, the succession crisis on Ecgfrith's death.

The revelation of Ecgfrith's fall in 685 involving Iurminburg recalls for us that first revelation in 684 at Coquet Island involving Ælfflæd. Abbess Ælfflæd had summoned Cuthbert to the island, apparently famed for its monasteries, to search out his opinions about the succession problem. She called on Cuthbert to use his "spirit of prophecy" (Bede, prose *Life*, cap. xxvii) to reveal how long her brother will live, who will succeed to the throne, and what Cuthbert's views might be about the episcopacy of Lindisfarne. It doesn't take divine inspiration to predict that Aldfrith will succeed after the death of his childless half-brother. The politics of dynasties turns often enough on the marriage bed. Nor do we need Cuthbert's spiritual powers to foresee Ecgfrith's downfall,

---

26. Bede, *Ecclesiastical History*, Book IV, caps.19–20.

given the prior evidence of his disastrous policies against the Irish.[27] As sister to the king and abbess of Whitby, Ælfflæd has considerable political insight and influence, which she clearly wishes to exert over the bishop-elect at Coquet Island. At stake are relations between abbesses and bishops—both of whom have considerable interest and influence in royal as well as church matters. In this regard, to follow Hollis, Bede's representation of the relationship between the holy man and holy woman as one of friendly alliance—spiritual kinship—is crucial.[28] What Bede manipulates in his account of the relations between Abbess Ælfflæd and Cuthbert at Coquet Island is the threat posed to the sacramental authority of monks, priests, and bishops by a powerful royal woman with strong ecclesiastical contacts, a credible amount of rational foresight, and concern for the future of family and Church. Bede reorients this relationship using the veiling metaphor of spiritual friendship: the abbess and monk are friends, but the latter has authority over the former. Ælfflæd may have summoned Cuthbert to meet with *her* at Coquet Island, but the soon-to-be bishop Cuthbert holds on to *his* powers of prediction (or influence).

Whatever the abbess, Ælfflæd, actually said to the soon-to-be bishop, Cuthbert, at Coquet Island in 684, Cuthbert has the upper hand by the time of his visit to Carlisle in 685, or so Bede would have us believe. Cuthbert undertakes this visit on his own initiative—no summons from a royal abbess here—and finds Iurminburg in the sister convent of a member of the royal family, possibly one of the daughter houses of Whitby, Ælfflæd's minster.[29] The second revelation of Ecgfrith's fall is unprompted by any woman (indeed, Bede offers an anonymous priest to witness Cuthbert's prophecy).[30] In place of Ælfflæd's impertinent questions, Bede supplies the image of that Roman wall and *fons*: an image of empire thus replaces that of the weeping royal woman in the earlier scene. Finally, the sacramental implications of Cuthbert's gift of prophecy are spelled out as Cuthbert justifies his authority by referring to a sermon with the theme of the power that bishops have by grace over and above lesser ministers of the Church. According to Bede, Cuthbert had first preached this sermon to the monks at Lindisfarne, who had interpreted it to be a prophecy about the plague, but he repeats it for the benefit of the nuns at Carlisle a week or so after the death of Ecgfrith was revealed to him. The theme of the sermon is vigilance.

---

27. Bede, *Ecclesiastical History*, Book IV, cap. 26.
28. See Hollis, *Anglo-Saxon Women and the Church*, especially ch. 8, "Rewriting Female Lives: Hild of Whitby and Monastic Women in Bede's *History*," 243–70.
29. "in monasterio suae sororis," Bede, prose *Life*, cap. xxvii.
30. Bede, prose *Life*, cap. xxvii, "presbiter."

What are we not hearing in these reported conversations? The key to the episode of Cuthbert at Coquet Island in 684 is the struggle for influence over Church and kingdom between Ælfflæd and an apparently reluctant Cuthbert, who is represented as hardly eager to become bishop. The struggle is between royal, ecclesiastical female power and divinely inspired, ecclesiastically sanctioned male authority. By 685 Cuthbert's authority has won out. In case we don't get the point, it is staged for us in front of the congregation at a minster associated with women if not explicitly with Ælfflæd herself. Score one for Cuthbert and Bede, and the masculinization of sacred as well as secular power. But what of Iurminburg? Does the fact that the abbess and the queen seem so distinctively separate in these narrative sources—the one associated with Coquet Island and the other with Carlisle—have anything to do with this overwhelming rescripting of power in masculine terms?

Iurminburg and Ælfflæd are not usually spoken of in the same breath, whether by medieval hagiographers or by modern critics. To the best of our knowledge of the sources, these two women are never found in the same narrative space. In the various *Lives* of Cuthbert, Iurminburg goes unnamed and barely mentioned although she is a highly visible "she-wolf" turned "lamb of God" in the *Life of Wilfrid*.[31] Ælfflæd, by contrast, is a prominent figure in both *Lives*. In terms of geographical space, it is possible to map the movements of these women individually but not collectively on the islands of Coquet, near Alnmouth, and Inner Farne, the cities of Carlisle and Bamburgh, and the monasteries of Carlisle, Whitby, and Coldingham.

Hollis's work on the individual stories of Iurminburg and Ælfflæd is fundamental to our understanding of these deeply attenuated and problematic sources. Hollis points out the overt misogyny of the representation of Iurminburg in the *Life of Wilfrid*, probably the result of Stephen of Ripon's disdain for Iurminburg's alleged influence over Ecgfrith.[32] By contrast, the *Life* has positive things to say about royal women who sponsor Wilfrid: Eanflæd, Ælfflæd's mother and Oswy's wife, under whose patronage Wilfrid first became a monk and was sent to Rome; Æthelthryth, Ecgfrith's pious first wife, during whose marriage the royal kingdom (if not the marriage) flourished and who gave Wilfrid land with which to build the church at Hexham; and Ælfflæd herself, who was later influential in healing the division between Wilfrid and Aldfrith. But the *Life* certainly demonizes those "wicked" secular women who stand in the way of power: Queen Baldhild of the Franks as well as Queen Iurminburg

---

31. *The Life of Wilfrid*, ed. Colgrave, cap. xxiv.
32. See Hollis, *Anglo-Saxon Women and the Church*, ch. 5, "The Advice of Women and Eddius's *Life of Wilfrid*," 151–78, especially 165–78.

of the Northumbrians.³³ The silence about Iurminburg in the Cuthbert *Lives* speaks volumes: she only features in the one episode of Cuthbert in Carlisle, and there she is unnamed, as already noted. It is also possible to trace chronologically the diminishing importance of Ælfflæd in the various *Lives* of Cuthbert, beginning with the Lindisfarne *Life*, then those by Bede and finally, much later in the tenth century, by Ælfric (by which time the scene at Carlisle has been erased).³⁴ In so doing, we can assess the gradual writing out of female presence and agency in the sources of the early medieval period.³⁵ We need, however, to go further and consider how we might reconstruct relations between women, not just their individual, insular stories.

So let us return one more time to Carlisle, the queen, the abbess, and Cuthbert in 685. Ostensibly, as we know, Iurminburg was in Carlisle to sit out Ecgfrith's battle against the Picts, and Carlisle was in the heartland of the former British kingdom of Rheged. If she went there for safety, to be as far away as possible from the east of the Northumbrian kingdom, the royal city of Bamburgh, and possible Pictish incursions, her relocation to Carlisle also sent another message. For Carlisle was a place that represented Northumbrian hegemony over this former British region, and Iurminburg's presence was a potent symbol of Northumbrian domination of Picts and Irish alike. The *Life of Wilfrid* tells us that Iurminburg and Ecgfrith were accustomed to staging royal tours around their kingdom (cities and villages) with some quite showy sense of ritual, wealth, and drama.³⁶ The presence of Iurminburg on her own in Carlisle in 685 suggests a similar political gesture. Indeed, she had taken up temporary residence in a minster that may have been under the jurisdiction of one of her sisters, if not Abbess Ælfflæd herself. And it is in this minster that Iurminburg will subsequently enter religious life, with the blessing of Cuthbert and the approval of Bede. Later still, as we know from the *Life of Wilfrid* (cap. xxiv), Iurminburg became an abbess (though where, we do not know).³⁷ Although neither Bede nor the earlier anonymous *Life of Cuthbert*

---

33. For Balhild, see *Life of Wilfrid*, cap. vii.

34. Bede does not refer to Ælfflæd in his account of Cuthbert in the *Ecclesiastical History*, Book IV, ch. 27–30, nor does Ælfric in his *Life of Cuthbert*; see Homily X in *Ælfric's Catholic Homilies: The Second Series*, ed. Malcolm Godden, Early English Text Society, SS 5 (Oxford: Oxford University Press, 1979).

35. For a related discussion, see Clare A. Lees and Gillian R. Overing, *Double Agents: Women and Clerical Culture in Anglo-Saxon England* (Philadelphia: University of Pennsylvania Press, 2001; repr. with new preface, Cardiff: University of Wales Press, 2009), 56–100.

36. See, for example, *Life of Wilfrid*, ed. and trans. Colgrave, cap. xxxix.

37. See also the probably spurious reference to Iurminburh, abbess in an early Kentish Charter (Sawyer 20); see the Electronic Sawyer: https://esawyer.lib.cam.ac.uk/charter/20.html (accessed May 3, 2021).

tell us that Ælfflæd was in Carlisle at the same time as Iurminburg, the connections between the secular queen, who will be abbess, and the royal abbess, who is sister to the queen, symbolized in and by the place of Carlisle, its city and its minister, are intriguing indeed.

Iurminburg had two other sisters according to the *Life of Wilfrid*. One, Osthryth, another of Ecgfrith's sisters like Ælfflæd, was married to Æthelred of Mercia, Northumbria's sometime ally, sometime enemy. The other, whose name we do not know, was married to Centwine, king of the West Saxons. The *Life of Wilfrid* (cap. xl) predictably names neither woman, but the evidence indicates the political clout of the royal sisters and their support of Iurminburg's dispute with Wilfrid (which is also, of course, a dispute with Ecgfrith).[38] Iurminburg, Osthryth, and their unnamed sister are elite secular women linking the kingdoms of Northumbria, Mercia, and Wessex by marriage and kinship alliances. It is worth recalling in this context of elite women that the *Life of Wilfrid* demonizes Iurminburg (as a "wicked Jezebel," cap. xxiv) for her apparent jealousy of Wilfrid's visible displays of wealth, status, and land. For one thing is clear from any reading of the *Life of Wilfrid*; he is himself a master at acquiring both material wealth and land.[39] Here is a conflict between a queen and a bishop for their influence over a king, then, but it is also a conflict about whether queens and bishops can use power in their own right. Iurminburg has her own understanding of the sociopolitical uses of ostentation, and she is quite familiar with the strategic importance of staging performances of power. Wilfrid, moreover, was a close spiritual advisor to Ecgfrith's first wife, the ever-virginal and increasingly saintly Æthelthryth. Wilfrid's distaste for Iurminburg, perhaps sharpened by the misogyny of his *Life*, is not just second-wife syndrome. It helps us map out a zone of relations between those jostling for power within the Church and royal families. Elite women are key figures in both ecclesiastical and secular spheres, and relations between women, however hard to recover, are crucial. If we align Wilfrid with Æthelthryth, apparently against Iurminburg, then it is equally clear that Iurminburg's royal sisters are aligned with her.

And what of Ælfflæd? More than just Ecgfrith's sister and Iurminburg's sister-by-marriage, Ælfflæd was another powerful woman in her own right. Daughter of Eanflæd and Oswiu of Northumbria, as we have seen, she was dedicated to the Church at the age of one and features in the *Lives of Cuthbert* and *Wilfrid* and in Bede's *History*, although she never quite gains the caché of the saintly Æthelthryth. In 684 Ælfflæd was joint abbess of Whitby—she had

---

38. *Life of Wilfrid*, cap. XL and note at 175.
39. Especially in the restoring or building of minsters. See, for example, *Life of Wilfrid*, ed. Colgrave, cap. xvii.

been from 680—with her mother, Eanflæd, who as Oswiu's wife was the queen mother (that is, Eanflæd was Ecgfrith's mother as well). Eanflæd's sister, Æbbe, Ecgfrith's and Ælfflæd's aunt, was abbess of Coldingham, a little farther north up the coast from Lindisfarne. Coldingham, the anonymous *Life of Cuthbert* tells us, is where Cuthbert was secretly witnessed wearing only a "loincloth" ("ad lumbare") worshipping in the sea and then being dried by the seals during a visit to Æbbe (Book II, cap. iii). But Coldingham was not Bede's favorite dual monastery, according to his *History*. It was a place of "feasting, drinking, gossip, and other delights" for both men and women, although the only "delight" that Bede can bring himself to name is a taste for fine, expensive clothes.[40] The nuns spent their spare time weaving "elaborate garments with which to adorn themselves as if they were brides, so imperiling their virginity, or else to make friends with strange men." What to make of this accusation? Elite religious women throughout the early medieval period were known for their weaving and embroidery, and secular elite women used their dress sense to display their status and wealth. Moreover, the nuns at Coldingham were brides of Christ. Even if Bede is inviting us to imagine Coldingham as a place where women might find a husband other than Christ, the alternate he offers—that the women are dressing up to "make friends with *strange* men" (our emphasis)—also seems implausible. Rather, at stake here is gender decorum in the monastery in a period when monastic dress was not firmly distinguished from secular clothing and when there was always the potential for gender panic about elite women, their sexuality, and their power.[41]

We recall that Ecgfrith's first wife, Æthelthryth, married twice and remaining intact throughout, first took the veil at Coldingham, under Æbbe, before she went on to be Abbess of Ely. Bede's life of Æthelthryth culminates in her death from a tumor on her neck which she interprets as divine punishment for wearing elaborate necklaces in her youth.[42] Whatever the women at Coldingham were making, it's clear that Bede doesn't think it appropriate for them: religious women shouldn't dress *like that*. It takes a particularly penitent priest to spot this, of course, one used to eating only on Thursdays and Sundays, who predicts, accurately, that the monastery will burn down, although not in Æbbe's lifetime. It's all a bit reminiscent of finding yourself out of place with a "shabby handbag" and "with no habits" in a Friary, to return to Allnutt's poem.

Coldingham is also the scene of a powerful moment in the life of Iurminburg. According to the *Life of Wilfrid* (cap. xxxix), Coldingham was where

---

40. Bede, *Ecclesiastical History*, Book IV, cap. 25.

41. Gale R. Owen-Crocker, *Dress in Anglo-Saxon England* (Woodbridge, Suffolk: Boydell, 1986, rev. 2004), 133.

42. Bede, *Ecclesiastical History*, Book IV, cap. xix.

Iurminburg fell seriously ill, apparently possessed by a "devil," and where Æbbe intervened to persuade Ecgfrith to give up his persecution of Wilfrid and thereby effect Iurminburg's recovery. Æbbe succeeds. Ecgfrith and Wilfrid are persuaded by the tearful abbess into a rapprochement, albeit a temporary one, and, as a result, Iurminburg is healed in this not-quite miracle. The relevant chapter laconically concludes "And the queen recovered." Wilfrid has papal authority for his reinstatement, so Æbbe's gesture of reconciling the royal couple—her kin—with Wilfrid is also one that maintains good relations between the Northumbrian church—her religious *familia*—and papal authority at Rome. The specific details of Æbbe's intervention in this dispute about royal and ecclesiastical power are what matters, however, for in the course of her intervention, Æbbe instructs Iurminburg to take off her necklace and return it to Wilfrid.

Indeed, the real problem with Iurminburg, the *Life of Wilfrid* (cap. xxxiv) insists, is that when Wilfrid's possessions were confiscated by Ecgfrith, she took a reliquary that Wilfrid had obtained while he was in Rome. Worse still, Iurminburg was in the habit of wearing it as a necklace, both at home and abroad while out riding around the kingdom as if, the *Life* repeats twice, carrying the Ark of the Covenant "from city to city," like the Philistines (cap. xxxiv, xxxix). It was on such a royal tour that she came to Coldingham. These are wonderful descriptions of female power on full display, and it is entirely appropriate to what we know about Iurminburg. Elite early medieval people displayed their wealth—they wore it around their necks, for example, and in the form of rings, brooches and pins—and they were also accustomed to wearing protective amulets. So, what is the specific nature of the problem that the *Life* can hardly bear to mention (cap. xxxiv)? Is it the fact that this secular woman has arrogated to herself the right to carry sacred relics outside the Church—at home and abroad, as the *Life* puts it? Is it that she is wearing *Wilfrid's* relics? Wilfrid, a relic collector himself, obtained this particular reliquary in Rome, and he is not averse to material displays of religious wealth either. Or is it that Iurminburg is wearing *relics*—bits and pieces of saintly bodies— around *her* neck, on *her* body?

It has been assumed by some, Hollis for example, that Iurminburg was a pagan at the time of this episode.[43] Though the *Life of Wilfrid* might tempt us in that direction, there is no real evidence for this. Iurminburg is described in Old Testament terms in the *Life of Wilfrid*, certainly, but that does not necessarily mean that she has no knowledge of Christianity. The reliquary has some power to attract Iurminburg, this much is clear, and she appears to take

---

43. Hollis, *Anglo-Saxon Women and the Church*, 168.

it at the same time as her Christian husband confiscates Wilfrid's property (cap. xxxiv). We see this episode, therefore, as evidence for an elite woman wearing her Christianity on her sleeve as it were, flouting—or perhaps better, establishing—convention much as those nuns at Coldingham seem to have done. The contrast with that other woman, Ecgfrith's first wife, Æthelthryth, who used to wear necklaces before she dedicated herself to God and who interpreted a growth on her neck as she lay dying as a sign of her former vanity, seems pointed. The first wife takes off her necklaces; the second likes to put them on. Another female relation and elder, Æbbe, commands that the relics be restored to Wilfrid, the queen does recover, and she goes on to visit Carlisle, stay in her sister's convent, and, ultimately, become an abbess herself. We are not entirely convinced that the best way to read this career trajectory is to assume that we are dealing with a troublesome woman who was eventually reformed and sent to a nunnery. Rather, here is a secular elite woman who moves fluidly and with some effect in worldly and spiritual domains and whose movements suggest that she is connected to and supported by a network of other elite women: Ælfflæd, Æthelthryth, Æbbe, and Eanflæd, to mention only those whose names have survived. Mapping connections between women in as many contexts and from as many perspectives as possible reminds us of the female relationships—elite and religious—that written evidence often obscures. There is some evidence that others later in the early medieval period thought so too. Iurminburg appears, *after life*, in the ninth-century list of queens and abbesses in the Durham *Liber vitae* between Eanflæd and Ælfflæd.[44]

CONVERSATIONS WE WISH WE HAD HEARD

Even when there is no evidence that firmly puts Iurminburg and Ælfflæd in the same place at the same time, we think it would be folly to assume that they didn't come into contact regularly and in ways that significantly impacted each of their lives. Consider what they have in common, in terms of status, profession, politics religious and regional, shared interests and acquaintances, locations, not to mention the various men in their lives, and one woman in particular, Æthelthryth. If we were to narrate the silence created by early medieval hagiographers' separation of Ælfflæd and Iurminburg, and bring them together—in any number of locations, but perhaps somewhere near Car-

---

44. For the Durham *Liber vitae*, see London, British Library, MS Cotton Domitian A. VII, fol. 16r (column 1); http://www.bl.uk/manuscripts/Viewer.aspx?ref=cotton_ms_domitian_a_vii_fs001r, accessed March 2022.

lisle in 685 where Ælfflæd might be host in one of her foundations—we speculate that the now dead and ever-virginal, not-yet saintly Æthelthryth, first wife of Iurminburg's husband, might feature in their conversation.[45] We certainly would like to know more about her, and so did Bede in one of his characteristic affirmations of the reliability of the conversational sources of his narrative:

> Though she lived with him for twelve years she still preserved the glory of perfect virginity. When I asked Bishop Wilfrid of blessed memory whether this was true, because certain people doubted it, he told me he had the most perfect proof of her virginity; in fact Ecgfrith had promised to give him estates and money if he could persuade the queen to consummate the marriage, because he knew that there was none whom she loved more than Wilfrid himself . . .[46]

If these two churchmen having a candid conversation about the "perfect proof" of Æthelthryth's virginity, demonstrable initially via her husband's bribery of her favorite and eventually by her dead but intact body, offers a somewhat partial narrative here, we ask what might two women who are possibly much closer to the situation want to know, or already know? One is the sister of the estranged husband and the other is married to him. How might they understand and discuss the same set of circumstances? There is a downright good-gossipy aspect to the Æthelthryth story, though the whiff of prurience, and any scent of a woman, is studiously if narcissistically redirected in the men's conversation by a material explanation for such determined and enduring abstinence. We don't presume or propose that, were Æfflaed and Iurminburg to discuss their mutual sister-by-marriage, her sexuality is the focus. We might assume that they would like to know "the truth" (wouldn't you?) but also that they are more likely to know it and a great deal more. As we outlined in the previous section, the choices of one powerful abbess intersect with those of her cohort, and any conversation about Æthelthryth would be both nuanced and fraught with a host of other considerations. The "truth," for example, is less important than the outcome: no sex equals no heirs, and this would surely be as pressing a question for the secular queen, who will be abbess, and the royal abbess, who is sister to her husband the king, as it is for the male players, both secular and religious. So too the play of influence of the

---

45. Iurminburg marries Ecgfrith in 678 while Æthelthryth is still alive (she dies in 679 or 680; *Life of Wilfrid*, cap. xxiv, and note at 167); however, her uncorrupted body, "buried for sixteen years" (Bede, *Ecclesiastical History*, Book IV, cap. xix), has yet to be exhumed to demonstrate the full extent of her saintliness.

46. *Ecclesiastical History*, Book IV, cap. xix.

two powerful bishops Wilfrid and Cuthbert is threaded through the women's shared context. As we have seen, the sisters-by-marriage as well as the virginal first wife are in distinct camps according to our male-authored sources; Iurminburg is flanked by her powerful royal sisters in opposition to Wilfrid and consecrated by Cuthbert, whereas Æthelthryth and Æfflaed are to varying degrees and at varying times allied with him. But as we have also pointed out, we can make no certain assumptions about the depth of their differences, or whether they might like, respect, or fear each other. Or all three. We can only speculate, too, about their differing tastes in adornment, their reasons for wearing jewelry, or which branches of Christianity they may or may not have chosen to identify with.

What we can do, however, is to keep expanding our imagining of how these women might narrate their own experience by continuing to interrogate the historical record, a point we made in our own early work on Hild.[47] We do not claim to be able to write that experience. We leave the storytelling and the creation of such conversations to those poets and writers of the sort we discuss in our first section.[48] And we can continue to pursue the concept of *gemæcce* offered to us by Nicola Griffith, that "of formal female friendship or partnership," of connection across, in spite of, and because of a plethora of differences, and offer in turn some concluding observations about female friendship, medieval and modern.

CONCLUSION: ON FRIENDSHIP AND ITS POSSIBILITIES

Is nū sēo nēawest swā hit nā wǣre,
frēondscipe uncer.

[Now our presence together, our friendship, is as it never were]
—"The Wife's Lament," lines 24–25

When we were asked to contribute to this volume, we revisited the phrase *female friendship* from a variety of perspectives. What did we mean by the phrase? The *we* evokes for us the Old English dual pronoun *wit* ("we two"),

---

47. Lees and Overing, *Double Agents*, 39.
48. Like many others, we, await *Menewood*, Nicola Griffith's sequel to *Hild*. According to Griffith's blog, this may be forthcoming in 2021; "A Writing Update: *Hild*, Aud, *Ammonite* and More," https://nicolagriffith.com/2019/11/18/a-writing-update-hild-aud-ammonite-and-more/ (accessed April 8, 2020).

but our evocation here of our own conversations is intended to expand the purview of friendship beyond early medieval friends to the friendships of those who study them. We have written recently about the long arc of our own collaborative scholarship.[49] We have collaborated on many projects over thirty-some years. We are friends. We are female. The intellectual arc of our ongoing conversation has intersected regularly with shared academic, professional, and personal challenges, with developments, even transformations, within our field and in our evolving thinking. It's a package deal. Professional, personal, intellectual, and also past and present.

We have long been preoccupied with women's absence in the primary sources of our field, and revisiting the idea of female friendship brought us squarely back (though perhaps we have never actually left) to the world of seventh- and early eighth-century Northumbria, to all those literate, savvy, powerful, usually aristocratic women whose presence and influence must have been palpable. Even when there is no clear evidence, we had long thought that given the tight world of aristocratic politics, some of these women must have been friends and/or acquaintances, competitors, collaborators, lovers, customers, providers, sisters by marriage, or sisters in Christ (or both), or some or all of the above. Then, as now, there are many forms of connection and ways of creating alliance and community among women.

Medieval feminists such as Stephanie Hollis and Lisa Weston, whose work we have drawn on for this essay, and Karma Lochrie and Ulrike Wiethaus, whose work has long inspired us, have profoundly affected and enriched our thinking about friendship on and off the page; they have created for us an intellectual community of sorts, one where we do not always agree but where we can connect on different levels.[50] And some of them are indeed friends, though our point here is rather that as we think about our current academic community, the "we" broadens and our conversation expands, as different connections and forms of friendship are made possible by shared interests. The "we" of this community is professional, intellectual, social, diverse, divergent; it collapses, too, at certain points, and tests the limits of community and connectivity. At times, it seems impossible, as the speaker in the Old English

---

49. See *The Contemporary Medieval in Practice*, ch. 2.
50. Hollis, *Anglo-Saxon Women and the Church*; Weston, "Where Textual Bodies Meet"; Karma Lochrie, "Between Women," *The Cambridge Companion to Medieval Women's Writing*, ed. Carolyn Dinshaw and David Wallace (Cambridge: Cambridge University Press, 2007), 70–88; Ulrike Wiethaus, "In Search of Medieval Women's Friendships: Hildegard of Bingen's Letters to her Female Contemporaries," in Wiethaus, ed., *Maps of Flesh and Light: The Religious Experience of Medieval Women Mystics* (Syracuse, NY: Syracuse University Press, 1993), 93–111.

poem "The Wife's Lament" concludes.[51] Friendship comes and goes, and it is also a work in progress. We approach its absence, whether in the seventh or the twenty-first century, with a similar set of questions and precepts. Interrogating the historical record and its silences and exclusions; engaging and challenging the means of creation of such a record whether in early medieval or modern cultural contexts; reimagining the possibilities of human connection; paying close attention to both what we study and how we study it. Doing the work, and (not but) doing it differently.[52]

---

51. Her "freondscip" is generally assumed to be straight. See "The Wife's Lament" in *Old English Shorter Poems*, vol. 2, *Wisdom and Lyric*, ed. and trans. Robert B. Bjork, Dumbarton Oaks Medieval Library (Cambridge, MA: Harvard University Press, 2014), 104–7.

52. See *The Contemporary Medieval in Practice*, 8–9.

AFTERWORD

Friendship at a Distance

PENELOPE ANDERSON

WOMEN'S FRIENDSHIP IN MEDIEVAL LITERATURE appears at an unprecedented moment of distance, amid the paired threats of a global pandemic that necessitates social distancing and growing acknowledgment of the deadly rifts of systemic racism. At the same time, even as the coronavirus pandemic enforces social distance across many relationships, it also heightens proximity, the hours and days and weeks that families of choice and chance spend sequestered together. The pandemic likewise illuminates the unequal burdens of care, as the closing of schools and child care highlights the gendered inequalities still shaping many households. Systemic racism's permeation of all aspects of life for people of color forces more harmful closeness, from everyday racism to police brutality to disproportionate vulnerability to coronavirus.

Medieval women's friendship can help illuminate these dynamics of distance and closeness in new ways. Vitally, the distance of historical time offers a new perspective: not, as the editors Karma Lochrie and Usha Vishnuvajjala carefully articulate, "the idea that women's friendships are a particularly modern development, and with it the oversimplified narrative of historical progress between the Middle Ages and today, especially with respect to gender," but rather a sketching of the range of possibilities of loving relationships, over and across time.[1] Overturning a false sense of periodization, this volume both

---

1. Lochrie and Vishnuvajjala, "Introduction."

amplifies and disperses a sense of what friendship might be, from alewives gossiping together to attendants laying out bodies of the dead to later readers acknowledging a felt kinship with the past. Like the best feminist work, this volume "examine[s]" "the connection between the histories we inherit and the futures we imagine," as Ania Loomba and Melissa Sanchez write in a recent collection.[2] This "practice of befriending past female friendships" thus offers a way to take up Audre Lorde's exhortation in "Poetry Is Not a Luxury": "But there are no new ideas still waiting in the wings to save us as women, as human. There are only old and forgotten ones, new combinations, extrapolations and recognitions from within ourselves—along with the renewed courage to try them out."[3] My own perspective, as a white queer feminist scholar of seventeenth-century English literature, views this volume of essays on medieval texts both through my historical specialization and through the urgent demands of our current historical moment.

Women's friendship, in medieval contexts, manifests Lorde's courage in both distance and closeness. Distance takes the form of historical remove, physical separation, and unlikeness. Closeness entails intellectual companionship, physical proximity, and likeness. The latter triumvirate describes the dominant model of classical friendship, following Aristotle and Cicero. In the tradition of *philia* and *amicitia perfecta*, friends share one soul, "an other the same."[4] The insistence on likeness imposes limitations on classical friendship: friends are almost always men of the same class, religion, nation, and race—so alike that many stories of friendship substitute their indistinguishable bodies for one another.[5] According to the literary evidence, women's friendships rarely ascend to these heights, as Michel de Montaigne, quoted in the introduction, reminds us: "the ordinary sufficiency of women, cannot answer this conference and communication, the nurse of this sacred bond: nor seeme their mindes strong enough to endure the pulling of a knot so hard, so fast, and durable."[6] The weight of this masculine tradition means that the authors

---

2. Ania Loomba and Melissa E. Sanchez, "Feminism and the Burdens of History," in *Rethinking Feminism in Early Modern Studies: Gender, Race, and Sexuality*, ed. Loomba and Sanchez (New York: Routledge, 2016), 15–41, at 41.

3. Lochrie and Vishnuvajjala, "Introduction"; Audre Lorde, "Poetry Is Not a Luxury," *Sister Outsider* (Trumansburg, NY: Crossing Press, 1984), 36–39, at 38.

4. Aristotle, *Nicomachean Ethics*, trans. and ed. Christopher Rowe, ed. Sarah Brodie (Oxford: Oxford University Press, 2002), IX.viii.2.

5. See Alan Bray, *Homosexuality in Renaissance England* (London: Gay Men's Press, 1982), and Laurie Shannon, *Sovereign Amity: Figures of Friendship in Shakespearean Contexts* (Chicago: University of Chicago Press, 2002).

6. Michel de Montaigne, "Of Friendship," in *Essayes*, trans. John Florio, ed. Desmond McCarthy (London: J. M. Dent and Sons, 1928), 199.

in this collection need to look closely and otherwise for the traces of medieval women's friendship, whether by investigating the silence between the lines in written texts, as Jennifer N. Brown does, or by recalibrating our sense of what constitutes friendship, as Lochrie does, or by searching for traces in later writers' responses, as Clare A. Lees and Gillian R. Overing do.[7]

The friendships that emerge from these texts thus often look quite different from the perfect pair of the classical tradition. Friendship spans both larger acts of "patronage and institution-building" and the everyday "intimacy, consideration, and ritual courtesy" in Stella Wang's analysis of Marie de France.[8] Friendship can be a group of women attending to the material needs of a visionary woman and receiving mentoring in return, as in Brown's essay. Friendship offers both a way to perfect the self and a means to protect vulnerable women from worldly society, in Andrea Boffa's investigation of the *vitae* of Clare of Rimini, Umiliana de' Cerchi, and Margaret of Cortona. As these examples show, women's friendships were more likely to be familial, cross-class, and multiple, rendering them less visible within a textual tradition dominated by Aristotle's and Cicero's idealized masculine pairs.[9] Alexandra Verini and Melissa Ridley Elmes thus align medieval women's friendship with another classical paradigm "based on fellowship with beneficial intent," that of the Epicurean garden in which multiple women and men share friendship, "an alliance of likeminded people who are joined in goodwill and reciprocally sharpen each other's virtue through philosophical conversations."[10] These emphases on ethical virtue and spiritual development resonate with the Aristotelian and Ciceronian models, which have similar didactic elements.

Another throughline from classical friendship through the medieval period and into the Renaissance lies in textuality. Classical writers on friendship emphasize its persistence across physical and temporal distances; Renaissance writers take up this adage to claim a friendship with the past, as in Francesco Petrarca's familiar *Letters to the Ancients*. While commentators often exclude women from this textual world, the essays in this volume depict a vibrant culture of female writers, scribes, and correspondents, and suggest that texts can forge friendship with later readers. Thus Wang discusses "the patronage, translation, reading, copying, and dissemination of vernacular lit-

---

7. Brown, "Female Friendships and Visionary Women"; Lochrie, "'All These Relationships Among Women': Chaucer and the Bechdel Test for Female Friendship"; Lees and Overing, "Conversations among Friends: Ælfflæd, Iurminburg, and the Arts of Storytelling."

8. Wang, "The Foundations of Friendship: *Amicitia*, Literary Production, and Spiritual Community in Marie de France."

9. Verini, "Sisters and Friends: The Medieval Nuns of Syon Abbey."

10. Elmes, "Female Friendship in Late Medieval English Literature: Cultural Translation in Chaucer, Gower, and Malory"; Verini, "Sisters and Friends."

erature for women," Brown analyzes fourteenth-century German sisterbooks that record women's lives and women scribes' letters for Catherine of Siena, and Elmes shows how female patrons and readers rewrite earlier misogynist texts.[11] In the work of Christine de Pizan, Christine Chism powerfully argues for "women's virtuous friendship as a form of needful solidarity in a hostile world and the crucial role of women's alliances with books as a form of friendship with and between women."[12] This reinterpretation and exemplary application of earlier texts forms a central component of Renaissance humanist practice; Chism reveals not only its medieval existence but also the underacknowledged work of women in this dynamic. Textual models can take on practical applications, as in Laurie Finke's work on the reappropriation of rituals of the medieval past.ABlees and Overing connect textual recovery in the period to later writers' friendship with the past in their analysis of Ælfflæd, Iurminburg, and the contemporary writer Gillian Allnutt.

For our current pandemic moment, these textual models offer both reassurance and a caveat. They demonstrate the affordances of distance, the potential flourishing of friendship and virtuous selfhood not despite but because of the perspective distance brings, enabled by the written word that prompts reflection. But such a process requires sustained qualities of attention—not the casual aside of a brief communication but the willingness to translate the self into writing with the expectation of a careful reader on the other end.

Those qualities of attention, made both more difficult and more necessary through distance, shape another form of friendship neglected in the classical models: the wider burden of care, often ministered to those very different from oneself. The need to value and account for the burdens and importance of care forms a central strand in much feminist thought, notably Sibyl Schwarzenbach's reimagining of care-oriented civic friendship in response to individual and communal vulnerabilities.[13] The essays on spiritual women's groups of friends, whether laywomen or nuns, illustrate one form of care: the practical attention to the body's needs that supports the spirit's flourishing. These repeated, often unappreciated acts of care resonate with the particular stresses of the pandemic, from the daily struggles of parents', disproportionately mothers', care for children at home to the life-or-death risks of essential workers providing medical care, food, and other services. In thinking about the pos-

---

11. Wang, "The Foundations of Friendship"; Brown, "Female Friendships and Visionary Women"; Elmes, "Female Friendship in Late Medieval English Literature."

12. Chism, "The Politics of Virtual Friendship in Christine de Pizan's *Book of the City of Ladies.*"

13. Sibyl A. Schwarzenbach, *On Civic Friendship: Including Women in the State* (New York: Columbia University Press, 2009), 60–62.

sibilities that care creates, Usha Vishnuvajjala's essay demonstrates that the friendship of a community might make space for an individual's emotions, in a recuperative reading of the Stanzaic *Morte*'s Gaynor. Most surprisingly and persuasively, Vishnuvajjala goes on to show that this dynamic of care can enable sympathy with a woman framed by the text as an enemy. In a contemporary moment of deadly political divisions, the possibility that women's friendship might reshape a community beyond itself, enabling a sympathy that recognizes difference, seems deeply appealing.

Frustratingly, the political aspects of friendship, central to the classical tradition, often appear least available to female friends. While my own work argues that seventeenth-century women writers use friendship's political valences to articulate the fractured politics of civil war, it also charts the diminishment of that political connection as friendship becomes feminized through history.[14] The writers in this volume trace varied modes of political friendship, such as Chism's strong statement that Christine de Pizan "recovers a history erased by authoritative Greeks and the Romans, hand in hand with the antique patristic writers and medieval clergy: a history of women's friendship in a staunch classical sense, where friendship is the bedrock of polity itself."[15] Women's friendship also appears political in its resistance to masculine authority, in the work of Boffa, Verini, Harris, and Lochrie. Whether through the threat of holy women turning to friends for support rather than church authorities or the bawdy exchange of strategies for managing men, these groups of women form political alliances, "teaching each other how to navigate the abuses enabled by marital power imbalances and larger structural inequalities."[16] Political alliances and didactic exemplarity form crucial elements of the friendship tradition, but women's appropriations become illegible as such because they explicitly challenge the patriarchal political system.

One subversive element of female bonds appears in this collection in very muted form: women's same-sex eroticism. The collection emphasizes friendship over queerness partly in response to the way that queer studies' early instantiations subsumed studies of female friendship, as Lochrie and Vishnuvajjala write in the introduction to this volume. Nevertheless, strands of queer affiliation and affection commingle with female friendships throughout the volume, from Wang's "subversive inclusivity of communal spiritual love"

---

14. Penelope Anderson, *Friendship's Shadows: Women's Friendship and the Politics of Betrayal in England, 1640–1705*, (Edinburgh: Edinburgh University Press, 2012).

15. Chism, "The Politics of Virtual Friendship."

16. Harris, "Cultivating Cummarship: Female Friendship, Alcohol, and Pedagogical Community in the Alewife Poem."

to Harris's connection between the queer elements of cummarship and lesbian bar culture.[17] In the ways that the collection conceives of a range of female bonds, the collection as a whole owes much to the foundational work of queer theory, from Adrienne Rich's "lesbian continuum" to Lochrie's own earlier works.[18] Queerness teaches us that bodies and desires do not behave in predictable ways. In another way, the depiction of friendship in this volume can help reorient a troubling strand within studies of same-sex eroticism: the very insistence on sameness that characterizes classical friendship. With a focus on *homo*, or the same, this type of queer studies creates a fiction of self-identical bodies, reinscribing binary sexual difference rather than acknowledging the continuum of bodily morphology. Like the physical interchangeability of the perfect classical friends, this emphasis on sameness disallows difference.

One of the contributions of *Women's Friendship in Medieval Literature*, then, is to write various types of difference back into the story of friendship. Across differences of religion, class, age, and nation, the women of these texts forge alliances. As Chism writes, "these historical women appeal not through likeness, or ideality, but through unlikeness and historicity. They do not model female virtue so much as measure the wider latitudes of virtuous femininity itself, across time and cultural difference."[19] Lydia Yaitsky Kertz's virtuosic reading of *Emaré* shows the forging of bonds across cultural difference via a luxurious Islamicate cloth that denotes "female skill-based transnational community."[20] Yaitsky Kertz goes on to link the "racialized alterity," when applied to a woman, to justifications of human trafficking, as long as those trafficked were of a different faith.[21] Lochrie also traces affinities across nations that highlight racist patterns, noting that Geoffrey Chaucer's Custance's "use of the Middle English word *thraldom*, meaning 'captivity, slavery, submission, and tyranny,'" links her to the Sultaness by "affinity in their shared experience of slavery and suffering under men's governance."[22] Like Vishnuvajjala, Lochrie offers hope for alliances between those imagined as enemies: "Female friendship, like female affinities through emotional identification, proves recalcitrant

---

17. Wang, "The Foundations of Friendship"; Harris, "Cultivating Cummarship."
18. Adrienne Rich, "Compulsory Heterosexuality and Lesbian Existence," *Signs* 5, no. 4 (Summer 1980), 631–60; and Karma Lochrie, *Heterosyncrasies: Female Sexuality When Normal Wasn't* (Minneapolis: University of Minnesota Press, 2005).
19. Chism, "The Politics of Virtual Friendship."
20. Yaitsky Kertz, "'Amonge maydenes moo': Gender-Based Community, Racial Thinking, and Aristocratic Women's Work in *Emaré*."
21. Yaitsky Kertz, "'Amonge maydenes moo.'"
22. Lochrie, "'All These Relationships between Women': Chaucer and the Bechdel Test for Female Friendship."

to fantasies of heterosexual containment, empirical expansion, and religious conversion."[23]

The medieval women's friendships in this book thus look very like what Judith Kegan Gardiner and Millie Thayer hope from friendship: they are "more pragmatic, more vulnerable, and contend more fully with difference."[24] This vulnerability takes varied forms, from Vishnuvajjala's articulation of Gaynor's shielding of the Maid's emotions as well as her own, to Finke's limning of the fragility and transience of friendships in Wiccan contexts, to the perilous deathbed visits of Marie de France's friends in Brown's essay. The latter example, especially, feels achingly out of reach in the current pandemic moment, when loved ones cannot even attend their dead. The pain of that historical rupture, the way that the casual physical closeness of the alewives and gossips, the nuns and laywomen, recedes into untouchable distance, also forms part of the meaning of this volume. But the vulnerability and resistance of these networks of women, exemplary both in their openness to each other and as a bulwark against outside threats, also helps us understand the risks of friendship now. In contrast to Schwarzenbach's argument, sometimes care produces rather than compensates for vulnerability, but that vulnerability can be the point rather than a problem.[25]

Vitally, then, an assessment of the risks and rewards of friendship's vulnerabilities must acknowledge that different people can experience shared vulnerabilities in vastly disproportionate ways. As Audre Lorde critiques Mary Daly, "you fail to recognize that, as women, those differences expose all women to various forms and degrees of patriarchal oppression, some of which we share, and some of which we do not."[26] The importance of differential vulnerabilities but also differential strengths means that while I agree with Ivy Schweitzer that "equality presumes differences and dissymmetry," I do not concur that "offer[ing] each person the same or equivalent opportunities and rights" requires "put[ting] aside differences temporarily."[27] Instead, the long history of women's friendship helps us imagine an equality that incorporates rather than puts aside difference.

---

23. Lochrie, "'All These Relationships between Women.'"

24. Judith Kegan Gardiner and Millie Thayer, "Preface," in "Women's Friendships," special issue, *Feminist Studies* 42, no. 2 (2016): 271–79, at 271.

25. Anderson, *Friendship's Shadows*, 17–18.

26. Audre Lorde, "An Open Letter to Mary Daly," in *This Bridge Called My Back: Writings by Radical Women of Color*, ed. Cherríe Moraga and Gloria Anzaldúa, 4th ed., paperback (Albany: State University of New York Press, 2015), 92.

27. Ivy Schweitzer, "Making Equals: Classical *Philia* and Women's Friendship," *Feminist Studies* 42, no. 2 (2016): 337–64, at 345–46.

Friendship at a distance—the distance of the past, the distance required by a responsible, humane approach to a highly infectious global pandemic, the distance of respect for other people's pasts and vulnerabilities—places us in "a memory palace of historically separated exemplary women, thereby bringing about a new allegorically asynchronic polity of women."[28] In this pandemic world where suddenly "synch" and "asynch" teaching are common parlance, medieval women's friendship gestures toward an asynchronic polity that does not set aside difference but recognizes it as foundational to practices of equality, that acknowledges differential vulnerabilities and uses both the openness and the bulwark of women's friendship, across lines of all kinds, to make a space for being.

---

28. Chism, "The Politics of Virtual Friendship."

WORKS CITED

Abel, Elizabeth. "(E)merging Identities: The Dynamics of Female Friendship in Contemporary Fiction." *Signs* 6, no. 3 (Spring 1981): 413–35.

Adgar, *Le Gracial*. Ottawa, CA: Editions de l'Université d'Ottawa, 1982.

Ælfric. *Ælfric's Catholic Homilies: The Second Series*. Ed. Malcolm Godden. Early English Text Society, SS 5. Oxford: Oxford University Press, 1979.

Aelred of Rievaulx. Aelredi Rievallensis, *De spirituali amicitia*. In *Aelredi Rievallensis Opera Omnia*. Ed. A. Hoste and C. H. Talbot. Turnhout: Brepols, 1971.

———. *Aelred of Rievaulx: Spiritual Friendship (De Spirituali Amicitia)*. Ed. Marsha L. Dutton, trans. Lawrence C. Braceland, SJ. Trappist, KY: Cistercian Publications, 2010.

———. *The Liturgical Sermons: The First Clairvaux Collection, Sermons One-Twenty-Eight*. Trans. Theodore Berkeley and M. Basil Pennington. Cistercian Fathers 58. Kalamazoo, MI: Cistercian Publications, 2001.

———. *A Rule of Life for a Recluse*. Trans. Mary Paul Macpherson. In *Treatises: The Pastoral Prayer, Works*, vol. 1. Ed. David Knowles. Spencer, MA: Cistercian Publications, 1971.

Ahmed, Sara. *Living a Feminist Life*. Durham, NC: Duke University Press, 2017.

Akbari, Suzanne Conklin. "The Saracen Body." In *Idols in the East: European Representations of Islam and the Orient, 1100–1450*. Ithaca, NY: Cornell University Press, 2009. 155–99.

Allnutt, Gillian. *How the Bicycle Shone: New & Selected Poems*. Tarset, Northumberland: Bloodaxe Books, 2007.

Ancelet-Hustache, Jeanne. *La Vie Mystique d'un Monastère de Dominicanes au Moyen Âge D'après la Chronique de Töss*. Paris: Perrin, 1928.

Anderson, M. L., ed. *The James Carmichaell Collection of Proverbs in Scots*. Edinburgh: Edinburgh University Press, 1957.

Anderson, Penelope. *Friendship's Shadows: Women's Friendship and the Politics of Betrayal in England, 1640–1705*. Edinburgh: Edinburgh University Press, 2013.

Anonymous. *Cryste crosse me spede* (*DIMEV* 986). London: Wynkyn de Worde, 1534?.

Anonymous. *Fowre Wittie Gossips Disposed to be Merry*. London: Printed for H. G., 1632.

Anonymous. *The Gossips Feast: or, a merry meeting of women kinde each other greeting*. London: Printed for Thomas Lambert, 1635–36?.

Anonymous. *The Gossips Meeting, or the Merry Market-Women of Taunton*. London: Printed for F. Coles, T. Vere, J. Wright, and J. Clarke, 1674.

Anonymous. *The Merry Gossips Vindication*. London: Printed for P. Brooksby, 1672–96?.

Anonymous. *The Seven Merry Wives of London: or, the Gossips' Complaint*. London: Printed for J. Blare, 1664–1703?.

Archibald, Elizabeth. "Some Uses of Direct Speech in the Stanzaic *Morte Arthur* and Malory." *Arthuriana* 28, no. 3 (Fall 2018): 66–85.

Aristotle. *Nicomachean Ethics*. Trans. and ed. Christopher Rowe. Ed. Sarah Brodie. Oxford: Oxford University Press, 2002.

———. *The Nicomachean Ethics*. Trans. H. Rackham. Loeb Classical Library, 2nd ed. Cambridge, MA: Harvard University Press, 1934.

———. *Nichomachean Ethics Books VIII and IX*. Ed. and Trans. Michael Pakaluk. Oxford: Clarendon Press, 1998.

Aungier, G. J. *The History and Antiquities of Syon Monastery, the Parish of Isleworth and the Chapelry of Hounslow*. London, 1840.

Baltzly, Dirk, and Nick Eliopoulus. "The Classical Ideals of Friendship." In *Friendship, a History*. Ed. Barbara Caine. London: Equinox, 2009. 1–64.

Barker, Hannah. *That Most Precious Merchandise: The Mediterranean Trade in Black Sea Slaves, 1260–1500*. Philadelphia: University of Pennsylvania Press, 2019.

Barr, Marleen S. *Feminist Fabulation: Space/Postmodern Fiction*. Iowa City: University of Iowa Press, 1992.

Barratt, Alexandra, ed. *Women's Writing in Middle English*. New York: Routledge, 1992.

Bartlett, Robert. *The Making of Europe: Conquest, Colonization, and Cultural Change, 950–1350*. Princeton, NJ: Princeton University Press, 1993.

———. "Medieval and Modern Concepts of Race and Ethnicity." *Journal of Medieval and Early Modern Studies* 31, no. 1 (2001): 39–56.

Batt, Catherine. "Clemence of Barking's Transformations of Courtoisie in *La Vie de Sainte Cathérine d'Alexandrie*." *New Comparison: A Journal of Comparative and General Literary Studies*, no. 12 (1991): 102–23.

Baudri de Bourgueil. *Poèmes*. Trans. Jean-Yves Tilliette. Baldricus Burgulianus. Paris: Les Belles Lettres, 1998.

Bechdel, Alison. "The Rule." In *Dykes to Watch Out For*. Ithaca, NY: Firebrand Books, 1985. 22.

Bede. *Bede's Ecclesiastical History of the English People*. Ed. and trans. Bertram Colgrave and R. A. B. Mynors. Oxford: Clarendon Press, 1969.

———. *The Ecclesiastical History of the English People*. Ed. and trans. Judith McClure and Roger Collins. Oxford: Oxford University Press, 1994.

Bell, Susan. "Medieval Women Book Owners: Arbiters of Lay Piety and Ambassadors of Culture." In *Sisters and Workers in the Middle Ages*. Ed. Judith M Bennett. Chicago: University of Chicago Press, 1989. 135–61.

Bell, Susan Groag. *The Lost Tapestries of the City of Ladies: Christine de Pizan's Renaissance Legacies* Berkeley: University of California Press, 2004.

———. "Medieval Women Book Owners: Arbiters of Lay Piety and Ambassadors of Culture." In Erler and Kowaleski, *Women and Power in the Middle Ages*, 149–87.

Bellotto, Carla Rossi. *Marie de France et Les Érudits de Cantorbéry*. Paris: Classiques Garnier 2009.

Benedict, Kimberly. *Empowering Collaborations: Writing Partnerships between Religious Women and Scribes in the Middle Ages*. New York: Routledge, 2004.

Bennett, Judith M. *Ale, Beer, and Brewsters in England: Women's Work in a Changing World 1300–1600*. Oxford: Oxford University Press, 1996.

———. "'Lesbian-Like' and the Social History of Lesbianisms." *Journal of the History of Sexuality* 9 (2000): 1–24.

———. "Public Power and Authority in the Medieval English Countryside." In Erler and Kowaleski, *Women and Power in the Middle Ages*, 18–36.

Bennington, Geoffrey. "Forever Friends." In *Interrupting Derrida*. Ed. Bennington. London: Routledge, 2000. 110–27.

Benson, Larry D. "A Brief Chronology of Chaucer's Life and Times." *The Geoffrey Chaucer Page*, July 27, 2000. https://chaucer.fas.harvard.edu/pages/brief-chronology-chaucers-life-and-times-0.

———, ed. *The Riverside Chaucer*. Boston: Houghton Mifflin, 1987.

Benson, Larry D., ed., and Edward E. Foster, rev. *King Arthur's Death: The Middle English Stanzaic Morte Arthur and Alliterative Morte Arthure*. Kalamazoo, MI: Medieval Institute Publications, 1994.

Bérat, Emma. "The Authority of Diversity: Communal Patronage in Le Gracial." In *Barking Abbey and Medieval Literary Culture: Authorship and Authority in a Female Community*. Ed. Jennifer Brown and Donna Alfano Bussell. Woodbridge, Suffolk; Rochester, NY: York Medieval Press, 2012. 210–32.

Bevegnati, Giunta. *Legenda de vita et miraculis Beatae Margaritae de Cortona*. Grottaferrata, Italy: Editiones Collegii S. Bonaventurae ad Claras Aquas, 1997.

———. *The Life and Miracles of Saint Margaret of Cortona*. Trans. Thomas Renna. St. Bonaventure, NY: Franciscan Institute, 2012.

Beveridge, Erskine, ed. *Fergusson's Scottish Proverbs, from the Original Print of 1641, Together with a Larger Manuscript Collection of About the Same Period Hitherto Unpublished*. Edinburgh: William Blackwood and Sons for the Scottish Text Society, 1924.

Bjork, Robert B., ed. and trans. *Old English Shorter Poems*. Vol. 2, *Wisdom and Lyric*. Dumbarton Oaks Medieval Library. Cambridge, MA: Harvard University Press, 2014.

Black Witch. "'Trolololo – She Ratchet': Is Wicca Just for White Folks?" Afropunk, https://afropunk.com/2012/07/black-witch-trolololo-she-rachet-is-wicca-just-for-white-folks/

Blake, E. O. *Liber Eliensis*. London: Offices of the Royal Historical Society, 1962.

Blamires, Alcuin. *Chaucer, Ethics and Gender*. Oxford: Oxford University Press, 2006.

Blanton, Virginia. "Chaste Marriage, Sexual Desire, and Christian Martyrdom in *La Vie Seinte Audrée*." *Journal of the History of Sexuality* 19, no. 1 (2010): 94–114.

———. "King Anna's Daughters: Genealogical Narrative and Cult Formation in the 'Liber Eliensis.'" *Historical Reflections / Réflexions Historiques* 30, no. 1 (2004): 127–49.

Bloch, R. Howard. *The Anonymous Marie de France*. Chicago: University of Chicago Press, 2006.

———. *Medieval Misogyny and the Invention of Western Romantic Love*. Chicago: University of Chicago Press, 1991.

Blunt, John Henry, ed. *The Myroure of oure Ladye, containing a Devotional Treatise on Divine Service. With a Translation of the Offices used by the Sisters of the Brigittine Monastery of Syon, at Isleworth, during the Fifteenth and Sixteenth Centuries*. Early English Text Society, ES 19. London: N. Trübner, 1873.

Boccaccio. *Famous Women*. Trans. Virginia Brown. Cambridge, MA: Harvard University Press, 2003.

———. *Il Filostrato*. Trans. Nathaniel Griffin and Arthur Myrick. Cambridge, ONT: In Parenthesis, 1999.

Boffey, Julia. "The Maitland Folio Manuscript as a Verse Anthology." In *William Dunbar, "The Nobill Poyet": Essays in Honour of Priscilla Bawcutt*. Ed. Sally Mapstone. East Linton, UK: Tuckwell, 2001. 40–50.

Boffey, Julia, and A. S. G. Edwards. "The Legend of Good Women." In *The Cambridge Companion to Chaucer*. Ed. Piero Boitani and Jill Mann. Cambridge: Cambridge University Press, 2003. 112–26.

Bogdan, Henrik. *Western Esotericism and Rituals of Initiation*. Albany: State University of New York Press, 2007.

Bolton, Brenda. "Mulieres Sanctae." *Studies in Church History* 10 (1973): 77–85.

Bond, Gerald. *The Loving Subject: Desire, Eloquence, and Power in Romanesque France*. Philadelphia: University of Pennsylvania Press, 1995.

Bourdieu, Pierre. *Language and Symbolic Power*. Trans. Gino Raymond and Matthew Adamson. Cambridge, MA: Harvard University Press, 1991.

Bovaird-Abbo, Kristin. "Is Geoffrey Chaucer's *Tale of Sir Thopas* a Rape Narrative? Reading Thopas in Light of the 1382 Statute of Rapes." *Quidditas* 35 (2014): 7–28.

Boyd, Nan Alamilla. *Wide-Open Town: A History of Queer San Francisco to 1965*. Berkeley: University of California Press, 2003.

Brandsma, Frank, Carolyne Larrington, and Corinne Saunders. "Introduction." In *Emotions in Medieval Arthurian Literature: Body, Mind, Voice*. Ed. Brandsma, Larrington, and Saunders. Woodbridge: D. S. Brewer, 2015. 1–12.

Bray, Alan. *The Friend*. Chicago: University of Chicago Press, 2003.

———. *Homosexuality in Renaissance England*. London: Gay Men's Press, 1982.

Brown, Jennifer N. "The Chaste Erotics of Marie d'Oignies and Jacques de Vitry." *Journal of the History of Sexuality* 19 (2010): 74–93.

———. *Fruit of the Orchard: Catherine of Siena in Late Medieval and Early Modern England*. Toronto: University of Toronto Press, 2018.

Brown, Jennifer N., and Donna Alfano Bussell, eds. *Barking Abbey and Medieval Literary Culture: Authorship and Authority in a Female Community*. Woodbridge, Suffolk; Rochester, NY: York Medieval Press, 2012.

Brown-Grant, Rosalind. "Christine de Pizan as a Defender of Women." In *Christine de Pizan: A Casebook*. Ed. Barbara K. Altmann and Deborah L. McGrady. New York: Routledge, 2015. 81–100.

Bullock-Davies, Constance. "Marie, Abbess of Shaftesbury, and Her Brothers." *The English Historical Review* 80, no. 115 (1965): 314–22.

Burge, Amy, and Lydia Kertz. "Fabricated Muslim Identity, Female Agency, and Cultural Complicity: The Imperial Project of *Emaré*." *Medieval Feminist Forum* 56, no. 1 (2020): 38–69.

Burgess, Glyn. "Symbolism in Marie de France's *Laüstic* and *Le Fresne*." *Bibliographic Bulletin of the International Arthurian Society* 33 (1981): 258–68.

Burgess, Glyn S., and Keith Busby, eds. and trans. *The Lais of Marie de France*. London: Penguin, 1986.

Burke, Janet M. "Freemasonry, Friendship and Noblewomen: The Role of the Secret Society in Bringing Enlightenment Thought to Pre-revolutionary Women Elites." *History of European Ideas* 10, no. 3 (1989): 283–93.

Burke, Janet M., and Margaret Jacob. "French Freemasonry, Women, and Feminist Scholarship." *Journal of Modern History* 68, no. 3 (1996): 13–49.

Burns, E. Jane. *Sea of Silk: Textile Geography of Women's Work in Medieval French Literature*. Philadelphia: University of Pennsylvania Press, 2010.

Caesarius of Heisterbach. *The Dialogue on Miracles*, vol. 1. Ed. G. G. Coulton and Eileen Power. New York: Harcourt, Brace, 1929.

Calderwood, David. *The History of the Kirk of Scotland Volume 5: 1589–1599*. Ed. Rev. Thomas Thomson. Edinburgh: Printed for the Wodrow Society, 1844.

Camp, Bayliss J., and Orit Kent. "'What a Mighty Power We Can Be': Individual and Collective Identity in African American and White Fraternal Initiation Rituals." *Social Science History* 28, no. 3 (2004): 439–83.

Canatella, H. M. "Friendship in Anselm of Canterbury's Correspondence: Ideals and Experience." *Viator* 38, no. 2 (2007): 351–68.

———. "Long-Distance Love: The Ideology of Male-Female Spiritual Friendship in Goscelin of Saint Bertin's *Liber confortartorius*." *Journal of the History of Sexuality* 19 (2010): 35–53.

Canatella, Holle. "Loving Friendship in Baudri of Bourgueil's Poetic Correspondence with the Women of Le Ronceray." *Medieval Feminist Forum* 48, no. 2 (2013): 5–42.

Cannon, Christopher. "Chaucer and Rape: Uncertainty's Certainties." In *Representing Rape in Medieval and Early Modern Literature*. Ed. Elizabeth Robertson and Christine M. Rose. New York: Palgrave Macmillan, 2001. 255–79.

Carman, J. Neale, trans., and Norris J. Lacy, ed. *From Camelot to Joyous Gard: The Old French La Mort le roi Artu*. Lawrence: University Press of Kansas, 1974.

Cartlidge, Neil. "Criseyde's Absent Friends." *Chaucer Review* 44, no. 3 (2010): 227–45.

Cavendish, Margaret. *The Convent of Pleasure*. In *Paper Bodies: A Margaret Cavendish Reader*. Ed. Sylvia Bowerbank and Sara Mendelson. Peterborough, ONT: Broadview, 2000. 97–35.

Caxton, William. *Book of the Knight of the Tower*. Ed. M. Y. Offord. Early English Text Society SS 217. London: Oxford University Press, 1971.

Cicero. "De Amicitia." In *Cicero de Senectute, De Amicitia, De Divinatione*. Trans. William Armistead Falconer. Cambridge, MA: Harvard University Press, 2001.

———. *Laelius, On Friendship and The Dream of Scipio*. Ed. and trans. J. G. F. Powell. Liverpool: Liverpool University Press, 1990.

Clark, David. *Between Medieval Men: Male Friendship and Desire in Early Medieval English Literature*. Oxford: Oxford University Press, 2009.

Classen, Albrecht. "From *Nonnenbuch* to Epistolarity: Elsbeth Stagel as a Late Medieval Woman Writer." In *Medieval German Literature: Proceedings from the 23rd International Congress on Medieval Studies: Kalamazoo, Michigan, May 5-8, 1988*. Ed. Albrecht Classen. Göppingen: Kümmerle Verlag, 1989. 147–70.

———. *The Power of a Woman's Voice in Medieval and Early Modern Literatures*. Berlin: de Gruyter, 2007.

Classen, Albrecht, and Marilyn Sandidge. *Friendship in the Middle Ages and Early Modern Age: Explorations of a Fundamental Ethical Discourse*. Berlin: de Gruyter, 2010.

Cnattingius, Hans. *Studies in the Order of St Bridget of Sweden*. Vol. 1, *The Crisis in the 1420s*, Acta Universitatis Stockholmiensis, Stockholm Studies in History 7. Stockholm: Almqvist & Wisk, 1963.

Coakley, John. *Women, Men, and Spiritual Power: Female Saints & Their Male Collaborators*. New York: Columbia University Press, 2006.

Cohen, Jeffrey Jerome. "On Saracen Enjoyment: Some Fantasies of Race in Late Medieval France and England." *Journal of Medieval and Early Modern Studies* 31, no. 1 (2001): 113–46.

Cohen, Rhaina. "'Text Me When You Get Home' Celebrates the Complexities of Female Friendship." *NPR*, February 11, 2018.

Coleman, Kristy S. *Re-riting Women: Dianic Wicca and the Feminine Divine*. Lanham, MD: Alta Mira Press, 2009.

Colgrave, Bertram, ed. and trans. *The Life of Bishop Wilfrid*. Cambridge: Cambridge University Press, 1927; repr. 1985.

———. *Two Lives of Saint Cuthbert*. Cambridge: Cambridge University Press, 1940; repr. 1985.

Constable, Giles. *Letters and Letter-Collections*. Turnhout: Brepols, 1976.

———. *Three Studies in Medieval Religious and Social Thought*. Cambridge: Cambridge University Press, 1995.

Constable, Olivia Remie. *Trade and Traders in Muslim Spain: The Commercial Realignment of the Medieval Iberian Peninsula, 900–1500*. Cambridge; New York: Cambridge University Press, 1994.

Cooper, Helen. "Providence and the Sea: 'No tackle, sail, nor mast.'" In *The English Romance in Time: Transforming Motifs from Geoffrey of Monmouth to the Death of Shakespeare*. Oxford; New York: Oxford University Press, 2004. 106–36.

Copland, Robert. *The Seven Sorowes That Women Have When Theyr Husbondes Be Deade*. In *Robert Copland: Poems*. Ed. Mary Carpenter Erler. Toronto: University of Toronto Press, 1993.

Crane, Susan. *Animal Encounters: Contacts and Concepts in Medieval Britain*. Philadelphia: University of Pennsylvania Press, 2012.

———. *Gender and Romance in Chaucer's "Canterbury Tales."* Princeton, NJ: Princeton University Press, 1994.

———. *The Performance of Self: Ritual, Clothing, and Identity during the Hundred Years War*. Philadelphia: University of Pennsylvania Press, 2002.

Cranstoun, James, ed. *Satirical Poems of the Time of the Reformation*. 4 vols. Edinburgh: William Blackwood and Sons, 1890–93.

Crocker, Holly. *The Matter of Virtue: Women's Ethical Action from Chaucer to Shakespeare*. Philadelphia: University of Pennsylvania Press, 2019.

Crosby, Everett Uberto. *Bishop and Chapter in Twelfth-Century England: A Study of the Mensa Episcopalis*. Cambridge: Cambridge University Press, 1994.

Dalarun, Jacques. "Gospel in Action: The Life of Clare of Rimini." *Franciscan Studies* 64 (2006): 179–215.

———. *L'impossible Sainteté: La Vie Retrouvée de Robert d'Arbrissel (v. 1045–1116) Fondateur de Fontevraud*. Paris: Cerf, 1985.

———. *"Lapsus Linguae": La Légende de Claire de Rimini*. Spoleto: Centro Italiano di Studi sull'Alto Medioevo, 1994.

———. "Robert d'Arbrissel et Les Femmes." *Annales. Histoire, Sciences Sociales* 39, no. 6 (1984): 1140–60.

———. *Robert of Arbrissel: Sex, Sin, and Salvation in the Middle Ages*. Trans. Bruce Venarde. Washington, DC: Catholic University of America Press, 2006.

Dargis, Manohla. "Sundance Fights Tide with Films like 'The Birth of a Nation.'" *New York Times*, January 29, 2016. https://www.nytimes.com/2016/01/30/movies/sundance-fights-tide-with-films-like-the-birth-of-a-nation.html.

Davis, Natalie Zemon. *Women on the Margins: Three Seventeenth-Century Lives*. Cambridge, MA: Harvard University Press, 1997.

Davis-Secord, Sarah. *Where Three Worlds Met: Sicily in the Early Medieval Mediterranean*. Ithaca, NY: Cornell University Press, 2017.

de Hamel, Christopher. "The Medieval Manuscripts of Syon Abbey and Their Dispersal." In *Syon Abbey: The Library of the Bridgettine Nuns and Their Peregrinations after the Reformation*. Otley, UK: Roxburghe Club, 1991. 48–133.

de Oya, Jeanine. *Portal into the Light of Truth: The First Book of Wicca for African Americans and All Seekers*. Publish America, 2002.

de Pizan, Christine. *The Book of Deeds of Arms and Chivalry*. Trans. Sumner Willard. Ed. Charity Cannon Willard. State College: Pennsylvania State University Press, 1999.

———. *The Book of the City of Ladies and Other Writings*. Ed. Sophie de Bourgault and Rebecca Kingston. Trans. Ineke Harde. Indianapolis, IN: Hackett, 2018.

———. *The Livre de la cité des dames of Christine de Pizan: A Critical Edition*. Ed. Maureen Curnow. Ann Arbor, MI: UMI Dissertation Information Service, 1975.

de Rogatis, Tiziana. "For Elena Ferrante, What Distinguishes Conventional Male and Female Friendships? The Liberating Messiness of the Neapolitan Quartet Friendship." *LitHub*, December 17, 2019. https://lithub.com/for-elena-ferrante-what-distinguishes-conventional-male-and-female-friendships/.

Dearnaley, Roger. "The Influence of Aleister Crowley upon 'Ye Bok of ye Art Magical.'" http://geraldgardner.com/dearnaley.php (accessed May 9, 2021).

Dembowski, Peter, ed. *La Vie de Sainte Marie l'Égyptienne: Versions en Ancien et en Moyen Français*. Genève: Droz, 1977

Denisoff, Dennis. "The Hermetic Order of the Golden Dawn, 1888–1901." In *BRANCH: Britain, Representation and Nineteenth-Century History*, n.d., ed. Dino Franco Felluga. *Extension of Romanticism and Victorianism on the Net*. http://www.branchcollective.org/?ps_articles=dennis-denisoff-the-hermetic-order-of-the-golden-dawn-1888-1901 (accessed May 9, 2021).

Denny-Brown, Andrea. *Fashioning Change: The Trope of Clothing in High- and Late-Medieval England*. Columbus: The Ohio State University Press, 2012.

Derrida, Jacques. *The Politics of Friendship*. Trans. George Collins. New York: Verso, 1997.

Dinshaw, Carolyn. *Chaucer's Sexual Poetics*. Madison: University of Wisconsin Press, 1989.

———. *How Soon Is Now? Medieval Texts, Actual Readers, and the Queerness of Time*. Durham, NC: Duke University Press, 2012.

Dinshaw, Carolyn, and David Wallace, eds. *The Cambridge Companion to Women's Writing*. Cambridge: Cambridge University Press, 2003.

Dronke, Peter. *Women Writers of the Middle Ages*. Cambridge: Cambridge University Press, 1984.

Duby, Georges. *The Knight, the Lady, and the Priest: The Making of Modern Marriage in Medieval France*. Chicago: University of Chicago Press, 1993.

Ducharme, Jamie. "Why Spending Time With Friends Is One of the Best Things You Can Do for Your Health." *Time*, June 25, 2019. https://time.com/5609508/social-support-health-benefits/ (accessed June 2, 2021).

Dunbar, William. *The Poems of William Dunbar*, 2 vols. Ed. Priscilla Bawcutt. Glasgow: Association for Scottish Literary Studies, 1998.

Duncan, Malcom C. *Duncan's Masonic Ritual and Monitor.* https://www.sacred-texts.com/mas/dun/dun02.htm#fr_2.

Duplessis, Rachel Blau. *Writing Beyond the Ending: The Narrative Strategies of Twentieth-Century Women Writers.* Bloomington: Indiana University Press, 1985.

Dutton, Marsha L. "The Sacramentality of Community in Aelred." In *A Companion to Aelred of Rievaulx.* Ed. Dutton. Leiden: Brill, 2017. 246–67.

Earenfight, Theresa. *Queenship in Medieval Europe.* Basingstoke: Palgrave Macmillan, 2013.

Echols, Alice. *Daring to Be Bad: Radical Feminism in America, 1967–1975.* Minneapolis: University of Minnesota Press, 1989.

Edwards, Robert R. "The Franklin's Tale." In *Sources and Analogues of the Canterbury Tales I.* Ed. Robert M. Correale and Mary Hamel. Woodbridge: D. S. Brewer, 2002. 211–65.

Elkins, Sharon K. *Holy Women of Twelfth-Century England.* Chapel Hill: University of North Carolina Press, 1988.

Elmes, Melissa Ridley. "'Compassion and Benignytee': A Reassessment of the Relationship Between Canacee and the Falcon in Chaucer's 'Squire's Tale.'" *Medieval Feminist Forum* 54, no. 1 (2018): 50–64.

———. "Public Displays of Affliction: Women's Wounds in Sir Thomas Malory's *Morte Darthur.*" *Modern Philology* 116, no. 3 (2019): 187–210.

———. "Treason and the Feast in Sir Thomas Malory's *Morte Darthur.*" In *Treason: Medieval and Early Modern Adultery, Betrayal, and Shame.* Ed. Larissa Tracy. Leiden: Brill, 2019. 320–39.

Epstein, Steven A. *Speaking of Slavery: Color, Ethnicity, and Human Bondage in Italy.* Ithaca, NY: Cornell University Press, 2001.

Erler, Mary. *Women, Reading, and Piety in Late Medieval England.* Cambridge: Cambridge University Press, 2002.

Erler, Mary, and Maryanne Kowaleski. *Women and Power in the Middle Ages.* Athens: University of Georgia Press, 1988.

Ewan, Elizabeth. "'For Whatever Ales Ye': Women as Producers and Consumers in Late Medieval Scottish Towns." In *Women in Scotland, c. 1100–c. 1750.* Ed. Elizabeth Ewan and Maureen Meikle. East Linton, UK: Tuckwell Press, 1999. 125–35.

———. "Mons Meg and Merchant Meg: Women in Later Medieval Edinburgh." In *Freedom and Authority: Scotland, c. 1050–c. 1650: Historical and Historiographical Essays Presented to Grant G. Simpson.* Ed. David Ditchburn and Terry Brotherstone. East Linton, UK: Tuckwell Press, 2000. 131–42.

Faderman, Lillian. *Surpassing the Love of Men: Romantic Friendship and Love Between Women from the Renaissance to the Present.* New York: William Morrow, 1981.

Fairweather, Janet. *Liber Eliensis: A History of the Isle of Ely from the Seventh Century to the Twelfth.* Woodbridge, UK: Boydell & Brewer, 2005.

Faivre, Antoine. *Western Esotericism: A Concise History.* Trans. Christine Rhone. Albany: State University of New York Press, 2010.

Farmer, Sharon. *The Silk Industries of Medieval Paris: Artisanal Migration, Technological Innovation, and Gendered Experience.* Philadelphia: University of Pennsylvania Press, 2017.

Farrar, Janet, and Stewart Farrar. *The Witches' Way: Principles, Ritual and Belief in Modern Witchcraft.* Custer, WA: Phoenix, 1986.

Febvre, Lucien, and Henri-Jean Martin. *The Coming of the Book: The Impact of Printing, 1450–1800.* Trans. David Gerard. Foundations of History Library. London: N.L.B., 1976.

Federici, Sylvia. *Caliban and the Witch: Women, the Body and Primitive Accumulation.* Brooklyn, NY: Atonomedia, 2014.

Fein, Susanna, with David Raybin and Jan Ziolkowski, ed. *The Complete Harley 2253 Manuscript: Volume 2*. Kalamazoo, MI: Medieval Institute Publications, 2014.

Fell, Christine. "Saint Æđelþryđ: A Historical-Hagiographical Dichotomy Revisited." *Nottingham Medieval Studies*, 38 (1994): 18–34.

Felten, Franz J. "What Do We Know about the Life of Jutta and Hildegard at Disibodenberg and Rupertsberg?" Trans. John Zaleski. In *A Companion to Hildegard of Bingen*. Ed. Beverly Mayne Kienzle, Debra Stoudt, and George Ferzoco. Leiden: Brill, 2014. 15–38.

Ferrante, Elena. "A Woman Friend Is as Rare as True Love." Trans. Ann Goldstein. *Guardian*, April 28, 2018. https://www.theguardian.com/lifeandstyle/2018/apr/28/elena-ferrante-woman-friend-rare-as-true-love.

Ferrante, Joan A. *To the Glory of Her Sex: Women's Roles in the Composition of Medieval Texts*. Bloomington: Indiana University Press, 1997.

Finke, Laurie A. "Fraternal Conspiracy and the Subject of Feminism." *Women's Studies* 47, no. 5 (2018): 485–503.

Fiske, Adele M. *Friends and Friendship in the Monastic Tradition*. Cuernavaca, Mexico: Centro Intercultural de Documentacion, 1970.

"The Five Points of Fellowship." *The Masonic Trowel*, last modified March 22, 2014. http://www.themasonictrowel.com/Articles/degrees/degree_3rd_files/the_five_points_of_fellowship_gltx.htm (accessed May 9, 2021).

Fletcher, John Rory. *The Story of the English Bridgettines of Syon Abbey*. South Brent, Devon: Syon Abbey, 1933.

Fox, John Charles. "Marie de France." *English Historical Review* 25, no. 98 (1910): 303–6.

———. "Mary, Abbess of Shaftesbury." *English Historical Review* 26 (1911): 317–26.

Francis, W. Nelson, ed. *The Book of Vices and Virtues*. Early English Text Society, OS 217. London: Oxford University Press for Early English Text Society, 1968.

Frappier, Jean, ed. *La Mort le Roi Artu*. 3rd ed. Geneva and Paris: Textes Littéraires Francais, 1964.

Friedman, Jamie. "Making Whiteness Matter: *The King of Tars*." *postmedieval: a journal of medieval cultural studies* 6 (2015): 52–63.

Furnivall, Frederick J., ed. *Early English Meals and Manners*. Early English Text Society, OS 32. London: Oxford University Press for the Early English Text Society, 1868.

Fyler, John M. "Domesticating the Exotic in the *Squire's Tale*." *ELH* 55 (1988): 1–26.

Gallo, Marcia M. *Different Daughters: A History of the Daughters of Bilitis and the Rise of the Lesbian Rights Movement*. Emeryville, CA: Seal Press, 2007.

Galloway, James A. "Driven by Drink? Ale Consumption and the Agrarian Economy of the London Region, c. 1300–1400." In *Food and Eating in Medieval Europe*. Ed. Martha Carlin and Joel T. Rosenthal. London: Hambledon Press, 1998. 87–100.

Gardiner, Judith Kegan. "Review: Women's Friendships, Feminist Friendships." In "Women's Friendships," special issue, *Feminist Studies* 42, no. 2 (2016): 484–501.

Gardiner, Judith Kegan, and Millie Thayer. "Preface." In "Women's Friendships," special issue, *Feminist Studies* 42, no. 2 (2016): 271–79.

Gibson, Gail McMurray. "Scene and Obscene: Seeing and Performing Late Medieval Childbirth." *Journal of Medieval and Early Modern Studies* 29, no. 1 (1999): 7–24.

Giffney, Noreen, Michelle M. Sauer, and Diane Watt, eds. *The Lesbian Premodern*. New York: Palgrave Macmillan, 2011.

Gilchrist, Roberta. *Contemplation and Action: The Other Monasticism*. London: Leicester University Press, 1995.

———. *Gender and Material Culture: The Archaeology of Religious Women*. New York and London: Routledge, 1997.

Góngora, María Eugenia. "Elizabeth von Schönau and the Story of St Ursula." In *Mulieres Religiosae: Shaping Female Spiritual Authority in the Medieval and Early Modern Periods*. Ed. Veerle Fraeters and Imke de Gier. Turnhout: Brepols, 2014. 17–36.

Gosh, Shami. *Writing the Barbarian Past: Studies in Early Medieval Historical Narrative*. Leiden: Brill, 2015.

Gower, John. *Confessio Amantis*. Ed. Russell A. Peck. TEAMS Middle English Text Series. Kalamazoo, MI: Medieval Institute Publications, 2000.

Gowing, Laura, Michael Hunter, and Miri Rubin, eds. *Love, Friendship and Faith in Europe, 1300–1800*. Basingstoke: Palgrave Macmillan, 2005.

Greene, Jody. "The Work of Friendship." *GLQ: A Journal of Lesbian and Gay Studies* 10, no. 3 (2004): 319–37.

Greene, Richard Leighton. *The Early English Carols*, 2nd ed. Oxford: Clarendon Press, 1977.

Greer, Mary K. *Women of the Golden Dawn: Rebels and Priestesses*. Rochester, VT: Park Street Press, 1995.

Gregersson, Birger. *Vita S. Birgittae in Scriptores rerum svecicarum medii aevi*. 3. Uppsala: Edvardus Berling, 1876.

———. Birgerus Gregorii, *Legenda S. Birgitte*. Ed. Isak Collijn. Uppsala: Almquist and Wiksells, 1946.

Griffith, Nicola. *Ammonite*. New York: Ballantine Books, 1993.

———. *Hild*. London: Blackfriars, 2013.

Gross, Jenny. "Can You Have More Than 150 Friends?" *New York Times*, May 11, 2021. https://www.nytimes.com/2021/05/11/science/dunbars-number-debunked.html (accessed June 14, 2021).

Hahn, Thomas. "Don't Cry for Me, Augustinius: Dido and the Dangers of Empathy." In *Truth and Tales: Cultural Mobility and Medieval Media*. Ed. Fiona Somerset and Nicholas Watson. Columbus: The Ohio State University Press, 2015. 41–59.

Hallett, Nicky. *The Senses in Religious Communities, 1600–1800: Early Modern "Convents of Pleasure."* Farnham: Ashgate, 2013.

———. "Women." In *A Companion to Chaucer*. Ed. Peter Brown. Oxford: Blackwell, 2000. 480–94.

Hamilton, John. *A facile traictise, contenand, first: ane infallible reul to discerne trew from fals religion*. Louvain: Laurence Kellam, 1600.

Hanawalt, Barbara A. "Lady Honor Lisle's Networks of Influence." In Erler and Kowaleski, *Women and Power in the Middle Ages*, 188–212.

———. *The Wealth of Wives: Women, Law, and Economy in Late-Medieval London*. New York: Oxford University Press, 2007.

———. "Widows." In Dinshaw and Wallace, *The Cambridge Companion to Medieval Women's Writing*, 62–65.

Hankin, Kelly. *The Girls in the Back Room: Looking at the Lesbian Bar*. Minneapolis: University of Minnesota Press, 2002.

Hanna, Ralph, and Traugott Lawler. "The Wife of Bath's Prologue." In *Sources and Analogues of the Canterbury Tales II*. Ed. Robert M. Correale and Mary Hamel. Cambridge: D. S. Brewer, 2009. 351–04.

Harris, Carissa M. *Obscene Pedagogies: Transgressive Talk and Sexual Education in Late Medieval Britain*. Ithaca, NY: Cornell University Press, 2018.

Harris, Marguerite Tjader, ed., and Albert Ryle Kezel, trans. *Birgitta of Sweden: Life and Selected Revelations*. New York: Paulist Press, 1990.

Harvey, Ruth. "The Wives of the 'First Troubadour' Duke William IX of Aquitaine." *Journal of Medieval History* 19, no. 4 (January 1, 1993): 307-25.

Harwood, W. S. "Secret Societies in America." *North American Review* 164 (1897): 617-24.

Haseldine, Julian, ed. *Friendship in Medieval Europe.* Stroud: Sutton, 1999.

———. "Monastic Friendship in Theory and Action in the Twelfth Century." In Classen and Sandidge, *Friendship in the Middle Ages and Early Modern Age*, 349-94.

Heidle, Alexandra, and Jan A. M. Snoek. *Women's Agency and Rituals in Mixed and Female Masonic Orders.* Leiden: Brill, 2008.

Heng, Geraldine. *Empire of Magic: Medieval Romance and the Politics of Cultural Fantasy.* New York: Columbia University Press, 2003.

———. *The Invention of Race in the European Middle Ages.* New York: Cambridge University Press, 2018.

———. "The Invention of Race in the European Middle Ages I: Race Studies, Modernity, and the Middle Ages." *Literature Compass* 8, no. 5 (2011): 315-31.

———. "The Invention of Race in the European Middle Ages II: Locations of Medieval Race." *Literature Compass* 8, no. 5 (2011): 332-50.

Herbert, Amanda. *Female Alliances: Gender, Identity, and Friendship in Early Modern Britain.* New Haven, CT: Yale University Press, 2014.

Herlihy, David. "Did Women Have a Renaissance? A Reconsideration." *Medievalia et Humanistica: An American Journal for the Middle Ages and Renaissance* 13 (1985): 1-22.

Herring, Scott. *Queering the Underworld: Slumming, Literature, and the Undoing of Lesbian and Gay History.* Chicago: University of Chicago Press, 2007.

Hildegard of Bingen. *Hildegard of Bingen: Scivias.* Trans. Mother Columba Hart and Jane Bishop. Introd. Barbara J. Newman; pref. Caroline Walker Bynum. New York: Paulist Press, 1990.

———. *Hildegardis Scivias.* Ed. Adelgundis Führkötter OSB. Turnholt: Brepols, 1978.

———. *The Letters of Hildegard of Bingen*, vol. 1. Trans. Joseph L. Baird and Radd K. Ehrmann. Oxford: Oxford University Press, 1994.

———. *The Letters of Hildegard of Bingen*, vol. 2. Trans. Joseph L. Baird and Radd K. Ehrmann. Oxford: Oxford University Press, 1998.

Hill, John. "Aristocratic Friendship in *Troilus and Criseyde*: Pandarus, Courtly Love and Ciceronian Brotherhood in Troy." In *New Readings of Chaucer's Poetry*. Ed. Robert G. Benson and Susan J. Ridyard. Cambridge: D. S. Brewer, 2003. 165-82.

Hodges, Kenneth. "Guinevere's Politics in Malory's *Morte Darthur*." *Journal of English and Germanic Philology* 104, no. 4 (2005): 54-79.

Hogg, James, ed. *The Rewyll of Seynt Sauioure.* Vol. 4, *The Syon Additions for the Sisters from the British Library MS Arundel 146.* Salzburg, Austria: Institut Für Anglistik und Amerikanistik Universität Salzburg, 1980.

Hollis, Stephanie. *Anglo-Saxon Women and the Church.* Woodbridge: Boydell Press, 1992.

Holmes, U. T. "New Thoughts on Marie de France." *Studies in Philology* 29 (1932): 1-10.

Hsy, Jonathan. *Trading Tongues: Merchants, Multilingualism, and Medieval Literature.* Columbus: The Ohio State University Press, 2013.

Hsy, Jonathan, and Julie Orlemanski. "Race and Medieval Studies: A Partial Bibliography." *postmedieval: a journal of medieval cultural studies* 8 (2017): 500-31.

Hult, David F. "The *Roman de la Rose,* Christine de Pizan, and the *querelle des femmes.*" In Dinshaw and Wallace, *The Cambridge Companion to Women's Writing*, 184-94.

Hunt, Mary. *Fierce Tenderness: A Feminist Theology of Friendship.* New York: Crossroad, 1992.

Hutchison, Ann M. "Devotional Reading in the Monastery and the Medieval Household." In *De Cella in Seculum: Religious and Secular Life and Devotion in Late Medieval England.* Ed. Michael G. Sargent. Suffolk: D. S. Brewer, 1989. 215–27.

———, ed. "The Life and Good End of Sister Marie." *Birgittianna* 13 (2002): 33–89.

———. "Mary Champney: A Bridgettine Nun under the Rule of Queen Elizabeth I." *Birgittiana* 13 (2002): 3–89.

Hutton, Ronald. *Triumph of the Moon: A History of Modern Pagan Witchcraft.* Oxford: Oxford University Press, 1999.

Hyatte, Reginald. *The Arts of Friendship: The Idealization of Friendship in Medieval and Early Renaissance Literature.* Leiden: Brill, 1994.

Ingham, Patricia Clare. "Little Nothings: *The Squire's Tale* and the Ambition of Gadgets." *Studies in the Age of Chaucer* 31 (2009): 53–80.

Jacoby, David. "Silk Economics and Cross-Cultural Artistic Interaction: Byzantium, the Muslim World, and the Christian West." *Dumbarton Oaks Papers* 58 (2004): 197–240.

Jacques de Vitry. *Exempla Ex Sermonibus Vulgaribus Jacobi Vitriacensis.* Ed. Thomas Frederick Crane. London, 1890.

Jaeger, C. Stephen. *Ennobling Love: In Search of a Lost Sensibility.* Philadelphia: University of Pennsylvania Press, 1999.

———. *The Envy of Angels: Cathedral Schools and Social Ideals in Medieval Europe, 950–1200.* Philadelphia: University of Pennsylvania Press, 1994.

Jambeck, Karen K. "Patterns of Women's Literary Patronage: England 1200–ca. 1475." In *The Cultural Patronage of Medieval Women.* Ed. June Hall McCash. Athens: University of Georgia Press, 1996. 228–65.

James, Edward, and Farah Mendlesohn, eds. *The Cambridge Companion to Science Fiction.* Cambridge: Cambridge University Press, 2003.

Jeep, John M. "Among Friends? Early German Evidence of Friendship among Women." *Women in German Yearbook: Feminist Studies in German Literature & Culture* 14 (1999): 1–18.

Johns, Susan M. *Noblewomen, Aristocracy and Power in the Twelfth-Century Anglo-Norman Realm* Manchester: Manchester University Press, 2018.

Johnson, Fern L., and Elizabeth J. Aries. "The Talk of Women Friends." *Women's Studies International Forum* 6, no. 4 (1983): 353–61.

Johnson, Penelope. *Equal in Monastic Profession: Religious Women in Medieval France.* Chicago: University of Chicago Press, 1993.

Jones, Claire Taylor. *Ruling the Spirit: Women, Liturgy, and Dominican Reform in Late Medieval Germany.* Philadelphia: University of Pennsylvania Press, 2017.

Jones, Ellen E. "Is *Big Little Lies* Selling Us a Version of Consumer Feminism That Is Just Too Good to Be True?" *Guardian*, June 19, 2019. https://www.theguardian.com/tv-and-radio/2019/jun/08/big-little-lies-reese-witherspoon-meryl-streep-nicole-kidman-zoe-kravitz-laura-dern.

Kahn, Janet, and Patricia A. Gozemba. "In and around the Lighthouse: Working-Class Lesbian Bar Culture in the 1950s and 1960s." In *Gendered Domains: Rethinking Public and Private in Women's History.* Ed. Dorothy O. Helly and Susan M. Reverby. Ithaca, NY: Cornell University Press, 1992. 90–106.

Karras, Ruth Mazo. "Friendship and Love in the Lives of Two Twelfth–Century English Saints." *Journal of Medieval History* 14, no. 4 (1988): 305–20.

Kaufman, Amy S. "Guinevere Burning." *Arthuriana* 20, no. 1 (Spring 2010): 76–94.

———. "Liberating Guinevere: Female Desire on Film." In *Medieval Women on Film: Essays on Gender, Cinema and History.* Ed. Kevin J. Harty. Jefferson, NC: McFarland, 2020. 19–32.

Kay, Sarah. *Courtly Contradictions*. Stanford: Stanford University Press, 2001.

Kellogg, Judith L. "Le Livre de la cité des dames: Reconfiguring Knowledge and Reimagining Gendered Space." In *Christine de Pizan: A Casebook*. Ed. Barbara K. Altmann and Deborah L. McGrady. New York and London: Routledge, 2003. 126–46.

Kennedy, Beverly. "Adultery in Malory's *Le Morte Darthur*." *Arthuriana* 7, no. 4 (Winter 1997): 63–91.

Kennedy, Edward Donald. "Caxton, Malory, Arthurian Chronicles, and French Romances: Intertextual Complexities." In *And Gladly Wolde He Lerne and Gladly Teche: Essays on Medieval English Presented to Professor Matsuji Tajima on His Sixtieth Birthday*. Ed. Yoko Iyeiri and Margaret Connolly. Tokyo: Kaibunsha, 2002. 217–36.

———. "Sir Thomas Malory's (French) Romance and (English) Chronicle." In *Arthurian Studies in Honor of P. J. C. Field*. Ed. Bonnie Wheeler. Cambridge: D. S. Brewer, 2004. 223–34.

Kennedy, Elizabeth Lapovsky, and Madeline D. Davis. *Boots of Leather, Slippers of Gold: The History of a Lesbian Community*. 20th anniv. ed. New York: Routledge, 2014.

Kertz, Lydia Yaitsky. "Literal and Literary Ekphrasis: A Medieval Poetics." *Medievalia et Humanistica* 45 (2019): 75–99.

Kienzle, Beverly Mayne. "Catherine of Siena, Preaching, and Hagiography in Renaissance Tuscany." In *A Companion to Catherine of Siena*. Ed. Carolyn Muessig, George Ferzoco, and Beverly Kienzle. Leiden: Brill, 2012. 127–54.

Kinoshita, Sharon. "Almería Silk and the French Feudal Imaginary: Towards a 'Material' History of the Medieval Mediterranean." In *Medieval Fabrications: Dress, Textiles, Clothwork, and Other Cultural Imaginings*. Ed. E. Jane Burns. New York: Palgrave Macmillan, 2004. 165–76.

———. *Medieval Boundaries: Rethinking Difference in Old French Literature*. Philadelphia: University of Pennsylvania Press, 2006.

———. "Two for the Price of One: Courtly Love and Serial Polygamy in the Lais of Marie de France." *Arthuriana* 8, no. 2 (1998): 33–55.

Knapton, Antoinette. "A La Recherche de Marie de France." *Romance Notes* 19, no. 2 (1978): 248–53.

Krishna, Valerie, ed. *Five Middle English Romances*. New York: Routledge, 1991; rpt. 2015.

Krug, Rebecca. *Reading Families: Women's Literate Practice in Late Medieval England*. Ithaca, NY: Cornell University Press, 2002.

Langland, William. *Piers Plowman: The B Version*, rev. ed. Ed. George Kane and E. Talbot Donaldson. Berkeley: University of California Press, 1988.

Laskaya, Anne, and Eve Salisbury, eds. *Emaré*, in *The Middle English Breton Lays*. TEAMS Middle English Text Series. Kalamazoo, MI: Medieval Institute Publications, 2001. 145–99. Also available at https://d.lib.rochester.edu/teams/text/laskaya-and-salisbury-middle-english-breton-lays-emare.

Lawton, David, ed. *The Norton Chaucer*. New York: Norton, 2019.

Lears, T. J. Jackson. *No Place of Grace: Antimodernism and the Transformation of American Culture, 1880–1920*. Chicago: University of Chicago Press, 1994.

Lees, Clare A. "Gender and the Subjects of History in the Early Middle Ages." In *The Cambridge History of Historical Writing: Britain and Ireland, 500–1500*. Ed. Emily Steiner, Jennifer Jahner, and Elizabeth Tyler. Cambridge: Cambridge University Press, 2019. 299–318.

Lees, Clare A., and Gillian R. Overing. *The Contemporary Medieval in Practice*. London: UCL Press, 2019.

———. *Double Agents: Women and Clerical Culture in Anglo-Saxon England*. Philadelphia: University of Pennsylvania Press, 2001; repr. with new preface, Cardiff: University of Wales Press, 2009.

———. "Women and the Origins of English Literature." In *The History of British Women's Writing*, vol. 1. Ed. Elizabeth McAvoy and Diane Watt. New York: Palgrave Macmillan, 2013. 31–40.

Lefler, Nathan. *Theologizing Friendship: How Amicitia in the Thought of Aelred and Aquinas Inscribes the Scholastic Turn*. Cambridge: James Clarke, 2014.

Legassie, Shayne Aaron. "Among Other Possible Things: The Cosmopolitanisms of Chaucer's 'Man of Law's Tale.'" In *Cosmopolitanism and the Middle Ages*. Ed. John M. Ganim and Shayne Aaron Legassie. New York: Palgrave Macmillan, 2013. 181–205.

Leitzmann, Albert, ed. *Kleinere mittelhochdeutsche Erzählungen, Fabeln und Lehrgedichte. I. Die Melker Handschrift*. Berlin: Weidmannsche Buchhandlung, 1904.

"The Lesbian Bar Project." https://www.lesbianbarproject.com/ (accessed May 13, 2021).

Lewis, Gertrud Jaron. *By Women, for Women, about Women: The Sister-Books of Fourteenth-Century Germany*. Toronto: Pontifical Institute of Mediaeval Studies, 1996.

Lie, Orlanda Soei Han, Martine Meuwese, Mark Aussems, and Hermina Joldersma. *Christine de Pizan in Bruges: Le Livre de la Cité de Dames as Het Bouc van de Stede der Vrauwen* (London, British Library, Add. 20698). Hilversum: Verloren, 2015.

Lightsey, Scott. *Manmade Marvels in Medieval Culture and Literature*. New York: Palgrave, 2007.

Lin, Suwen, Louis Faust, Pablo Robles-Granda, Tomasz Kajdanowicz, and Nitesh V. Chawla. "Social Network Structure Is Predictive of Health and Wellness." *PLOS One* 14, no. 6 (2019): Article e0217264. https://doi.org/10.1371/journal.pone.0217264.

Livy. *History of Rome*, I.9.16. In *Livy in XIV Volumes, 1–2*. Cambridge MA: Harvard University Press; London: William Heineman, 1962.

Lochrie, Karma. "Between Women." In Dinshaw and Wallace, *The Cambridge Companion to Medieval Women's Writing*, 70–88.

———. *Covert Operations: The Medieval Uses of Secrecy*. Philadelphia: University of Pennsylvania Press, 1999.

———. *Heterosyncrasies: Female Sexuality When Normal Wasn't*. Minneapolis: University of Minnesota Press, 2005.

———. "Preface." In Giffney, Sauer, and Watt, *The Lesbian Premodern*, xiii–xviii.

Lomuto, Sierra. "The Mongol Princess of Tars: Global Relations and Racial Formation in *The King of Tars*, c. 1330." *Exemplaria* 31, no. 3 (2019): 171–92.

Loomba, Ania, and Melissa E. Sanchez. "Feminism and the Burdens of History." In *Rethinking Feminism in Early Modern Studies: Gender, Race, and Sexuality*. Ed. Loomba and Sanchez. New York: Routledge, 2016. 15–41.

Lorde, Audre. "An Open Letter to Mary Daly." In *This Bridge Called My Back: Writings by Radical Women of Color*. Ed. Cherríe Moraga and Gloria Anzaldúa. Albany: State University of New York Press, 2015. 101–5.

———. "An Open Letter to Mary Daly." In *This Bridge Called My Back: Writings by Radical Women of Color*. Ed. Cherríe Moraga and Gloria Anzaldúa. 4th ed., paperback. Albany: State University of New York Press, 2015. 90–93.

———. "Poetry Is Not a Luxury." In *Sister Outsider: Essays and Speeches*. Trumansburg, NY: Crossing Press, 1984. 36–39.

———. *Sister Outsider: Essays and Speeches*. Freedom, CA: Crossing Press, 1984.

———. *Zami: A New Spelling of My Name*. Freedom, CA: Crossing Press, 1982.

Lugones, Maris, and Pat Alake Rosezelle. "Sisterhood and Friendship as Feminist Models." In *Feminism and Community*. Ed. Penny A. Weiss and Marilyn Friedman. Philadelphia, PA: Temple University Press, 1995. 135–46.

Lumiansky, R. M., and David Mills, eds. *The Chester Mystery Cycle*, 2 vols. Early English Text Society, SS 3. London: Oxford University Press, 1974.

Lynch, Andrew. "Making Joy / Seeing Sorrow: Emotional and Affective Resources in the Stanzaic *Morte Arthur*." *Arthuriana* 28, no. 3 (Fall 2018): 33–50.

Lynch, Kathryn L. "East Meets West in Chaucer's Squire's and Franklin's Tales." *Speculum* 70, no. 3 (July 1995): 530–51.

Lyndsay, David. *Ane Satyre of the Thrie Estaitis*, ed. Roderick Lyall. Edinburgh: Canongate, 1989.

Maitland, Sara. "After Life." In *Far North and Other Dark Tales*. London: Maia Books, 2008. 59–74.

Malory, Sir Thomas. *Le Morte Darthur*. Ed. P. J. C. Field. Cambridge: D. S. Brewer, 2017.

Marie de France. *Lais de Marie de France*. Ed. Karl Warnke. Trans. Laurence Harf-Lancner. Paris: Librairie Générale Francaise, 1990.

———. *Saint Patrick's Purgatory*. Ed. Michael J. Curley. Binghamton, NY: Medieval & Renaissance Texts & Series, 1993.

Marloff, Sarah. "The Rise and Fall of America's Lesbian Bars." *Smithsonian Magazine,* January 21, 2021, https://www.smithsonianmag.com/travel/rise-and-fall-americas-lesbian-bars-180976801/.

Matter, E. Ann. "'My Sister, My Spouse: Woman-Identified Women in Medieval Christianity." *Journal of Feminist Studies in Religion* 2 (1986): 81–93.

Mayor, Adrienne. *The Amazons: Lives and Legends of Warrior Women Across the Ancient World*. Princeton, NJ: Princeton University Press, 2016.

McCash, June Hall. *The Cultural Patronage of Medieval Women*. Athens: University of Georgia Press, 1996.

———. "*La vie seinte Audree*: A Fourth Text by Marie de France?" *Speculum* 77, no. 3 (2002): 744–77.

McDougall, Sara. *Royal Bastards: The Birth of Illegitimacy, 800–1230*. Oxford: Oxford University Press, 2017.

McElroy, Tricia A. "The Uses of Genre and Gender in *The Dialogue of the Twa Wyfeis*." In *Premodern Scotland, Literature and Governance 1420–1587: Essays for Sally Mapstone*. Ed. Joanna Martin and Emily Wingfield. Oxford: Oxford University Press, 2017. 198–210.

McGuire, Brian Patrick. *Friendship and Community: The Monastic Experience, 350–1250*. Ithaca, NY: Cornell University Press, 2010.

McIntosh, Marjorie Keniston. "Drink Work." In *Working Women in English Society 1300–1620*. Cambridge: Cambridge University Press, 2005. 140–81.

McLoughlin, Sarah Annette. "Gender and Transgression in the Late Medieval English Household." Ph.D. diss., University of York, 2013.

McNamer, Sarah. *The Two Middle English Translations of St Elizabeth of Hungary*. Heidelberg: Universitätsverlag C. Winter, 1996.

McWebb, Christine. *Debating the Roman de la Rose: A Critical Anthology*. New York: Routledge, 2013.

Michel de Montaigne. "Of Friendship." In *Essayes*. Trans. John Florio. Ed. Desmond McCarthy London: J. M. Dent and Sons, 1928. Book 1, chapter 28.

———. "Of Friendship." In *The Complete Works: Essays, Travel Journal, Letters*. Trans. Donald M. Frame. New York: Knopf, 2003. 164–76.

Midorikawa, Emily, and Emma Claire Sweeney. *Secret Sisterhood: The Literary Friendships of Jane Austen, Charlotte Brontë, George Eliot, and Virginia Woolf*. Boston: Houghton Mifflin Harcourt, 2017.

Mieszkowski, Gretchen. *Medieval Go-Betweens and Chaucer's Pandarus*. New York: Palgrave Macmillan, 2006.

Miles, Laura Saetveit. "Queer Touch between Holy Women: Julian of Norwich, Margery Kempe, Birgitta of Sweden, and the Visitation." In *Touching, Devotional Practices, and Visionary Experience in the Late Middle Ages*. Ed. David Carrillo-Rangel, Delfi I. Nieto-Isabel, and Pablo Acosta-García. New York: Palgrave, 2019. 203–35.

Mills, Robert. "Gender, Sodomy, Friendship, and the Medieval Anchorhold" *Journal of Medieval Religious Cultures* 36, no. 1 (2010): 1–27.

Mitchell, Linda E. "Joan de Valence and Her Household: Domesticity, Management, and Organization in Transition from Wife to Widow." In *Royal and Elite Households in Medieval and Early Modern Europe*. Ed. Theresa Earenfight. Leiden: Brill, 2018. 95–114.

Mooney, Catherine, ed. *Gendered Voices: Medieval Saints and Their Interpreters*. Philadelphia: University of Pennsylvania, 1999.

Morrison, Toni. *Beloved*. New York: Knopf, 1987.

Mortimer, Julia. "Reflections in the Myroure of Oure Ladye: The Translation of a Desiring Body." *Mystics Quarterly* 27, no. 2 (2001): 58–76.

Murphy, Kate. "How to Rearrange Your Post-Pandemic 'Friendscape.'" *New York Times*, June 7, 2021. https://www.nytimes.com/2021/06/01/well/family/curate-friends.html (accessed June 14, 2021).

Nehamas, Alexander. *On Friendship*. New York: Basic Books, 2016.

Nelson, Deborah. "The Implications of Love and Sacrifice in 'Fresne' and 'Eliduc.'" *The South Central Bulletin* 38, no. 4 (December 1, 1978): 153–55.

Nelson, Janet. "Society, Theodicy and the Origins of Heresy." *Studies in Church History* 9 (1972): 65–77.

Nelson, Venetia, ed. *A Myrour to Lewede Men and Wymmen: A Prose Version of the 'Speculum vitae.'* Middle English Texts 14. Heidelberg: Carl Winter, 1981.

Németh, Attila. *Epicurus on the Self: Issues in Ancient Philosophy*. New York: Routledge, 2017.

Nestle, Joan. *A Restricted Country*, 2nd ed. San Francisco: Cleis Press, 2003.

Newman, Barbara. *God and the Goddesses: Vision, Poetry, and Belief in the Middle Ages*. Philadelphia: University of Pennsylvania Press, 2003.

———. "Hildegard of Bingen: Visions and Validation." *Church History* 54 (1985): 163–75.

Nievergelt, Marco. "The Place of Emotion: Space, Silence, and Interiority in the Stanzaic *Morte Arthur*." *Arthurian Literature* 32 (2015): 31–58.

Noffke, Suzanne, trans. "Letter T61/G183/Dt2 To Monna Agnessa Malavolti and the *Mantellate* of Siena." In *The Letters of Catherine of Siena*, volume 1. Tempe: Arizona Center for Medieval and Renaissance Studies, 2000.

Nussbaum, Martha. *The Therapy of Desire*. Princeton, NJ: Princeton University Press, 1994.

O'Keefe, Tim. *Epicureanism*. Berkeley: University of California Press, 2010.

Owen-Crocker, Gale R. *Dress in Anglo-Saxon England*. Woodbridge, Suffolk: Boydell, 1986; rev. 2004.

Page, William, and H. Arthur Doubleday, eds. *The Victoria History of the Counties of England*, vol. 2. London: A. Constable, 1903.

Painter, Sidney. "To Whom Were Dedicated the Fables of Marie de France?" *Modern Language Notes* 48, no. 6 (1933): 367–69.

Patersen, Linda. "Women, Property, and the Rise of Courtly Love." In *The Court Reconvenes: Courtly Literature across the Disciplines*. Ed. Barbara Altmann and Carroll Carleton. Woodbridge, Suffolk: Boydell & Brewer, 2003. 41–56.

Paul the Deacon. *History of the Langobards, by Paul the Deacon.* Trans. William Dudley Foulke Philadelphia: University of Pennsylvania, 1907.

Paxton, Jennifer. "Monks and Bishops: The Purpose of the 'Liber Eliensis.'" *The Haskins Society Journal* 11 (1998): 17–30.

Pearson, Jo. "Embracing the Lash: Pain and Ritual as Spiritual Tools." *Scripta Instituti Donneriani Aboensis* 23 (2011): 351–63. https://doi.org/10.30674/scripta.67394.

Pester, Holly. "Archive Fanfiction: Experimental Archive Research Methodologies and Feminist Epistemological Tactics." *Feminist Review* 115 (2017): 114–29.

Petroff, Elizabeth. *Consolation of the Blessed.* Millerton, NY: Alta Gaia, 1980.

Pezzini, Domenico. "Aelred's Doctrine of Charity and Friendship." In *A Companion to Aelred of Rievaulx.* Ed. Marsha Dutton. Leiden: Brill, 2017. 221–45.

Phillips, Susan E. *Transforming Talk: The Problem with Gossip in Late Medieval England.* University Park: Pennsylvania State University Press, 2007.

Phillips, William D. Jr. *Slavery from Roman Times to the Early Transatlantic Trade.* Minneapolis: University of Minnesota Press, 1985.

———. *Slavery in Medieval and Early Modern Iberia.* Philadelphia: University of Pennsylvania Press, 2014.

Pizarro, Jaoquin Martinez. *Writing Ravenna: The Liber pontificalis of Andreas Agnellus.* Ann Arbor: University of Michigan Press, 1995.

Plutarch. "On Having Many Friends." In *Plutarch's Moralia,* vol. 1. Trans. F. C. Babbitt. Loeb Classical Library. Cambridge, MA: Harvard University Press, 1927.

Poirier, Paris, dir. *Last Call at Maud's.* Frameline, 1993.

Poole, R. L. "Gascoigne, Thomas (1403–1458)." In *Dictionary of National Biography, 1885 1900,* Vol. 21. Ed. Leslie Stephen. London: Smith, Elder & Co, 1900. 41–44.

Poquet, A. E., abbé. *Les Miracles de La Sainte Vierge Traduits et Mis En Vers Par Gautier de Coincy.* Paris: Parmantier, 1857.

Power, Eileen. *Medieval English Nunneries, c. 1275 to 1535.* New York: Biblo and Tannen, 1964.

Pugh, Tison. "'For to be Sworne Bretheren til They Deye': Satirizing Queer Brotherhood in the Chaucerian Corpus." *The Chaucer Review* 43, no. 3 (2009): 282–310.

Rapp, Beverlee Sian. "A Woman Speaks: Language and Self-Representation in Hildegard's Letters." In *Hildegard of Bingen: A Book of Essays.* Ed. Maud Burnett McInerney. New York: Garland, 1998. 3–24.

Raymond, Janice. *A Passion for Friends: Toward a Philosophy of Female Affection.* Boston: Beacon Press, 1986.

Raymond of Capua. *The Life of St. Catherine of Siena by Blessed Raymond of Capua.* Trans. George Lamb. Rockford, IL: Tan Books and Publishers, 1960, repr., 2003.

———. *Legenda maior.* Ed. Silvia Nocentini. Firenze: Edizioni del Galluzzo, 2013.

Regardie, Israel. *Outer Order Rituals and Commentaries.* Vol. 6 of *The Complete Golden Dawn System of Magic.* Ed. David Cherubim. Phoenix, AZ: New Falcon, 2014 (ebook).

Reider, Alexandra. "Ic ane geseah idese sittan: The Woman and Women Apart in Old English Poetry." *The Heroic Age: A Journal of Early Medieval Northwestern Europe* 19, August 13, 2019. https://www.heroicage.org/issues/19/reider.php.

Rich, Adrienne. "Compulsory Heterosexuality and Lesbian Existence." *Signs* 5, no. 4 (Summer 1980): 631–60.

Riddy, Felicity. "'Women Talking about the Things of God': A Late-Medieval Sub-culture." In *Women and Literature in Britain 1150–1500.* Ed. Carol Meale. Cambridge: Cambridge University Press, 1996. 104–27.

Rist, John M. "Epicurus on Friendship." *Classical Philology* 75, no. 2 (1980): 121–29.

Robbins, Russell Hope. "Good Gossips Reunited." *British Museum Quarterly* 27, no. 1/2 (1963): 12–15.

Robertson, Duncan. "The Anglo-Norman Verse Life of 'St. Mary the Egyptian.'" *Romance Philology* 52, no. 1 (1998): 13–44.

Rollason, D. W., Lynda Rollason, Elizabeth Briggs, and A. J. Piper, eds. *The Durham Liber vitae: London, British Library, MS Cotton Domitian A. VII: edition and digital facsimile with introduction, codicological, prosopographical and linguistic commentary, and indexes*. London: British Library, 2007.

Rosenberg, Alyssa. "In 2019, It's Time to Move Beyond the Bechdel Test." *Washington Post*, December 21, 2018. https://www.washingtonpost.com/opinions/2018/12/21/its-time-move-beyond-bechdel-test/.

Rosenblatt, Louise. *The Reader, The Text, The Poem: The Transactional Theory of the Literary Work*. Carbondale, IL: Southern Illinois University, 1978.

Rowlands, Samuel. *Tis Merrie When Gossips Meete*. London: W. White, 1602.

———. *A Whole Crew of Kind Gossips, All Met to be Merry*. London: W. Jaggard for John Deane, 1609.

Russ, Joanna. *Magic Mommas, Trembling Sisters, Puritans, and Perverts*. New York: Crossing Press, 1985.

Russell, Delbert. "The Campsey Collection of Old French Saints' Lives: A Reexamination of Its Structure and Provenance." *Scriptorium* 57 (2003): 51–83. Electronic Campsey Project, University of Waterloo, http://margot.uwaterloo.ca/campsey/cmphome_e.html.

Ryerson, Kathryn. *Women's Networks in Medieval France: Gender and Community in Montpellier, 1300-1350*. New York: Palgrave Macmillan, 2016.

Saul, Nigel. "John Gower: Prophet or Turncoat?" In *John Gower, Trilingual Poet: Language, Translation, and Tradition*. Ed. Elisabeth M. Dutton, John Hines, and Robert F. Yeager. Cambridge: D. S. Brewer, 2010. 85–97.

Saunders, Corinne J. *Rape and Ravishment in the Literature of Medieval England*. Cambridge: D. S. Brewer, 2001.

Scala, Elizabeth. "Canacee and the Chaucer Canon: Incest and Other Unnarratables." *The Chaucer Review* 30, no. 1 (1995): 15–39.

———. "The Texture of *Emaré*." *Philological Quarterly* 85, no. 3–4 (2006): 223–46.

Schachter, Marc D. *Voluntary Servitude and the Erotics of Friendship: From Classical Antiquity to Early Modern France*. Aldershot: Ashgate, 2008.

Schaefer, Kayleen. *Text Me When You Get Home: The Evolution and Triumph of Modern Female Friendship*. New York: Dutton, 2018.

Schiavone de Cruz-Sáenz, Michèle, ed. *The Life of Saint Mary of Egypt: An Edition and Study of the Medieval French and Spanish Verse Redactions*. Barcelona: Puvill, 1979.

Schibanoff, Susan. "Hildegard of Bingen and Richardis of Stade: The Discourse of Desire." In *Same-Sex Love and Desire among Women in the Middle Ages*. Ed. Francesca Canadé Sautman and Pamela Sheinborn. New York: Palgrave, 2001. 49–84.

———. "Worlds Apart: Orientalism, Antifeminism, and Heresy in Chaucer's Man of Law's Tale." *Exemplaria* 8, no. 1 (1996): 59–96.

Schirmer, Elizabeth. "Reading Lessons at Syon Abbey: The Myoure of Oure Ladye and the Mandates of Vernacular Theology." In *Voices in Dialogue: Reading Women in the Middle Ages*. Ed. Linda Olsen and Kathryn Kerby-Fulton. Notre Dame: University of Notre Dame Press, 2005. 345–76.

Schotland, Sara Deutch. "Talking Birds and Gentle Heart: Female Homosocial Bonding in Chaucer's 'Squire's Tale.'" In Classen and Sandidge, *Friendship in the Middle Ages and Early Modern Age*. 525–42.

Schuchman, Anne M. "The Lives of Umiliana De' Cerchi: Representations of Female Sainthood in Thirteenth-Century Florence." *Essays in Medieval Studies* 14 (1997): n. pag.

Schulenburg, Jane Tibbets. *Forgetful of Their Sex: Female Sanctity and Society ca. 500–1100*. Chicago: University of Chicago Press, 1998.

Schwarzenbach, Sibyl A. *On Civic Friendship: Including Women in the State*. New York: Columbia University Press, 2009.

Schweitzer, Ivy. "Making Equals: Classical *Philia* and Women's Friendship." *Feminist Studies* 42, no. 2 (2016): 337–64.

Scorpo, Antonella Liuzzo. *Friendship in Medieval Iberia: Historical, Legal and Literary Perspectives*. Burlington, VT: Ashgate, 2014.

———. "Friendship in the Middle Ages." *The History of Emotions Blog*, March 20, 2014. https://emotionsblog.history.qmul.ac.uk/2014/03/friendship-in-the-middle-ages/ (accessed June 29, 2021).

Shannon, Laurie. *Sovereign Amity: Figures of Friendship in Shakespearean Contexts*. Chicago: University of Chicago Press, 2002.

Short, Ian. "Patrons and Polyglots: French Literature in Twelfth-Century England." *Anglo-Norman Studies* 14 (1991): 229–49.

Signori, Gabriela. "Muriel and the Others . . . or Poems as Pledges of Friendship." In *Friendship in Medieval Europe*. Ed. Julian Haseldine. Stroud: Sutton, 1999. 199–212.

Silvas, Anna, ed. *Jutta and Hildegard: The Biographical Sources*. Turnhout: Brepols, 1998.

Simone, Gail. "Women in Refrigerators." https://www.lby3.com/wir/ (accessed January 29, 2020).

Skelton, John. *The Complete English Poems of John Skelton*, rev. ed. Ed. John Scattergood. Liverpool: Liverpool University Press, 2015.

Sklar, Elizabeth. "'Stuffed with Ymagerye': Emaré's Robe and the Construction of Desire." *Medieval Perspectives* 22 (2007): 145–56.

Smith, Gwendolyn. "Sister Act: From Killing Eve to Little Women, Female Friendships Finally Get Top Billing." *Guardian*, December 22, 2019. https://www.theguardian.com/film/2019/dec/22/little-women-female-friendships-top-billing-tv-shows-plays-films.

Smith, Lesley, and Jane H. M. Taylor, eds. *Women, the Book, and the Worldly*. Woodbridge: Boydell and Brewer, 1995.

Smith, Nicole D. *Sartorial Strategies: Outfitting Aristocrats and Fashioning Conduct in Late Medieval Literature*. Notre Dame, IN: University of Notre Dame Press, 2012.

Smith-Rosenberg, Carroll. "The Female World of Love and Ritual: Relations between Women in Nineteenth-Century American." *Signs* 1, no. 1 (Autumn 1975): 1–29.

Snyder, Jane McIntosh. *The Woman and the Lyre: Women Writers in Classical Greece and Rome*. Carbondale: Southern Illinois University Press, 1989.

Southern, R. W. *St. Anselm: A Portrait in a Landscape*. Cambridge: Cambridge University Press, 1990.

———. *Western Society and the Church in the Middle Ages*. London: Hodder and Stoughton, 1970.

Staples, Kathryn Kelsey. *Daughters of London: Inheriting Opportunity in the Late Middle Ages*. Leiden: Brill, 2011.

Starhawk. *The Spiral Dance: A Rebirth of the Ancient Religion of the Great Goddess*. New York: Harper, 1999.

Stefaniw, Blossom. "Spiritual Friendship and Bridal Mysticism in an Age of Affectivity." *Cistercian Studies Quarterly* 41, no. 1 (2006): 65–78.

Stevenson, Jane. "Anglo-Latin Women Poets." In *Latin Learning and English Lore (Volumes I & II): Studies in Anglo-Saxon Literature for Michael Lapidge*. Ed. Katerine O'Brien O'Keeffe and Andy Orchard. Toronto: University of Toronto Press, 2005. 86–107.

Stretter, Robert. "Rewriting Perfect Friendship in Chaucer's 'Knight's Tale' and Lydgate's 'Fabula Duorum Mercatorum.'" *The Chaucer Review* 37, no. 3 (2003): 234–52.

Strohm, Paul. *Social Chaucer*. Boston: Harvard University Press, 1989.

Stuard, Susan Mosher. *Gilding the Market: Luxury and Fashion in Fourteenth-Century Italy*. Philadelphia: University of Pennsylvania Press, 2006.

Talbot, C. H. *The Anglo-Saxon Missionaries in Germany*. London: Sheed and Ward, 1954.

Tannen, Deborah. *You're the Only One I Can Tell: Inside the Language of Women's Friendships*. New York: Ballantine Books, 2017.

Taylor, Judith. "Beyond 'Obligatory Camaraderie': Girls' Friendships in Zadie Smith's *NW* and Jillian and Mariko Tamaki's *Skim*." *Feminist Studies* 42, no. 2 (2016): 445–68.

———. "Enduring Friendship: Women's Intimacies and the Erotics of Survival." *Frontiers: A Journal of Women's Studies* 34, no. 1 (2013): 93–113.

Thacker, Alan. "Hild [St Hild, Hilda] (614–680), Abbess of Strensall–Whitby." *Oxford Dictionary of National Biography*, September 23, 2004. https://o-www-oxforddnb-com.catalogue.libraries.london.ac.uk/view/10.1093/ref:odnb/9780198614128.001.0001/odnb-9780198614128-e-13255 (accessed April 6, 2020).

Thomas, Alfred. *Reading Women in Late Medieval Europe: Anne of Bohemia and Chaucer's Female Audience*. New York: Palgrave Macmillan, 2015.

Thompson, Sally. *Women Religious: The Founding of English Nunneries after the Norman Conquest*. Oxford: Oxford University Press, 1991.

Thorpe, Rochella. "The Changing Face of Lesbian Bars in Detroit, 1938–1965." In *Creating a Place for Ourselves: Lesbian, Gay, and Bisexual Community Histories*. Ed. Brett Beemyn. New York: Routledge, 1997. 165–81.

———. "'A House Where Queers Go': African-American Lesbian Nightlife in Detroit, 1940–1975." In *Inventing Lesbian Cultures in America*. Ed. Ellen Lewin. Boston: Beacon Press, 1996. 40–61.

Tolhurst, Fiona, and K. S. Whetter. "Standing Up for the Stanzaic-Poet: Artistry, Characterization, and Narration in the Stanzaic *Morte Arthur*." *Arthuriana* 28, no. 3 (Fall 2018): 86–113.

Tracy, Larissa. "Silence and Speech in the Female Lives of the *Gilte Legende* and Their Influence on the Lives of Ordinary Medieval Women." In *Women of the Gilte Legende: A Selection of Middle English Saints Lives*. Ed. and trans. Tracy. Woodbridge: D. S. Brewer, 2003. 101–27.

Traub, Valerie. *The Renaissance of Lesbianism in Early Modern England*. Cambridge: Cambridge University Press, 2002.

Trouillot, Michel-Rolph. *Silencing the Past: Power and the Production of History*. Boston: Beacon Press, 1997.

Turner, Marion. *Chaucerian Conflict: Languages of Antagonism in Late Fourteenth-Century London*. London: Oxford University Press, 2006.

Utley, Francis Lee. *The Crooked Rib: An Analytical Index to the Argument about Women in English and Scots Literature to the End of the Year 1568*. Columbus: The Ohio State University Press, 1944; repr., New York: Octagon Books, 1970.

van Dijk, Mathilde. "Female Leadership and Authority in the Sisterbook of Diepenveen." In *Mulieres Religiosae: Shaping Female Spiritual Authority in the Medieval and Early Modern Periods*. Turnhout: Brepols, 2014. 243–64.

Venarde, Bruce L., trans. *Robert of Arbrissel: Sex, Sin, and Salvation in the Middle Ages*. Washington, DC: Catholic University of America Press, 2006.

———. *Women's Monasticism and Medieval Society: Nunneries in France and England, 890–1215*. Ithaca, NY: Cornell University Press, 1997.

Verini, Alexandra. "Medieval Models of Female Friendship in Christine de Pizan's *The Book of the City of Ladies* and Margery Kempe's *The Book of Margery Kempe*." *Feminist Studies* 42, no. 2 (2016): 365–91.

Vines, Amy N. "'Who-so wylle of nurtur lere': Domestic Foundations for Social Success in the Middle English *Emaré*." *The Chaucer Review* 53, no. 1 (2018): 82–101.

———. *Women's Power in Late Medieval Romance*. Cambridge: D. S. Brewer, 2011.

Vishnuvajjala, Usha. "Adventure, Lealté, and Sympathy in Marie de France's Eliduc." *Texas Studies in Literature and Language* 59, no. 2 (2017): 162–81.

Vitus Cortonensis. "Vita Beatae Humilianae De Cherchis." In *Acta Sanctorum*. Antwerp, 1685.

Wack, Mary. "Women, Work, and Plays in an English Medieval Town." In *Maids and Mistresses, Cousins and Queens: Women's Alliances in Early Modern England*. Ed. Susan Frye and Karen Robertson. Oxford: Oxford University Press, 1999. 33–51.

Walker, Alice. *In Search of Our Mothers' Gardens: Womanist Prose*. New York: Harcourt, 1983.

Wallace, David. *Chaucerian Polity: Absolutist Lineages and Associational Forms in England and Italy*. Stanford: Stanford University Press, 1994.

Warren, Nancy. *Spiritual Economies: Female Monasticism in Later Medieval England*. Philadelphia: University of Pennsylvania Press, 2001.

Watson, Henry, trans. *The Fyftene Joyes of Maryage*. London: Wynkyn de Worde, 1507.

———. *The Gospelles of Dystaves*. London: Wynkyn de Worde, 1510.

Watt, Diane. *Women, Writing and Religion in England and Beyond, 650–1100*. London: Bloomsbury, 2019.

Waugh, Patricia. "Feminism and Writing: The Politics of Culture." In *The Cambridge History of Twentieth-Century Literature*. Ed. Laura Marcus and Peter Nicholls. Cambridge: Cambridge University Press, 2005. 600–618.

Webb, Diane. *Saints and Cities in Medieval Italy*. Manchester: Manchester University Press, 2007.

Weinstein, Donald, and Rudolph M. Bell. *Saints and Society: The Two Worlds of Western Christendom, 1000–1700*. Chicago: University of Chicago Press, 1982.

Weston, Lisa M. C. "Virgin Desires: Reading a Homoerotics of Female Monastic Community." In Giffney, Sauer, and Watt, *The Lesbian Premodern*, 93–104.

———. "Where Textual Bodies Meet: Anglo-Saxon Women's Epistolary Friendships." In Classen and Sandidge, *Friendship in the Middle Ages and Early Modern Age*, 231–46.

Whetter, K. S. "Love and Death in Arthurian Romance." In *The Arthurian Way of Death*. Ed. Karen Cherewatuk and K. S. Whetter. Cambridge: D. S. Brewer, 2009. 94–114.

Whitaker, Cord J. "Black Metaphors in the *King of Tars*." *Journal of English and Germanic Philology* 112, no. 2 (2013): 169–93.

White, Ethan Doyle. *Wicca: History, Belief, and Community in Modern Pagan Witchcraft*. Brighton: Sussex Academic Press, 2016,

White, Hayden. *Tropics of Discourse*. Baltimore and London: Johns Hopkins University Press, 1978.

Wicher, Andrzej. "The Fairy Needlewoman Emaré: A Study of the Middle English Romance Emaré in the Context of the Tale of Magic." In *Evur happie & glorious, ffor I hafe at wille grete riches*. Ed. Liliana Sikorska and Marcin Krygier. New York: Peter Lang, 2012. 145–53.

Wiethaus, Ulrike. "In Search of Medieval Women's Friendships: Hildegard of Bingen's Letters to Her Female Contemporaries." In *Maps of Flesh and Light: The Religious Experience of Medieval Women Mystics*. Ed. Ulrike Wiethaus. Syracuse, NY: Syracuse University Press, 1993. 93–111.

Wills, David. "Full Dorsal: Derrida's *Politics of Friendship*." *Postmodern Culture* 15, no. 3 (May 2005). https://doi.org/10.1353/pmc.2005.0032.

Wogan-Browne, Jocelyn. "'Clerc u lai, muïne u dame': Women and Anglo-Norman Hagiography in the Twelfth and Thirteenth Centuries." In *Women and Literature in Britain, c. 1150–1500*. Ed. Carol M. Meale. Cambridge: Cambridge University Press, 1993. 61–85.

———. "Recovery and Loss: Women's Writing around Marie de France." In *Women Intellectuals and Leaders in the Middle Ages*. Ed. Kathryn Kerby-Fulton, Katie Buygyis, and John Van Engen. Cambridge: D. S. Brewer, 2020. 169–91.

———. "Rerouting the Dower." In *Power of the Weak: Studies on Medieval Women*. Ed. Jennifer Carpenter and Sally-Beth MacLean. Urbana: University of Illinois Press, 1995. 27–56.

———. *Saints' Lives and Women's Literary Culture, 1150–1300: Virginity and Its Authorizations*. Oxford: Oxford University Press, 2001.

Woledge, Brian, and Ian Short. "Liste provisoire de manuscrits du XIIe siècle contenant des Textes en langue française." *Romania* 102, no. 405 (1981): 1–17.

Wong, Kristen. "The Curious Disappearance of the Lesbian Bar." *The Story Exchange*, June 28, 2019. https://thestoryexchange.org/the-curious-disappearance-of-the-lesbian-bar/.

Woodbridge, Linda. *Women and the English Renaissance: Literature and the Nature of Womankind, 1540–1620*. Urbana: University of Illinois Press, 1984.

Woolf, Virginia. *The Death of the Moth and Other Essays*. London: Hogarth, 1942.

———. *A Room of One's Own*. New York: Harcourt Brace, 1981.

Wyatt, Siobhán M. *Women of Words in "Le Morte Darthur": The Autonomy of Speech in Malory's Female Characters*. New York: Palgrave Macmillan, 2016.

Yeager, Robert F. *John Gower's Poetic: The Search for a New Arion*. Cambridge: D. S. Brewer, 1990.

Yoon, Joo Ok. "Medieval Documentary Semiotics and Forged Letters in the Late Middle English *Emaré*." *English Studies: A Journal of English Language and Literature* 100, no. 4 (2019): 371–86.

Zeikowitz, Richard E. *Homoeroticism and Chivalry: Discourses of Male Same-Sex Desire in the Fourteenth Century*. New York: Palgrave, 2003.

Zieman, Katherine. "Playing Doctor: St. Birgitta, Ritual Reading, and Ecclesiastical Authority." In *Voices in Dialogue: Reading Women in the Middle Ages*. Ed. Linda Olsen and Kathryn Kerby-Fulton. Notre Dame, IN: University of Notre Dame Press, 2005. 307–34.

Zimmerman, Margarete. "Christine de Pizan: Memory's Architect." In *Christine de Pizan: A Casebook*. Ed. Barbara K. Altmann and Deborah L. McGrady. New York and London: Routledge, 2003. 57–81.

Ziolkowski, Jan. "Twelfth-Century Understandings and Adaptations of Ancient Friendship." In *Mediaeval Antiquity*. Ed. Andries Welkenhuysen, Herman Braet, and Werner Verbeke. Leuven, Belgium: Leuven University Press, 1995. 59–81.

CONTRIBUTORS

PENELOPE ANDERSON is an Associate Professor of English at Indiana University, where she teaches Early Modern British Literature with a focus on gender and political theory. Her first book, *Friendship's Shadows: Women's Friendship and the Politics of Betrayal in England, 1640–1705,* was published by Edinburgh University Press in 2012, and she is currently completing her second book, *Humanity in Suspension: Gender and International Law in Seventeenth-Century Literature.* She is co-editor of the English Civil Wars and Protectorate section of the Palgrave *Encyclopaedia of Early Modern Women's Writing.*

ANDREA BOFFA obtained a PhD in History from Stony Brook University. She is an Adjunct Assistant Professor in the History and Philosophy Department at CUNY York College.

JENNIFER N. BROWN is a Professor of English and World Literatures at Marymount Manhattan College, where she is also currently serving as Chair of the Division of Humanities and Social Sciences. Her work centers on women's writing and reading in late medieval England. Her most recent books are a monograph, *Fruit of the Orchard: Catherine of Siena in Late Medieval and Early Modern England* (University of Toronto, 2018), and a co-edited collection with Nicole R. Rice, *Manuscript Culture and Medieval Devotional Traditions: Essays in Honour of Michael G. Sargent* (York Medieval Press, 2021).

CHRISTINE CHISM teaches medieval literature at UCLA. She is revising a manuscript on friendship in Middle English writing, *Mortal Friends: The Politics of Friendship in Late Medieval England,* forthcoming from University of Pennsylvania Press.

MELISSA RIDLEY ELMES is an Assistant Professor of English at Lindenwood University. She is co-editor, with Misty Urban and Deva Kemmis, of the collection *Melusine's Footprint: Tracing the Legacy of a Medieval Myth* (Brill, 2017). She is also co-editor, with Kristin Bovaird-Abbo, of the volume *Food and Feast in Premodern Outlaw Tales* (Routledge, 2021), and her articles have appeared in journals including *Modern Philology, Arthuriana, Medieval Perspectives*, and *Medieval Feminist Forum*.

LAURIE A. FINKE, Professor of Women's and Gender Studies at Kenyon College, is the author of *Women's Writing in Middle English* (1998) and *Feminist Theory, Women's Writing* (1992) and co-author, with Martin Shichtman, of *King Arthur and the Myth of History* (2004) and *Cinematic Illuminations: The Middle Ages on Film* (2009); she is also one of the editors of the *Norton Anthology of Criticism and Theory* (2001, 2010, 2018). Her articles have appeared in *postmedieval, Exemplaria, Arthuriana, Feminist Studies, Theatre Survey, Signs*, and *Theatre Journal*.

CARISSA M. HARRIS is Associate Professor of English at Temple University. Her research focuses on gender and sexuality in late medieval England and Scotland, with a particular emphasis on histories of gendered emotion, rape and consent, manuscript studies, and connections between past and present sexual cultures. She is the author of *Obscene Pedagogies: Transgressive Talk and Sexual Education in Late Medieval Britain* (Cornell University Press, 2018) and co-editor, with Sarah Baechle and Elizaveta Strakhov, of *Rape Culture and Female Resistance in Late Medieval Literature* (Pennsylvania State University Press, 2022).

LYDIA YAITSKY KERTZ is an Assistant Professor of English at SUNY Geneseo. Her research situates medieval romance's discourse of luxury within a global framework of intellectual and material history. Her work has appeared in *Medieval Feminist Forum, Medievalia et Humanistica, Medieval Perspectives*, the *Journal of the Early Book Society*, and *Word and Image*.

CLARE A. LEES is Professor of Medieval Literature, Director of the Institute of English Studies, and Vice Dean, School of Advanced Study, University of London. She is a Fellow of the English Association and a Fellow of King's College London. Clare's research interests include early medieval literatures, languages, and cultures of Britain and Ireland, gender and sexuality studies, and histories of place and belief. Her most recent work explores how modern and contemporary poets, writers, and artists engage with early medieval cultures. Her long-term co-author and friend is Gillian R. Overing; together they published *The Contemporary Medieval in Practice* in 2019.

KARMA LOCHRIE is Provost Professor of English Literature at Indiana University Bloomington. They have written books on female mysticism, women's secrecy, queer sexuality in the Middle Ages, and medieval utopianism. Friendships have sustained them throughout their scholarly career.

GILLIAN R. OVERING is Research Professor of English at Wake Forest University. She has published widely on early English literature, with a focus on gender, landscape studies, and Beowulf. She is a long-time collaborator and friend of Clare A. Lees; their most recent book is *The Contemporary Medieval in Practice* (UCL Press, 2019).

ALEXANDRA VERINI is Assistant Professor of Medieval Literature at Ashoka University. She is currently working on a monograph about medieval and early modern English women's spiritual utopias.

USHA VISHNUVAJJALA is a fixed-term lecturer in English Literature at Cardiff University. Her work focuses on medieval romance, medievalism, gender, and the history of emotions and has appeared in journals including *Arthuriana, Arthurian Literature, Studies in Medievalism,* and *Texas Studies in Literature and Language*. She is completing her first monograph, *Feminist Medievalisms: Embodiment and Vulnerability,* forthcoming from Arc Humanities Press / Amsterdam University Press.

STELLA WANG teaches as a Visiting Assistant Professor at Holy Cross and is presently a Visiting Research Fellow at Harvard University, where she received her PhD in English Literature.

INDEX

Ælfflæd, abbess, 11, 241, 243, 245, 247, 248–59
Aelred of Rievaulx, 5, 17–18, 37, 39–40, 48n41, 42, 43, 53–56, 70–71, 78
affect, 1, 2, 10, 51, 54–55, 56, 71n31, 77, 115–17, 119, 120–28, 129, 133–34, 135, 142, 163, 164, 181–82, 197–98, 200, 201, 203, 207, 208, 211, 217
Alewife Poem, 137n8, 157–67, 171, 172, 173, 176, 266n6
Alliterative *Morte Arthur*, 117, 121n18
Allnutt, Gillian, 241, 242, 243, 245–46, 247, 249
Amazons, 181, 197–98, 201, 209
Amicitia, 4, 10, 17, 26, 36, 37–38, 39, 43, 49, 50, 52–53, 55, 56, 57, 70, 74, 83n24, 98, 182, 194, 198, 199, 263
Anne of Bohemia, 137, 139
Aristotle, 4, 19, 70, 77, 78, 138, 163, 166, 182, 263, 264
Augustine, 78

Baudri of Bourgueil, 40, 55, 56
Bechdel test, 172, 177–78, 180, 182, 195–96

Bede, the Venerable, 43, 243n8, 244, 246, 248, 249–53, 255, 258
Boccaccio, Giovanni, 51, 137, 140, 142, 143, 145, 201–2, 213–14
Bray, Alan, 6, 77n7, 199–200, 263n5
Bridget, Saint, 79, 80–81, 84–88, 91, 93

caritas, 54
Catherine of Siena, 9, 15n1, 16, 29–35, 265
Cavendish, Margaret, 76–77, 80, 84, 90, 93
Champney, Marie, 32–34
chastity, 15n1, 23, 44, 45, 50, 59, 60, 162, 214
Chaucer, Geoffrey, 3, 10, 50, 99, 110, 112, 135, 136, 137, 138–45, 147, 149, 150n44, 151, 153, 177–80, 195, 216, 264n10, 267; *Book of the Duchess*, 178; *Canterbury Tales*, 10, 179, 180, 181, 195; Franklin's Tale, 138, 143–45, 153; Knight's Tale, 181; Man of Law's Tale, 99, 100, 110, 112, 181–86, 191; Squire's Tale, 191–95; Wife of Bath's Prologue, 3, 187–89 Wife of Bath's Tale, 8, 187, 189–91; *Legend of Good Women*, 139, 178; *Parliament of Fowles*, 178; *Troilus and Criseyde*, 138–43, 153
Chrétien de Troyes, 115

Cicero, 5, 39, 70, 77, 78, 79, 82, 138, 140n22, 141, 182, 194, 198, 199, 208, 211–12, 214, 217, 263, 264

Clare of Rimini, 10, 58–75, 263

Copland, Robert, 160n11, 161, 171, 172, 173

courtly love, 6–7, 51n49, 56, 140n22, 178

Crowley, Aleister, 222, 233–34, 236, 240; Thelema, 233, 240

cummar/cummer, 165–66, 167, 168–72, 187, 188; cummarship, 159, 162, 164, 167–72, 221

Cuthbert, 243–45, 246

Dante, 199, 201, 211

de France, Marie, 10, 37–42, 263, 268; *Guildelüec and Guilliadun*, 42, 52–57; *La vie seint Audree*, 10, 37, 42, 43–48, 54, 56, 57; *Le Fresne*, 10, 49–52, 53

de Pizan, Christine, 10–11, 98, 263, 265, 266; *Book of the City of Ladies*, 197–218; *querelle des femmes*, 137

Derrida, Jacques, 8n24, 9, 219n2, 220–21, 232

Dido, 144n32, 203, 204, 213, 214

Dunbar, William, 157–59, 160

Elisabeth of Schönau, 25–26

Elizabeth of Töss, 18–19

Elsbeth of Stagel, 16, 28–29

Emaré, 10, 97–113, 267

emotions, 1, 10, 16, 19, 33, 34, 114–34, 141, 142, 143, 145, 186, 193, 200, 201, 212, 220, 224, 239, 266, 267, 268. *See also* affect

esotericism, 221–24, 228, 236–37

female religious communities, 16, 18, 19, 24, 26–28, 29–30, 33, 37–39, 41, 42, 59, 61, 63–65, 67, 68, 69–70, 72–73, 74, 75, 76–77, 80–84, 87–88, 89, 90. *See also* female same-sex communities

female same-sex communities, 158, 159, 164, 168. *See also* female religious communities

femininity, 40, 159, 180, 184, 187–89, 203–4, 208, 216, 220, 237, 267

Ferrante, Elena, 1, 3–4, 8

fraternity, 219, 221, 223–24, 226, 231, 233–34, 239

Freemasonry, 221–29, 234, 235–39

friendship, chaste, 6, 71; cross-species, 191–95; epicurean, 78–79, 263; epistolary, 16, 20, 24, 40, 52, 56, 179n7; in film, 2–3; male/masculine, 4, 5–6, 7, 8, 10, 39, 70–71, 77–78, 82, 98, 138, 140n22, 182, 198, 199, 208, 212, 263, 264; prosthetic, 8, 219, 220, 224, 225, 230, 236, 238–39; secular, 9–10, 179; spiritual, 4, 5, 6, 9–10, 15–93, 179

Godsibbe femininity, 180, 187–89

gossip, 63, 67, 131, 158, 160–61, 167, 171–72, 175, 176, 180, 186–91, 196, 217, 255, 258, 263, 268. *See also* godsibbe femininity

Gower, John, 99, 135, 137, 145–49, 151, 153, 172

Griffith, Nicola, 11, 241, 242, 243, 246–47, 259

Hildegard of Bingen, 9, 16, 19–26

homosocial bonds, 7n21, 124, 150, 160, 164n26, 166, 172, 192n27, 208, 218, 236, 237, 244

Hutchison, Anne, 33, 34nn62–63

intimacy, 21–22, 23, 24, 29, 30, 32, 34, 36, 40, 48, 52, 55, 65, 68, 71, 82–83, 86–88, 89–90, 93, 115, 116, 141n25, 158, 159, 160–68, 171, 172, 173, 176, 179, 180, 185, 187–89, 193, 195, 199, 209, 217–28

Iurminburg, queen, 11, 241, 243, 247, 248–57

Jutta, 20–22, 26

Kempe, Margery, 18n10, 72–73, 98, 181n7

King of Tars, The, 112

lesbian bar culture, 173–76

Liber Eliensis, 43, 44, 46, 47

Livy, 204–8

Lorde, Audre, 174n67, 263, 268

Maitland, Sara, 241, 242, 243–45

Malory, Thomas, 10, 115, 116n6, 117, 128nn19–20, 135, 136, 137, 138, 145, 149–53, 264n10

Margaret of Cortona, 10, 59–75, 263
masculinity, 4–7, 8, 10, 11, 40, 59, 75, 79, 133, 138, 149, 154, 159, 178, 180, 181, 182, 183, 187, 188, 191, 199, 200, 202, 206, 207, 208, 209, 213, 219, 220, 230n50, 237, 247, 252, 263, 264
Medieval Mediterranean, 101, 103, 105, 107–8, 111
Michel de Montaigne, 5, 263
Myroure of Oure Ladye, The, 80–89, 92
misogyny, 137–38, 139, 140, 171, 172, 182, 184, 196, 197, 198, 201, 202; misogynisms, 201–9
mysticism, 15, 19, 22n23, 29, 34, 66, 71n31, 77n5, 179, 230, 231

pandemic, 2, 11, 262, 265
patriarchy, 59, 62, 64, 70, 73, 75, 77, 93, 165, 185, 198, 238, 266, 268
Paul the Deacon, 137, 146–49
pedagogy (and female community), 157, 159, 160–62, 164, 166, 168–70, 172, 180
Petrarch, 50, 264
Philia, 4, 78–79, 135n1, 220n6, 263
Plato, 78
Plutarch, 78, 201

queer, 18, 159, 164, 167, 172, 173, 174n67, 175, 179, 181n13, 201n13, 242, 263, 266–67; queer studies, 7

racialized difference, 1, 97, 101–5, 109, 110–13, 267
Rich, Adrienne, 9n25, 267

Richardis, 10, 19, 22–26, 29, 179n6
Roman de la Rose, 138, 211
romance, 98, 99n5–6, 100, 102–6, 109n29, 111–12, 114, 115, 116n4, 117, 118–19, 132, 136n3, 143, 149, 181nn13–14, 186n19, 191, 194n32, 197, 214, 223

saint's life, 41, 43–48, 61, 74, 75, 85–88, 191, 248
sexuality (female), 44–45, 50, 236, 255, 258; heterosexuality, 6, 9n25, 172, 178, 186, 189, 195, 236, 237, 267n18, 268; same-sex desire, 76, 83, 99, 102, 157, 168, 172, 173, 266–67; feminine desire, 162, 187–90, 192; female pleasure, 4, 76, 78n9, 80, 93, 162, 164–65, 169, 173, 180, 181n10, 189
Sir Gawain and the Green Knight, 106, 115, 117
Skelton, John, 161
space, feminine, 10, 61–70, 88, 115–25, 158, 159, 169, 171–74, 194, 195n3 and n5, 200, 207, 208, 219, 221, 214
Stanzaic *Morte Arthur*, 10, 114–34, 150
Syon Abbey, 10, 76–93, 138n10, 179, 241

Umiliana de' Cerchi, 10, 58–75, 263

visionary women, 9, 19, 20, 21, 25–26, 28–29, 32, 34–35, 264
voice, female, 10, 27n40, 31, 40, 63, 80n19, 116, 119–20, 190, 202, 242, 249

Wicca, 11, 221–25, 232–40, 268; African American Wiccan Society, 239–40
Woolf, Virginia, 4, 7, 177–79, 186–87, 195, 231n52

INTERVENTIONS: NEW STUDIES IN MEDIEVAL CULTURE
Ethan Knapp, Series Editor

Interventions: New Studies in Medieval Culture publishes theoretically informed work in medieval literary and cultural studies. We are interested both in studies of medieval culture and in work on the continuing importance of medieval tropes and topics in contemporary intellectual life.

Women's Friendship in Medieval Literature
EDITED BY KARMA LOCHRIE AND USHA VISHNUVAJJALA

Courtly and Queer: Deconstruction, Desire, and Medieval French Literature
CHARLIE SAMUELSON

Continental England: Form, Translation, and Chaucer in the Hundred Years' War
ELIZAVETA STRAKHOV

Material Remains: Reading the Past in Medieval and Early Modern British Literature
EDITED BY JAN-PEER HARTMANN AND ANDREW JAMES JOHNSTON

Translation Effects: Language, Time, and Community in Medieval England
MARY KATE HURLEY

Talk and Textual Production in Medieval England
MARISA LIBBON

Scripting the Nation: Court Poetry and the Authority of History in Late Medieval Scotland
KATHERINE H. TERRELL

Medieval Things: Agency, Materiality, and Narratives of Objects in Medieval German Literature and Beyond
BETTINA BILDHAUER

Death and the Pearl Maiden: Plague, Poetry, England
DAVID K. COLEY

Political Appetites: Food in Medieval English Romance
AARON HOSTETTER

Invention and Authorship in Medieval England
ROBERT R. EDWARDS

Challenging Communion: The Eucharist and Middle English Literature
JENNIFER GARRISON

Chaucer on Screen: Absence, Presence, and Adapting the Canterbury Tales
EDITED BY KATHLEEN COYNE KELLY AND TISON PUGH

Chaucer, Gower, and the Affect of Invention
STEELE NOWLIN

Fragments for a History of a Vanishing Humanism
EDITED BY MYRA SEAMAN AND EILEEN A. JOY

The Medieval Risk-Reward Society: Courts, Adventure, and Love in the European Middle Ages
  WILL HASTY

The Politics of Ecology: Land, Life, and Law in Medieval Britain
  EDITED BY RANDY P. SCHIFF AND JOSEPH TAYLOR

The Art of Vision: Ekphrasis in Medieval Literature and Culture
  EDITED BY ANDREW JAMES JOHNSTON, ETHAN KNAPP, AND MARGITTA ROUSE

Desire in the Canterbury Tales
  ELIZABETH SCALA

Imagining the Parish in Late Medieval England
  ELLEN K. RENTZ

Truth and Tales: Cultural Mobility and Medieval Media
  EDITED BY FIONA SOMERSET AND NICHOLAS WATSON

Eschatological Subjects: Divine and Literary Judgment in Fourteenth-Century French Poetry
  J. M. MOREAU

Chaucer's (Anti-)Eroticisms and the Queer Middle Ages
  TISON PUGH

Trading Tongues: Merchants, Multilingualism, and Medieval Literature
  JONATHAN HSY

Translating Troy: Provincial Politics in Alliterative Romance
  ALEX MUELLER

Fictions of Evidence: Witnessing, Literature, and Community in the Late Middle Ages
  JAMIE K. TAYLOR

Answerable Style: The Idea of the Literary in Medieval England
  EDITED BY FRANK GRADY AND ANDREW GALLOWAY

Scribal Authorship and the Writing of History in Medieval England
  MATTHEW FISHER

Fashioning Change: The Trope of Clothing in High- and Late-Medieval England
  ANDREA DENNY-BROWN

Form and Reform: Reading across the Fifteenth Century
  EDITED BY SHANNON GAYK AND KATHLEEN TONRY

How to Make a Human: Animals and Violence in the Middle Ages
  KARL STEEL

Revivalist Fantasy: Alliterative Verse and Nationalist Literary History
  RANDY P. SCHIFF

Inventing Womanhood: Gender and Language in Later Middle English Writing
  TARA WILLIAMS

Body Against Soul: Gender and Sowlehele *in Middle English Allegory*
  MASHA RASKOLNIKOV

www.ingramcontent.com/pod-product-compliance
Lightning Source LLC
Chambersburg PA
CBHW021214240426
43672CB00026B/78